THE OTHER DESERT WAR

The Libyan desert. Photograph taken by Major Ralph A. Bagnold; Department of Archives/Manuscripts, No. D3/007434, courtesy of the Royal Geographical Society.

THE OTHER DESERT WAR

British Special Forces in North Africa, 1940–1943

JOHN W. GORDON

Foreword by Theodore Ropp

Contributions in Military Studies
Number 56

GREENWOOD PRESS
NEW YORK • WESTPORT, CONNECTICUT • LONDON

Library of Congress Cataloging-in-Publication Data

Gordon, John W.
  The other desert war.

  (Contributions in military studies, ISSN 0883–6884 ; no. 56)
  Bibliography: p.
  Includes index.
  1. World War, 1939–1945—Campaigns—Africa, North.
2. World War, 1939–1945—Commando operations—Africa,
North.   3. World War, 1939–1945—Commando operations—
Great Britain.   4. Great Britain. Army—Commando
troops.   I. Title.   II. Title: British Special Forces.
III. Series.
D766.82.G57 1987   940.54'23   86–9969
ISBN 0–313–25240–8 (lib. bdg. : alk. paper)

Library of Congress Catalog Card Number: 86–9969
ISBN: 0–313–25240–8
ISSN: 0883–6884

First published in 1987

Greenwood Press, Inc.
88 Post Road West, Westport, Connecticut 06881

Printed in the United States of America

The paper used in this book complies with the
Permanent Paper Standard issued by the National
Information Standards Organization (Z39.48–1984).

10 9 8 7 6 5 4 3 2 1

To My Mother and Father

Contents

Abbreviations   ix

Illustrations   xi

Foreword by Theodore Ropp   xiii

Preface   xvii

Acknowledgments   xxi

Chapter 1. First Experiments: World War I   1

Chapter 2. The Penetration of the Desert   17

Chapter 3. The Formation of a Desert Special Force   33

Chapter 4. First Missions: A Huge Bluff Played Out   53

Chapter 5. Against the Germans   69

Chapter 6. The Raiding Partnership   87

Chapter 7. A Daring Gamble That Failed: The Raids on Tobruk,
             Benghazi, Jalo, and Barce   109

Chapter 8. The Road Watch and the Verification of Ultra   131

Chapter 9. The Last Act: A Left Hook Around the Mareth Line   155

Epilogue   179

Notes   189

Essay on Sources   225

Index   235

Abbreviations

AOC	Air-Officer Commanding
BBC	British Broadcasting Corporation
C&SC	Command and Staff College, United States Marine Corps, Quantico, Virginia
CIGS	Chief of the Imperial General Staff
C-in-C	Commander-in-Chief
Des Force	Desert Force
DF	Direction-Finding
DMI	Director of Military Intelligence
DMO	Director of Military Operations
FSR	*Field Service Regulations*
G(RF)	General Staff Operations, Raiding Forces
GHQ-ME	General Headquarters, Middle East
GOC-BTE	General Officer Commanding British Troops in Egypt
HQ-BTE	Headquarters, British Troops in Egypt
LCP	Light Car Patrol
LRDG	Long Range Desert Group
MP	Member of Parliament
NATO	North Atlantic Treaty Organization
NCO	Noncommissioned officer

OBE	Officer, Order of the British Empire
OKW	Oberkommando der Wehrmacht (German Armed Forces High Command)
OSS	Office of Strategic Services (U.S.)
POW	Prisoner of war
PPA	Popski's Private Army
Pzkw	Panzerkampfwagen (armored fighting vehicle)
RAF	Royal Air Force
Recce	Reconnaissance
RFC	Royal Flying Corps
RNAS	Royal Naval Air Service
SAS	Special Air Service
Sd Kfz	Sonderkraftfahrzeug (armored special-purpose vehicle)
SIG	Special Interrogation Group
Sigint	Signal Intelligence (intelligence gained from interception and decryption of enemy signals)
SOE	Special Operations Executive (British)
USAAF	United States Army Air Forces
USA	United States Army
USMC	United States Marine Corps
WDLO	Western Desert Liaison Officer
W/T	Wireless Telegraphy
Y	Y Service (interception, decryption, and analysis of enemy tactical messages)

Illustrations

Frontispiece: The Libyan desert

Map 1: The desert   3

Map 2: The desert area, eastern half   55

The following photographs appear between pages 86 and 87:

Major Ralph Alger Bagnold, shortly after his posting to China in the early 1930s.

Sir Archibald Wavell with U.S. Army Lieutenant General Brehon B. Somervell in India in 1943.

Rommel understood very clearly that British special forces could be used to mount interdictive raids against his supply lines and rear areas. He was slow, however, to grasp the scale of that effort or the value of such forces for intelligence-gathering operations.

A meal in the LRDG's command post: Lieutenant Colonel Guy Prendergast is far right, with Major W. B. Shaw, the unit's intelligence officer, facing the camera.

Captain David Stirling, SAS, awaiting message traffic at an LRDG wireless truck in 1942. The LRDG's Captain Donald G. Steele is at right.

SAS and LRDG men the morning after a raid, Wadi Tamet, January 1942.

Lieutenant Colonel John Haselden, intelligence agent and originator of the idea for the Tobruk raid.

The aftermath of the raids on Tobruk, Jalo, Benghazi, and Barce: members of an LRDG patrol wait to evacuate the wounded by RAF aircraft from a landing ground deep in the desert.

G(RF)'s Colonel John W. Hackett, flanked here by Generals Montgomery and Urquhart in 1944

Breakdown in the desert: a truck belonging to the LRDG's Yeomanry Patrol under repair.

One of the camouflaged positions from which the Road Watch surveillance was maintained. A new team of watchers was moved up every night, while the rest of the patrol and the vehicles remained hidden in a wadi a few miles to the south.

Y1 Patrol's Captain David L. Lloyd Owen at the LRDG's Siwa base, November 1941. It was Lloyd Owen's task, in the wake of the Dodecanese disaster, to convert a desert special force into one capable of mounting operations in the Balkans and other areas of southeastern Europe.

Map 3: The desert area, western half   161

Foreword

This is exciting, well-written military history. It can be read with pleasure and profit by anyone from a teen-aged war gamer to a National War College student concerned with the role of special forces in twentieth-century warfare. How such forces were employed—particularly in the second of the century's two world wars, and particularly by the Anglo-Americans—has remained an issue given only limited exploration in existing assessments. In this sound analysis, Professor Gordon has succeeded in unraveling the partly legendary story of a key period in the evolution of special forces—the period when, in the first half of World War II, the British sent small, self-contained, highly mobile units raiding, reconnoitering, and intelligence-gathering into the deserts of North Africa. In so doing he makes clear the differences between elite forces, special forces, and the task force organizations almost always preferred by military professionals. Elite forces—the "few good men" of the U.S. Marines, the Brigade of Guards, the Gurkhas—are selected, trained and disciplined to do something well, anywhere at any time. A task force, on the other hand, comprises an all-arms, all-service force that is formed for a given operation—rescuing the Falklands or Grenada, say, or perhaps punishing a state that supports terrorism. But a special force is a rather newer phenomenon in modern warfare than these two types. It is a force that is recruited, trained, and equipped solely for a particular kind of operation, one that is regarded as difficult and hazardous and often involves actions deep behind enemy lines.

The Libyan desert, in which the British employed precisely this sort of force, is a jumble of mountains and oases with artesian wells in the eastern third of the Sahara between Egypt and the Sudan. It lies adjacent to the Mediterranean coastal strips and uplands of Libya and Cyrenaica, and the Western Fezzan, to which an east-west caravan route leads to join the north-south ones from Tripoli and Benghazi. Other routes extend down from the eastern end of the Gulf of Sirte, finally reaching Lake Chad and the Western Sudan in the far south. In ancient times, from the opening of the metal trades onwards, the inland and coastal routes were fought over by Phoenicians, Greeks, and Carthaginians. Darius of Persia once lost an army in Egypt's Western Desert, while Alexander and Hannibal both consulted the Oracle of Ammon at Siwa Oasis. Two millenia later, the Europeans added the old Ottoman pirate states of Morocco, Algiers, Tunis, and Tripoli to Egypt as European colonies or protectorates. Tripoli was conquered by Italy in 1911–1912, but the conquerors abandoned all but the coastal sections of their new possession in World War I. The interior remained in the hands of the Islamic fundamentalist order of the Senussi, whose leaders had finally fled to the Oasis of Kufra in Cyrenaica to escape the attentions of the Turks and their European successors.

Between world wars, Marshal Rodolfo Graziani, Benito Mussolini's empire builder, pacified the Bedouin in 1929 and 1934, but he cleared his supply lines for his advance to "liberate" Egypt at the start of World War II by withdrawing the Italian settlers and administrators to Italy. This step cleared the way for British sabotage and demolition strikes against his supply lines from deep in the interior—and a clean, romantic, and special war waged by the Anglo-Egyptian civil servants, reservists, and frustrated military careerists who had been experimenting in desert crossings with light trucks and aircraft, just as their French allies had been doing in their better known north-south crossings of the Western Sahara. With the loyalty of the Senussi assured by the promise that they would never be returned to Italian rule, and with most of the Italian colonial population out of the way, the British unleashed a series of delaying actions, surprises, and demolitions using first the Long Range Desert Group and then the two additional special forces that joined it. The various operations, including raids from the sea, were carefully controlled and coordinated under the command of the outnumbered regulars. The reward of their success for their Senussi supporters was to make Idris, the grandson of the original Grand Senussi, the king of a united Libya (Tripoli, Cyrenaica, Fezzan) at the end of World War II. How this outcome led to Idris's overthrow and to the place where American forces were hunting his successor Mohammar Quadaffi in the 1980s is, of course, another story. These British operations had not, strictly speaking, been independent guerrilla operations per se, but had instead been more in the nature of partisan operations that developed from the new flank established in the desert.

After the Allied conquest of North Africa was achieved in May 1943, a few officers felt that the desert special forces should be kept alive and given new missions. Part of the Long Range Desert Group, for example, was used in a series of disastrous operations against German-held islands in the Aegean. The survivors thereafter either returned to their original formations or else formed the nucleus of a Group that had to adapt itself to the conditions of special operations in a new arena. In retrospect the desert special forces were less the counterparts of the contemporary Delta Force or the British Special Air Service than they were a body of wartime volunteers who had considerable previous experience in utilizing a particular terrain for a specific strategic purpose. The career of the World War II special units ends in a clear triumph. The men of these forces accomplished the mission that circumstances gave them. Just how they got the mission and what it was and what they did with it is admirably told in this expert military history.

Theodore Ropp
Duke University

Preface

This study seeks to clarify the role of the British special forces employed in the North African desert from 1940 to 1943. It is neither a history of all British special forces nor of special forces of all kinds in World War II, although the role in that war of unconventional forces of elitist cast and specialized ground-combat function remains an inadequately explored one. These were the kinds of formations that the British, by 1940, had begun categorizing as "special forces"—not civilian saboteurs but uniformed soldiers specifically organized to carry out the high-risk functions of raiding, harassing, and intelligence gathering on the flanks or behind enemy lines. Their creation was predicated upon the assumption that the missions they undertook either fell outside the "normal operations of war" or else were impossible for standard units to perform efficiently within time and space constraints.

The fielding of the special forces, including the desert units with which this study is concerned, was a process adjunctive to those same developments in tactics, mobility, and communications that made the first half of World War II the era of blitzkrieg warfare. In contrast to the linear, static fronts of the previous world war, armored, mechanized, and air armies could now strike deeply into enemy territory. But the corollary was that the network of bases and lines of communication that sustained them was itself vulnerable to disruptive attacks carried out by small units able to operate behind enemy lines. That such forces could act with new effectiveness in this role was expressly a function of twentieth-century technology and the strategic constraints prevailing in the early stages of the war. Among the key preconditional developments were: (1) infiltration and access to enemy rear areas—provided by light motor vehicles, aircraft, assault landing craft, motorboats, submarines; (2) greater lethality and portability of weapons—provided by automatic weapons and new types of explosives; and (3) high-level control and coordination—provided by long-distance radio apparatus linking the special forces to the overall direction of a strategic headquarters. Given these favorable conditions, it was perhaps inevitable that the special forces would be regarded by some as a means of compensating for conventional-force failures elsewhere—a way to strike back during periods of defeat, retreat, and stress when no other method was available.

Of the various campaigns of that war, it is perhaps the particular geographical, strategic, and command relationships of the desert campaign in North Africa that permit the contributions and implications of such forces to stand out in sharpest relief. There the two sides for the greater portion of the campaign had to grapple with each other within a narrow, 1000–mile-long, east-west running corridor of desert. The northern limit of this corridor was the Mediterranean coast, the southern the impassable (to tanks and most heavy vehicles) dune ranges of the Sand Seas and the salt-marsh sump of the Qattara Depression. The corridor itself was sterile, mostly flat, mostly empty terrain that stretched from El Alamein in the east to Tripoli in the west. Arid and lacking features to block or slow movement, it seemed the arena *par excellence* of armored warfare. South of the corridor the vast, even harsher territory of the "true" or "inner desert" represented a medium through which small, highly mobile forces might pass in order to raid or reconnoiter an enemy's rear areas and lines of communication. The existence of a substantial body of primary-source material and accounts by participants makes possible a detailed examination of the process by which the British, to their considerable advantage and in contrast to their enemies, did just that—how they in fact made an early and fundamental commitment to the evolution of forces and means precisely to achieve the fullest possible exploitation of this open desert flank.

The three special forces so evolved were the Long Range Desert Group (raised in 1940), the "L" Detachment of the Special Air Service (1941), and the No. 1 Demolition Squadron/PPA (1942). Like most other special forces of World War II, these three were accorded elite unit status, their high-quality, selectively recruited personnel, intensive preparation, and assignment to very hazardous missions supposedly setting them apart from other ground-combat formations of the era. Certainly they appeared to differ in kind from types of *corps d'élite* more familiar in the history of warfare. In contrast to the Grenadiers, Scots, Coldstreamers, and other components of the British Army's Brigade of Guards—whose regiments, based upon their centuries-old reputation for selective recruitment, precision drill, and rigid, disciplined performance on the battlefield, comprise a sort of "designated elite"—these special forces performed nothing like the panoply of ceremonial duties associated with the Guards. Nor could they adequately be categorized as a "combat-proven" or "functional elite" in the same sense as those various types of standard units whose ranks, filled by the rush to volunteer or by conscription or both, have from time to time managed through hard training and good leadership to win a reputation for superlative performance on the battlefield. An example of a unit of this type might be the U. S. Army's 3rd Infantry Division, which won distinction in both the North African and European theaters of World War II. Nor, last, did the special forces quite fit into the mold of a "prototechnological elite" on the order of the German Wehrmacht's 21st Panzer Division. The personnel of that formation's tank units, comprising men selectively recruited as well as those acquired by conscription, had had to receive specialized training requisite to the operation of the gun, turret, and engine mechanisms that made up the vital weapon of blitzkrieg warfare. Instead, it was depth-of-mission, and the small parties in which they operated, that most immediately distinguished the special forces from these and other types of elite units. They were "elite" in the qualitative sense of their choice personnel and excellent preparation, but they were "special" in the functional military sense that what they did, if not wholly new or unconventional in concept, at the time seemed to lie outside or at least on the fringes of existing capabilities. In that regard the special forces existed precisely because they could exploit the gaps, voids, and backwaters arising from the playing out of the dominant machine-warfare paradigm in its desert setting. They were special forces for a special habitat with whose alien character conventional forces were by training, organization, and equipment less adequately shaped to deal.

Finally, the fielding of these three forces was the product of a process compatible with British military practices and institutions, a process which reached back to experiments with motorized forces for desert operations in World War I. Their employment twenty years later shows how experimentation in World War I evolved—as crucially influenced by the desert exploratory efforts and punitive campaigns against tribes conducted in the 1920s and 1930s—into a highly successful component of British combat in the difficult North African arena of World War II, an approach to warfare that could exist independently of the reverses suffered by the conventional formations. Representing only a modest investment in men and resources, the desert special forces secured for British arms the mastery of a unique dimension of warfare that the succession of general officers sent to command in the Middle East theater exploited to the fullest extent.

Acknowledgments

This book was made possible by the encouragement and support of many people. My first debt of gratitude is owed to Dr. Theodore Ropp, Professor Emeritus of History at Duke University, who saw the project launched, offered patient criticism of its themes and interpretations, and at length provided an essay by which to introduce it. Hardly less profound are my debts to two other professors at Duke, Dr. I. B. Holley, Jr., and Dr. Richard A. Preston, both of whom influenced my preliminary investigations into this aspect of the World War II experience.

Not only did colleagues in the Department of History, The Citadel, thereafter encourage the continuation of such investigations, but they suggested many helpful new themes for evaluation as well. Conspicuous has been the help of Dr. Larry H. Addington, who read and criticized the entire manuscript; it is my hope that he will recognize that his counsels have greatly influenced both the book's title and what appears on these pages. Likewise, Dr. John L. Brittain and Dr. Jamie W. Moore have each unfailingly contributed advice, support, and perspective, as has Dr. David H. White, Jr., who also read and offered suggestions on major portions of the manuscript. Professor W. Bland Mathis, Department of English, recalling his earlier role of mentor in undergraduate days, reviewed the manuscript for style and errors of grammar and spelling. And, at early and critical junctures, colleagues in other departments at The Citadel, in particular Dr. Harold W. Askins, Dr. Dennis Forsythe, and Dr. W. Bruce Ezell, now President of Erskine College, each contributed encouragement invaluable to the moving forward of this project.

Colleagues at the United States Military Academy, where I was privileged to serve as visiting professor of military history, further assisted my endeavors. In particular, Brigadier General Roy K. Flint, USA, currently Dean of the

Academic Board at West Point but then the Professor and Head, Department of History, made every effort to secure for me favorable teaching loads and other advantages that did much to advance the task of writing. Special thanks must be expressed as well to three other members of the History Department: to Colonel Robert A. Doughty, himself now Professor and Head, who shared results gleaned from his own research, read portions of the manuscript, and was one with whom it was always a pleasure to have intellectual exchanges; and to Colonel W. Scott Dillard and Lieutenant Colonel Kenneth E. Hamburger, both of whom offered ideas that improved the focus of particular portions of the manuscript. Colonel Paul F. Miles, Lieutenant Colonel S. L. Bowman, Major Donovan F. Jagger, and many others eased administrative burdens and helped the work to proceed. For their cooperation and hospitality I am very much indebted to my former departmental colleagues at West Point, as well as to John Keegan, Senior Lecturer in War Studies at the Royal Military Academy, Sandhurst, a careful observer of military practices on both sides of the Atlantic.

I owe the same debt of gratitude to many individuals associated with the Adjunct Faculty Program of the United States Marine Corps Command and Staff College, Quantico, Virginia. Dr. Allan R. Millett, Professor of History, Ohio State University, and the present head of C&SC's Adjunct Faculty, has followed the development of this project with interest and good advice, as have Dr. William J. Hatcher, Dr. James J. McNamara, Dr. Milton Shaw, and Dr. James R. Weinlader. Their ideas, and those of Lieutenant Colonel Donald F. Bittner, USMC, C&SC's staff military historian have sharpened the analysis in this book. The opportunity to offer lectures before Quantico's officer-students, drawn from a variety of armed forces, both U. S. and foreign, was an additional benefit. The individual experiences of these officers in special operations did not fail to add perspective, and provided a useful counterpoint to those undertaken four decades ago.

That much is owed to another group of officers—those who, as members of the LRDG, SAS, and PPA, were active participants in the mounting of dangerous operations in an alien environment—will be apparent from the extensive use I have made in the text of their thoughts, recollections and, in some cases, personal papers. I can only attempt to thank them for their kindnesses to my family and efforts in my behalf.

Generous assistance from several sources provided funds for the research and writing of this book. These include grants from Duke University, The Citadel Development Foundation, the Military History Institute/U. S. Army War College, and the National Endowment for the Humanities. Support of this excellent sort made it possible for me to conduct research in the following repositories, whose archival and library staffs I wish to thank for providing me access to holdings: the British Museum; the Ministry of Defence (Old War Office) Library; the Staff College, Camberley; King's College, University of London; the Royal Geographical Society; the Public Record Office;

the Service Historique, Château de Vincennes, Paris; the James C. Breckinridge Library, MCDEC Quantico, Virginia; the Duke University Library; the Daniel Library, The Citadel; The Citadel Archives and Museum; the Military History Institute, U. S. Army War College; and the U. S. Military Academy Library. Critical administrative support for the production of this book came, at West Point, from Mrs. Sally French and Miss Debbie Bittle, and, at The Citadel, Mrs. Glenna Bird, Mrs. Linda Pope, and Mrs. Thelma Pitts. Miss Bittle and Mrs. Pitts typed chapter drafts with efficiency and fortitude.

The three maps appearing in this book were drawn by Richard L. Cook, Jr., BSCE.

Finally, I wish to thank my wife, Betsy, whose steady encouragement has meant so much for so long. So also has the patient interest of my daughters, Ashley and Caroline, and I thank them for it.

All of these people contributed much; it must be with them that I share the credit for what value this book has. It remains only to be said that any errors of omission or commission are mine alone.

THE OTHER
DESERT WAR

First Experiments: World War I

They [the new armored and scouting cars] were worth hundreds of men to us in these deserts.
—T. E. Lawrence, *Seven Pillars of Wisdom*[1]

Stretching 3,000 miles across the northern third of Africa and a thousand miles below the coast of the Mediterranean, the "Great Desert" or Sahara is the world's largest mass of arid land. Two smaller deserts, the Sinai and the Arabian, lie just to the east and are almost equally hot and dry. It was to deal with the conditions of warfare in these three that the British Army commenced, in the second year of World War I, its experimentation with motorized forces for desert reconnaissance and raiding operations. The failure of their amphibious thrust at the Dardanelles in 1915–1916 committed the British, if they were to defeat Germany's ally, Ottoman Turkey, to a full-scale land campaign waged in some of the most difficult desert terrain on earth. This effort the historian B. H. Liddell Hart—characterizing Turkey as "a bent old man"—later pronounced as being like trying "to swallow . . . him from the feet upwards." Other measures having failed, that is, the British Army was left with no recourse but, python-like, to drag "its endless length across the desert" from Egypt to Palestine and thence north to Damascus.[2]

It was a campaign that ultimately required enormous efforts and three difficult years to win, as well as the diversion away from the main seat of war in France of more than 80,000 British troops. The Turks began by resorting to the traditional measure, the proclamation of a *jihad*. But the called-for holy war failed in its strategic purpose of igniting all the faithful of Islam to join in a general crusade against the British marshaling forces in

Egypt. And in one sector, it conspicuously backfired. In the Hejaz region of the Arabian peninsula it helped, in fact, to drive Prince Feisal, eventually backed by Colonel T. E. Lawrence and liberal inducements of British money and guns, to launch the guerrilla war afterwards famous as the Arab Revolt.[3]

In the vast desert lying west of Egypt's Nile Valley, however, the response to the *jihad* was quite different. Focusing their attentions on the bands of Bedouin tribesmen who inhabited the chain of oases astride the Libyan-Egyptian border, the Turks soon sent emissaries and promises of arms. In particular, the Senussi, a nomadic people of fundamentalist Islamic belief, proved receptive to Turkish overtures and plans for sending raids against the British from the west. These Senussi were hard cases indeed. Having fiercely resisted the Italian conquest of Libya's coastal regions four years before, they now were more than ready to make common cause against hated Italy's allies, the British. Certainly their leader or "Grand Senussi," Sayed Ahmed (described by a captured British naval officer as a "shrewd-looking . . . powerful man with a greyish beard and hawkish features"[4]) did not long delay in accepting the offers of Ottoman assistance. The result was that Austrian submarines, slipping through the British blockade, began arriving in the late months of 1915 with the promised arms and munitions. These included Mauser rifles, machineguns, and various types of light artillery pieces. Such weapons, along with German and German-trained Turkish officers, plus a small contingent of Turkish regular troops, were to serve as the nucleus for a Senussi desert army to be raised in the main oases.[5]

Rounding up additional tribesmen as it moved east towards Egypt, this Senussi force therefore commenced its attacks in the winter months of early 1916. While Sayed Ahmed's array never amounted to more than 10,000 men, it shortly proved able to cause the British plenty of trouble. Superb raiders mounted on camels and operating in their own element, the Senussi irregulars could find their way across a trackless region to stage hit-and-run attacks against a string of outposts. These thrusts soon succeeded in precisely the purpose the Turks had intended. As the intelligence reports came in, the British commander, General Sir Archibald Murray, had no choice but to begin shifting forces away from the Sinai front to block the raids now being sent against him, 400 miles away, on the other side of Egypt.[6]

Murray's troops faced a difficult task: to patrol and defend against raiders more mobile than themselves an empty region of desert running from the Mediterranean coast down to the scattered oases lying 500 miles to the south. His first step was to juggle his forces to best advantage. Combining selected British, Indian, Australian, and New Zealand units, Murray soon created what the staff colleges refer to as a "task-organized" force. This entity, styled the Western Frontier Force, contained a mixture of infantry, cavalry, and artillery elements supported by the light bombing aircraft of the Royal Flying Corps' (RFC's) No. 17 Squadron. But Murray also went a step further. Following the military wisdom laid down in *Small Wars: Their Principles and*

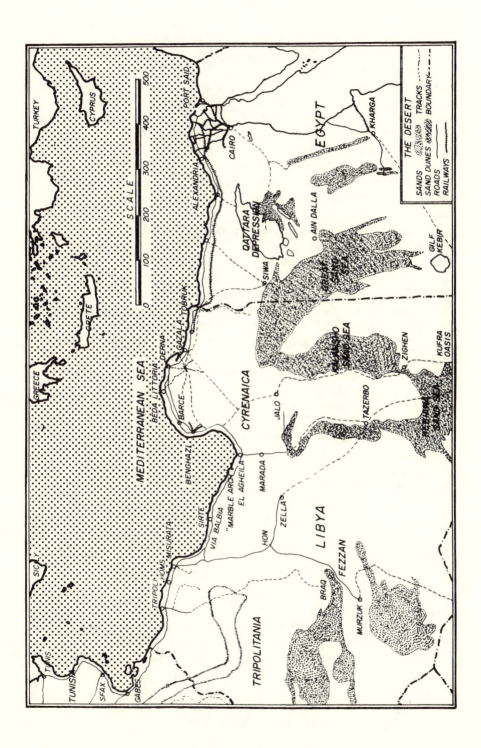

Practice (1896) to the effect that "the conditions . . . [of desert warfare] are so diversified, [and] the enemy's mode of fighting is often so peculiar . . . that irregular warfare must generally be carried out on a method totally different from the stereotyped system," he sought to give his troops a degree of mobility approaching that of the nimble enemy they were to fight.[7] At the suggestion of a veteran colonel who had won the Victoria Cross fighting in the desert twenty years before, he directed that a large segment of this force be mounted and formed into a special Camel Corps. Thus, nearly a thousand men drawn from British and Australian light cavalry units soon found themselves unhorsed in order to undertake the trials of learning to ride temperamental camels, all in hopes of beating the Senussi at their own game.[8]

This was an approach that had been tried before. Certainly in earlier desert wars British—and for that matter, French and Italian—commanders had also found it necessary to mount a portion of their forces on camels in order to fight a highly mobile opponent. The camel was, after all, the mainstay of desert travel. Even so, some old desert hands still doubted that large numbers of new troops could learn to handle camels with any sort of effectiveness, much less learn to endure the privations of the desert. These privations were indeed formidable—the lack of water, the burning hot sun, the awesomeness of empty spaces, violent sandstorms, and mysterious fevers that could reduce whole companies of men to the shakes. It was true, for example, that one entire contingent of troops sent beyond the oases soon "had sores all over their faces," flies swarmed about them constantly, and heatstroke cases reduced their numbers to a handful.[9] Overall, it was clear to Murray from the start that the Camel Corps approach could at best yield but very limited results. The seemingly pragmatic step of mounting troops on camels might indeed serve to lessen the edge in mobility enjoyed by their Bedouin opponent. At the same time, however, closing the mobility gap by this means would also impose upon his men some of the same limitations faced by the enemy. As a price for their enhanced mobility, Camel Corps troops could expect to forfeit at least some of that superiority of firepower (for example, fewer machineguns and artillery pieces and less ammunition could now be carried) that had usually given European troops the edge in previous desert fights.[10]

Actually, a far more efficient and promising method for moving troops across the desert already existed. Moreover, it was one that had already been put to the test of desert warfare and been found reasonably workable. Nearly a decade before, French forces in Morocco had begun using motor vehicles— both armored cars and light, unarmored models for scouting and patrolling— to run down and defeat desert tribesmen. Thereafter, in the desert just south of their newly acquired coastal enclaves in Libya, the Italians also had begun employing vehicles of this sort to batter these same Senussi who, with their Turkish allies, now vexed Murray. But the British were about to carry the employment of such vehicles, as a crucial element of desert warfare, to levels unmatched by either the French or the Italians in any previous campaign. In the process and given the greater scale and centrality of role with which these vehicles were ultimately employed, Murray's forces would help to alter forever the old equation of desert warfare, an equation that had generally given the odds to the Bedouin enemy as long as that enemy avoided positional warfare. Mounted on fast camels, such raiders could usually strike some isolated post and then escape back into the desert again before European forces could react and bring them to battle. Putting regular forces on camels might improve their mobility, but it markedly decreased their hitting power; in effect, it reduced them, in terms of firepower, to the same level as their irregular opponents. But motor vehicles were now, in the first large-scale test of their employment in major desert operations, to change the old relationship. They would prove able to give European forces a degree of mobility equal to if not greater than that of their desert enemies. More importantly, they would make it possible for those forces to bring their superior firepower to bear even at points deep in the desert's interior.[11]

Murray thus came to seize upon the use of motor vehicles as a means of solving the problems of desert warfare. As it happened, however, his first contingent of armored cars came not from the British Army but from the Royal Navy. That vehicles so well suited to the open spaces of the Libyan desert should have been in the possession of the navy stemmed from early notions as to the nature of the aerial reconnaissance mission. The cars had originally been obtained to serve as a sort of ground adjunct to the Senior Service's brand-new air arm, the Royal Naval Air Service (RNAS). The idea, and this had held particular appeal for First Lord of the Admiralty Winston Churchill, himself a cavalry officer by training, was that they would somehow be useful for scouting and for rescuing the RNAS's downed fliers. The cars and their volunteer crews were promptly sent to France in 1914, where they just as promptly proved unusable on battlefields whose trenches and mud the cars could never hope to negotiate. Thereafter they were shunted off to Egypt. Of excellent design and durability, most of the cars were 1914–model Rolls Royces that, covered with a thin crust of armor, weighed better than three tons. Carrying a crew of four men and mounting machineguns, they were certainly enough to take on any band of lightly armed desert guerrillas. On the other hand, as their first forays into the desert shortly revealed, they had a tendency to bog down in soft sand, they consumed enormous quantities of gasoline, and they required an elaborate train of "tenders" (still in the naval parlance) to support and maintain them.[12]

Murray formed them into striking units called Light Armoured and Motor Machinegun Batteries. His initial idea seems to have been that the armored cars would give him a force able to hit quickly and powerfully against concentrations of Senussi, while the Camel Corps, whose training was now nearly completed, took on the more sedentary job of patrolling the isolated oases to the south. But since it was also clear that the weight and limited radius of action of the armored cars would act to restrict their operations, Murray looked about for some form of lighter, faster motor vehicle, one better suited to the task of scouting the enemy over longer ranges. Trials with motorcycles, using the standard models employed by military dispatch riders, proved a total failure. What came next, undertaken as a makeshift, soon led to the adaptation of the simple, unpretentious but rugged Model T Ford car as a vehicle useful for desert warfare. There were plenty of these cars available, since the army had already shipped hundreds to Egypt for use as transport vehicles on the lines of communication. Making these "Tin Lizzies," with their twenty-horsepower, four-cylinder engines, into the dependable mechanical mounts of a long-range scouting force required little more than the mounting of a .303–caliber Lewis gun or two on them. The volunteers to man them were drawn from British and Australian units already in the Middle East. Using the structure of the Light Armoured Motor Batteries as a model, they were, early in 1916, formed into independent units officially designated the Light Car Patrols (LCPs). Ultimately there would be six of these LCPs, each with two officers and twelve "other ranks" riding in five or six vehicles.[13]

Assisted by their Turkish artillery, the Senussi forces had by now thrust into Egypt as far as Matrûh on the Mediterranean coast, a point about a hundred miles west of the El Alamein battlefield of World War II. But here Sayed Ahmed made the mistake of listening too much to his chief military advisor, Ja'far Pasha, described by British intelligence as a "Germanized Turk of considerable ability."[14] Rather than sticking to the traditional Senussi mode of warfare—mounting sudden raids and then retiring into the desert— he let himself be talked instead into trying to hold fixed positions. This set him up for attacks by the British, and Murray made the best of his opportunity. Spearheading the Western Desert Force, the armored car units— their way scouted by No. 17 Squadron's biplanes—were sent racing forward into the desert. In short order, they began to head off and then systematically to drive the Turks and Senussi back towards Libya. Under this kind of pressure the Senussi army, by now running short of food and munitions, began disintegrating into various separate and disjointed bands, many of them encumbered by their women and children and flocks of sheep and goats.

Two clashes in 1916 served in particular to illustrate to British commanders the potency of the new motorized weapons for desert warfare. In one, a large contingent of Turks and Senussi, exhausted from the retreat and thinking itself safely beyond the range of their pursuers, committed the fatal error of settling down to camp along a major caravan route. But guided by one of the RFC's BE-2C biplanes, a full squadron of British armored cars almost immediately arrived to mount an attack. By nightfall, the squadron had managed to kill a considerable number of the enemy and had captured so many prisoners that they had to be herded along like cattle. A second episode followed in short order and succeeded in capturing the imagination of the British public even in the grim year of the Somme battle, not least because of the dashing and flamboyant character of the cars' commander. A former Guards officer educated at Eton, Hugh Richard Arthur Grosvenor, second duke of Westminster, had served in the Boer War before entering politics, where he had become a close friend and associate of Winston Churchill. Learning that British seamen and soldiers (the survivors of H.M.S. *Tara* and the S.S. *Moorina*, earlier torpedoed off the North African coast by a German submarine) had fallen into the hands of the Senussi, Westminster prepared a daring rescue operation. Intelligence reports indicated that the prisoners were being held across the Libyan border at a place called Bir Hacheim, a collection of native huts clustered around an ancient Roman well (or, in Arabic, a *bir*). Pushing west before dawn, Westminster's armored cars led a force of twenty vehicles loaded with infantry, plus a number of ambulances. The column slipped past Senussi watchpoints and arrived at the objective by midafternoon. Immediately the cars fanned out in line-abreast formation to attack. Despite the fears of ambush, the rescue operation itself proved surprisingly easy. Quickly scattering the handful of guards, the force rounded up the *Tara-Moorina* survivors—who, though suffering from hunger, dysentery, lice, and various fevers, had under the circumstances been fairly well treated—and got away before the large body of Senussi in the area could react. The whole operation had cost the rescue force not a single casualty.[15]

In less than two months, this and other armored-car operations in the portions of the desert proximate to the Mediterranean coast had done much to smash what had started as a Turkish-Senussi advance. The cars, assisted by infantry, cavalry, and artillery elements and supported by aircraft that could spot and strafe the enemy, had made short work indeed of a poorly equipped array of desert irregulars. While the British had not yet used tanks for desert warfare (the first tanks, developed in great secrecy, would receive their first trial in combat on the Western Front a month or two after Westminster's exploit), it was by now abundantly clear that the armored car had great potential as a device for catching and mauling the retreating Senussi. In fact, most of Sayed Ahmed's army, so pounded, had pulled back into the safety of Libya. But having thus far listened to Turkish military advice with disastrous results, Sayed Ahmed now elected to go back to the standard Senussi mode of fighting. By shifting his main effort to the south and to the deep inner desert which was the Bedouin's true element, he believed that he could avoid the dangerous concentrations of British force in the north. In particular, by using Siwa—a major oasis that hugged the edge of the vast dunes that ran south into the interior—as a base, he would have an excellent and sheltered jump-off point from which to advance in stages along a series of undefended oases. Such an approach might even make possible the launching of raids against the Nile Valley itself. Thus, with British forces gathered in the north, guarding the Egyptian coastal towns, Sayed Ahmed could hope to fight in the traditional way, attacking and then fading into the desert.[16]

His bands indeed soon managed to take Siwa. Thereafter, they commenced their harassing operations in the direction of the Nile. Hopeful that aircraft might be useful in the task of spotting and attacking them as they moved across the open desert from one oasis to another, the British promptly shifted RFC squadrons to begin flying a fan of air patrols. But the extreme distances and the flying conditions of the southern desert were too much for the aircraft of 1916. A 19–year-old pilot—the future Sir John Slessor, marshal of the Royal Air Force—recalled that his biplane's ninety-horsepower engine tended to get clogged with sand, the aircraft lacked anything like the fuel-carrying capacity needed to fly the distances required, and it could, moreover, quickly come to grief in one of the sudden sandstorms. It was precisely these obvious limitations of the airpower of that day that prompted the British to begin making use of their Light Car Patrols (LCPs). Thus, in mid-1916, these half-dozen reconnaissance patrols were ordered south to cover the southern Egyptian oases. There they very quickly proved themselves more than just an auxiliary to the air and the Camel Corps patrols trying to contain the Senussi. In fact, the LCPs very soon acquired the primary role. As a first step, the establishment of hidden caches of reserve gasoline, food, and water at various points in the desert acted to increase both the range and the duration of their missions. With the main goal in warfare against desert tribesmen being to gain control of the few waterholes, the British soon discovered that this step helped the LCPs to move faster and farther than the Senussi. They proved able, in fact, to cordon off and hold the raiders to one or two oases. Finally, in terms of firepower, the machineguns and Lewis guns which the LCPs mounted were far too much for the Senussi to take on. The patrols indeed were successful to the point that, after a hard travail in the 120° temperatures of the Libyan desert's summer, Sayed Ahmed's bands, prevented from extending their raids closer to the Nile and forced out of key oases, eventually had to give up. By the autumn of 1916, they began falling back to Siwa, 250 miles distant. As they did so, the LCPs kept up their pursuit, in some cases occupying an oasis within an hour or so of the enemy's departure.[17]

With his southern desert thrust and traditional mode of combat defeated by a handful of motorized patrols, Sayed Ahmed kept his force (now down to fewer than 2,000 men) concentrated at Siwa. The British, meanwhile, were determined to finish him off with one good battle. But to attack Siwa, 200 miles from their nearest base, was an undertaking beyond anything yet attempted in the desert. In particular, little if any information of real military value was known about the oasis or the approaches to it. Sheltered by the desert which encircled it, Siwa had the reputation of being a picture-book oasis, known for its sweet-date palms, deep pools, native mud huts, and

elaborate baths (still functional) constructed by the Romans. It had, in ancient times, been the seat of the god Jupiter Ammon, and was most famous
for the visit Alexander the Great made to it in 332 B.C. But early in 1917,
the British commenced the extensive logistical preparations necessary to
move a large force of all arms against the place. As these preparations were
just getting underway, however, Senussi deserters brought in news which
threatened to upset the whole plan. The wily Sayed Ahmed—either learning
or guessing what the British were up to—had suddenly decided to get out
of Siwa before his enemies could strike. Other deserters reported that he
was planning to decamp and move west over the desert to Jarabub, an oasis
just across the Libyan border. With a full-scale effort now out of the question
because of the time factor, General Murray at once authorized the formation
of a special attack column made up solely of armored cars and the Light Car
Patrols. Accordingly, three complete Light Car Patrols—No.'s 4, 5, and 6,
comprising about forty officers and men and nearly two dozen Fords—received orders to join the armored cars. Of these, a full squadron had already
reached an assembly point far out in the desert. The armored cars and the
LCPs were placed under the overall command of a brigadier.[18] While these
forces were hurriedly being moved into position, a separate supply column
of trucks began setting up, at intervals in the desert, the dumps of gasoline
and water necessary to get the attackers all the way to Siwa. "No motor
column," noted a war correspondent who had covered the desert campaign
since the beginning, had yet contemplated a move "on so large a scale."[19]

The force began its advance early in February 1917. The weather was
bitterly cold, and time was lost trying to start cars whose radiators had frozen
during the night. But thereafter the column made good progress and arrived,
by the end of the second day, at the junction of two main caravan tracks.
This put the attackers near the place where, they knew from maps and from
what the deserters had told them, the broad, flat, sandy expanses of the Libyan
plateau suddenly dropped off to the much lower desert floor that harbored
Siwa itself. Pressing on, they came finally to the edge and looked down from
the top of a high, almost vertical escarpment. Far in the distance they could
just make out the dark blur of the date palms that marked the northern
limits of the oasis—and presumably the enemy camp. As one officer put it,
the sensation of standing atop the escarpment and looking down to the desert
floor below was the disquieting one of "looking down into a hole," by which
he meant that going down the escarpment looked like a one-way trip.[20] That
is, the column might be able to get its vehicles down but, once down, might
not be able to get them back up again, especially if the enemy subsequently
proved too strong and the only recourse was a hasty retreat. It was evident
that the Senussi had used great care in employing demolition charges to
blow in the good approaches; certainly none appeared useable. Eventually
locating a narrow defile, the attackers began sending their Fords and the big
armored cars lurching down its steep grade. Aside from a broken spring or

two, the cars were, in this manner, one by one, brought safely to the bottom. The column's only hope of getting its vehicles out again was to defeat the Senussi—and so gain time to try to level out the defile by digging—or else to search for a new way back up.

Thus committed, the force headed off in the direction of Siwa. Neither the brigadier in command nor any of his officers had anything approaching a clear idea as to what they could expect to find. In fact, after wallowing through sand dunes and some tamarisk scrub, they eventually found the enemy before they found Siwa. There followed what one of the participants described as "an *opera bouffe*' affair," an episode characterized by "an immense amount of noise and very little blood-shed" as the British cars charged forward towards a low hill dotted with huts and tents.[21] Machineguns chattering, the armored cars almost immediately blundered into a kind of depression or mud flat. Bogged down in the mud, they spent some hot moments under the fire of an estimate 700 or 800 Senussi and Turks while their crews worked to get them out. The two sides thereafter settled down to shoot at each other for the rest of the day. While the Turks' pair of light artillery pieces and two Maxim guns did little real damage, the armored cars were likewise unable to get close enough to the enemy to be effective. Moreover, the British position grew increasingly precarious as, towards dusk, one of the Light Car Patrols brought in the unsettling news that another 500 Senussi were located just a few miles away and might be preparing to attack from the rear at any time. This possibility caused the brigadier, as he later phrased it, "some little anxiety." What he could not know was that the sudden approach of the armored cars at this seemingly unreachable spot had so shaken the Senussi that they were already giving thought to pulling out. In fact, as night fell, Sayed Ahmed's force began slipping away and moving west over the desert towards Libya. By the time the British guessed what was afoot, it was already too late. Although some armored cars and the Fords of No. 6 LCP were sent to cut them off, virtually all of the Senussi managed to escape when their pursuers were halted by rough ground,[22] and while the official account of the operation boasted that upwards of 150 Senussi had been killed or wounded, a "native 'doctor' who had served with the enemy" told one of the LCP officers that there had actually been only "nine casualties," none of them more than "slightly wounded."[23]

Still, General Murray was sufficiently pleased with the results to scrawl "Excellent Operation" across the top page of the after-action report.[24] And well he might: in addition to giving the British control of this crucial oasis—and thus of an enormous expanse of surrounding desert—the Siwa attack had served as the *coup de grace* to the whole Senussi campaign. These desert irregulars had had enough, and they soon proved willing to negotiate. Their fatal mistake, noted Lieutenant Colonel Archibald Wavell—who would command British forces against Rommel in this same desert twenty-five years later—had been that of forfeiting "their natural methods of warfare by adopting the . . . tactics of regular armies.''[25] But if their employment of conventional methods had played into the hands of the British, it was equally clear that their best efforts at fighting in their customary style had also been defeated by the introduction of motorized forces, the armored cars and the Light Car Patrols. For the first time, the circumstances of desert warfare had been changed to favor one of Wavell's ''regular armies,'' rather than the bands of camel-riding desert tribesmen who moved and fought in their own element. As the official report noted, though a small affair, the Siwa attack had actually been ''the first operation ever carried out by the British Army on an entirely mechanised basis.''[26] But the ability to field the Light Car Patrols as a specialized desert scouting force—the ''eyes of the army,'' as they were already being characterized—had not come about overnight. Nor was it the result of some special expertise contained exclusively within the army itself. Rather, in building up the LCPs as an effective force, Murray's headquarters had been able to call upon the services of perhaps the most expert desert explorer then available anywhere.

Geologist and avid archeologist rather than soldier, that expert, Dr. John Ball, was a British civilian employee of the Egyptian government's survey department. At age 50 and having spent years examining the wastelands on both sides of Egypt, Ball, in his knowledge of the desert and its habitat, was unmatched. Early in 1916, the army began putting this knowledge to use with the formation of the Light Car Patrols. Ball began by working to adapt the basic Model T Ford to meet the conditions of an environment that no one had ever expected that particular vehicle to face. The first problem was water. When the Model T's engine overheated in the extreme temperatures, its water-cooled radiator usually boiled over, thus spilling the desert's most precious commodity. Ball rigged up a special hose-and-condenser arrangement in order that the water, rather than being lost when the radiator boiled over, could instead be collected and recycled.[27] His second critical problem was navigation: a method by which to find the way across hundreds of miles of flat wasteland lacking, for the most part, recognizable features. Away from established caravan tracks, standard military map-and-compass techniques were of little use. Compasses—even aircraft compasses, as Ball discovered—proved unworkable when mounted on a Model T (the changing magnetic fields set up by the engine and transmission constantly threw them off). Moreover, stopping every mile or so to dismount and walk far enough away to take a new reading was manifestly impractical for a fast-moving scouting force. Giving up on the magnetic compass altogether, Ball helped to design a sun compass—a sort of sundial device, consisting of a vertical spike and a circular card or plate marked off in degrees. With practice this instrument could be read by noting how the sun's shadow fell across the card. It gave an accurate course heading, and could be used while the car was moving.[28]

Perhaps more than any other, it was this development which acted to permit the LCPs to reach and to conduct surveys of hitherto unknown sections of the desert. Taken together, the compass and the various techniques and practical desert lore which Ball imparted to the LCPs' Australian and British volunteers proved a vital step in the defeat of the Senussi. In addition to their scouting activities, the topographic data which the patrols brought back helped to supply the Western Desert Force with accurate maps of its area of operations. Attached to No. 3 Light Car Patrol, civilian Ball spent the last months of the campaign doing what he liked to do best: knocking about in the desert, happily applying the techniques he had worked to impart to the army. These techniques were eventually compiled in an official manual entitled *Desert Reconnaissance by Motor-Car: Primarily a Hand Book for Patrol Officers in Western Egypt,* issued in 1917.[29]

With the Senussi raids defeated and the threat to Egypt's western frontier now eliminated, the British were free once again to concentrate efforts on the Sinai front and the drive towards Palestine. Certainly the results of that endeavor had so far proved disappointing. Despite a superiority in men and equipment and extensive logistical preparations, the efforts of General Murray's six-division Egyptian Expeditionary Force to overcome the Turkish defenses at Gaza and Beersheba—the gateway to Palestine—had twice failed. In fact, Murray, who had been exceedingly innovative in fielding the Light Car Patrols and armored cars to cope with the Senussi, was eventually removed from command. He was replaced by thickset cavalryman Sir Edmund Allenby, whom the troops shortly nicknamed "Bull." An aggressive commander, Allenby did not fail to make good use of the apparatus which his predecessor had fashioned. Moreover, by the time he was ready to initiate his main offensive, he possessed a very significant advantage indeed. The Turks, and their sizeable reinforcing contingents of German and Austrian troops, were by now being raided, jabbed at, and dislocated on their flank and along their lines of communication by a British-led (or at least influenced) force of Arab guerrillas.[30]

The name of the one British officer, among the score sent to work with or to assist Feisal, that eventually became virtually synonymous with the exploits of these guerrillas was, of course, that of T. E. Lawrence. Affecting the robes and *kaffiyeh* headdress of an Arab sheikh and assisted by a not inconsiderable flair for showmanship, Lawrence received, both during and after the war, the lion's share of the credit. The 29–year-old Colonel Lawrence, as "Lawrence of Arabia," emerged as a figure whose actual contributions became increasingly difficult to separate from the powerful imagery of the legend that began to grow up about him even while the war was still in progress. For the British, having just used their new motorized weapons to defeat one army of desert guerrillas, in the last two years of the conflict turned their hand to the task of employing their own army of guerrillas. In the process, the powerful and appealing imagery of Lawrence— an Oxford-educated "English sheikh of Araby," a "brilliant natural soldier," and the "brains, . . . organizing force, . . . and military technician"[31] of the whole effort—came finally to symbolize a sense of British mastery of all of the elements of desert warfare.[32] This sense of mastery persisted long after the successes of the armored cars and Light Car Patrols had been forgotten.

Initially, however, the British were slow in acting to exploit Feisal's 1916 "Arab Revolt" against the Turks. Probably their own difficulties in defeating the Senussi from 1916 to early 1917 were a necessary learning experience in helping first Murray and then Allenby to see how, in Lawrence's rich rhetoric, the Hejaz Arabs' "loose shower of sparks" could be fanned, with appropriate British support, into "a firm flame" that would eventually serve to tie down the enemy in a futile effort to guard a long desert flank.[33] Certainly the last episodes on the final front of the desert campaign came quickly to overshadow the earlier struggle against the Senussi, and eventually emerged as the classic example of desert guerrilla warfare. Lawrence's main targets were the Turks' isolated desert outposts and their vital but exposed Hejaz rail line. Well aware of how the Senussi had gone wrong with their conventional attacks on Egypt, he began by rejecting efforts to reinforce Feisal's tribesmen with units of British or French regulars. He perceived that the Turkish army, deployed in the desert and dependent upon its long lines of communication, was like a plant: it was "immobile, firm-rooted, [and] nourished through long stems to the head." Feisal's guerrillas, by preserving their mobility and "drifting about [the desert] like a gas," could hope to destroy these stems—the Hejaz rail line in particular—with a series of carefully orchestrated moves.[34] By the time Allenby was ready to attack the main Turkish defenses guarding Palestine, the British discovered that far more enemy troops were engaged in trying to contain Lawrence than were actually deployed on the key front. Thereafter, in the autumn of 1918, and supported by Camel Corps, armored-car, and LCP elements that would enhance their striking power without diminishing their essential mobility, Lawrence's guerrillas played a crucial role in Allenby's winning of the Turkish stronghold of Damascus. A month later the Turks, facing the advance of additional British forces converging on them from Macedonia and Iraq, finally capitulated, just over a week before the Armistice ending the war was signed on the Western Front.[35]

Although Allenby may at times have regarded Lawrence as "something of a charlatan," his name had, well before the termination of the desert campaign, caught the popular imagination in a way that was unique.[36] The generals and diplomats with whom he worked may have found him pretentious and pushy: he was the "little Lawrence" who "lacked social position as well as inches."[37] Yet his exploits had come to suggest the distinctive features of the desert war, a war of movement remote and far different from the stalemate, mud, and slaughter of the European theater's Western Front. Even before the American journalist Lowell Thomas began his

highly popular lecture series entitled "With Allenby in Palestine and Lawrence of Arabia," Lawrence's place as desert-fighter *par excellence* was secure. Liddell Hart, for example, believed that Lawrence's strategy for
waging guerrilla warfare was so brilliant as to elevate him to the Napo-
leonic orbit of Great Captain. Lawrence, in his view, had possessed "a
theoretical mastery of war that was . . . unique." It was a mastery supposedly the product of extensive reading in what Lawrence tried to toss off as
"the usual schoolboy stuff"—virtually every military classic from Jomini
and Clausewitz to Mahan.[38]

In any case, he emerged as "the only old-style hero" of a war which had
killed off anonymous masses of men in futile assaults.[39] The image of Lawrence as hero was altogether too powerful and fascinating to be resisted. In
the English-speaking world of the 1920s and 1930s, his name soon came to
rival even those of major commanders Haig and Pershing. The actual in-
gredients of British victory in the desert had been the conventional infantry,
cavalry and artillery forces—supplemented by the resourceful employment
of the new motorized weapons for the effort against the Senussi—that had
borne the real brunt of the fighting. But the role of the Light Car Patrols
was soon forgotten, and even the highly publicized exploits of the Duke of
Westminster's armored cars gradually faded from the public memory (and
would even more so, as Westminster eventually and publicly began to express
admiration for Germany's Adolf Hitler). The value of the LCPs and armored
cars for use as scouting units against desert tribes remained a matter of interest
chiefly to professional soldiers who might, should the need for these forces
ever arise in the future, have to make use of them again. But Lawrence's
name and his role in the Arab Revolt did not fade. Rather, he seemed to
encompass and to stand for everything the British had done in the desert
from 1916 to 1918. Lawrence himself, by his enigmatic personality and
strange antics, helped to contribute to this image; he managed, along the
way, to enthrall some of the leading lights of his day, including George
Bernard Shaw, the poets Robert Graves and Siegfried Sassoon, and Winston
Churchill. Awarded a prestigious position as a fellow of Oxford University's
All Souls, he eventually wrote the book entitled *Revolt in the Desert*. This,
and the full, epic version of the work which appeared after his death in 1935
as *Seven Pillars of Wisdom: A Triumph*, sealed forever his legend.[40] To Churchill, *Seven Pillars of Wisdom* had to be ranked with the very "greatest books
ever written in the English language."[41]

Thus, Lawrence's name and image cast a powerful spell, and the legend
surrounding his exploits grew during the years of the interwar decades. It
helped, in the 1920s, to inspire exploration of the region where he had
fought and in other desert areas as well. Twenty years later the legend would,
in a future world war and in combination with "native romanticism, schoolboy
yearning for high adventure," but above all, through the inspiration of Lawrence "as the great guerrilla fighter," send "dozens of young Englishmen

raiding in the desert or along the shores of the Aegean."[42] And in a critical moment in the summer of 1940, the legacy of that name would help to ensure official backing of the first British special force to be formed for desert operations in World War II.

CHAPTER 2

The Penetration of the Desert

A few of us, beginning with no really deep interest in exploration at all, evolved techniques by which we could penetrate to places in the far interior of the Libyan desert.

—Major Ralph A. Bagnold[1]

Allenby's army had scarcely been disbanded before British troops were once again forced to confront the problems of desert warfare. In the early 1920s, the necessity of bringing Iraq's refractory Bedouin tribesmen under control ensured that British military attentions remained focused on the techniques of combat in arid regions. Concurrent with that interest, a handful of officers, acting independently and sometimes having to overcome official resistance, undertook to develop the techniques of long-range desert exploration. It was these techniques that ultimately made it impossible for them to use standard motor vehicles to push far into the largest desert on earth.[2]

Awarded Iraq as well as Palestine and Transjordan as League of Nations mandates, the British had to deal, in the desert west and south of Baghdad, with tribesmen almost as difficult as the Senussi of 1916–1917. By 1921, with units of the British Army trying to contain these Bedouin in an increasingly bitter and costly campaign, desert expert Lawrence proposed an alternative solution. Serving as a special advisor to Churchill, who now headed the Colonial Office, Lawrence argued that the war just ended had conclusively demonstrated the great utility of the new motorized weapons for desert combat. The British, he said, should at once replace their slow-moving columns of infantry with an efficient, quick-reacting "combination of armoured-cars and aircraft." These weapons "could rule the desert," and could do so on a basis far more economical than the means then being employed.[3]

When the army, however, proved chary about sharing control of this sort of air-ground endeavor, Lawrence concentrated his efforts on the new Royal Air Force, independent since 1918. Ardent for any opportunity to show what air power could do, RAF officers proved eager to accept the new mission. Thus their service was duly given responsibility for bringing order to Iraq's deserts.[4]

The concept first proposed by Lawrence was soon being referred to as "Air Control." Its application flowed from the principle of war known as "economy of force." That is, a handful of airplanes, concentrated at one or two easily defended points, could be launched over great distances in order to deliver a telling blow but with minimum expenditure of resources. The RAF began its task of policing a vast territory by adding, as Lawrence had suggested, a ground element to its airplanes. This element, comprising armored cars, was manned and operated exclusively by air force personnel. In addition, the division of the desert into a series of districts, each monitored by an intelligence network of Arabic-speaking British officers and linked by radio to a central base, made possible the launching of aerial strikes on extremely short notice and after the issuance of official warnings. The standard *modus operandi* that emerged for Air Control operations was relatively simple—it worked, as one of its key practitioners put it, on the basis of "a fire brigade."[5] When a district intelligence officer radioed word of the latest tribal foray, a combined force of airplanes and armored cars was dispatched immediately. In this way, "refractory tribesmen" could be "attacked . . . in five or six hours," even at distances approaching 200 miles.[6] After the aircraft had visited their repeated bombing and strafing attacks on the Bedouin and their villages and livestock, the armored cars arrived to finish the job. It was hardly surprising that, having endured the ordeal of air attack in the open desert, the survivors generally could be counted upon to go back to their allotted tribal preserve without further resistance.

As the 1920s continued, the RAF's formula for Air Control successfully pounded the Iraqi tribes into submission. But Lawrence himself soon gave up his post under Churchill. In fact, he eventually hid himself in the enlisted ranks of the RAF, then the army, then the RAF again. Changing his name to Shaw, he sought not the anterooms of the great but the obscurity of a string of RAF and army stations. He was killed a decade later in a motorcycle accident. Among the small crowd of mourners attending his funeral were Winston Churchill and a rising star in the British Army, Brigadier Archibald Wavell. As Allenby's staff officer, Wavell had witnessed the last stages of the Senussi campaign, and he was also directly familiar with the issues relating to Lawrence's role with Feisal's Arabs. It happened that both figures, the one as the future prime minister and the other as the British general in the Middle East theater, would within five years find themselves championing a form of warfare which Lawrence had helped to render comprehensible and appealing to his countrymen. In the interim, by its very success, the Air Control experiment encouraged within the British military apparatus a belief in the efficacy of nonstandard solutions when it came to coping with the problems of desert warfare.[7]

Yet the British could hardly claim exclusive monopoly or even first application of such solutions. What amounted to variations of Lawrence's formula also held enormous appeal for French and Italian soldiers faced with relatively similar problems in other deserts. In any event, the use of aircraft and armored cars in combination, in order to "pacify" tribesmen, was to be tested throughout the interwar decades and in campaigns a good deal more extensive than the one in Iraq. French efforts to pacify the Saharan interior of Morocco and Italian efforts to bring Libya's Senussi to heel had, after all, only been temporarily interrupted by World War I. With the termination of that war these efforts could now be resumed. More than that, these other efforts soon came to surpass the British one not only in numbers of men and amounts of resources involved, but also in terms of the inventiveness and scope of the operations undertaken.[8]

French military forces operating in the Moroccan and Algerian fringes of the Sahara had, as already indicated, begun using armored cars well before the start of the British campaign against the Senussi. A final effort to achieve desert pacification, however, had to await the successful conclusion of the so-called Riff War, fought out in stand-up battles in the rugged Middle Atlas range and against the considerable native forces of Abd el Krim. But with the end of that war in 1926, French military authorities could turn their full attention to the region of the Sahara below the mountains. In order to get at the tribesmen there, General Henri Giraud fashioned a combination of forces comprising aircraft, armored cars, and camel-mounted infantry. Giraud also employed many of the same elements already found useful to the Air Control formula in Iraq. Much the same sort of network of intelligence officers, for example, sent back information and called forth aerial bombing attacks whenever the tribesmen tried to move out of their oases. Special mobile groups, made up of heavy armored cars and lighter scouting vehicles, projected French firepower deep into the desert. Mixed units of these vehicles, designated the *compagnies sahariennes*, quickly impressed Giraud's officers by their ability to move in from over the horizon and completely surround an oasis, bringing fire to bear on it from all sides. Such forces at length became the decisive element in this final campaign. Once they reached and attacked a particular oasis, they gave defending tribesmen little choice but to surrender. Within a very short span, Giraud's resourceful employment of these new units had begun to wear down the warring tribes of the Sahara just as effectively as had the RAF's airplanes and armored cars the Bedouin of the Iraqi desert.[9]

But the Italian experimentation carried out in the Libyan portion of the desert forming the vast Sahara soon went beyond anything which Giraud's forces had yet tried. The Senussi had so far managed to hold their Italian invaders to the shallow coastal enclaves gained in 1911–1912. As envisioned by Benito Mussolini, however, Libya was now to become Italy's "Fourth Shore" and, with its ruins of ancient baths, amphitheaters, and forums, the centerpiece of a new Roman empire.[10] In 1923, therefore, Il Duce's "new Romans" set out to complete the business of conquering what had been the ancient provinces of Proconsular Africa, Tripolitania, and Cyrenaica. In just over two years, the full field army sent south from Tripoli had succeeded in mastering all of Tripolitania, Libya's westernmost province. Moreover, outposts and airfields were also established well to the south and in the desert region called the Fezzan. The first phase of the pacification program was completed with little difficulty. But the process of subduing Cyrenaica—whose inner-desert portions formed the seat of Senussi strength—proved a far more arduous undertaking. When standard methods failed, Mussolini's favorite field commander, 48–year-old General Rodolfo Graziani, concentrated instead on trying to contain the Senussi within specific areas. To keep them from fleeing to the safety of the Egyptian oases, for example, his engineers erected a sixteen-foot-high fence made up of triple-concertina barbed wire. Anchored with metal stakes, the fence was protected by a string of forts. It paralleled the frontier and ran from the Mediterranean far down into the desert.[11]

With the Senussi now more or less cornered, Graziani commenced the actual seizure of key oases and waterholes. Backed up by infantry and artillery, his armored cars began systematically to move against these points and also to drive the Senussi bands into the open desert—where aircraft of Italy's air force, the Regia Aeronautica, could hammer them at will. This approach was effective to the point that, cut off from their oases and grazing lands, many of the Senussi soon surrendered. The few diehards still holding out fled south towards their last remaining stronghold, the oasis of Kufra. But by late 1930, Graziani—already relishing the title of "Butcher" for his ruthless efficiency—was ready to move against even this final point. The problems facing him were immense. Five hundred miles south of the coast, Kufra, mysterious and unknown, was the sacred, carefully guarded center of Senussi religion and culture. Only a handful of Europeans had ever visited the place, and Graziani's intelligence officers remained far from clear even as to its exact location. Certainly no European force had ever attempted something so risky as venturing a large expedition that deep into the interior of a hostile desert. The perils included the obvious lack of water as well as the enemy's potential for staging sudden ambushes.[12]

Finding the logistical problems of preparing a full-sized force altogether insurmountable, Graziani at length decided to rely solely upon a mobile column made up of forces specifically formed for desert warfare. One type of these was his own recent creation: the special unit combining armored cars, scouting vehicles, and motorized infantry and designated the "Auto-Saharan" company. Similar to one of Giraud's *compagnies sahariennes*, the

Auto-Saharan company employed Fiat armored cars as well as light vehicles for reconnaissance. Units of camel-mounted native troops (or *meharisti*) could easily be added for sustained operations. But Graziani's special desert unit was superior to the similar French and British forces of the period in one crucial respect: each Auto-Saharan company also contained its own organic contingent of aircraft. The Italians, going a step further, had managed to incorporate within their units the observation and bombing capabilities of light aircraft. Moreover, Italian practice called for the Auto-Saharan companies to be commanded by trained ground officers who were also qualified pilots. When it came to hunting down scattered bands of tribesmen over wide areas, the tactical benefits of this fully integrated air-ground combination were manifest. Once the aircraft had spotted and then presumably pinned the enemy with strafing attacks, the armored cars and motorized infantry could be brought in for the kill. The whole operation was directed by a commander who coordinated from overhead in one of the planes. Thereafter, having occupied a particular string of oases, one of these Auto-Saharan units could remain on station to patrol a really large expanse of desert. Of the European powers conducting major desert campaigns between the two world wars, only the Italians had reached the stage of fusing—within a single unit and under a single commander—both the air and the ground elements shown to be crucial to operations against hard-to-get-at tribesmen.[13]

Graziani's faith in what this approach might yield was soon borne out in the campaign for Kufra. Taking advantage of the cold winter months, his Auto-Saharans commenced their push against the distant oasis in late 1930. Moving south along a desert track used by the Senussi, the Italians planted a ten-foot high *paletto di ferro* (iron post) at every kilometer, to mark the route for the supply convoys which followed. When they were nearing their objective early in the new year, their scout planes spotted a band of Senussi just a few miles north of the oasis. Additional aircraft, followed by the Auto-Saharans' potent armed vehicles, were quickly called up to mount an attack. The fight was brief; of the Senussi who survived, most gave up. Those who did not fell back into the date palms. As the Italians pushed into the oasis, a handful of tribesmen, including women, children, and old people, began a desperate trek across some of the worst territory in the desert. Some made it to the Egyptian oases, but many others did not. For years thereafter, explorers continued to find their remains, long since mummified in the desert's aridity, scattered along the tracks leading towards Egypt.[14]

Meanwhile, Graziani consolidated his conquests. Kufra became his major outpost in southern Libya. Near its major village, which consisted of a mosque, a market, and various mud-walled buildings, his forces began construction of a well-fortified compound. Complete with radio station, troop barracks, maintenance facilities, and adjoining airfield, it became a key base of operations for the Auto-Saharans. Graziani himself described the taking of Kufra and the subsequent building of a base there as "the greatest operation ever accomplished in the Sahara." "It places us," he boasted, "indisputably in the forefront of desert armies." By its audacity it "has stunned our French and British neighbours [in North Africa]."[15] The conclusion of the campaign meant that, after a protracted struggle of nearly twenty years' duration, the Italians could at last count themselves masters of a country and a people they had been battling since 1911. In the north, Italian colonists planted their olive groves, vegetables, and other crops. Their clusters of stuccoed, whitewashed houses, always protected by small forts and pillboxes, dotted the areas near the coast. A hard-surface highway paralleling that coast and running east towards the Egyptian border was named, in honor of Libya's governor general, Italo Balbo, the "Via Balbia." Two well-marked main tracks led down to the outposts far to the south. Following the Kufra campaign and aside from the routine patrolling operations of the Auto-Saharans, however, the Italians lost interest in the desert country which comprised so much of their colony. Their interests were confined to the north and to the limited areas which supported agriculture. Although sporadic efforts were made to map the territories around Kufra, these focused almost exclusively on the areas immediately adjacent to the main routes. Libya's empty interior was thought of as "the big sandbox," a place remarkable for its scorpions, vipers, utter dryness, and little else. Even after the conquest of Kufra, most of Libya south of the coast and away from the tracks remained a blank spot on the map.[16]

Ten thousand years before, and prior to a major climatic shift, much of that country had apparently been a most fertile zone. It had been inhabited by a Stone Age people whose pictographs, which could still be seen on rock formations, would eventually draw explorers and archeologists. But the desert that harbored the artifacts of a previous age was fundamentally a zone formed by aridity and wind erosion. Scouring the surface for thousands of years, the wind had constantly shifted the grains of sand, smoothing out some areas but heaping up the sand in great chains of dunes in others. The Arab invaders who arrived in the seventh Century A.D. had largely avoided the regions sheltered by these high dune ranges, as did the Italians in the 1920s and 1930s. Awesome in their size, these ranges seemed to go on forever. The largest was marked on the maps as the "Great Sand Sea" because its high crests of sand and shallow troughs called to mind rolling swells at sea. By the time of the Kufra campaign, the Italians had come to believe that the various "Sand Seas" together formed a sort of giant S. Turned on its side, this S apparently extended from Egypt and much of the way across Libya. Above all, the Sand Seas were regarded as barriers. Why they were avoided would have been apparent to anyone traveling down to Kufra on Graziani's new "Palificata" desert track. Visible off to the left, on the eastern horizon, was a sight which never failed to awe the few Europeans who had seen it: the first actual "breaker" dunes of the Sand Sea. Yellowish white and rising above the flat desert surface, the high dunes stretched off as far as the eye could see. Utterly without water or plant or animal life, they were the ultimate desert, seeming to make even the barren flats out of which they rose almost hospitable by comparison. To enter them at all was to risk disorientation and slow death from thirst.[17]

Certainly every previous expedition attempting to push in had come close to disaster. For example, sixty years before Graziani took Kufra, the German explorer Gerhard Rohlfs had nearly died when he had become lost and his camels had run out of water. Only the fortuitous arrival of rain (perhaps the only shower in that region for decades) had saved him. In the early 1920s another major expedition, this one led by one of the most experienced desert soldiers in the British Army, Lieutenant Colonel N. B. de Lancey Forth, had likewise attempted to use camels to traverse the Great Sand Sea. But despite the extent of his preparations, Forth also ended up having to turn back. The failure of his determined, skillfully led expedition seemed to suggest that only track-driven types of motorized vehicles might have any hope of success.[18] The example of French explorers in using such special vehicles—most especially the new version of the half-track car manufactured by the Citroën-Kégresse automotive firm—seemed encouraging. For example, a party sent out by French tank theorist General J. E. Estienne had recently succeeded in pushing some 800 miles into the Algerian Sahara. The French accomplishment sparked the purchase by one of the wealthiest men in Egypt, Prince Kamal-al-Din, cousin to the future King Farouk, of Citroën-Kégresse "caterpillars" of this same variety. The cars were brought to Egypt and readied for a major expedition into the Libyan desert. Assisted by the same Dr. Ball who had worked with the Light Car Patrols, Prince Kamal found, on this and subsequent expeditions in the mid-1920s, much to fill in the blank spaces on the map. Even he, however, ultimately failed to get across the Sand Sea, principally because the Citroëns' intricate gears proved temperamental and tended to break down. As his money began to run short, Prince Kamal's passion for desert exploration likewise began to wane. The trouble was that such exploration, using the dozens of vehicles and mounted on the grand scale which he regarded as essential for safety, was enormously expensive. In the absence of substantial funding either from governmental or from large corporate sources, it seemed a task far beyond the resources of private individuals. At any rate, neither the ventures employing camels nor those employing motor vehicles of the special track-driven type had succeeded in traversing the Sand Sea. The great dunes remained a barrier that had consistently defeated the best efforts of resourceful and experienced explorers.[19]

The British Army officer who ultimately succeeded in overcoming that barrier arrived in Egypt at about the time that Prince Kamal was losing interest in the task of desert exploration. Captain Ralph Alger Bagnold had graduated near the top of his class from "The Shop," the Royal Military Academy, Woolwich, in 1915, and was now in his late twenties. He had, as a Royal Engineers officer, survived wounds and the trench warfare which killed off so many of his generation. War service had been followed by advanced study at Cambridge University's Gonville and Caius College. Eventually, drawn by its developing communications technology, Bagnold had switched to the Royal Corps of Signals, his branch at the time of his arrival on the fringes of the great desert about to become for him a place of fascination and challenge. Garrison life in Egypt, after the upheaval of the war years, soon proved routine, even monotonous. Perhaps his frustration grew all the more intense as his sister Enid—as Lady Enid Bagnold Jones, the wife of Sir Roderick Jones, head of the Reuters news service—meanwhile continued to win a growing reputation as a novelist and playwright of promise. The most famous of her works, *National Velvet*, would eventually appear on stage in London and on Broadway (and, later still, would be made into the movie starring Elizabeth Taylor and Mickey Rooney).[20] But Bagnold himself, stuck in Egypt, apparently faced rather less attractive prospects. Increasingly bored by the routine, he eventually turned to the desert as an outlet for his energies. His interest was already stirred by Lawrence's role in the war just past, and he soon found himself lured even more by "whatever relics and mysteries there might be out there in the desert beyond the Pyramids." The "desert-walloping" accounts he heard from one or two of the former Light Car Patrol officers still around inclined him to believe that motor vehicles, rather than camels, represented the most promising means for carrying out exploration. In any event, within a year of his arrival in Egypt, Bagnold had begun to organize his own small group of friends for the purpose of investigating "the desert beyond the Pyramids."[21]

The initial members of this group were, like himself, junior officers drawn primarily from the Royal Tank Regiment, the Engineers, or the Signals. The original idea was that exploration was to be a hobby—that "there was fun to be got out of a 'holiday' in the desert." By pooling funds, the group bought equipment, supplies, and Model T Ford cars of the type that had served the LCPs so well ten years before. These vehicles were modified in the LCP way, most importantly by the addition of radiator condensers like those devised during the war. The group also, after trying out several different types of compasses, fell back on the kind of sun compass that the LCPs had used. But here Bagnold soon showed his own considerable inventive talents. While workable, the LCP-type compass was awkward to use. By designing an improved type of rotating circular plate or compass card, however, Bagnold developed an instrument that was far more efficient and, with other modifications, was eventually patented for manufacture. Further experimentation with this compass saw the development of various formulas, tables, and techniques into an effective procedure for navigation. Short jaunts to known features, primarily in the region west of the Nile, taught valuable lessons and built up confidence for trying larger endeavors. Above all, the Bagnold explorers developed the ability to navigate with such precision that they could reach virtually any point, no matter how far it might be from some known landmark. They also worked out precise tables for the amounts of gasoline, food, and water they could expect to consume under different weather conditions and in different types of desert terrain. As these expeditions grew more ambitious in scope, the policy followed with regard to them by British civil and military authorities was one of benign neglect. Bureaucratic resistance stemmed primarily from concerns about paying "for a rescue party—and perhaps death benefits—should the group become lost."[22]

The year 1926 marked the beginning of the Bagnold group's involvement with really long expeditions—the extension of its forays, in fact, from conservative jaunts to large-scale efforts. Bagnold himself had long wanted to visit the sites of Lawrence's battles in the Hejaz and on the fringes of the Holy Land. Eventually securing the necessary permission from the authorities, he led his group east into the Sinai and off on its first 1,000–mile push. The party in due course reached the same country where Lawrence's tribesmen had raided the Turks. The explorers found plenty of evidence of those battles: spent rifle cartridges, twisted rails, and the blackened hulks of the Turkish locomotives that Lawrence had destroyed. Even longer forays followed over the next two years, as Bagnold shifted back to the Libyan desert and to the main oases lying east of the great dunes. As Dr. Ball himself soon recognized, what Bagnold was accomplishing had already surpassed, in terms of the expertise acquired, the best efforts of the old Light Car Patrols. For Bagnold and the others, as they admitted, had caught a bad case of "horizon fever." The desert represented for them an "incredible sense of freedom, [a sense] of being able to go on forever." "You could get in a car, set your [sun-compass] bearing for whatever direction you wanted, and go off on a straight course for mile after mile. The desert was empty, clean. And no one had been there before you."[23]

It was this attitude which helped drive the group, three years later, to the ultimate test: taking on the Sand Sea's dunes. To traverse the dunes had already been pronounced impossible by the reigning master of desert exploration, Prince Kamal. No one knew how far the dunes extended, and Kamal remained convinced that their high crests of loose sand were absolutely beyond the capabilities of any existing motor vehicle, wheeled or tracked. But Bagnold's experience to date had led him to think otherwise. Skill and proper technique, he believed, might make it possible to get a vehicle all the way to the top of the first large dune. Just as his preparations for an assault on the Sand Sea began to take shape, however, official military demands intruded. Bagnold was already due for a transfer; he now received orders posting him to India, 2,000 miles from the Libyan desert and a whole continent away from the attempt on the Sand Sea. When efforts to secure a delay in the orders failed, he duly reported to the Northwest Frontier and to the outposts guarding the Khyber Pass. He remained determined, nonetheless, to overcome this setback to his plans. For nearly a year he continued to coordinate all necessary preparations from far-off India, sending cables to his friends, still in Egypt, instructing them to fetch this or that essential item of equipment. The party had agreed upon the winter of 1929 as the best time for the expedition. But as the starting date approached, a second problem arose to threaten the whole enterprise. These same cooler months were also the season when the Egypt-based British forces regularly staged their annual field maneuvers, and of the six explorers, five were officers serving in units needed for the exercises. At this point, with everything else nearly ready, the senior British general officer in Egypt flatly refused to grant leave for Bagnold's officer-explorers to make the expedition. So far as he cared, the Sand Sea business "could wait forever."[24]

Bagnold remained determined not to be undone. But getting the general's decision reversed eventually required no less than an airline flight (in 1929, still very much of an adventure) all the way to London, and going straight to the Chief of the Imperial General Staff. Still, his personal interview with the CIGS proved successful in every regard. With the necessary permission now granted (to the chagrin of the general in Egypt), the expedition was back on. Thus it was that the whole party—Bagnold and five others, relying upon their three specially fitted Fords, this time Model A's—prepared to head into the desert in late 1929. The troubles with the military authorities in Cairo notwithstanding, Bagnold had also succeeded in gaining some important outside support. The Royal Geographical Society, an institution which in the previous century had sent out expeditions to locate the sources of the Nile and in general had acted to foster exploration of the fringes of Queen Victoria's vast empire, had supplied a number of crucial scientific instruments. Bagnold, who was himself a fellow of the society, therefore led, for the first time, an expedition equipped with chronometers, barometers, and surveyor's theodolites adequate for the first really scientific observations in the Sand Sea. While Bagnold had informed the Royal Geographical Society that there were indeed "many chances" that the expedition might not be able to reach the far side of the Sand Sea, "we shall have the advantage of being entirely self-contained [as to food, water and fuel] for [a range of] 2,000 miles."[25]

Bagnold and his friends headed west out of Cairo in November 1929. Leaving the rich bottomland cultivation of the Nile Valley and driving past the Pyramids of El Giza, they almost immediately entered the barren world of the desert. Each of the vehicles carried a heavy load of fuel and supplies, and the weight caused problems almost from the start. Because of the delay in securing leave, Bagnold had been forced to make "the bad mistake" of not experimenting with the vehicles "fully loaded . . . over the actual country we were going to cross."[26] Alarmingly, the vehicles began "to devour petrol at a rate we hadn't reckoned on." But the group pressed on. Five days later and 300 miles west of Cairo, the explorers reached the eastern edge of the

Great Sand Sea. They paused at the base of a "glaring wall of yellow sand" stretching across the western horizon. But there was still plenty of daylight left, and Bagnold could see no reason why he should not make at least one attempt on the "outermost rampart of sand." This particular "rampart" rose to a steep knife-edge crest perhaps 400 feet high. Leaving the rest to watch while he tried to force a motorized vehicle all the way to the top, he climbed into one of the Fords. Bagnold braced himself as the vehicle, lurching forward and spewing sand, plowed into the steep slope. He had expected to stall. But instead, the Ford seemed to "float . . . upwards," almost like "riding in a lift [elevator] in a high building." The motor whined, but there was almost no sense of forward motion. Only when Bagnold, now practically mesmerized, glanced down to see the 40 mph reading on the speedometer did he stop. He had reached the top. As the others came laboring up the slope after him, Bagnold indulged himself in an impish grin. It had been easy: rather than sticking deep in loose sand as "instinct and experience . . . foretold," the Ford, its wheels churning away, had smoothly ground a path all the way to the crest.[27] The Bagnold group had reached and conquered its first great obstacle—and had done what Kamal had said was impossible.

In the days that followed, the expedition repeated this performance again and again, driving the vehicles up dunes and deeper into the Sand Sea. Frequent halts, however, were necessary in order to dig the vehicles out of soft spots. What really saved them in these soft troughs between the dunes were the metal planks that had been brought along almost as an afterthought. Laid in front of the wheels, these five-foot-long planks—"channels," Bagnold called them—were just the thing for extricating "a car or a lorry which no amount of pushing could move."[28] The difficulty, though, was that these exertions began to consume far too much of their limited gasoline reserves. When a gear box in one of the vehicles eventually gave out, Bagnold had reached the limit of penetration, at least for this trip. Still short of the far side of the Sand Sea and with no real idea yet as to how far to the west the dunes actually extended, he had no choice but to turn back. But he and the others were far from disappointed in their performance. They had secured precise, useful data about the nature and configuration of the dunes themselves. And what was most important was that they had proved what Bagnold had believed all along: motor vehicles, with the right preparation and skillful handling, could actually climb and traverse the most difficult dunes of the Sand Sea. They had also proved that relatively inexpensive standard vehicles—not the French-built Citroëns, whose purchase costs were considerably beyond the means of these officers—could be used to conquer the Sand Sea. In the absence of government funding, this was a crucial point indeed. If the task of exploring the desert was to be left to "a few army officers, with no . . . desire to do anything unusual except to see the country they were in," as Bagnold later put it, then the vehicles and equipment that they employed needed above all to be affordable.[29]

A second expedition was prepared for October 1930. This time Bagnold had to face none of the military-leave problems that had plagued him the year before. Everything was based on the lessons of the previous effort, with the vehicles being stripped of their fenders, hoods, windshields, and other nonessential items. Caches of gasoline and water were set up in advance to provide ample reserves along the way. Three vehicles, all brand new, were fitted with the special "box bodies" that Bagnold had designed and which permitted the hauling of extra cans of gasoline and water. The goal was to penetrate the Sand Sea as far as "the western limit of the great crested ranges."[30] If this endeavor succeeded, the plan was that the group would then return by heading south through the dunes and finally east in a giant loop of nearly 3,000 miles. Joining Bagnold for the first time was a nonmilitary participant, William Kennedy Shaw, a civilian official of the Sudan Colonial Service and a veteran of numerous camel treks into the desert. Shaw's specialty was navigation. Riding in the lead car, he would use dead-reckoning techniques to keep the course during each day's run. This task necessitated taking directional readings from the sun compass and mileage readings from the odometer. A running plot was kept on a 1:500,000 map. At night, Shaw checked the dead-reckoned or "estimated" position that this process yielded, using star shots taken with a theodolite. Employed in combination, the two systems—dead-reckoning and celestial or astrofix—gave the party an extremely efficient and reliable means of navigation.[31]

The explorers at length reached Dalla, a desolate, uninhabited oasis 200 miles west of the Nile and their first stopping point. From there they proceeded across the flat desert and finally came once again to the edge of the great dunes. Shaw had seen these walls of sand before but had never actually been in them. Bagnold, impatient to show off his new skill, could not resist recing his vehicle, with Shaw in it, towards the first big "breaker." As a confirmed believer in the camel, Shaw up until this point had remained "politely but firmly skeptical of this business of trying to cross dunes by car."[32] But the previous year's performance was "repeated exactly" and, with its wheels churning into the soft slope, the vehicle carried Bagnold and Shaw safely to the crest. Thereafter, the party continued in a generally southwesterly direction and in weather hot enough to make the air above the dunes "shimmer . . . like that above a red-hot stove."[33] Finally, four days after entering the Sand Sea, they came to the crest of its very last dune. They had completely crossed the Sand Sea, a nearly 200–mile-wide range of dunes. Looking to the south and west, they could see nothing but flat, empty desert (and, although they could not know it, the route by which Graziani's Auto-Saharans would attack Kufra just two months later). Only five years after their introduction to "desert-walloping," Bagnold's group had succeeded in surmounting the wide belt of dunes comprising the Great Sand Sea. In the days ahead, they turned south to find and reach the lower limits of the Sand Sea. This was a success that, weeks later, following their return to Cairo, attracted the attention of *The Times* of London. In an article published in January 1931, that newspaper hailed the crossing of the Sand Sea as one of the great feats of exploration, an accomplishment that had opened up a mysterious and unknown region. Five months after the crossing, Bagnold and Shaw journeyed to London to present their findings before the Royal Geographical Society. Their paper, read before the assembled fellows, ensured that additional aid would be forthcoming from the society's exploration fund. It also helped them obtain a modest grant from the University of Chicago's Oriental Institute, assistance that would help to make possible a third major expedition.[34]

The explorers were ready to leave by late September 1932. In addition to Shaw, by now a "regular," the group this time numbered in its ranks no less than an Oxford University professor of paleolithic archeology. It would also, in the person of Squadron Leader H. W. G. H. Penderel, have some help from the Royal Air Force. The commanding officer of the RAF's No. 216 Squadron, Penderel had been a fighter ace ("with . . . twenty-three Huns to his credit") in the last war.[35] His squadron was a bomber unit whose crest bore the Latin motto *Dona Ferens* (Bearing Gifts), and the plan was for Penderel, based at the RAF airfield at Heliopolis, to fly out, "Bearing Gifts" of extra tires and the like, and join the expedition at selected points. The difficulty, however, was that Penderel's aircraft, a twin-engined Vickers biplane called a "Valencia," had insufficient range to keep up with Bagnold's group as it moved south. Instead, Penderel would have to make preliminary flights just to set up various dumps of fuel along the way. He would then, miles from anywhere and flying over featureless terrain, presumably have to take his chances on finding his way from dump to dump before the fuel in the airplane ran out.[36]

The main objective for this exploration was a place called Jebel al Uwaynat, a mountain perhaps 700 miles south of Cairo. The area was believed to harbor some tribesmen, possibly hostile, known as the Tebu. Although Bagnold himself tended to discount the danger of these supposedly "fierce tribesmen," British military authorities insisted that his party go well armed and prepared for trouble.[37] The participants were therefore issued Enfield service rifles as well as a box of hand grenades. But the journey itself proved uneventful. Penderel flew out and joined them as planned, although in the glare and heat haze he had had great difficulty in following their tracks. Eventually reaching Uwaynat safely and on schedule, the group found no natives. Instead, they set up their camp and spent a leisurely morning poking around some giant boulders. Yet they were not alone after all. Sitting down to the noon rations, Bagnold and the others suddenly looked up as, from over a rise, a half-dozen tan-painted trucks came bearing down on them. At almost the same moment, a light aircraft zoomed in low over their camp. On this, their third long desert venture, Bagnold and his group had at last encountered an air-ground force of Auto-Saharans.[38]

After the plane landed nearby, an Italian major came over to enquire, in "passable English," exactly what this British party was doing at Uwaynat and in territory claimed by Italy. But the occasion turned into an amicable one, and the Italian soon suggested, after the arrival of Penderel, that the two groups share a meal together. This event, as Bagnold noted somewhat grandly, brought together, in a spot deep in the desert, "representatives of the armies and air forces of Britain and Italy, and of the Universities of Oxford and Chicago."[39] After a few days the Italians left, and the British also departed soon thereafter. But Bagnold observed that the Italians evidently "had no intention of losing track of our movements," since they left a detachment to keep watch from a point nearby.[40] The encounter with the Italians impelled Bagnold, immediately upon returning to civilization, to go to the British military headquarters in Egypt, the high-walled structure called the Cairo Citadel. There he "reported our finding the Italians" in territory then claimed by the Anglo-Egyptian Sudan, and this information was dispatched "direct to the Foreign Office in London."[41] Bagnold's had been virtually the first British party ever to see an Auto-Saharan patrol, and the information which he supplied soon found its way into the reports dealing with intelligence on Italian units. On the whole, however, he and the others had rather enjoyed their meeting with the Italians. They were fascinated by what they could see of the Auto-Saharans' vehicles, equipment, and techniques. Most of all, they were impressed by the quality and know-how of the Italian officers. Tough, long-service colonial soldiers, they seemed to fit none of the stereotypes left over from Italy's poor showing at Caporetto and in other battles of World War I.[42]

One Italian officer in particular, a *maggiore* or major, had managed to leave a lasting impression on Bagnold. He was a veteran desert soldier named Lorrenzini, and he recounted in great detail his first-hand experiences of the Kufra operation of the year before. Major Lorrenzini seemed to like Bagnold. Yet, half seriously, he also baited him about how easy it might be—should their two countries ever go to war—for the Italians to send their crack Auto-Saharans on raids against the British. In Lorrenzini's view, the whole Nile Valley represented a "long, unguarded flank."[43] It was, he argued, completely vulnerable to a force capable of staging raids across the empty region south of the Sand Sea's dunes. Using a map to point out the route that might be employed, he showed in detail how an Auto-Saharan force could push across from Uwaynat to the Nile. Striking from out of the desert, such a force could blow up the large dam at Aswan, demolish the key Sudanese railhead at Wadi Halfa, and perhaps even mount additional raids further to the north. Having wrecked the dam at the Nile's first cataract, as well as destroying the important river communications link between the British and the Sudan, the raiding force could then easily escape before the British could ever hope to react. Bagnold recognized that Lorrenzini's scheme, at least in the purely military terms in which it was laid out, was not quite as outlandish as it might have seemed. Certainly it was clear to him that the Auto-Saharans appeared to have the potential to do precisely what Lorrenzini said. If so, they could raid Egypt's exposed outposts and lines of communications in a way that the Senussi, fifteen years before, could never have matched. The remembrance of Lorrenzini's conversation would stay with Bagnold over the years. In 1940, it would lead him finally to go over the head of his superior officer in order to get a British special desert force formed, one that was capable of penetrating into the area sheltered by the great dunes in order to find out just what the Italians were up to.

CHAPTER 3

The Formation of a Desert Special Force

Without Bagnold, I very much doubt that anything of the kind would ever have been tried.
—Brigadier Eric J. Shearer,
Director of Military Intelligence, Middle East Forces, 1940–1942[1]

The findings of the 1932 expedition were written up in the Royal Geographical Society's *Journal*, as well as in other journals concerned with the process of desert exploration. Moreover, the series of articles which appeared in *The Times* of London helped to spark other probes into the region sheltered by the Sand Sea. One of these, led by Squadron Leader Penderel, eventually succeeded in reaching a vast, steep-sided plateau called the Gilf Kebir. Rearing up about where the southernmost dunes of the Sand Sea left off, the Gilf, situated far from oases or caravan routes, had long been regarded as one of the Libyan desert's largest and most unusual features.[2]

To reach it Penderel used the same sort of air-ground approach employed by Bagnold on the Uwaynat effort. While he and a fellow aviator, Lieutenant Sir Robert Clayton, Royal Navy, flew their Gypsy Moth two-winger down a series of prestaged dumps of gasoline, the ground element moved south under Patrick Clayton, a World War I veteran and professional surveyor with Dr. Ball's Department of Egyptian Surveys. But what tended to make this expedition unique was the participation of a new and somewhat mysterious volunteer, a man whom the British Foreign Office's intelligence apparatus would, as World War II approached, come to regard with mounting suspicion. Like Penderel and Clayton, the new participant, Ladislas de Almaszy, was also a skilled pilot—a veteran of considerable flying service in the forces of the Austro-Hungarian Empire in the war of 1914–1918. He also claimed to be a count in the Hungarian nobility. Whether his money came from landed estates or from some other source was, however, never clear. Certainly he always seemed to have resources ample to pay for a whole series of desert explorations conducted in the mid-1930s. But in the "conquest" of the Gilf Kebir, Almaszy, urbane and personable, more than proved his worth to Penderel and the others. His efforts aided them in locating and then climbing the high plateau, and the observations taken of its topography, geology, and general configuration greatly helped to flesh out the knowledge of the desert.[3]

While the British Foreign Office manifested increasing interest in Almaszy's various comings and goings between Cairo, Rome, and Berlin, the Italian military command in Libya kept, for its part, an equally watchful eye on the series of British expeditions poking around south of the Sand Sea. Within days of the Gilf Kebir effort, for example, the commander of the Auto-Saharan patrols based at Kufra sent a full report to his supreme headquarters at Tripoli, commenting upon virtually every aspect of the "Count de Almaszy-Squadron Leader Penderel *Spedizione*." His report noted that the *"cinque europei"* and *"tre arabi"* (Patrick Clayton's Bedouin guides) had traveled in several specially fitted Ford cars and *"uno auto 'pick-up'."* An earlier Auto-Saharan report had commented with equal thoroughness on Bagnold's trip and the encounter at Uwaynat.[4] On the whole, however, neither the Italian nor the British authorities were then inclined to regard these forays as anything particularly significant, much less the substance of some international incident. Nonetheless, the British command in Egypt gradually began, as Bagnold recalled, to "discourage enterprising young officers from spending their leave [periods] on desert motor trips." Why this was so probably had more to do with bureaucratic strictures against "wasting funds on search efforts, should an expedition get itself lost," than with any actual fear of provoking the Italians. No general officer wanted, after all, to "get a black mark" if a member of his command "were to get lost and the family have to be compensated."[5]

Late in 1935, however, British perceptions of Italy—and particularly of the long desert border which Egypt shared with Libya—altered drastically. The catalytic event which induced that change was Mussolini's invasion of a backward, poorly armed country situated well south of Egypt and in the Horn of Africa: Ethiopia. However distant from Egypt, the invasion of the Emperor Haile Selassie's weak nation, and the ensuing "Ethiopian Crisis" so ineffectually dealt with by League of Nations economic sanctions, compelled British military planners increasingly to regard Egypt as the possible target of a future Italian advance. Not only did it force them to look to the defense of that nation's western frontier, but it also induced them, for the first time since the Senussi raids of two decades before, to contend with the threat of attacks mounted from Libya and sent across Egypt's expanses of desert. Mussolini's Libyan-based ground forces seemed larger and better equipped than anything the British had in Egypt at that point, and a new

Italian bomber, the Savoia Marchetti-79, possessed the range to reach and attack targets in the Nile Valley.[6] In short order, therefore, the General Officer Commanding British Troops in Egypt (GOC-BTE) rushed off to London his analysis of how a potential Italian attack might proceed. There was, he informed his superiors at the War Office, only one practicable route for such a move: due east, like the first Senussi attack of early 1916, and over the hard surfaces of the Libyan plateau. That plateau, generally trafficable to tanks and heavy vehicles, formed the obvious gateway to Egypt for an attack from the west. It formed a long, funnel-shaped corridor lying just south of the Mediterranean coast and pointing east towards the Royal Navy's fleet base at Alexandria, and, ultimately, at the Nile Valley itself. Blocked off by the Sand Sea and the Qattara Depression, the rest of the desert seemed impassable to large forces whose logistical problems alone would have presented a nightmare to enemy staff officers.[7]

On the whole, however, actual British military knowledge of the vast region identified on the maps as the "Western Desert of Egypt" still remained surprisingly vague. A year or two before the Ethiopian crisis, for example, Bagnold discovered that the maps in use at the British headquarters still dated from World War I: very little effort, if any, had been made to update them with the new information which his expeditions had provided. Until the onset of the crisis, the British forces stationed in Egypt (almost exclusively in its Nile Valley and Delta) had as their mission the maintenance of internal security, not the repelling of an external invasion from Libya.[8] Senior officers appeared to take little interest in the desert to the west, and few of them had ever actually seen the region through which the Italians might try to attack. Therefore British general staff officers now, in the autumn of 1935, found themselves in need of precise information. Of the Bagnold group of desert experts, however, all had been transferred; Bagnold himself had been sent off to a posting in China. The best man the staff officers could locate in the time available was his old exploring colleague, William Kennedy Shaw. At the time on leave in England, Shaw was asked if he thought the Italians could "move an armoured force along the [desert] escarpment" that rose up just inland from the coast. But as a civilian with no military experience whatsoever, and who, perhaps more importantly, had never in his life even "seen an 'armoured force'" of any kind, he reckoned that the advice he gave "was of little value." Indeed, it appeared to do little to help clarify matters for the "very harassed staff officer" who had gone to such lengths to seek him out.[9]

However, the explorers' information had already made some impact. In the eyes of the military planners in Cairo, the most important of the Bagnold reports was the one about meeting the Auto-Saharans at Uwaynat three years before. It alerted the GOC-BTE to the fact that the Italians possessed first-quality, highly specialized desert units capable of operating over long ranges. On the basis of this information, he therefore suggested to London that such "light mobile forces in desert cars" might, at the same moment that the Italians should commence a full-scale attack over the Libyan plateau, "be sent... to divert our attention."[10] Such a diversion might take the form of raids against the lines of a number of vulnerable outposts and the lines of communication. The enemy's mobile forces could also act to help establish "advanced landing grounds," hidden far out in the desert, from which bombing aircraft could be flown in order "to strike... Cairo and the Nile Valley." Furthermore, it seemed reasonable to suppose that the Auto-Saharans might also set up secret caches of arms for use by the "Fascist-leaning elements" among the 50,000 or so "well-organized... Italian nationals" estimated by British intelligence to be in Egypt. These, it appeared, possessed a "very great... potential indeed for sabotage."[11]

The threat of some sort of raiding activity developing from the interior of the desert thus caused the British to examine carefully the apparatus available for watching that sector. What they found was hardly reassuring. By the mid-1930s, the old Light Car Patrols of World War I had long since either been disbanded or handed over to the civilian control of the Egyptian Frontiers Administration. The handful of these motorized patrols in existence—supplemented by camel-mounted forces—increasingly were under Egyptian, not British, officers. Moreover, as border patrol elements, they had as their primary mission police and anti-smuggling work. It was clear that these units would require time and considerable training before they could be expected to act as a source of "military intelligence and as a first line of defence" in the desert in time of war.[12]

Fortunately their ability to function in this LCP-style role did not have to be put to the test. Nor, for that matter, were the overall defensive assessments of the GOC-BTE—not just yet, that is. Despite the brief flurry of war scare preparations associated with the Ethiopian crisis, there was no Italian thrust into Egypt in 1935–1936. Rather, the crisis passed as attentions were instead drawn to other areas of conflict, most immediately to the civil war erupting in Spain. But it did nonetheless help to produce an important alteration in the complex mosaic of Anglo-Egyptian relations. The Anglo-Egyptian Treaty finally signed in 1936 at last granted Egypt full independence, and formally terminated a half-century of British occupation. Though the large British garrisons remained, they were perceived (if only for the moment) by a fragmented but growing nationalist movement as something of a necessary evil in order to protect against Italian predation developing from Libya. The treaty not only pledged the British to defend the Suez Canal, but also to send large-scale military assistance in the event of war. At the same time, they promised as well to make every effort to upgrade the Egyptian Army, regarded by some as little more than a parade-ground body of quasi-police forces and cavalry squadrons.[13] As World War II approached, however, relations between the British and the Egyptians once again began to manifest signs of strain. Indeed the British soon suspected no less a figure than King Farouk (who succeeded to the throne in 1936) of favoring Nazi Germany. In addition, in 1938, two years after the signing of the treaty, the Egyptians, infuriated by British efforts to put down the anti-Zionist rebellion that broke out among Palestine's Arabs, retaliated by replacing the last of the Frontiers Administration's British officers with Egyptians. In the eyes of the GOC-BTE, this step effectively terminated any hope of turning the motorized patrols into a "vital covering screen for Intelligence and Security" in those desert regions through which the Italians might attempt to attack.[14]

By early 1939, the British found themselves increasingly uncertain of the reliability of the Egyptian armed forces in time of war. Mussolini's sudden invasion of Albania in the spring of that year prompted a complete re-examination of the whole program for defending not just Egypt but the entire Middle East area as well. The chief result was the decision to create a single, unified command entity. Designated Middle East Command, it was intended to bring together the plans and preparations of the senior RAF, British Army, and Royal Navy commanders in the region. Sir Archibald Wavell was appointed General Officer Commanding-in-Chief, with responsibility for the prosecution of all British land operations within the command. Now nearly 60 years old and a lieutenant general, the new C-in-C had seen extensive service as a staff officer under Allenby, had dealt with Lawrence in 1917–1918, and had held a range of important staff and command appointments since. He seemed by far the best possible choice for accomplishing the twin tasks of coordinating British war plans with those of the French and yet acting to develop "the Egyptian Forces . . . into efficient modern forces capable of cooperating . . . in the defence of Egypt."[15] Himself the son of a decorated general officer, Wavell was reckoned far and away one of the best brains in the British Army. Forty years before, his intellectual gifts had been such that the headmaster of his school, Winchester, had recommended against the younger Wavell's entering the Royal Military College, Sandhurst: so much obvious talent could only be wasted in an army whose officer corps was not generally noted for its cerebral distinctions.[16]

But following service with the Royal Highland (the Black Watch) Regiment and combat duty in World War I (in which he lost an eye to a shell splinter), Wavell had gone on to command units in the very forefront of experimentation in the new mobile-operations theories then being advanced by the paramount "prophets" of armored warfare, J. F. C. Fuller and Basil H. Liddell Hart. Under their influence Wavell developed an early interest in what he termed "the motor guerrilla." He believed that small forces of these highly mobile raiders might become, by virtue of their ability to infiltrate and strike at enemy lines of communication, a "prominent feature of the next war."[17] Thus it was that Wavell, in August 1939, brought to his new post as C-in-C, Middle East, not merely an extensive, firsthand knowledge of the desert terrain in and on both sides of Egypt, but a thorough grounding as well in the latest theories and doctrines by which the British Army would attempt to prepare fast-moving, highly mobile operations. He found, however, that the "one incomplete armoured division" then based in Egypt, plus a hodgepodge of other garrison units, had been trained not for operations in the desert but along more conventional lines, for combat in Europe.[18] He found also that the traditional rites of peacetime colonial soldiering—polo first thing in the morning, a brief stint at work before breaking away during the heat after lunch, perhaps a final game of polo after tea, and then a visit to Shepheard's Hotel (the main evening watering spot)—seemed to be very much intact. Despite the war scare associated with the Ethiopian crisis of four years before, realistic preparations for combat appeared, at this point, to be minimal.[19]

Establishing his General Headquarters, Middle East (GHQ-ME), in the Cairo Citadel, he devoted his first weeks to planning, learning, and finding out.[20] He learned, for example, that the 1936 war scare had prompted the development of British plans for fostering a revolt of Senussi tribesmen against the Italians in Libya. Staff officers informed Wavell that the Senussi were ready, with the proper encouragement in the form of arms and money, to go at the hated Italians at any moment. The plans for creating a full-blown, Lawrence-style "desert revolt" of this sort called for British officers to coordinate the recruitment of certain tribal leaders and their followers into a partisan force which would operate out of the southern oases. Known as the "Arab 'G' Expansion Scheme," the whole thing bespoke the strong influence of the Lawrence legend, and also the fact that Lawrence's best-selling book, *Seven Pillars of Wisdom*, had been published in the same year in which the Ethiopian crisis occurred.[21] Wavell himself was hardly immune to the appeal of that legend. Indeed, to him, T. E. Lawrence remained easily "the most impressive . . . man I ever met."[22]

The revolt scheme was originally envisioned as an efficient and viable way to raid and dislocate the Italians—a way, that is, to force them to divert resources away from their main attack if and when one actually developed. But even before Wavell's arrival in Cairo, the plan had already encountered problems. In particular, it had run afoul of certain influential Egyptians, both civilian and military. In their eyes a scheme to arm what they regarded as a bunch of desert ruffians, culturally alien and, worst of all, politically unreliable, was sheer folly. They pointedly objected to the fact that the British would have the controlling say in any operations of this irregular force. But British staff officers had themselves also raised doubts as to the efficacy of the Arab "G" Scheme; several key officers, in fact, regarded "the idea of a Senussi rising as an absurdity."[23] For one thing, the numbers of Senussi tribesmen actually available were a mere fraction of the numbers of Hejaz Arabs available to Lawrence in 1916–1918. Even more critically, the impending arrival of British and Empire-Commonwealth troops promised to tie up the motor transport and other limited resources necessary for supporting such a revolt. By September 1939, with Hitler's invasion of Poland and the commencement of World War II in Europe, Wavell was at best extremely skeptical as to the prospects of applying a mode of warfare that had worked so well for the British twenty years before. While Mussolini for the moment held back from joining his Axis partner in the war (but made use of the time to add to his forces in Libya), Wavell was forced, as he complained, to follow a London-dictated "policy of doing nothing whatever that could annoy the Italians."[24] In the months of uneasy calm that followed while Italy sat on the fence, Wavell was, by that policy, prevented from sending intelligence agents into Libya, although his own areas of responsibility were regarded as being "full of Italian agents." By early 1940, as the Germans began preparations for their blitzkrieg into France and the Low Countries, Wavell felt compelled to voice his doubts about the desert-revolt concept: the basic preparations remained "necessarily incomplete," and, until the exact policy "to be followed with regard...[to Libya] becomes known, the plans for insurrectionary activities... cannot be decided upon."[25] Given the diplomatic realities of the moment, the task of developing these various plans could only seem more hopeless all the time. Most important of all, however, Wavell had sensed that a Lawrence-style desert guerrilla war, no matter how appealing the precedent of twenty years before, could have but little real chance of success against the modern air, armored, and motorized forces of the Italians. Arab guerrillas, even British-led ones, could no longer "drift... about [the desert] like a gas," as had Lawrence's, applying their hit-and-run tactics at will.[26] The equation had altered. The new motorized weapons and units evolved since World War I could now hunt down, isolate, and defeat those guerrillas, as Giraud, Graziani, and the British themselves, with their Air Control formula in Iraq, had already demonstrated. The planning for the revolt scheme was allowed to go on; Wavell, however, increasingly placed little faith in what desert guerrillas could hope to accomplish against Italian forces able to move faster and hit harder than they themselves.

By the time the Germans launched their offensive into France in May 1940, Wavell's intelligence sections estimated that the Italians had in Libya a force at least five times greater than anything he could muster against them. In Egypt, to meet the Italian army of nine divisions of various types then positioned in Libya, Wavell had (or would soon have) elements of two infantry divisions, the 4th Indian and 2nd New Zealand, plus a further contingent of various infantry battalions. The crucial 7th Armoured Division, however, remained incomplete. An additional threat was an Italian army far to the south, and commanded by the Duke of Aosta, that seemed poised for thrusting into the Sudan from the Italian colonies of Eritrea and Ethiopia.[27] Also, what staff officers had come to refer to as the "Siwa diversion"— the possibility, first advanced in 1935, that the Italians might try to use the Auto-Saharan and other motorized units to seize Siwa Oasis as a base for diversionary and spoiling attacks against the Nile Valley—could not reasonably be overlooked.[28] But finding out about Italian preparations (if any) for such a move presented considerable problems. Underlying the difficulties stemming from the policy against sending out agents was the overall lack of detailed information regarding the trafficability of routes and the location and quality of waterholes and other features in those inner-desert sectors south of the Sand Sea. On the eve of World War II, the main briefing map kept in the office of the GOC-BTE, for example, was dated 1916. Despite the extensive exploring efforts carried out in the early 1930s, this map still carried the notation that the "limits of [the] sand dunes" and other key features were "unknown."[29] In fact, those limits had long since been extensively worked out by the explorers. It was this lack of information, or the presence of inaccurate or incomplete information, which ultimately caused Wavell to turn to Bagnold and to as many of the old nucleus of desert explorers as could be found and made available for service.

When World War II started, however, Bagnold was nowhere near the Libyan desert. Moreover, he was now a civilian. At age 43 and having apparently reached his terminal rank (major), he had retired from the army after twenty years of service. Now back in England, he devoted his efforts to conducting experiments with homemade wind tunnels, totally absorbed in the process of compiling data for a book on the nature of sand formations and wind erosion. When finally published, that work, entitled *The Physics of Blown Sand and Desert Dunes*, was almost immediately lauded as a unique and pioneering effort. In fact, both it and his other contributions would eventually be judged worthy of elevating Bagnold to his nation's very highest scientific-intellectual orbit: the Royal Society, founded in 1662 and since its formation characterized by an array of notables including Newton, Faraday, Pepys, and Franklin. Actually, Bagnold had already produced a book of rather more immediate relevancy to the interests of the British military apparatus in 1939–1940. Five years before, since "we all thought . . . that [our Uwaynat] expedition had been the last," he had, almost as a way of tidying up the last details of the desert trips, published *Libyan Sands: Travels in a Dead World*.[30] A narrative of the expeditions from 1925 to 1932, it explained in detail the techniques which his group had evolved for using a handful of standard motorized vehicles by which to penetrate some of the most difficult desert country in the world. In literary terms it was hardly a work to rival Lawrence's *Seven Pillars*, which appeared that same year. Yet in its own way, *Libyan Sands* was a fascinating, even exciting account. And among its readers was one who had known Lawrence and had already commented upon the potential of "the motor guerrilla": Lieutenant General Sir Archibald Wavell, newly appointed C-in-C, Middle East, and now vitally concerned with the "dead world" of the Libyan desert as a possible battleground.[31]

As things turned out, Wavell's first actual meeting with Bagnold was the result of a fortuitous accident. With hundreds of other retired-officer "dug-outs," Bagnold was recalled to Army service in the autumn of 1939. Rather than ordering him to the desert world he knew best, however, the War Office instead elected to send him to join the British units deployed in Kenya, a place Bagnold had never visited before and knew next to nothing about. But fortune prevailed. Entering the Suez Canal, his transport ship suffered a collision. As a result the passengers, including Bagnold, were forced to disembark at Port Said until the necessary repairs could be effected. Wel-coming this opportunity to see a country he had last visited years before, Bagnold lost no time in getting to Cairo; there he checked into Shepheard's Hotel. A reporter who spotted him soon wrote up a brief article for the *Egyptian Gazette*, declaring that the "renowned desert-explorer R. A. Bag-nold" had arrived in Egypt and that this represented clear evidence indeed that the Army was, in contrast to 1914–1918, "at last trying to fit square pegs into square holes."[32] In a way it was: Wavell, who noticed the newspaper sketch, promptly sent for "the renowned desert-explorer." Ushered into the C-in-C's office, Bagnold was offered the chance to stay in Egypt rather than proceeding on to Kenya. In short order, therefore, he found himself reas-signed and heading out into the Western Desert to take over duties as a signals officer with the 7th Armoured Division.[33]

During his interview with Wavell, Bagnold had decided not to bring up the matter of his meeting with Maggiore Lorrenzini seven years before, and the question of whether or not the Italians might be contemplating Auto-Saharan raids in the southern desert. Italy, after all, had not yet come into the war, and Bagnold had no way of knowing what intelligence, if any, might be reaching Wavell regarding the potentiality of hostilities in North Africa. Moreover, he had not wanted the C-in-C to size him up, on first encounter, as some sort of alarmist eccentric. But Bagnold was soldier enough to see, thereafter, that his new unit, the 7th Armoured, had "only enough motor transport for a radius of action of a paltry 100 miles," and that the forces currently available could expect to cover only very limited portions of Egypt's long desert border with Libya.[34] At the same time, the rumors, already rife, of war with Italy only intensified as spring 1940 approached. One of them he found at least partially believable. Air Marshal Italo Balbo, the flamboyant governor-general of Libya who had led Italian seaplanes on record-setting flights in 1931 and to the Chicago World's Fair of 1933, was said to be setting up a network of secret bases in the far interior of the desert. These bases, supposedly located in the region below Kufra, could be used as refueling points for bomber flights to the south. If war came—as the wealthy Egyptians who frequented Cairo's clubs and nightspots were already predicting—the Italians might use these bases to push into French Equatorial Africa's Chad Province, and perhaps to attack the key airfields by which the British hoped to fly aircraft across Africa and thence up to Egypt.[35]

To Bagnold, the key to Italian activities in the inner desert, whether Auto-

Saharan raids or Balbo's potential thrusts into Chad, seemed to be Kufra. But the Italian base there was a mystery. RAF reconnaissance planes could, by using prestaged refueling points, conceivably fly there and return. But they might not spot the vehicles, aircraft, and supply dumps that could be hidden away under Kufra's thick cover of date palms, and, in any case, could not detect movements made by night. Also, given the state of peace existing between Great Britain and Italy, to violate Libyan airspace by blatantly sending aircraft to reconnoiter Kufra seemed clearly out of the question. Bagnold, carrying out his routine duties at Matrûh on the Mediterranean coast and picking up rumored tidbits about this or that Italian activity, increasingly convinced himself that the only reliable way to find out was to send a small motorized patrol across the desert to Kufra. But such a patrol need not go directly or even all the way to that base. Instead, Bagnold believed that a small party using motorized vehicles could push across the Sand Sea and then slip, undetected, across the border. From there it could continue on until it reached the Palificata, the stake-marked, main north-south route which Graziani had opened up nine years before and along which all Italian military convoys heading down to Kufra had to travel. At some selected point along that route, the party would halt, hide itself, and set up a surveillance post. Just "track-reading" alone—estimating, that is, from the number of tire tracks left in the sand the volume of vehicular traffic recently passing over the route—seemed likely, Bagnold believed, to give a fairly reliable indication of the level of activity.[36]

After carefully analyzing all the steps that would make such a move possible, Bagnold at length decided to propose the organization of a small patrol capable of reconnoitering the desert track above Kufra. He submitted his proposal in the prescribed military way—up through channels, in the standard From-To-Subject format. A "few suitable vehicles" should be acquired, he argued, with training "to begin at once . . . [in preparing] a nucleus of men in long-range patrolling operations through the western sands."[37] He encountered no difficulty at all in selling his division commander, Major General Percy C. S. Hobart, on the project. Counted one of his army's keenest, most innovative tank warfare theorists, Hobart was always ready to try out a new idea (and, indeed, would go on to play a key role in developing the special amphibious tanks and vehicles so successfully employed by the British in the D-Day invasion of Normandy). Hobart accepted Bagnold's proposal enthusiastically; he at once forwarded it up to his own immediate superior, Lieutenant General Sir Henry Wilson, the GOC-BTE. But here the idea ran into solid resistance. Hobart and Wilson had apparently, as Bagnold learned later, already come to be at professional if not personal odds with each other. Given this circumstance, Hobart's positive endorsement of what Bagnold proposed could only guarantee trouble. The result was that Wilson's headquarters rejected the plan almost at once, and it got no further. Its submission alone was sufficient, at HQ-BTE, to win Bagnold the reputation of being an "impudent, even suicidal" glory-seeker, an "obscure, retired major" who apparently wanted to make himself into some sort of new Lawrence of Arabia.[38]

Wilson, in fact, soon relieved Hobart and sent him home (where he promptly enlisted as a corporal in the Home Guard before being given command of another armored division). But Bagnold decided to try again, only to have the second edition of his proposal receive the same rejection as before. At this point he resolved to dispense altogether with following the chain of command: next time, he would go directly to the top—to the C-in-C, Wavell himself. He also had good cause to believe that, for this final try, he might be on rather better ground. Early in June 1940, having waited until the German victory in France was all but assured, Mussolini had finally taken the plunge. Ending his vacillation, he finally brought Italy into the war on the side of German power. To the British in Egypt it seemed only a matter of time before Libya's full weight of Italian troops, tanks, and aircraft came sweeping east towards the Nile Valley.[39]

Bagnold arranged for an old service friend (who conveniently happened to be Wavell's head of operations) to place a copy of his desert proposal on the C-inC's desk. The move succeeded; a short while later the proposal's author was summoned to the office and motioned to a chair. Wavell began by saying that he "had read . . . [the] plan with interest," but now wanted to hear more about it.[40] Bagnold told him about Lorrenzini and Uwaynat, about the distinct possibility, in his view, that the Italians might be preparing raids, and about his opinion that the only foolproof way to find out was to send a ground force to reconnoiter above Kufra. Wavell asked detailed questions as to how such a force would be organized, trained, and controlled. Finally, he asked Bagnold pointblank what would happen "if we let you go to all this trouble and you end up finding nothing—no sign at all that the Italians are really up to something. Won't we just have wasted a whole lot of time and effort?" But Bagnold had had plenty of time to contemplate that same issue, and he had a ready answer. "Any force," he said, that could "get over the desert for recce [i.e., reconnaissance] jobs could also do something rather more potent if it has to," and he told Wavell that the British should act at once to begin "exploit[ing] the advantages of a secret route deep into the heart of Libya."[41] Indeed, his suggestion that a small motorized force might profitably engage in—for want of a better phrase—"some old-fashioned 'piracy on the high desert'" certainly did not fall on deaf ears.[42] For Wavell, a general who had himself already given thought to "the motor guerrilla who may be a prominent feature of the next war," now, June 1940, was indeed "the next war."[43] Faced with the prospects of trying to stop an enemy whose numerical strength was greater than his own, Wavell felt that any measure that might help to buy time seemed worth trying. Since the tribal revolt scheme seemed unlikely to produce good results, perhaps what Bagnold offered might help to even up the odds somewhat. By the time

Bagnold left the office, he carried with him the C-in-C's personal authorization for the formation of a motorized desert unit. Designated the Long Range Patrols, it was to function directly under the control of the C-in-C and his Cairo-based theater staff, GHQ-ME. It was also—to use the term increasingly coming into vogue within the British military structure—to be regarded as a "special force."

In fact, it was the second British force of that type to be created in World War II. At almost the same moment and more than 3,000 miles to the northwest, in London, Winston Churchill, now the prime minister, had recently backed the raising of a hand-picked force of seaborne light infantry. These troops, initially called "Leopards" but soon given the Boer War title of "Commandos," were intended to stage hit-and-run raids on the coast of German-occupied Europe. Churchill took his model from the classical Age of Sail and the days of William Pitt's "conjunct operations"—the joint British Army-Royal Navy raids mounted against France in the war of 1756–1763. With the British driven off the Continent in the same month as Bagnold's meeting with Wavell, Churchill, following Dunkirk, sought a way to strike back and restore fighting spirit in a nation about to endure the Battle of Britain. But Luftwaffe control of the skies over the Continent and the obvious mobility of German ground forces appeared to rule out the sort of large-scale, daylight amphibious ventures characteristic of the operations of Pitt's day. Instead, attacks against enemy installations would now have to rely on surprise, would have to be made primarily under cover of darkness, and would demand correspondingly smaller numbers of troops. These conditions suggested that the troops themselves would require special weapons, tactics, training, and organization. More significant, the demands of such operations seemed to require, in a qualitative sense, "special" men as well. In Churchill's view, certainly, only the very best, most physically fit, most highly motivated "hunter-class" volunteers could be expected to endure the greater rigors and hazards of Commando service.[44]

Increasingly, therefore, the term "special force" came to stand for a unit whose primary function was to carry out certain types of extremely hazardous infiltration and raiding missions. These missions were regarded as being either beyond the normal operations of war or else too difficult for a standard unit, even one given special training, to undertake with any sort of efficiency during the time when it would have to be pulled away from its regular duties. Almost from the start, and perhaps inevitably, the tendency was to regard a force of this variety as both "special" and "elite." It was "special" as to military function because it performed a limited variety of exceedingly demanding functions, for which "special operations" seemed a convenient generic description. And it was "elite" as to status because it seemed to display, in discharging these operational functions, markedly superior fighting prowess and skill. This status was underpinned by the belief that only the most carefully selected personnel could hope to measure up, and that they had to receive "rites of passage" training more demanding than that afforded other troops. The fact that units of this type often came to attract a rather generous share of political and press attention could only serve to reinforce their *corps d'élite*, set-apart status.[45]

But the type of unit which Bagnold was about to form would be a special force in an additional sense as well. The operational functions that it would ultimately carry out were not dissimilar to those undertaken by various other types of special forces in the war of 1939–1945, and, like them, it also would come to be accorded a reputation as an elite unit. But it was the first to be created in order to function in a particular type of unconventional habitat, one whose harsh and unique conditions could place great stress on the capabilities of existing forces. Because it was specifically created to function in the habitat of the Libyan desert, it thus originated not merely as a special force but as a habitat-particular special force as well. In the end, this circumstance would cause an intensive degree of concentration upon a narrow range of operational undertakings, and it would further serve, in a very beneficial sense, to protect the unit from misapplication in roles more appropriately left to conventional units.[46]

As conceived by Wavell and Bagnold, the Long Range Patrols would comprise a headquarters element and three complete patrolling units, each consisting of approximately thirty men and a dozen vehicles (or a total of just under a hundred men and forty vehicles). Wavell had instructed Bagnold to write out his own operation orders and to show them only to Wavell personally. Everything—the men, the vehicles, the equipment—was to be ready to go in six weeks' time at the latest. Above all and for obvious reasons the existence of the unit had to be kept absolutely secret. Bagnold began by rounding up as many of his old exploring group as possible. He succeeded in locating Captain E. C. Mitford, a tank officer who had made most of the prewar trips. But others, such as Guy Prendergast, now a major, were stationed elsewhere and could not be available on such short notice. Bagnold finally located W. B. Kennedy Shaw, and sought, through channels, to obtain his services. But Shaw, who had already volunteered and been turned down once for military service, was told that his present official duties ("helping to censor the Palestine newspapers") were far too important for him to be released. At age 39 and a product of University College, Oxford University, he was admittedly old to be embarking on a soldier's career. But with Wavell's help, it was arranged that he was at last "sprung" from his Colonial Service commitment and given a temporary commission as an intelligence officer. A similar appointment for World War I Royal Artillery veteran Patrick Clayton rounded out the initial nucleus of desert-expert officers. While these old hands ran down needed items of equipment, Bagnold turned to the larger task of securing the "ORs"—the "other ranks" or enlisted personnel—who would obviously have to make up the bulk of the unit.[47]

His preference as to where these men should come from very much reflected the British regular officer's Boer War– and World War I–induced high regard for the toughness and resourcefulness of the troops from the Empire-Commonwealth's dominions. In particular, Bagnold wanted men from Australia's "outback," an arid region whose similarities of climate and terrain presumably would have hardened them to the conditions of the Libyan desert. When Australian commanders objected to having their troops parcelled out among British units, Bagnold turned to those New Zealand Division elements already in Egypt. While New Zealand's cool, damp climate was admittedly no more similar to the Libyan desert than was England's, Bagnold understood that many of this division's personnel were farmers in civilian life; consequently, they were probably well versed in such practical matters as keeping vehicles and engines in working order. Then, too, their commander, Lieutenant General Bernard Freyberg, who had won the Victoria Cross in World War I, was an old friend and professional colleaque of long standing of Wavell's. With the C-in-C's personal help Bagnold was thus able to procure, on little more than the strength of the officially advertised call for "volunteers for a dangerous mission," not fewer than ninety men and several junior officers from the New Zealand Division. More importantly, he seems to have been given some of the very best men available within that division. Arriving for the short interviews conducted by Bagnold or the other old desert hands, they had little of the ferocious "Commando" image built up later in the war. Most, indeed, appeared to be rather serious; they were "settled men" in their late twenties and therefore somewhat older than might have been expected. With the exception of a lance corporal named Croucher, who had earned a merchant-seaman mate's ticket (and was thus spotted by Shaw for training as a navigator), virtually none had ever actually been outside New Zealand before, much less to a desert. But it soon became apparent to Bagnold that he had been given the first-class material of a division that would consistently, in the campaigns ahead, go on to prove itself one of the most distinguished of the war.[48]

The volunteers reported to Bagnold's temporary headquarters at the Abassia Ordnance Depot located just outside Cairo. He had already concluded that the best all-around vehicle for the unit to use was the one-and-a-half-ton truck built by Chevrolet. But virtually none of these models seemed to be available. Learning that twenty or so had recently been assigned to the Egyptian Army, however, he used Wavell's assistance to get them handed back to the British and thence to the Long Range Patrols. Fourteen more, all brand new, were obtained by direct purchase from a civilian dealership in Alexandria. Like the ones from the Egyptian Army, they came fitted British fashion, with the right-hand-side steering wheel. Some three-quarter-ton Fords were also acquired to serve as "pilot" or command vehicles. Additional five-ton heavy "lorries," which would be used as supply trucks, gave Bagnold a total of something over thirty-five vehicles. As soon as they were acquired, the vehicles were run into the maintenance shops, where they were fitted with mounts for weapons and painted in desert-tan camouflage.[49]

Other items of equipment proved rather more difficult to obtain than the trucks. The problem was that, with the Battle of Britain now commencing and German U-boats preying upon convoys, much of the needed equipment was in critically short supply in the Middle East. Moreover, at least some of what Bagnold needed struck supply officers, accustomed to the more stable, long-established requirements of peacetime service, as altogether exotic. An example was the theodolite. Bagnold needed at least three of these standard surveying devices for navigation, one for each of the three patrols. His attempts to borrow, as a substitute, standard navigators' sextants from the RAF had netted three hopelessly defective instruments. Those theodolites held by Royal Engineers units were already being put to good use in helping to build the roads and fortifications that might help to stop the Italians. Finally, and only after a flurry of messages and the C-in-C's personal intervention, two of the crucial instruments were located. A third, apparently the only spare then available in the entire Middle East Command, was located in Nairobi and flown north to Cairo by the RAF. The celestial almanacs and logarithmic tables necessary for use with the theodolites were obtained at the Royal Navy's fleet base at Alexandria, along with a full complement of protractors, dividers, and the like. While obtaining something as rare as a sun compass would normally have presented major difficulties, there were, by good fortune, already plenty of these available close at hand. Three years before, as part of the short-lived program for upgrading the Frontiers Administration desert patrols, the Egyptian government had been induced to order about two hundred of these compasses. Of the model that Bagnold had designed and patented, a consignment had arrived in Egypt only to spend the next three years languishing on the shelves of a Cairo arsenal. Told only that they were now needed for a routine training exercise, Egyptian military authorities duly handed them over for installation on the dashboards of the pilot vehicles and some of the trucks. A hundred pairs of sunglasses were furnished by the RAF, and various army units contributed camouflage nets, map boards, and virtually the last sets of military binoculars available in the Middle East. The Army's medical branch provided a specially treated refrigerator for storing medicines, and the quantity of tires piling up around Bagnold's headquarters was soon at least three times greater than that normally issued to a unit of comparable size.[50]

By now Shaw had begun training some of the New Zealanders in desert navigation. It was essential as well that each of the officers have at least a working knowledge of the sun compass and the dead-reckoning techniques developed in the previous decade. If the principle of the sun compass was simple (it worked, after all, like a sundial), in practice its operation could be tricky. Having noted where the sun's shadow fell across the card (the compass obviously could not be used at night), the navigator next had to keep adjusting it to correspond with the movement of the sun across the sky. Shaw began the novice navigators with blackboard-and-chalk sessions; a program of practice runs in the desert beyond the Pyramids followed.[51] Clutching map boards, protractors, and dividers, the New Zealanders found themselves riding over the sands and learning how to set and follow a course. Celestial navigation, using the theodolite, came next. At noon and at night, taking sun and star shots, they learned how to do the lengthy calculations that, when finally worked out, would give their precise position.[52]

By mid-August most of the trucks were out of the shops and ready. Reinforcing strips of metal had been welded onto each chassis and extra leaves added to the springs for greater strength. Any feature judged "extraneous" in Bagnold's view—the windshields, roofs, doors, mirrors, and anything else that added to weight but did not improve performance—was stripped off. Radiator condensers were fitted on, and brackets, installed on the sides, carried the five-foot-long pieces of steel planking or "sand channels" which the early expeditions had shown to be essential. For its weapons the unit received an assortment dictated more by availability than by mission. In addition to small arms, including rifles, revolvers, and Thompson submachineguns, Bagnold acquired World War I–vintage Lewis guns, some .303–caliber Browning machineguns, and a dozen antitank guns. Each truck carried one of the Brownings, mounted on a swivel-rig behind the driver. Bolted to the passenger's side of the cab, a .303 Lewis gun gave additional firepower to the front. Bagnold briefly experimented with trying to add armorplate to protect the trucks, but soon gave this up as hopelessly impractical. It added drastically to the weight and, in any case, there was no longer any time left for trying to turn the trucks into makeshift armored fighting vehicles.[53]

The process of organizing the three patrols was completed well before the trucks were ready. Assignments were made, as Bagnold put it, "so as to get the optimum use out of the people available."[54] Of the three patrols, designated R, W, and T Patrols, two were therefore given to old desert hands and the third to a New Zealand officer who had done well in Shaw's desert-navigation course. The experienced Captain Patrick Clayton thus assumed command of T Patrol, and Captain Mitford—the only regular officer besides Bagnold in the unit at the time, and a prewar explorer—got W Patrol. R, the third patrol, was placed under Lieutenant D. G. Steele, 28 years old and previously a farmer in New Zealand. The concept was that, led by the commander and his navigator riding in the pilot vehicle, the rest of the patrol would follow in the Chevrolet trucks. One truck in each patrol, fitted with the British Army's standard radio, the Type No. 11 Wireless Unit, would serve as the communications vehicle. A "W/T" (wireless-telegraphy) apparatus, the No. 11 used Morse dot-dash rather than direct-voice communication.[55] For signaling between the vehicles, Bagnold made everyone learn a signal-flag system that recalled men-of-war in the Age of Sail. One variety of pennant, for example, specified a line-ahead formation, a second flag dictated a turn to the right, and so on. In the brief time available, the patrols were taken for practice jaunts into some low dunes west of Cairo. The machinegunners were able to practice with their guns, and the signals specialists set up their gear and made contact with a base station. The whole unit was to be ready to go by the end of August.

In the little time remaining, Bagnold gave considerable effort to going over the final aspects of his plan with Wavell and his staff. One of the most important of these officers was the head of GHQ-ME's intelligence department, Colonel (later Brigadier) Eric J. Shearer. As Director of Military Intelligence (DMI), Shearer had increasingly become, after the first meetings with Wavell, Bagnold's chief point of contact. Like Bagnold, Shearer was a "dug-out," having been brought back from retirement (and a top executive slot at London's Fortnum and Mason, Ltd.) in 1939. Educated at Wellington and Sandhurst, he had won the Military Cross in World War I, had graduated from the Staff College, and had served on the general staff. His initial interest in Bagnold's unit was obvious, since it could furnish him with crucial intelligence. In Shearer's view, very little "actual hard . . . information" on Italian activities in "the Qufra region" had ever been supplied by French sources, and even these had dried up when France surrendered in June.[56] But now, and well before the end of Bagnold's six weeks' deadline, Shearer received new information that could only tend to lend credence to fears that the Italians might indeed be up to something in the far south: Marshal Graziani, the Mussolini-favored general who, ten years before, had made his reputation in conquering that same region of the desert, was now returning to Libya. Named commander-in-chief of Italian forces in North Africa, he was to replace Marshal Balbo, recently and accidentally shot down and killed over Tobruk by his own antiaircraft guns. Apart from some border skirmishing, the Italians had so far made no overt move towards Egypt. But the arrival of Graziani, a former governor of Cyrenaica and recently the chief of the Italian Army Staff, gave fresh impetus to the task of getting the Long Range Patrols ready as soon as possible.[57] It suggested to Shearer, at least, that precisely the kinds of actions about which Lorrenzini had joked with Bagnold might well be imminent.

He and Bagnold therefore, as time was running out, presented to Wavell an idea for sending over Captain Clayton and a small party for the purpose of setting up a watch-post on the track north of Kufra. This had been Bagnold's original concept, and it was clear that the full unit could never be ready in time to carry out this first probe. In addition, this approach would give the patrols an opportunity to begin ferrying out the stocks of reserve fuel by which Bagnold hoped to establish a secret base on the western edge of the Sand Sea. Wavell, with little to lose by it, accepted the plan. Early in August, Clayton, with two Fords, five of the New Zealanders, and an Arab guide from his surveying days, was sent west out of Cairo. Wearing

blue RAF caps, they pretended, in order to confuse anyone who might be
unduly interested in their activities, to be engaged in a routine survey of
auxiliary airfield sites.[58]

With Clayton thus launched on the unit's first actual mission into enemy
territory, Bagnold concentrated on the final details of preparation for the
move into the desert. Six weeks exactly from the date of his meeting with
Wavell, the Long Range Patrols were at last ready. A formal inspection was
held so that the C-in-C himself could see the men—each of them wearing,
straight out of Lawrence, the Arab *kaffiyeh* and *agal* (headcloth and cords)
that Bagnold had selected as the unit's official (and already, with the men,
less-than-popular) headgear—as well as the vehicles and special desert par-
aphernalia. Apart from the unique headdress, however, there was little else
to give away their identity as a special unit. The trucks bore standard army
insignia, and the personnel wore the cotton drill shorts and shirts, standard
summer-service field uniform for British units in the Middle East. But Wavell
apparently liked what he saw. That night, in a coded message to the War
Office in London, he was able to report that "the Long Range Patrols were
ready to take the field."[59] His backing of this newly formed band of "motor
guerrillas" had not been without certain costs, however. Merely to get Bagnold's unit equipped had meant taking nearly forty scarce vehicles and pulling them away from critical needs elsewhere. Also, the very last machineguns
available anywhere in the entire command had been given to Bagnold so
that he might have a chance against the Auto-Saharan patrols he expected
to encounter on the far side of the Sand Sea.

Indeed, Shearer and Shaw alike later came to recognize that only Bagnold
could have succeeded in persuading Wavell—no matter how drastic his need
for a means to distract the Italians until British strength could be built up—
to back the formation of this special unit. To them, only Bagnold had possessed both "the necessary knowledge of the Army *and* the necessary experience of the desert, plus the vision and driving power, to extract . . . [what
he wanted] from [GHQ] Middle East."[60] At any rate, the moment for action
was nearly at hand. His "one good eye glinting," the C-in-C appeared before
the unit for a final time to wish them "good hunting."[61] With that, the Long
Range Patrols drove out of Cairo. Leaving in groups of two or three vehicles
so as not to attract attention and with their trucks piled high with equipment
and supplies, they threaded their way past mosques and shops and through
streets crowded with city Arabs. Picking up the road that ran through mango
groves and the lush cultivation on the city's western side, they drove out of
the Nile Valley and up to the edge of the desert. The Pyramids marked
their entry into a world of glare and searing heat. After reaching their rendezvous point, the vehicles, now together, continued west along the old
caravan route that led to Siwa Oasis. But after a few miles, Bagnold's patrols,
setting their sun compasses on a southwesterly course, pulled off the track
and vanished into the emptiness of the desert that would be their element

for the next two and a half years. What had begun in the middle 1920s as an exploring venture and had been given military impetus by a chance encounter with an Italian patrol nearly ten years later, was about to win for the British the domination of the vast spaces lying south of the Libyan plateau.[62]

CHAPTER 4

First Missions: A Huge Bluff Played Out

Only later did I begin to realize how much the C-in-C was gambling on a "huge bluff." We were to create sufficient havoc that Graziani would be forced to recalculate the real British strengths and intentions.
—Brigadier Ralph A. Bagnold,
Commanding Officer, LRDG, 1940–1941[1]

Bagnold's first objective was Ain Dalla, a desolate, spring-fed waterhole where he had built a wooden shack ten years before. The patrols reached it three days and 300 miles out of Cairo. There was little to look at: merely the shack, still sheltering some gasoline cans (and a scorpion or two), and a collection of stunted palms dotting the hot sand. But to the west, just a few miles beyond, loomed the first great dunes and the unit's real jump-off point for Libya. Unloading their cargoes of gasoline cans, for the next week the patrols took turns making the run to fetch in more fuel from the north.[2]

While this process was going on, Clayton returned from the unit's first venture into enemy territory. Nearly three weeks had elapsed since his departure from Cairo. He and his party had pushed west and directly into the Sand Sea, pausing only to set up a reserve dump of fuel and water to cover the line of retreat. Coming out of the dunes at a point approximately 200 miles inside Libya, they eventually reached the vicinity of the north-south Kufra track. There had so far been no sign at all of enemy planes or patrolling activity. But Clayton, deciding to wait until dark to approach the tracks, showed his men how to hide the vehicles and brush over the last few hundred yards of tire tracks. Then, with their vehicles safely hidden in some low hills, they moved forward on foot to watch for enemy movement down the Palificata. First light revealed one or two of the iron stakes which marked the route. But as the sun climbed higher nothing came—no enemy trucks, no enemy patrols, and no Auto-Saharans. Italian aircraft of different types passed overhead several times, but there was no vehicular movement down the track. That night Clayton went forward to "track-read." He found only a few deep ruts, and these appeared to be weeks old. In the days ahead, enduring temperatures that climbed to perhaps 130°, he and his men continued to maintain their watch over an empty track. But at length, with no sightings of enemy movements to report, they pulled back into the dunes for the long return push to Egypt. Not until much later did they learn the reason for the strange absence of enemy traffic down this main route. The Italians, when convoys of recent months had begun to chew up the Palificata's loose sand, had merely shifted their traffic to a new route just a few miles to the west. Enemy movement had indeed been there all the time, but apparently too far away for the party to spot the telltale dust clouds.[3]

Clayton's effort had not been totally without success, however. For one thing, enemy aircraft had consistently failed to spot his hidden vehicles, a fact that could only bode well for the safety of future operations. Of even greater significance was the fact that Clayton had located a practicable route for traversing this sector of the dunes. Indeed he had found the route that would serve, for the next two years and with only slight variation, as the unit's primary (and, by the enemy, never discovered) avenue of approach for slipping behind first Italian and then German lines.[4]

Bagnold was by now ready to commence the patrols' main thrust into Libya. He had selected, after consultation with Clayton, as the site for his secret base a place known as "Big Cairn"—a collection of rocks piled up on a survey of years before. Located on the far side of the Sand Sea and just a few miles from the Libyan border, Big Cairn had the advantage of being fairly close to Kufra. But to reach Big Cairn demanded that the whole unit would first of all have to drive its overloaded vehicles across 150 miles of difficult Sand Sea dunes. The problem was that, given the short time available for training, none of the New Zealand drivers had as yet been introduced to the difficulties of moving vehicles over these great sand formations. Bagnold himself was far from certain as to how it would go, especially as the prewar expeditions had used—as opposed to these heavy trucks crammed full of weapons, munitions, spare parts, and extra fuel—only the very lightest vehicles. Moreover, his previous efforts had all been made in the cooler winter months, rather than in a season whose temperatures could quickly rise to the low hundred-plus degrees range.[5]

Early in September, however, he led the initial patrol, Mitford's W, towards the first dune. Despite the heat of the day, the sight of its 300–foot-high crest momentarily chilled the New Zealanders into silence. But one by one they lined up their trucks for the run to the top. The first vehicle, with Bagnold riding in it, lurched forward and into the climb—and got about halfway up before stalling in the sand. Only after repeated attempts, and

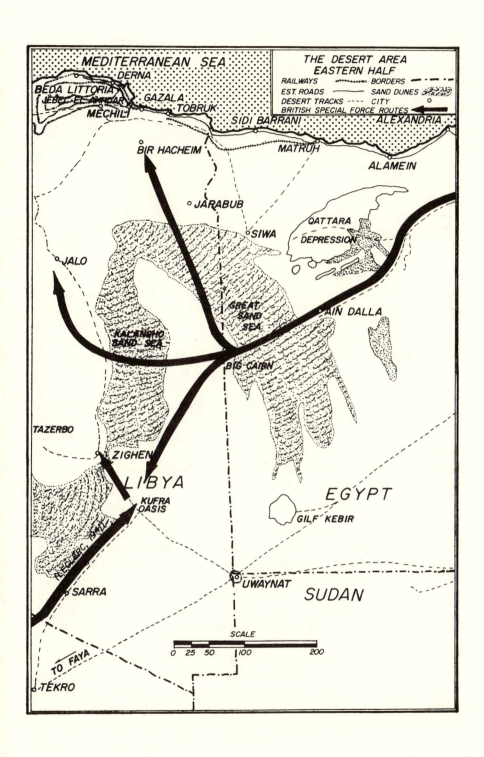

after Bagnold began to doubt that "we should ever get across . . . with such loads," did this first truck finally make it all the way up.[6] The rest of the day was spent in this way: attempt after attempt, with each of the trucks floundering, and interspersed with endless digging and using the sand channels to extract vehicles stuck axle-deep in soft sand. Yet by late afternoon all of W Patrol had safely conquered the first dune. Furthermore, it seemed to Bagnold that the new desert drivers were actually "catching on marvellously fast."[7] Certainly progress improved the next day and even more the day after that. At length, after a full day's good running, they topped the very last dune. They were across the Sand Sea at last. Excepting Clayton's small party of the month before, they were the first military unit ever to accomplish such a feat. Once again, as they stood on a dune looking west towards Libya, it was proved to Bagnold, as he had believed all along, that a properly organized force, with sufficient food and fuel to operate for weeks on end, could, with perseverance and the right skills and equipment, get across this barrier after all.

He had half expected to find the Auto-Saharans, perhaps with Lorrenzini himself, waiting in ambush. But they were not. After sweeping the horizon with his binoculars, he led the column down and onto the flat sandy plain. Reaching Big Cairn a few miles further on, they posted lookouts, dispersed the vehicles, and "laagered up" for the night. The crucial cargo of gasoline cans was cached nearby. When the signals specialists got the antenna set up, Bagnold radioed Clayton to begin bringing over the other two patrols. These arrived a few days later, having endured the same initially difficult travail as Mitford's, but also without having spotted or having been spotted by enemy patrols or aircraft. Bagnold spent a day or two thereafter going over plans with the patrol commanders. Finally, on a night towards the middle of September 1940, the unit settled down, cooking fires hidden, to a hot meal and a welcome shot of rum with the evening tea. (The rations-scale specified by the unit's medical officer, in civilian life a general practitioner in Auckland, included extra allotments of chocolate, canned milk, marmalade, lime juice, and fruit. It also included rum, supposedly issued to units in the field only upon the express authorization of at least a local "divisional commander or the equivalent."[8]) As the men wrapped themselves against the growing chill, the regular evening BBC broadcast from London came on, giving the navigators their standard Greenwich time signals. It also carried the soft "swing" rhythms of a new American hit by Glenn Miller, whose orchestra "was always the patrols' favourite."[9] But this night the routine transmission from GHQ-ME in Cairo, received over the No. 11 set, carried news that was anything but routine. As the operators finished decoding the dot-dash message, Bagnold learned that the long-expected had finally occurred. Up north, in the Libyan plateau, the Italians had finally launched their offensive into Egypt, and the lengthy transmission concluded with a terse message: the Long Range Patrols were to commence their operations immediately.

Bagnold's first and most compelling priority was to carry out the intelligence-gathering mission used as justification for the formation of a special unit in the first place: to find out precisely what, if anything, the Italians were up to in the south. In short order, therefore, Bagnold sent the patrols, each assigned a specific sector, to investigate the tracks and outposts connecting Kufra with the coast and with the region down towards Uwaynat. These probes soon revealed the obvious presence of enemy air and ground forces. But neither enemy strengths nor enemy activities seemed to indicate anything like the levels of preparation necessary for the full-scale raiding ventures which Lorrenzini had mentioned many years before. This Bagnold found indeed exceedingly puzzling. Had the threat of such raids in reality been an empty one all along, or had some unknown factor arisen to alter Italian intentions? Certainly Bagnold found it odd that his unit had so far apparently gone undetected by the Auto-Saharans, whose aggressive employment against him might have spelled disaster in the early stages. It was not until much later, well after the conclusion of these first reconnaissance efforts, that he gained firm evidence of the inadequacy of Italian preparations for combat in the inner desert. Lorrenzini, for example, recently promoted to colonel, was himself actually nowhere near the Libyan desert when the war commenced. Instead, he had earlier been sent south to Ethiopia to take command of infantry forces for the campaign in East Africa (and was ultimately to be killed there, in 1941, in operations against the British). Unlike Bagnold, there had been for him no intervention by a higher commander to ensure that an invaluable desert expert was kept in the country he knew so well. This misapplication of talent and expertise had thus deprived the Italians of a "gifted desert commander whose abilities," in Bagnold's judgment, could have "caused us a great deal of trouble."[10]

But the first reconnaissance efforts at least proved that the threat of sizeable enemy raids could now be safely ruled out for the present. Bagnold's unit was directed to turn to the task which Wavell had intended for it all along— to attack and harass in such a way that Graziani would have to divert forces in order to protect those desert outposts he had won a decade earlier. Its success in the role of diverting enemy forces from their main thrust into Egypt ultimately won for the unit "a reputation [for competence and sheer audacity] which we never lost."[11] The raids commenced almost on the heels of the sort of fearsome desert storm the Arabs called a *qibli*. Its thick, choking clouds of hot sand sorely vexed the patrols, producing heat casualties and wearing paint off the trucks, but had the positive virtue of masking their movements from enemy eyes. Mitford's W Patrol became the first to strike when, north of Kufra, it spotted the red "wind socks" by which the Italians marked their auxiliary airstrips. Mitford planted charges and blew up, in rapid succession, the fuel dumps and pumping facilities at several landing grounds. Thereafter, intercepting part of a supply convoy on its way south, the patrol bagged the unit's very first prisoners. It also captured the pouch of mail and official dispatches intended for Kufra's garrison commander. This act in particular soon provoked a whole flurry of worried Italian signals. Intercepted by the British "Y Service's" radio-monitoring stations and analyzed by Shearer's DMI staff, these signals encouraged Wavell to instruct Bagnold to do even more. While Wavell and Major General Richard O'Connor's newly formed Western Desert Force prepared a British counterstroke in the north, the Long Range Patrols were to mount a full program of raids that would "stir up trouble in . . . [every] part of Libya."[12]

Bagnold decided to attack a whole string of widely separated points at more or less the same moment. W Patrol, with intelligence officer Shaw riding along, was sent against Uwaynat's airstrip and protecting outposts. Approaching the southernmost of these, however, W was spotted and attacked by a pair of Caproni-309 light bombers, the sort which the Italians called "Ghiblis." These bombed and strafed but eventually, running low on fuel, broke off and gave the patrol a chance to get away before other planes could arrive. Finally reaching the enemy positions, W Patrol's vehicles attacked at two points before returning to the safety of the desert. Steele's R Patrol next planted mines along the main track to the north of the airfield and blew up a munitions dump. Steele also caught and destroyed on the ground one of the Uwaynat-based Ghibli bombers, and he later set charges on a large aviation fuel dump as well. The raids continued throughout the month of October and into November 1940. Clayton's patrol, sent the furthest north, eventually crossed the Sand Sea to plant mines within eighty miles of the coast and almost on the fringes of the Italian colonial settlements. He also ambushed a Kufra-bound convoy and raided various small forts and outposts. These operations netted prisoners (most of whom were let go since there was no room for them on the trucks) as well as documents useful to Shearer's intelligence staff. The pace of these attacks did not let up as Wavell continued to follow a policy of hold and hit: to hold in the north until O'Connor could be ready to initiate the major counteroffensive, by now taking shape under the code name Operation Compass; and to use Bagnold's patrols to hit in the south so as to distract Graziani and thus gain time for O'Connor to move. Wavell's judgment was that his opponent, the Italian general who had conquered the southern desert, might be susceptible to the "huge bluff" of a diversionary scheme that would throw him off as to "the real British strengths and intentions."[13] The Long Range Patrols, by their program of raids deep inside enemy territory, were to change Graziani's string of deep-desert outposts from assets into liabilities.

Wavell's plan worked. As the raids intensified, they gave the impression of "simultaneous appearances at places 600 miles apart."[14] Intercepted and decoded messages began to reveal that Italian commanders were pressing for more troops and more air patrols to cover their supply convoys and distant outposts. Graziani himself soon took the bait. Rather than keeping every available unit concentrated for his main thrust, which had pushed only about sixty miles into Egypt and then stalled, he made the mistake of diverting forces, especially some of his mobile units and aviation elements, to the task of protecting Kufra and the tracks above it. This step prompted Wavell to heighten the pressure on his opponent by extending the raids into even more distant parts of Libya.[15] To do so, however, required that the size of Bagnold's unit be expanded, and Wavell permitted him to recruit new volunteers from the pick of the British units available in the Middle East. Among the new arrivals were contingents furnished by two of that army's most distinguished regiments, the Scots Guards and the Coldstream Guards. The hand-picked Guardsmen supposedly were physically taller than the soldiers of "the Line" regiments, and they brought to the unit the sort of regimental discipline that had prevailed at Blenheim and Waterloo. They differed from Bagnold's proven New Zealanders—very much "colonials," who tended to make fun of the Guardsmen's precise and formal military courtesy. Rather than trying to mix the two groups, Bagnold opted instead to form G (Guards) Patrol, placing it under the senior of the two Guards officers who had been sent.[16] In addition to the Guardsmen, a contingent from various Yeomanry units—the volunteer mounted forces that had traditionally formed a sort of British "national guard"—were organized into a separate Y (Yeomanry) Patrol.[17] The last group of volunteers, like the New Zealanders, was also made up of "colonials": farmers-turned-soldiers from Southern Rhodesia (now Zimbabwe), who were formed into S (Southern Rhodesia) Patrol. Together the three new patrols gave the unit a sixty percent increase in strength. The overall gain would have been even higher had not General Freyberg, trying to prepare his division for its role in Compass, at this time succeeded in securing the return of one of the three original New Zealand patrols. Even with the loss of these trained men, however, Bagnold's unit was in vastly better shape than before. Its greater size demanded its reorganization into a more flexible, two-squadron arrangement, as well as the adoption of a new title. The Long Range Patrols therefore now became officially the Long Range Desert Group (LRDG), a title which the patrols would keep until 1945 and their disbandment at the end of the war. Bagnold himself put on, as commanding officer of this expanded force, the crowns-and-pips insignia of a lieutenant colonel.[18]

Well before the task of recruiting and training these new volunteers had been completed, Wavell and Shearer informed Bagnold that a major "raid or two—perhaps on the far side of Libya and in the far limits of enemy territory—would do a good deal to add to Graziani's difficulties just now."[19] Bagnold did not long delay in choosing a likely target, and one that was indeed on the far side of Libya. Murzuk, the Italian district headquarters of the Fezzan province, was over 1,300 miles from the nearest British position. Bagnold counted on catching Murzuk's garrison—located in a back-water of the war and "sure to be asleep"—totally by surprise.[20] Almost certainly a sudden raid there would indicate to Graziani that the British could now reach and hit even his supposedly most secure outposts. Bagnold chose Clayton, now promoted to major, to lead the raid. His veteran T Patrol New Zealanders would be joined by G Patrol, whose new commander, a 23–year-old Scots Guards captain named Michael Crichton-Stuart, had at first found Bagnold to be a scholarly type who seemed more like a professor than a soldier. But the attempt on Murzuk would involve more than just these two LRDG patrols. For some time, Wavell's GHQ-ME in Cairo had wanted to approach the French forces in Chad with the possibility of joint operations. When a visit in October by General de Gaulle successfully won that province over to the Free French cause, the stage was set for Bagnold to be flown south for discussions with the French authorities at Fort Lamy. Not only did the French officers promise Bagnold to assist the LRDG effort by setting up forward dumps of gasoline at a point just across the Libyan border, but one of them, Fort Lamy's second-in-command, requested permission to join personally in the Murzuk raid.[21]

Bagnold returned by early December to find Clayton's preparations well advanced. Intelligence sources suggested that Murzuk's thick-walled fort and outlying airfield were held by perhaps three hundred Italian and native troops. By the time that G and T Patrols were at the point of completing the final tasks of readying their trucks for the LRDG's most ambitious operation to date, news was received which could only give fresh impetus to their preparations. At dawn on December 9, O'Connor's Compass tanks, infantry, and artillery, supported by the RAF, had suddenly smashed into Graziani's exposed forward elements. The Italians were sent reeling back in confusion and disarray. Surging west, the British forces, so recently on the defensive (and still numerically inferior), soon reached the frontier and stood poised to push into Libya itself. Their attack, superbly planned and executed, had caught Graziani totally by surprise. From London, Churchill signaled Wavell to "maul the Italian Army and rip them off the African shore."[22] Thus it was that, early in the second week of December, Clayton led his combined patrols out of Cairo on a mission well-calculated to "add to Graziani's difficulties just now."[23]

Bundled up against the bitter cold, Clayton's men were just settling down for the long pull when the column made a surprise stop on the outskirts of the city. Pulling out from behind a building, a black sedan quickly drove up and let out two men, both wearing the loose garb of Bedouin dress. As soon as these two figures had mounted, the column headed off again. Not until they were well out into the desert did the patrols learn the identity of their new passengers. Both were genuine desert Arabs and both looked to be hard cases indeed. (One of them proudly displayed a hand mangled by Italian bullets in some previous fight.) In fact, the elder of the two turned out to be no less than a full-fledged sheikh. Ten years before, as one of the most powerful of the Senussi leaders, he had survived Graziani's last attack by taking what was left of his family across 500 miles of desert. His tribal holdings had been in the area around Murzuk. And while Wavell, Shearer, and GHQ-ME had long since given up on the prospects of trying to stage a full-scale tribal revolt, letting the sheikh suddenly reappear at this particular juncture was altogether too good an opportunity to let pass by. In conjunction with the raids, it seemed a superb way by which to exploit and exacerbate Italian difficulties as the Compass force pushed deeper into Libya.[24]

G and T Patrols reached their first major goal, some lava beds east of Murzuk, early in January 1941. To the Guards' Crichton-Stuart, "no remoter spot in North Africa" could have been found.[25] While the column laagered its vehicles, the signalmen rigged up a pair of seventeen-foot-high wooden poles. These supported a horizontal Windom aerial, and made it possible to transmit and receive messages over distances approaching a thousand miles.[26] So far no Italians had been seen. With his force now well hidden in this remote position, Clayton took a small party and headed south to look for the Frenchmen who had promised to help. He found them, as arranged, at a rendezvous point in the foothills of the Tibesti Mountains, just inside Libyan territory. The promised cache of gasoline was there, and so also were the French officers who had pledged to come along. These included the "tall, monocled, turbaned" Lieutenant Colonel d'Ornano, Fort Lamy's second-in-command, and his assistant, Captain Jacques Emile Charles Marie Massu.[27] Both were St. Cyr graduates and long-service colonial soldiers, but the shaven-headed Massu (who would eventually rise to full general's rank in the French Army and to commands prominent in the Indochina, Suez, and Algerian wars) was perhaps the more flamboyant-appearing of the two. A real *Beau Geste* type in his gold-braided officer's *képi*, he also affected the same baggy trousers and burnous—and bare feet—as his camel-mounted irregulars. The Frenchmen insisted on bringing along a *tricolore* to show that this was now genuinely an Anglo-French endeavor. So reinforced, Clayton loaded up and returned north to the patrols' position. That night, the incoming dot-dashes of a radio signal told GHQ-ME in Cairo that Clayton had linked up with his patrols again and was ready to proceed against Murzuk.[28]

Early the next day, however, the column almost immediately encountered nomads and grazing camels. Clayton, pretending he was leading an Italian patrol, lost no time in shifting course just as soon as his vehicles were safely over the horizon. Next, intersecting one of the enemy's iron post-marked main routes, Clayton carefully led the whole column, vehicle by vehicle, across the track at exactly the same spot. Thereafter a tense hour was spent in carefully brushing over all signs of their tire tracks—a broad daylight job, as one of the officers commented, that one would not like "to do often."[29] A day later, approaching from the north as the least likely direction from the enemy's viewpoint, they came at last to a low sand ridge just above

Murzuk. The target was clearly visible through binoculars two miles off to the south. To the left of its white-domed mosque, native huts, and clusters of date palms could be seen the radio mast, airfield hangar, and high watch-tower which marked the enemy's fort and main compound.[30]

Clayton was still in the act of going over plans with the officers when an Italian plane suddenly zoomed over his position. With no time to lose now, he signaled the patrols forward. His vehicle, with d'Ornano's *tricolore* flying, led. Racing through the date palms, Crichton-Stuart's G Patrol peeled off to take the fort under fire while Clayton continued on towards the airfield. The Guardsmen almost immediately succeeded in blowing up an enemy vehicle trying to get inside the gate. As the volume of enemy return fire increased, Crichton-Stuart lost one of his sergeants but managed, with a well-aimed mortar round, to set part of the fort on fire. After continuing to fire away at the fort for awhile longer, he finally broke off, as arranged, to link up with Clayton at the airfield. By the time he arrived, its hangar, maintenance sheds, operations shack, and other facilities were already on fire, as was the enemy's main fuel point. Black smoke and orange flames also poured from the fuselages of the three Ca-309s that Clayton had caught on the ground. Furthermore, T Patrol's vehicles were already rounding up a flock of prisoners, and enemy dead seemed to be all over the place. But the sudden attack on the airfield had not been accomplished without cost. In the back of Clayton's vehicle lay the bloodsoaked body of Lieutenant Colonel d'Ornano, killed in a burst of fire when a machinegun had opened up from behind the hangar.[31] But the raid had caught the enemy by surprise, and, under a darkening sky and with the cold wind whipping up a sandstorm, Clayton soon led the patrols out of Murzuk. He paused a few miles away to treat casualties and to bury d'Ornano in the sand beside the track. In all, five men had been wounded. One of them, French Captain Massu, had used a lighted cigarette to cauterize the bullet wound in his leg—an act which managed to win even the admiration of the hardened old sheikh. Moving east and south in the days ahead, the patrols molested other enemy outposts along the way. One of these outposts, however, protected by thick walls and apparently alerted by radio from Murzuk, put up a good fight. The aircraft which it called in caught and pounded the patrols as they moved south. But by holing up in a wadi and throwing out a heavy volume of fire, the two LRDG patrols kept the planes from inflicting more than superficial damage.[32]

Finally, twenty days after they had left Cairo, the patrols departed the Fezzan altogether and moved into the safety of Free French territory. GHQ-ME had already begun learning the effects of Clayton's raid. Within hours of the attack on Murzuk, Y Service intercepts indicated that Italian outposts were frantically now "wirelessing to one another in alarm." Even better, the enemy had apparently decided that the raiders had come not from Egypt but from the French outposts in West Africa. The radio intercepts also confirmed that the Italians were particularly alarmed by the appearance of the Senussi sheikh, and now feared that plans might be afoot to arm and organize his tribesmen as guerrillas. With O'Connor's Western Desert Force rapidly closing in on the vital Italian port of Tobruk in the north, Graziani found himself confronted by raiders who apparently could fall upon virtually any fort, airfield, or outpost in the southern desert. This encouraged Bagnold to try for greater cooperation with the French. Taking an RAF bomber back to Chad again, he eventually met the officer whom de Gaulle had selected to replace the fallen d'Ornano. Bagnold was introduced to a "Colonel Leclerc," a charming, "most striking figure" who in actuality was Colonel the Viscount de Hautecloque.[33] Escaping after the fall of France seven months before, "Leclerc," another career-officer St. Cyrian, had taken on his *nom de guerre* in order to protect his family, who had been left behind in the German-occupied zone while he joined the resistance effort overseas. Although he had "no real desert experience at all," Bagnold found him "already and absolutely keen to do no less than to take Kufra."[34]

Leclerc's conviction was that, with O'Connor pressing the Italians in the north, the quest to seize Graziani's primary inner-desert position should commence at once. Bagnold agreed. But since the best jump-off point, the French outpost at Faya, was over 500 miles south of Kufra, and Leclerc had only a hodgepodge collection of vehicles by which to get there, Bagnold also agreed to place Clayton under him for the operation. The two LRDG patrols would act to screen the advance and take care of the navigation. Well before the push to the north began, however, Clayton and the LRDG officers had already developed a very considerable uneasiness over their French comrades' rather cavalier approach to security arrangements. Even the French officers admitted that Faya was probably full of enemy agents. That Leclerc's soldiers were already greeting each other on the streets with *"Vers Koufra!"* was a fact that hardly suggested that the attackers would find the element of surprise on their side when the crucial moment came.[35]

Their fears, as it turned out, were well founded, for this time it was the Italians who managed to do the surprising. Late in January, as Leclerc's column finally began the move up from Faya, Clayton took T Patrol to advance and scout out the waterholes along the route. Arriving at the first of these, he was alarmed to find that it had been carefully blown in by demolition charges. Then, while still moving north, the patrol spotted an enemy plane, another of the Ca-309s, circling overhead in the distance. Rather than diving to attack, however, the plane unexpectedly veered off to fly away at low altitude. Clayton's guess was that an enemy force, perhaps a sizeable one, was probably lurking close by and preparing to ambush Leclerc. He therefore continued moving north to investigate, eventually halting his vehicles in a shallow wadi. While his men were still getting their trucks camouflaged, however, the lookouts shouted that they could see an enemy ground force heading straight for the LRDG position. At almost the same moment, an enemy aircraft swooped in directly over the wadi. Clayton and everyone else ran for the trucks as the Italians, now practically on top of them, opened fire. In seconds, several of T Patrol's vehicles were hit and burning. The rest of the patrol, led by Clayton, raced for the open end of the wadi before the enemy could cut them off. But as their trucks spilled out onto the flat desert plain, a full flight of Italian aircraft pounced. Their strafing attacks wounded Clayton, and his truck, riddled in the tires and the radiator, was finally halted. Although his second-in-command, Lieutenant Ballantyne, succeeded in getting the rest of the patrol away, Clayton and the crew of his vehicle, stranded in the middle of the plain, were captured.[36]

He had been bagged, in fact, by a large contingent of those same Auto-Saharans who had so impressed Bagnold ten years before. Indeed, to ambush Clayton, No. 19 Auto-Saharan Company had brought to bear the full weight of a flight of Ca-309s, Fiat armored cars (which mounted 20–mm Breda cannon), at least five machinegun-mounted trucks, and a large reinforcing complement of motorized infantry. The LRDG learned later that the whole attack had been carefully planned by a Capitano Moreschini, a veteran of years of Auto-Saharan service. It was also learned that the Italian radio-monitoring stations at Kufra had easily picked up the heavy volume of traffic being generated by Leclerc's northward-moving main body. Furthermore, as Clayton had feared all along, Italian spies in Faya had indeed managed to send word of the advance.[37] Still, T Patrol, for the loss of its commander, seven men, and four trucks, had succeeded in triggering an ambush un-doubtedly intended to catch Leclerc's column when it was strung out and vulnerable along the line of march.

It also turned out that T Patrol's losses in men were not quite so great as was first believed, for in the confusion of the Italians' sudden attack, four of the New Zealanders had been left behind. Hiding out in the wadi until the victorious enemy tired of pulling souvenirs from the wreckage of the trucks, these four men began trudging, in darkness, back along the tracks their vehicles had made that morning. Two of them were wounded, they had less than a gallon of water between them, and the night temperatures were near the freezing mark. As far as they knew, Leclerc's force, the nearest help, was a good 150 miles to the south. But their refusal to give up became an epic feat of endurance rivalled only by the tragic march of the crew of the American B-24 bomber, the *Lady Be Good,* two years later. For six days they kept on until, with each man gradually succumbing to exhaustion, only one was still walking. A reconnaissance party sent north by Leclerc luckily found him. This same force then kept on until, two days later, the other three had also been located, all of them still alive. One man, however, despite the best efforts of the French doctor to save him, soon died. It seemed almost certain that all four would have been lost had they attempted their long walk in the desert's hotter months, when the soaring temperatures would have finished them off, as happened with the crew of the *Lady Be Good*, in a few days at most.[38]

Leclerc meanwhile pressed on with his approach, T Patrol guiding. The patrol code books which the Auto-Saharans had found in Clayton's vehicle inspired the Italians to begin sending all sorts of bogus messages and forced the LRDG to switch to an alternate code. But the Free French-LRDG force made good progress, and a small party, mounted in the column's best vehicles, was soon dispatched ahead to hit Kufra hard enough to keep the Italians off balance. This element managed to knock out Kufra's DF ([Radio] Direction-Finding) Station as well as some planes parked on the airfield. Ten days later, the main body reached the fringes of the date palms surrounding the oasis. Just above Kufra, Leclerc met and defeated Moreschini's No. 19 Company, recently victorious over Clayton, the remnants of which now fled up the Palificata to the north. After that, with the Free French entering the oasis proper, the attack on the main compound settled down to an old-fashioned siege operation. There were at least 450 enemy troops holding the fort, a strong position in which they had sufficient supplies, ammunition, and water to hold out for weeks. In addition, radio contact with Graziani held forth the promise of calling in air support or other assistance from the north. Leclerc's situation, on the other hand, bordered on the precarious. He had fewer men than the Italians, and, far more critically, his supplies of food, ammunition, and gasoline were already dangerously low. The siege, as it wore on, therefore became very much a do-or-die effort for the French. Having used up their wherewithal in fuel and food in just getting to Kufra, they were now stranded. Should they fail to take the fort, their chances of making it back to Faya across 500 miles of desert were practically nonexistent. But by the time Leclerc was down to half-rations and just about out of shells for his largest piece of artillery, a single 75–mm gun, the fort raised a white flag. While the Italian officer who came out did his best to put on the bold face, at dawn a day later the fort's commander finally surrendered. Leclerc's prize consisted of the full garrison of Italian and native troops, abundant supplies, numerous vehicles and light artillery pieces, and twice as many machineguns as the French had had in their whole force.[39]

In Bagnold's view, the flight of Moreschini's Auto-Saharans to the north had probably done more than anything else to break the morale of the fort's defenders. Their sense of being cut off had caused them to surrender "only a day or two before . . . [Leclerc's] supplies would have run out."[40] Leclerc's taking of Kufra not only capped off Wavell's "huge bluff" program of using LRDG raids to divert Italian resources, but also won a key inner-desert base by which to extend the scope of those raids in the future. Despite the loss of Clayton, who spent the rest of the war in POW camps (where he devoted his considerable drafting skills to forging escape documents), the success of the LRDG operations so far had very much "warmed the cockles of Wavell's heart."[41] He informed the commanding officer of the LRDG that a "full report of your activities has already been telegraphed to the War Office." In the operations that will follow, "you will be making an important contribution towards . . . adding to the anxieties and difficulties of our enemy."[42]

The problem, though, was that the nature of "our enemy" was now about to change. Rumors of impending German intervention in North Africa had already been circulating for some time. The Germans, it was said, were in the process of forming a special Afrika Korps and training it in "artificially heated indoor deserts on the Baltic coast."[43] Since the start of Compass in December, the operations of the Western Desert Force had succeeded beyond even the most optimistic expectations, thrusting ever deeper into Libya. O'Connor had taken vital harbors and position after position as his tanks had rolled west over the Libyan plateau. At the point when the British were fully halfway across Libya and poised to drive forward into the westernmost province, Tripolitania, Mussolini had at least replaced the hapless Graziani with a new general, Italo Gariboldi, and Hitler, in order to save Mussolini's North African empire before it fell to the British, at length decided to dispatch sizeable German air and ground contingents to join the war in the desert. In January 1941 and at about the same time that Clayton's patrols were linking up with Leclerc at Faya, the Fuhrer's Oberkommando der Wehrmacht (OKW or Armed Forces High Command) issued the directive which called for selected German forces to be sent to Libya as quickly as possible.[44] The initial elements of these forces began arriving in Tripoli not long after the Western Desert Force managed to smash nine Italian divisions in the desert south of Benghazi, and O'Connor jubilantly signaled Wavell: "Fox killed in the open."[45] Unfortunately for the British, the new "Fox" with whom they were about to contend was 49-year-old Lieutenant General Erwin Rommel, and he would shortly make the desert his own special arena. Moreover, the coming of Rommel and the Germans coincided with a British strategic blunder: Churchill's decision not to finish the job in Libya but instead to send O'Connor's best formations across the Mediterranean in order to block the Italian invasion of Greece then commencing.

In the face of this decision, Wavell had to hope that Cyrenaica could be held by two partially trained and equipped British divisions, and that it could form an effective buffer for the time being. He expected to have sufficient time in which to prepare for Rommel, who, with his 5th Light Division, the nucleus of the Afrika Korps, probably would not be able to mount any sort of "effective counter stroke" much "before May [1941] at the earliest."[46] Indeed the Germans themselves, regarding Libya as very probably lost anyway, intended Rommel's force to be a stopgap only.[47] General Franz Halder, the chief of the German General Staff, instructed Rommel "not to court action" prematurely.[48] But where Halder saw difficulty and lost cause, Rommel saw opportunity. The man who, in World War I, had won Imperial Germany's highest medal, the *Pour le Merite*, and who, two decades later, had slashed across France in command of the 7th Panzer "Ghost" Division, had always triumphed by his audacity. With supreme faith in his own *Fingerspitzengefühl*—the true soldier's sixth sense, the ability to sense an opponent's weak points and to strike accordingly—Rommel prepared to fall upon the British and drive them all the way back to Egypt.

The desert war was about to enter a new phase. Late in March Rommel's forces—some of his "tanks" actually cardboard bodies rigged up on Volkswagens and raising impressive clouds of dust—slammed into the British forward position at El Agheila. Even as his troops fell back in retreat, Wavell remained unconvinced that Rommel's sudden attack had behind it any "persistent weight."[49] This new attack came at a time when the Long Range Desert Group, because of the exploits in the south, was being touted as the British Army's "intrepid desert raiders." Given a special press conference, the unit "overnight . . . developed glamour," as well as "a slightly cock-eyed halo of publicity."[50] This new standing ultimately helped lead to a demand that the patrols be pressed into service not as a special force but as a forward reconnaissance element against advancing German armor. But first Bagnold, now regarded at GHQ-ME as "the new Lawrence," was instructed to move his headquarters down to Kufra and to begin using that oasis as a base by which to do to the Germans what he had already done to the Italians.[51] Only time would tell whether or not another "huge bluff" program of raids could work the same profitable mischief against Rommel as it had against Graziani.

CHAPTER 5

Against the Germans

[Special forces] can best be used to affect the enemy's morale. Their use against airfields, administrative establishments and the like ... can and does engender very considerable uneasiness in the mind of the enemy.

—Major General Neil M. Ritchie,
Deputy Chief of Staff, Middle East Forces, 1941[1]

Bagnold dispatched Mitford's A Squadron (G Patrol and the newly trained Yeomanry Patrol) forward to support the Western Desert Force. But the "DesForce" staff of General Sir Philip Neame—who had replaced the victorious O'Connor, recalled recently to Cairo for rest and theater-level consultation with Wavell—harbored unrealistic notions as to what form that support should take. Short of armored cars and vague as to what Rommel might try next, Neame's officers wanted LRDG patrols to act, in effect, as armored cavalry units. A close-reconnaissance role of this sort would undoubtedly take the patrols' unarmored vehicles out onto the Libyan plateau and thus dangerously close to major concentrations of German forces. Yet Mitford's objections were lost in the "intrepid desert raiders" aura now surrounding the LRDG; in the end, he had no choice but to deploy his patrols as directed.[2]

The staff had informed him that the earliest a large-scale German attack could be expected was "in about a month's time." Less than a week later, however, Rommel launched the full weight of his armor against the British, with devastating effect. In an effort to stem the tide of retreat, Wavell ordered O'Connor back into the desert, with the unfortunate result that, in the confusion of the battle, both O'Connor and Neame were captured by the

Afrika Korps. Mitford himself narrowly escaped being trapped by the advancing Germans. Having suffered casualties after blundering into an area seeded with small, air-dropped mines called "Thermos bombs," he had hidden out near one of the main tracks in some Roman ruins. He had not had long to wait before the Germans arrived; located on a prime route that cut across the desert just south of the broken ground on the Jebel al Akdar (Green Mountain) region of the Libyan hump, he was right in the middle of Rommel's avenue of approach. Mitford held on as long as he could, radioing back detailed reports on the enemy forces now streaming past him. But when a force of armored cars—Sd Kfz-222s and the heavier, six-wheeled, 77–mm-cannon-mounted Sd Kfz-234s—arrived, he ran for it. Even so, his trucks had to dodge dive-bombing Stukas (the LRDG's first exposure to these Luftwaffe planes that would prove a major nemesis of the patrols for the rest of the campaign), and large columns of panzers and motorized infantry trying to cut off the British at the key harbor of Tobruk.[3]

At this point, Mitford received radioed orders to do everything possible to slow down or disrupt the enemy's advance. A convenient sandstorm blew up to hide his movements as he turned back to the west. Attacking an enemy battery, he managed to capture one of the Germans' deadly 88–mm guns, probably the first such gun to be taken in the whole desert campaign. Thereafter he surprised a convoy of vehicles and came away with a large bag of prisoners. These were the first German troops the LRDG had seen up close, and their Afrika Korps uniforms, special desert goggles, and other items of uniform and equipment were carefully noted. (Of almost greater interest, though, were the Germans' portable gasoline containers: the compact, strongly constructed "jerry cans" that were superior to anything the LRDG had. These soon became much sought after items, with each patrol striving to capture as many as possible for its own use.) But with the enemy by now thoroughly alerted to his presence, Mitford had to cut short his marauding and run for it. As he did, a twin-engined Heinkel-111 bomber arrived to strafe him. Later, he had to dodge his way past another large column of motorized infantry, and he again encountered an area seeded with Thermos bombs. By the time he reached the safety of the open desert, he had lost vehicles and suffered additional casualties, and was running low on gasoline. Yet, on balance, his two LRDG patrols—initially employed in a close-reconnaissance role for which they were hardly suited—had given a good account of themselves. They had met the unit's first Germans and, by using their mobility and superior knowledge of the desert to offset the lack of armor, had given back better than they got.[4]

Meanwhile, the British forces had been driven all the way back to Egypt. Of Cyrenaic Libya, only the vital port of Tobruk, held by a single division of Australians, remained in British hands. As Rommel mounted assault after assault against that position, Churchill pressed Wavell to send back into Libya an offensive which would secure its relief. But when that offensive, code-named Battleaxe, was finally launched in June 1941, it ran into heavy opposition and soon faltered in the fierce fighting that took place. Finally the British, after losing a thousand men and nearly a hundred tanks, gave up and fell back. In many respects Battleaxe typified the kind of fighting that would take place in the next year and a half of this new phase of the desert campaign. Lacking obstacles to rapid movement such as rivers, mountain ranges, or large built-up areas, the desert's open spaces formed a veritable "arena *par excellence* of armoured warfare."[5] To Australian war correspondent Alan Moorehead, the armored battles in the desert suggested battles at sea rather than battles on land. Given the vastness of the arena, the tanks functioned almost like fleets at sea, maneuvering against each other in the same way that one "warship will hunt another warship."[6] The key strategic points were the few hill features where the infantry could dig in and protect itself, and those crucial passes or cuts in the coastal escarpment which permitted the tanks to grind their way up to the flat ground of the Libyan plateau.

The fundamental problem for the British was that the Germans had brought to the desert levels of tactical organization, doctrine, and training that were manifestly superior to their own. Nearly two decades before, British armored-warfare theorists Fuller and Liddell Hart had sown the seeds of such mobile combat, but the Germans, most notably through the efforts of General Heinz Guderian, had evolved those theories into the tactical doctrines of blitzkreig warfare. These doctrines combined the use of Luftwaffe tactical aircraft to supplement or replace artillery fire, the use of motorized infantry to keep up with the tanks, and above all the employment of tanks in mass in the panzer division. By the time Rommel arrived in North Africa, such divisions, refined and sharpened in the campaigns in Poland and France, had become a honed cutting edge of cohesive formations of tanks, infantry, and artillery acting in close cooperation. Each of these divisions was, in fact, an armored task force whose various elements were trained to function together as a well-organized team. Rommel's successes so far, and especially those during Battleaxe, had shown that the Germans had been quick to adapt their system to the special characteristics of desert warfare. Despite their initial advantage of knowing the terrain far better than their enemy, a good deal of time would pass before the British began to master the techniques of armored warfare on a level to match the Germans.[7]

Wavell's failure to beat the Germans and relieve Tobruk exasperated Churchill and soon cost him his job as C-in-C. Almost a year to the day since he had met with Bagnold and authorized formation of the Long Range Patrols, Wavell was relieved. Chosen to replace him was Lieutenant General Sir Claude Auchinleck, an officer whose career had been in the Indian Army and who was virtually an unknown quantity at GHQ-ME. The loss of its chief patron at headquarters hardly seemed a development that boded well for the LRDG. During the course of the desert war, the LRDG was several times "shown off" to the press and several times turned out for official inspection, once by a secretary of state for war and twice by a commander-in-chief, Middle East. But, as Shaw remembered it, Wavell would always remain the "one whose praise we valued [most]."[8]

By the time Auchinleck arrived in Egypt, Bagnold had his headquarters element and B Squadron positioned at Kufra, watching the tracks that led down from the Libyan plateau. To the north, operating out of Siwa, Mitford's A Squadron continued to linger near the Afrika Korps' southern flank. His patrols managed to pick up shot-down RAF pilots and crewmen, as well as stragglers from the main battles. Soon, however, a new decision by GHQ-ME had the effect of revising Bagnold's role and adding responsibilities which did little to enhance the effectiveness of the LRDG. Bagnold, designated "Military Commander of Kufra," was given the mission of using his patrols to hold the oasis should the Germans attempt to move down from the north.[9]

This decision put the LRDG's patrols on roughly the same disadvantaged basis as Graziani's Auto-Saharans of six months before. Rather than being sent aggressively against the enemy, they were instead to be tied down defending a static position. Also, Bagnold was cut off from direct contact with GHQ-ME by 700 miles of desert. This ruled out the kind of personal liaison he had enjoyed up to this point. But he was told that Leclerc's Free French had had to pull back to Chad in order to prepare for future offensives, and that no other troops could be spared at the moment for Kufra. GHQ-ME had no intention of permitting the Germans to install themselves in this important oasis, since they might use it to begin mounting desert raids of their own.[10]

As the summer of 1941 wore on, Bagnold found himself less the commander of a special deep-penetration force and more the officer responsible for defending an oasis. When he wanted to be in Cairo, convincing the new C-in-C of the capabilities—and limitations—of his patrols, he was instead stuck far away at Kufra. Almost immediately, problems developed. The most critical factor in determining the radius and scope of LRDG operations was gasoline—both the quantity the patrols could actually carry and what could be stashed in advanced dumps. But the unit now began to run out of fuel, and for the simple reason that the whole apparatus for sending out the required gasoline began to break down. In this critical period Bagnold, geographically removed from GHQ-ME, found himself in a poor position to intervene directly in order to work out an improvement.[11]

Just getting the gasoline hauled out to Kufra was a major operation in itself, and one far beyond the capabilities of the LRDG alone to handle. Large, ten-ton Royal Army Service Corps tanker trucks were required. These slow and cumbersome vehicles had to pick up the fuel from the rail line at Wadi Halfa and then, from the Nile, haul it across 750 miles of desert to Kufra. A complete round trip could take up to three weeks. Bagnold had received his last big shipment of gasoline (some seventy tons) in May. After that, the flow of gasoline virtually stopped. As their fuel began to run out, the patrols found themselves isolated and immobilized. By midsummer, they were doing little more than occupying the oases north of Kufra; the patrolling of Rommel's southern flank had ceased.[12] Of their operations during the two and a half years of the desert war, it was this period, early to midsummer 1941, that LRDG officers always remembered as "the real low point" of their unit's existence.[13]

Bagnold first tried to remedy the situation by sending urgent radio signals to GHQ-ME. These had little effect. By now, Major Guy Prendergast, one of the original desert hands from the early expeditions, had arrived to serve as the unit's second-in-command. Both he and Bagnold finally determined that personal liaison trips were the only answer if their unit were to gain proper representation at the higher levels. The fastest way to do this seemed to be by airplane. Bagnold asked the RAF for help in the form of scheduled liaison flights. But the air force, pleading heavy commitments elsewhere, could offer no assistance. In the end Prendergast, who held a private pilot's license, gave up on the RAF and solved the problem by actually procuring an LRDG "air force" of two small and antiquated planes. These were two "old and slow" (neither could fly more than about 120 mph), fabric-covered monoplanes called "Wacos."[14] Built by the Western Aircraft Corporation of Ohio, they carried no radios and seemed frail in construction. They were acquired by official purchase, using British Army funds, from their private owner, an Egyptian pasha. But Prendergast had had great difficulty in selling the RAF on the idea. The fact that this small army unit wanted to fly its own planes had immediately sparked interservice rivalries. The RAF had at first refused to share control of the British military aviation operating in North Africa's air space, and had tried to prevent the LRDG from getting the two Wacos painted up with the official roundel insignia on wings and fuselage. But such opposition was eventually overcome. With the acquisition of its own aircraft, the LRDG gained an efficient means of getting its commanding officer up to deal directly with the staff at GHQ-ME. In the next year and a half, the Wacos would also save a number of lives by evacuating men wounded in the various operations conducted deep in the desert.[15]

As Bagnold recalled, a trip in one of the stubby Wacos could "take years off one's life."[16] Except for compasses, the planes lacked any sort of navigational equipment. They were kept on course by the same methods that guided the patrols. To make the ten-hour trip to Cairo required stopping at special dumps of fuel positioned along the way. These were hard to find, and the planes sometimes got lost. Bagnold, who had to stuff himself into the cockpit behind Prendergast (a lanky six-footer), admitted later that he found flying, particularly in the bumpy, "hot haze" of the sandstorms that blew up and blotted out the features below, "quite hair-raising."[17] But the visits to GHQ-ME began to pay off. Also, as Bagnold's ally, Shearer had already been doing his best to make sure that Auchinleck saw that it was necessary for the LRDG to be able to reach and harass the Afrika Korps' flank and rear areas.[18] Because of his efforts and the liaison visits, arrangements that built up adequate stocks of fuel and regularized the gasoline convoys out to Kufra were eventually put into effect. Finally, after two months of frustration and inactivity at Kufra, GHQ-ME assigned the British-officered Sudan Defence Force to the defense of the oasis. With this step, "we were," as Shaw put it, "free to be LRDG again."[19]

But under a new commanding officer. Performing the difficult task of straightening out the logistical and communications problems of the summer was Bagnold's last contribution to the unit. The new procedures he had set up with GHQ-ME worked well; they lasted, with little modification, until the very end of the campaign and were sufficient to support LRDG bases even further distant than Kufra. But Bagnold had decided to leave. Even with the help of the Wacos, it seemed clear to him that "one of us—either Prendergast or I—would have to be back in Cairo all the time."[20] Someone with a special knowledge of the desert was needed to advise the staff. Since the Murzuk raid, GHQ-ME had developed altogether unrealistic and potentially disastrous expectations of what the LRDG's 150 men in twoscore vehicles might accomplish. Put simply, the LRDG needed a friend at headquarters. Bagnold had already demonstrated his capacity for working closely with Shearer, and he seemed the perfect choice. Moreover, it was his personal view that he had already made his contribution to the LRDG (a contribution generously mentioned in the official dispatches forwarded to London), and that it was now time to let Prendergast take the helm. Prendergast, an armor officer (the Royal Tank Regiment), had nearly two decades of service behind him, much of it in Egypt and the Sudan. Bagnold knew him to be a good organizer, with the kind of practical mind that converted broad concepts into precise, detailed plans. With Clayton gone, no one else could match Prendergast's knowledge of the desert, gained on the early expeditions and in extended service while commanding a Sudan Defence Force Mobile Machinegun Company.[21]

Thus, early in August 1941, Bagnold put on the red tabs of a general staff officer and moved up to the planning levels of GHQ-ME. He was 46 years old, and he had created and for over a year commanded a unit which had raided the distant outposts of an enemy-held desert. For his accomplishments with the LRDG and other service, he was awarded the OBE, or Officer, Order of the British Empire. Eventually achieving the rank of brigadier (three grades higher than the rank he had held at his "retirement" before the war), he would serve for three more years on the staff of GHQ-ME. Guy Prendergast, ten years younger than Bagnold, gained the insignia of a lieutenant colonel and assumed command of the Long Range Desert Group. He would remain in that position for the rest of the desert campaign.[22]

The unit's new commanding officer kept Mitford's A Squadron up north, operating from Siwa. Fighting off the malaria contracted from the mosquitoes infesting Siwa's ancient pools, that squadron's patrols were sent on a number of missions into the area along Rommel's flank. Increasingly these patrols found themselves involved in a new role: inserting British or Arab agents behind enemy lines to watch particular sectors near the coastal strip. It was this new mission, coordinated by Shearer's DMI staff at GHQ-ME, that Prendergast's men soon referred to as the "taxi service."[23] The first such effort was led by a newcomer to the LRDG, Captain J. R. (Jake) Easonsmith. A native of Bristol, England, and briefly a salesman in civilian life, he had enlisted in the Royal Tank Regiment at the start of the war, and had eventually been commissioned from an officer-candidate school. New orders took him to the Middle East, where he had promptly volunteered for the LRDG. There Easonsmith soon established a reputation, in that hackneyed phrase, as a "natural soldier and born leader." LRDG officers came to regard him as one of their ablest patrol commanders, perhaps even "the finest . . . we ever had."[24]

He certainly showed great ability on this first "taxi-service" job. The operation required that he get two Arab agents into the hills of the Jebel al Akdar, a maze of rough, tamarisk-dotted hills and gulleys. The appeal of the Jebel was that it sat astride the routes by which Rommel received his supplies—both the hard-surface coastal Via Balbia and the network of tracks running across the flat desert to the south—and it seemed an excellent place from which to watch the enemy. Also, throughout the broken foothills were scattered Senussi Arabs who, bearing no love for the Italians, were expected to be helpful or at least sympathetic to the British. In a long and demanding operation, Easonsmith succeeded in slipping past German patrols and eventually got his agents safely installed in the hills. That done, he attacked an outpost or two, bagged some prisoners, and finally picked up one of the RAF's downed Hurricane pilots. A second taxi-service mission followed in short order. On this one he deposited perhaps the most successful of the British intelligence agents in the desert, Captain John A. Haselden. An ex-cotton broker who had spent most of his life in Egypt, Haselden could speak various Bedouin dialects with great fluency. Bearded, wearing native clothing, and with his skin and hair dyed, he proved able to pass for a Bedouin on many occasions in the year ahead. The organization that he built up among the Jebel's Arabs ensured the acquisition of useful information on enemy movements. For the next months Easonsmith's or other patrols acted to keep his string of agents supplied with sufficient food and radio spare parts so that the flow of information back to GHQ-ME could be maintained.[25]

Other efforts turned out less well. Crichton-Stuart's G Patrol, for example, was sent north into the Libyan plateau to link up with the armored cars of the 11th Hussars, whose horse-cavalry forebears had charged with the Light Brigade at Balaclava during the Crimean War. Rather than the "Cherry Pickers," however, his patrol ran instead into the Germans, a pair of Panzer Mk IIIs that knocked out Crichton-Stuart's vehicle in the opening exchange of fire. When he grabbed his code books and made a run for it, he and his remaining trucks were next chased across thirty miles of desert by Sd Kfz-222 armored cars. This, as Prendergast later tried to point out to GHQ-ME, once again showed the folly of using LRDG trucks—which were nothing more than "thin-skinned containers of explosives"—in any sort of role better left to British armored cars.[26] Perhaps more importantly, this and other operations of the same period showed that the LRDG patrol, as presently structured, was too large. In the Libyan plateau, thirty men in twelve trucks presented too large a target to German armored cars and aircraft. Also, the new missions now being assigned differed from the long probes previously undertaken in the vast southern desert. Reconnaissance trips, hauling agents, and operating along Rommel's supply lines could be accomplished more efficiently with smaller patrols. In fact, one or two of the so-called "half patrols" had already been tried experimentally. Also, a full year's operations had given the new officers plenty of experience; it was no longer necessary to send them out under the watchful eyes of the old explorers. Prendergast thus completely revamped the patrol structure. His new "War Establishment" (Table of Organization) halved each of the five existing patrols, giving him a total of ten new patrols. By decreasing the size but doubling the total number, he was convinced that he could achieve a considerable magnification of operational effort. In this way, the two New Zealand patrols, R and T, became four patrols: R1 and R2, and T1 and T2. The same procedure was used for the others. G Patrol became G1 and G2; the Yeomanry, Y1 and Y2, and so forth. Each patrol ended up comprising twelve men riding in five or six vehicles, one of which was the radio truck. For ease of control, the patrols were grouped into two operational squadrons. These were A Squadron, the controlling entity for the four New Zealand patrols; and B Squadron, which coordinated the operations of the six Guards, Rhodesian, and Yeomanry patrols. An expanded Heavy Section, for logistical support, and a mobile maintenance unit, for effecting a wide variety of repairs, were placed under the Group Headquarters. To speed up the process of collecting topographic data from behind enemy lines, a special Royal Engineers survey section was added, headed by Lieutenant Kenneth Lazarus.[27]

This structure would, with only slight modification, endure for the rest of the campaign. It also permitted the recruitment of additional junior officers, of whom Prendergast, as had Bagnold, took care to pick from among the best available. He was aided by the fact that at least some commanders were willing to let promising junior officers volunteer, apparently on the rationale that a stint with the LRDG would enable these same junior officers to return with a knowledge of new desert techniques that might enhance the overall effectiveness of their units. An additional recruiting factor was Britain's entrenched "old-boy network"—that matrix of interconnected elite educational, family, and regimental ties. This factor ensured that the LRDG would gain its share of actual blue-bloods, most particularly among its Guards officers. Even so, "Lieutenant the Honourable" this or that still had to win his place next to the proven New Zealand officers (several of whom Prendergast and Bagnold had promoted from the ranks), and the Long Range Desert Group's reputation as an efficient and reliable force drawn from the British Army's best was to be sustained throughout the rest of the desert war.[28]

Certainly that reputation would be enhanced in the test of the great offensive now being planned. Since arriving in Cairo, Wavell's successor, Auchinleck, had spent his time trying to rebuild an army defeated by Rommel. He remained convinced, despite Churchill's insistence on immediate action, that no offensive should be undertaken until everything was ready. But by autumn 1941, he had available triple the number of forces that had tried to stop Rommel in the spring. What had been the original Western Desert Force now became instead a full-fledged army, the Eighth Army, whose striking elements comprised two full corps. The two corps together amounted to some 118,000 men and more than 700 tanks. To command the Eighth Army and defeat Rommel, Auchinleck now chose a general who had won his laurels by smashing the Italians in the East African campaign recently concluded. There, Lieutenant General Sir Alan Cunningham, a "magnificent-looking chap" who imparted an air of confidence, vitality, and decisiveness, had taken just over two months to defeat the Italians in some of the most difficult terrain in Africa.[29] This performance, however, obscured the fact that he knew as little about tank warfare as he did about the Libyan desert.

Auchinleck and Cunningham prepared as meticulously for their offensive as, a year earlier, Wavell and O'Connor had prepared for theirs. This new effort, designated Crusader, was set for November. The plan called for the Eighth Army to outflank Rommel and then hook north to link up with the Australians still holding out at Tobruk. Auchinleck understood from intelligence reports that Rommel now commanded a force entitled Panzer Group Africa. This comprised the Afrika Korps—his original 5th Light (recently redesignated the 21st Panzer) Division, the 15th Panzer Division, and a new unit assembled from various formations and named the 90th Light (or Africa) Division—and two Italian corps. Counting these two formations, Rommel had slightly more men but fewer tanks than the British. Auchinleck guessed that the colossal, 142–division, 2,000–plane Barbarossa onslaught now surging deeply into Russia would reduce to a trickle the resources and reinforcements available to Rommel for the war in North Africa. And he was determined to finish his opponent before even this trickle of resources and reinforcements could arrive.[30]

He was, moreover, determined "to get away from the idea, which seemed to be prevalent, of clinging to the coastal strip."[31] Hence the desert-based, flanking nature of the Crusader plan. As Prendergast discovered at the end of October, the whole operation seemed, at least to GHQ-ME, absolutely made to order for the LRDG. The patrols were to be placed under the direct control of the Eighth Army, and were to scout the section of desert through which Cunningham's armored forces would outflank the Germans. They would also be employed to "observe and report back on enemy reactions"— and enemy reinforcements or withdrawals—once the offensive actually commenced.[32] Prendergast thus decided to move his base and Group Headquarters from Kufra up to Siwa. He made repeated trips to the Eighth Army to coordinate plans. These trips did little to dispel his doubts, however, about using the LRDG as a "tactical" force in direct support of Cunningham. From the start, the unit had operated as a "strategic" force belonging to the C-in-C and under the direct control of his theater headquarters, GHQ-ME. Departures from that practice—the last-minute assignment of Mitford's patrols to fill in as armored cavalry during Rommel's advance, for example— had not turned out well. As Prendergast discovered, however, observing enemy reactions for the Eighth Army would not be the sole mission he would be called upon to undertake. Two additional assignments were "strategic" in that they came directly from Auchinleck's staff, and both would take the LRDG deep behind enemy lines. But in neither assignment would the patrols be playing the central special-force role. Instead, the LRDG was to be sent out for the purpose of assisting other parties of special troops. British experimentation with "special operations"—certainly not least because of the favorable example of the LRDG—had now reached the point where GHQ-ME was willing to use additional special means in order to devastate and cripple the Germans at the moment of decision. And the new special operations being planned were nothing if not ambitious. Just hours before the great offensive began, a party of Commandos, landed by submarine on the Libyan coast, would attempt to reach Rommel's own headquarters and there kill or capture him. At the same time, but farther east, a second special unit was to be dropped by parachute to infiltrate a key enemy airfield, and destroy, by means of demolition charges, as many as possible of the scores of planes parked there.[33]

The Commandos destined for the raid on Rommel had come to the Middle East as part of a contingent styled "Layforce" and operating under the command of Lieutenant Colonel (later Major General) Robert E. Laycock. Although Laycock's Layforce was disbanded shortly thereafter, one of his units, No. 11 (Scottish) Commando, had continued to practice night landings from submarines. These were made with rubber rafts and with the lightweight, canvas-covered canoes called folbots. No. 11's folbotists were commanded by Lieutenant Colonel Geoffrey C. T. Keyes, the son of Admiral of the Fleet Sir Roger Keyes, whom Churchill had chosen to direct all Commando operations from the headquarters of Combined Operations. The younger Keyes, just 24, had been educated at Eton and Sandhurst and had served in the Royal Scots Greys. A well-regarded and competent officer, he had insisted that he be allowed to lead in person the raid on Rommel's headquarters. By the time the decision was made to go ahead with the planning for such an attack, GHQ-ME's intelligence analysts believed that they had identified the precise location of that headquarters almost beyond a shadow of doubt. On a night in October, the same Captain Haselden whom Easonsmith's patrol had earlier inserted in the Jebel country had been dropped by parachute behind the enemy lines for the express purpose of pinpointing the location of that headquarters. For some time "Sigint" (Signals Intelligence), based on radio intercepts of enemy traffic, had pointed to a little village called Beda Littoria, situated in the Libyan hump, as the probable site. Disguised as an Arab once again, Haselden had watched the village—not far from Hannibal-son-of-Hamilcar's birthplace, the ancient city of Cyrene—in an effort to verify the Sigint information. He observed stuccoed Italian colonial buildings clustered in groves of cedars and cypresses, and a small village full of German troops. Off to one side could be seen a villa and the official building that the Italians called the Prefettura, around which were parked a score of Afrika Korps communications trucks. A steady stream of vehicles disgorged and retrieved officers and dispatch riders. Finally Haselden hit the jackpot: Rommel himself emerged from the Prefettura and headed off in his personal command vehicle. This seemed proof positive that Beda Littoria's Prefettura was indeed Rommel's headquarters. Rendezvousing with the LRDG two days later, Haselden was fetched back to Cairo with his information. Thereafter, plans and preparations went forward that would bring Keyes and his Commandos to the Prefettura at just the right moment. Timing their arrival carefully, they would dispose of Rommel just as, across the desert far to the east, Cunningham's armor was commencing the Crusader attacks.[34] By killing or capturing Rommel, the Commandos would throw the enemy's entire command system into chaos at the very instant that the British were mounting their main offensive.

The second special operation being planned for that offensive was to be led by Captain A. David Stirling. Two years older than Keyes and, like him, the product of a patrician education, Stirling had gone into the Scots Guards on the outbreak of war. When his cousin, the seventeenth Lord Lovat and twenty-fourth Chief of the Clan Fraser, had volunteered for the Commandos (eventually to win distinction in both the Dieppe raid and the D-Day landings), Stirling himself had promptly followed suit. His Commando training completed, he, as had Keyes, had then journeyed to the Middle East with Layforce. There he managed to take up parachute-jumping on a wholly unofficial basis, without benefit of training of any kind, and using standard aircrew parachutes and rides begged from friends in the RAF. This informal approach to a dangerous activity soon netted him a broken leg and a three weeks' stay in a military hospital in Cairo. It was during the time that he was thus laid up that Stirling began working out the details of a new method by which to conduct raiding operations. Previous Commando operations in the desert had been unsuccessful because such troops lacked the mobility to reach and attack enemy targets. But the parachuting experience had convinced Stirling that parties of raiders could be air-dropped under cover of darkness in order to reach enemy targets, especially airfields. Stirling believed that, once on the ground, such specially trained airborne raiders could use their infiltration skills to penetrate enemy perimeter defenses and then plant charges on the aircraft parked on any of a number of desert airfields used by the Germans and Italians. Once they had planted as many charges as possible and set the time-fuses, the raiders would then flee the airfield, link up with an LRDG patrol, and make their getaway into the open desert before the enemy could react.[35]

The proposal for this new concept Stirling did not bother submitting to higher headquarters via the normal chain of command. Rather, in what turned out to be the bold fashion characteristic both of his operations and of his relations with senior officers, the 6'6" Stirling talked his way into the Cairo Citadel and the staff offices of GHQ-ME. Still limping from his parachuting injury, he wound up in front of Auchinleck's deputy chief of staff, Major General Neil Methuen Ritchie. Ritchie was also a Scot (The Black Watch); he found himself much persuaded by the ideas that Stirling lost no time in laying out. Indeed, a short time later he took Stirling in to see Auchinleck himself. His plan for an airborne force of Commandos was accepted on the spot, and Stirling was promised a promotion and the men and resources he needed. One of Auchinleck's staff officers proposed that the new unit be called the "Special Air Service," of which Stirling's element would form the "L Detachment" of ostensibly a brigade-sized force. Of course, no such "brigade" actually existed. The whole idea was to deceive the Germans— whose own airborne forces had descended upon Crete just four months before—into thinking that the British order of battle now included a powerful airborne element. While the British were at the time striving to build up large airborne formations among the forces located in Britain itself, there were as yet no such forces in the Middle East and certainly no schools or instructors to train them. Not only might Stirling's handful of men do serious damage to the enemy's Stukas, Heinkels, and ME-109s parked on the ground, but they could also, with their purposely misleading title, induce the Germans to believe that a large British airborne force was already available for operations in the desert.[36]

Stirling's conviction was that only the physically toughest, most confident and resourceful men were suitable for Special Air Service operations. Detractors—and there would be more than a few of these as the campaign wore on—liked to say that Stirling tended to recruit most of his SAS officers in the bar at Shepheard's Hotel. Whatever the methods he employed, a full complement of officers, men, and equipment was soon assembled. With the training underway, experiments were begun with a kind of charge, based on plastic explosive and rigged up with a time-fuse, which could quickly be placed on the fuselage of an enemy plane. These were called "sticky bombs" or "Lewes bombs" after their inventor and early Stirling recruit, a lieutenant recently an honors student at Cambridge University.[37] But the main effort was on parachute training. Stirling tested his volunteers by making them learn to jump by doing backward rolls off a truck moving over the desert at 30 mph; for the survivors, jumping from airplanes with real parachutes followed. Although Stirling on first impression struck many as something of a risk-taker not always inclined to bother about the details of planning, his force was nonetheless ready and trained to a high pitch of performance well before the jump-off date for Crusader.[38]

By now the other special forces were also ready. The LRDG, as the retrieving element both for Stirling's SAS force and for any of Keyes' Commandos who might not be able to get back to the submarines, had begun its own planning and movements well before that date. In fact, Prendergast had gathered most of his patrols at Siwa a full five days before the offensive was to commence. He selected T2 Patrol for the task of taking Haselden, along with two other British officers and their teams of Arab agents, up to the coast. Once in position, Haselden's task was to link up with and then guide the submarine-landed Commandos to Rommel's headquarters. At the same time, a second patrol, Easonsmith's R1, would move north, take up a suitable waiting position, and be ready to meet Stirling's L Detachment, SAS, after the completion of its raid on the key enemy airfields located near Gazala. The patrols were thoroughly briefed on the timetable that had to be maintained, and were sent off to make their way north across the Libyan plateau. Despite the heavy enemy patrols in that region, the two LRDG units got through undiscovered. By midnight four days before Crusader, Haselden had reached his designated point and was sending the prearranged signal out to sea. The two Commando-carrying submarines, H. M. S. *Torbay* and H. M. S. *Talisman*, were already in position. Standing offshore since midafternoon, they had studied the landing site, a small cove, through their periscopes. As soon as they sighted the lights blinking from the beach, they flashed the recognition signal back to Haselden. The Commandos then began launching their folbots and rubber rafts. But heavy seas had built up, and many of the boats were lost. The sea grew so rough that only a fraction of the Commando force could get off before launching had to be suspended. Although buffeted by a howling wind, Keyes and Laycock (who was along to command the overall operation and to raid several other targets in the area) pressed on and led their men toward the shore. There the Commandos were furnished with directions and a native guide, and Haselden helped them hide their boats. These steps accomplished, he then slipped away to prepare for the second part of his mission, which was to blow up a German communications center on the same night that Keyes hit Rommel's headquarters.[39]

Keyes and his men began their approach to Beda Littoria, some twelve miles south of the coast, and spent the next two days hiding out in the rough country north of the village. The same foul weather that had prevented the landing of most of the Commandos also helped conceal his group from German patrols. By the night of November 17, they were poised on a ridge just above the target. Edging forward, their faces blackened and Thompson submachineguns at the ready, they approached the Prefettura that Haselden had identified the month before. Unfortunately for Keyes, however, the man already being called the "Desert Fox" was nowhere near the Prefettura nor, for that matter, was he at this moment even in North Africa. Unknown to British intelligence, Rommel had been flown back to Italy two weeks earlier for a rest and the celebration of his fiftieth birthday. Moreover, the Desert Fox had long since shifted his lair from Beda Littoria to a point much closer to the fighting front. The British Sigint of the month before had been correct: the Prefettura had indeed been the site of his headquarters, but only briefly. By great mischance Haselden had happened to spot him there on some routine visit to the staff group that had since taken over the building, the Afrika Korps Quartermaster-General's department. Although the Commandos could not know it as they crept forward, their prey was far away and safe on the other side of the Mediterranean.[40]

Their mission swiftly turned into a disaster. After killing a German sentry, the Commandos burst through the front door of the Prefettura. Their opening spray of fire dispatched a duty officer but aroused German troops asleep elsewhere in the building. As he ducked aside to let one of his men throw a grenade, Keyes was hit by a bullet just above the heart. He was dead by the time the Commandos could get him outside. His second-in-command was also hit, and the rest of the party beat a retreat, although they managed to blow up a generator and some vehicles. Most were captured by the force of Afrika Korps infantry sent out in reaction; Laycock, however, successfully eluded his pursuers and eventually made it back to the British lines. Only Haselden and his group enjoyed any real success. After carrying out their program of demolition on several targets, they reached the LRDG rendezvous unscathed. Yet T2 Patrol, Haselden's transportation back to safety, had already taken losses. While waiting for Haselden's party to reach the rendezvous, T2 had been discovered and attacked by an enemy already alerted by the raiding attacks. The patrol lost its commander and two men before it could escape. Perhaps the most admirable act of all was that of the man whom the raid had been intended to kill. When Rommel returned to North Africa and learned what the British had attempted, he reacted by ignoring Hitler's newly issued order calling for the immediate execution of all captured Commandos. Indeed, he saw to it that the fallen Keyes (to whom the British awarded the Victoria Cross) was buried with full military honors beside the four German soldiers his raid had killed.[41]

In terms of numbers of men lost, however, Stirling's SAS operation turned into an even greater disaster than the raid on Rommel. It had begun to go sour even before it started. The same bad weather that had interfered with the launching of the Commandos blew gale-force winds and sandstorms across the desert to Egypt. The RAF, which had the task of flying Stirling's men to their drop zones through the darkness and wild weather, recommended that the raid be cancelled. But Stirling was determined to go. Not only had his men trained hard, but he believed there were enemies in high GHQ-ME staff circles who would have greatly relished it had "we chucked in our hand at this late hour."[42] Thus, at about the same time that Keyes and his Commandos were preparing to close in on Rommel's "headquarters," the SAS climbed into their Bristol Bombay transport planes and flew into the blackness over the Mediterranean. The flight, turbulent and disorienting to the SAS soldiers, seemed to take far too long. At last, well past the point when the planes should have reached the drop-zone area, the navigator came back to tell Stirling that they were starting their approach. Stirling was the first one to jump. Coming down in a choking sandstorm, he was knocked unconscious when his billowing parachute dragged him across some rocks. He came to after a while and then took out a flashlight to begin signaling the others. An hour of this, however, brought him only a handful of men. Nor could any of the special containers be located in which most of the weapons and all of the crucial time-fuses had been dropped.[43]

It was by then clear that the RAF, thrown off by the high winds, had dropped him miles from his target. The situation Stirling now faced was that of being deep inside enemy territory and leading a handful of men who lacked even basic infantry weapons. It was obvious that without his explosives he could not hope to blow up any German planes even if he could reach the Gazala airfields. He and a sergeant went off to search the area to the north. Guided by the hurricane lantern that Easonsmith's R1 Patrol had placed on top of a low hill, they eventually reached the LRDG rendezvous point. A few other SAS men straggled in over the next few days. But although Easonsmith sent truck after truck to search for the others, none turned up. Finally, having waited as long as possible, R1 loaded up the SAS survivors and started the long journey back to Siwa. For Stirling it was a long and painful journey. On his very first mission he had lost good men and had never even reached the vicinity of his target. Of his original sixty-two officers and men, he now had only four officers and twenty men left. He learned later that two whole groups of SAS parachutists had been dropped so far off course that they probably came down in the Sand Sea. These men were never found; presumably they died of thirst trying, as did the crew of the *Lady Be Good* two years later, to make their way out of the high dunes. One other feature of the RAF's performance rankled Stirling even more—how the Germans had managed to capture a whole planeload of SAS troops without even firing a shot. Using good English and standard RAF radio procedure, they had actually tricked the plane's hopelessly lost pilot into landing on what he believed to be a British field. By the time the pilot discovered his error, it was too late and every man aboard was captured.

Ironically, the plane had been lured down to one of the very airfields that Stirling's force was to have raided.[44]

But the failure of Stirling's effort at Gazala and the Commando debacle at Beda Littoria were, if anything, a fitting prelude to the larger failure of Crusader. That operation, so carefully prepared, had begun right on schedule and with every hope of success. At first, everything went well and according to plan. At dawn on November 18, Cunningham's armor knifed through the enemy defenses, reached its initial objectives, and then wheeled north. The Tobruk garrison, alerted well in advance, prepared to break out of the enemy ring and link up with the advancing Eighth Army. But the Germans were merely biding their time and holding their counterattack until the British intentions could become clear. Then, sending first the 21st Panzer and next the 15th Panzer after the British at Sidi Rezegh, Rommel, now returned to Africa, succeeded in mauling a succession of the Eighth Army's armored brigades. By the end of the day, the British had repeated their performance in Battleaxe by again losing a hundred tanks. Auchinleck pressed the shaken Cunningham to lash out at Rommel, who—given the heavy German losses of the preceding days—was "probably in as bad a shape as we were."[45] But the Desert Fox was too quick for the British. Six days after Crusader started, he raced east towards Egypt to cut into Cunningham's exposed and vulnerable supply lines, a move which soon forced the Eighth Army once again to fall back from Libya.[46]

None of this was known to those LRDG patrols sent deep in order to "observe enemy reactions," and, presumably, thereby to aid Cunningham in making needed adjustments in what was to have been the unfolding of the Crusader victory. In actuality, the patrols, set up in a wide screen, were in the wrong place to have had any real effect. They were all too far to the west and therefore well away from the scene of the major actions. Instead, they spent their time scanning an empty desert and at night listening, on the Axis' Radio Belgrade, to a German song already a British favorite: "Lili Marlene." The error of positioning the patrols so far to the west was an outgrowth of the decision to use them under the direct tactical control of the Eighth Army in the first place. And Cunningham's failure to coordinate properly the actions of the patrols with those of other elements ultimately led to casualties. RAF Beaufighters, for example—large, twin-engined fighter-bombers—attacked and badly mauled at least one patrol in the belief that it was an enemy unit.[47]

But positioning the patrols so far to the west was soon turned into an advantage. For as the Eighth Army began its retreat and Rommel's tanks surged towards Egypt, Auchinleck became desperate for any means which could slow down the enemy. For the second time during one of Rommel's advances, the LRDG again received last-ditch, attack-at-all-costs orders. On the afternoon of November 24 and six days into the battle, Prendergast received over the radio on "Emergency Ops" priority the message that told him to cease the observation role forthwith and instead to "advance on and attack" any target that his patrols could find. Hard on the heels of this first message came a second one that told Prendergast to "act with utmost vigour offensively against any targets or communications within your reach."[48]

This effort commenced almost immediately. Given the dire straits of the Eighth Army, Prendergast decided, for the first time in the desert war, to take the bold step of sending his patrols against the Via Balbia itself. G1 Patrol, now commanded by Captain Anthony Hay of the Coldstream Guards (who had replaced Crichton-Stuart, recently stricken with malaria), became the first to hit the enemy in the region of the Via. A brief account of its operations gives some idea of the effectiveness of the LRDG patrols acting in this new role. Although Hay's patrol was several times attacked by Italian and Luftwaffe aircraft as it moved north, he nonetheless was able to reach the coastal road with little more than light damage to his vehicles. A large convoy of trailer-hauled Panzer Mk IIIs and Italian M13/40 light tanks presented a tempting target, but Hay had to pass it up: it was still daylight and this was too much to take on with just one patrol.[49] But that night he led his patrol out onto the road itself and towards one of the Italians' "Casa Cantonieri" or road houses. These way stations comprised squat, stuccoed clusters of buildings positioned every fifteen miles or so along the Via, and served as the headquarters for local patrolling activities, road-repair efforts, and the like. Several enemy convoys buzzed by Hay in the other lane but, in the darkness, apparently failed to spot his vehicles—painted in the same desert camouflage colors as their own—as belonging to a British patrol. Finally reaching the road house, Hay led G1 up to a group of perhaps twenty or thirty vehicles parked in front. German and Italian troops milled about, talking and enjoying a cigarette in the quiet evening. Suddenly Hay yelled "Fire!" and G1 opened up with everything it had. From a distance of thirty feet every machinegun in the patrol unleashed a shattering spray of armor-piercing bullets. Enemy soldiers were cut down as their vehicles exploded into blazing masses of orange flames. Hay hid out the next day as enemy planes crisscrossed overhead looking for him, but that night led his patrol back to the road. G1 shot up a whole convoy of Afrika Korps tanker trailers, and then ran for it, moving as far south as possible to get away from the next day's air search. By the time he finally reached the LRDG's Group Headquarters again, the British Y Service radio-intercept stations had picked up enough to learn that Hay's two raids had forced the enemy to halt, at least for several days, all traffic in this particular sector of the Via. Moreover, the enemy apparently believed that it was "British armored cars" that had reached and attacked the road. In the future, because of Hay's attacks, all enemy convoys would be guarded by at least an escort of light tanks and armored cars.[50]

Similar LRDG attacks were carried out to the east of G1's sector. By carefully juggling his patrols, Prendergast coordinated events so that a whole series of raids was sent against the Via at about the same time but at a number of different points. Two patrols—New Zealand R2, under Lieutenant Tony Browne (an accountant in civilian life), and S2, under Lieutenant John Olivey (from Salisbury, Rhodesia)—joined forces and concentrated on the area around Barce. They cut telephone wires and attacked enemy convoys on the Via, managing to destroy tanker trucks similar to those that Hay had attacked. Eighty miles to the east, in the next sector over, Y1 Patrol destroyed or damaged additional enemy vehicles. Y2 Patrol, led by Captain David L. Lloyd Owen of the 2nd Foot or Queen's Royal Regiment, succeeded in laying an ambush which netted a number of prisoners. When one of them told him, in broken English, that there was a small Italian outpost fort nearby, Lloyd Owen decided to try to capture it intact. Displaying the sort of panache that did credit to his days as a standout soccer player at Sandhurst and subsequent service in one of the British Army's most distinguished line regiments, Lloyd Owen drove his patrol boldly up to the fort's front gate. His demand that the Italians surrender immediately produced, however, not the white flag but machinegun fire, and the patrol had to run for cover behind a rise. Thereafter, its weapons seemed to have little effect on the fort, and it looked as though the Italians could hold out forever. Finally, with nothing else to try, Lloyd Owen resorted to his last option: a rifle-grenade fired from the muzzle of a service rifle. When his shot all but demolished the fort's observation tower, the garrison gave up, and Y2 took documents and prisoners. That night the patrol returned to the Via, blowing up still more tanker trucks and killing enemy troops.[51]

These hit-and-run LRDG attacks—"beat-ups," the patrols were beginning to call them—continued, and added to the enemy's mounting difficulties. As were the British, Panzer Group Africa was reeling from exhaustion and high losses. Rommel's supply situation, particularly the shortage of fuel for his panzers, was especially strained at the moment. It was precisely because of the fuel shortage that his Afrika Korps commander, Lieutenant General Ludwig Crüwell, had not favored his chief's idea of dashing to Egypt in the first place. The RAF pounded the German supply lines by day; and at night, in these critical days while Auchinleck needed time to get the Eighth Army in hand again, LRDG patrols continued their attacks on the Via. Their efforts had already destroyed or damaged a considerable number of scarce tanker trucks, and they had managed to disrupt a supply line that was already overextended. Added to Rommel's other woes, even these pinprick "beat-ups" helped the British situation. At any rate, after penetrating a few miles into Egypt, Rommel's panzers at last had to halt and wait until their fuel could catch up with them.[52] As the second winter of the desert campaign began, the Commando raid to kill Rommel and the SAS raid to blow up enemy aircraft had failed, but the Long Range Desert Group had continued to show that special-force operations could be used to good advantage, even against the masters of blitzkrieg warfare and the Desert Fox who commanded them.

Major Ralph Alger Bagnold, shortly after his posting to China in the early 1930s. Photograph from the Department of Archives/Manuscripts, No. D3/00735, courtesy of the Royal Geographical Society.

Sir Archibald Wavell with U.S. Army Lieutenant General Brehon B. Somervell in India in 1943. Photograph is Signal Corps No. 208-PU–219T–2, courtesy of the National Archives.

Rommel understood very clearly that British special forces could be used to mount interdictive raids against his supply lines and rear areas. He was slow, however, to grasp the scale of that effort or the value of such forces for intelligence-gathering operations. Photograph No. HU5625 (LRDG Collection), courtesy of the Imperial War Museum.

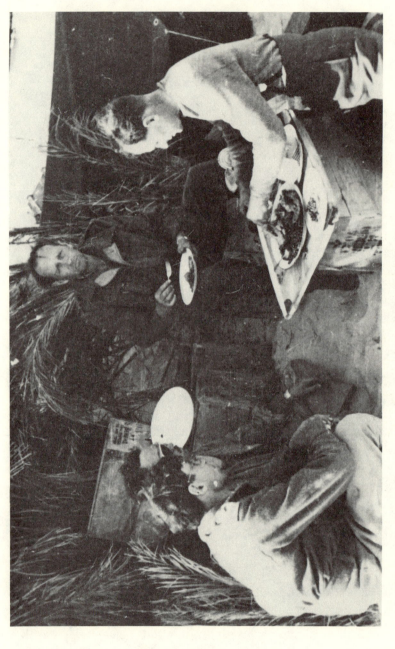

A meal in the LRDG's command post: Lieutenant Colonel Guy Prendergast is far right, with Major W. B. Shaw, the unit's intelligence officer, facing the camera. Photograph No. HU25097 (LRDG Collection), courtesy of the Imperial War Museum.

Captain David Stirling, SAS, awaiting message traffic at an LRDG wireless truck in 1942. The LRDG's Captain Donald G. Steele is at right. Photograph No. HU24994 (LRDG Collection), courtesy of the Imperial War Museum.

SAS and LRDG men the morning after a raid, Wadi Tamet, January 1942. Photograph No. HU24979 (LRDG Collection), courtesy of the Imperial War Museum.

Lieutenant Colonel John Haselden, intelligence agent and originator of the idea for the Tobruk raid. Photograph No. HU25145 (LRDG Collection), courtesy of the Imperial War Museum.

The aftermath of the raids on Tobruk, Jalo, Benghazi, and Barce: members of an LRDG patrol wait to evacuate the wounded by RAF aircraft from a landing ground deep in the desert. Photograph No. HU25286 (LRDG Collection), courtesy of the Imperial War Museum.

G(RF)'s Colonel John W. Hackett, flanked here by Generals Montgomery and Urquhart in 1944. Photograph courtesy of the Imperial War Museum/ General Sir John Hackett.

Breakdown in the desert: a truck belonging to the LRDG's Yeomanry Patrol under repair. Photograph No. HU25176 (LRDG Collection), courtesy of the Imperial War Museum.

One of the camouflaged positions from which the Road Watch surveillance was maintained. A new team of watchers was moved up every night, while the rest of the patrol and the vehicles remained hidden in a wadi a few miles to the south. Photograph No. HU24993 (LRDG Collection), courtesy of the Imperial War Museum.

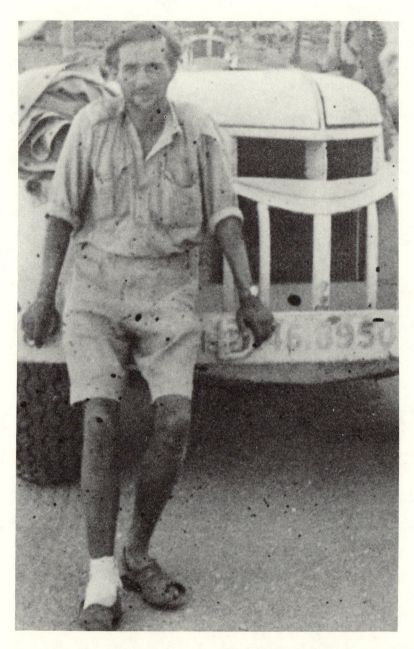

Y1 Patrol's Captain David L. Lloyd Owen at the LRDG's Siwa base, November 1941. It was Lloyd Owen's task, in the wake of the Dodecanese disaster, to convert a desert special force into one capable of mounting operations in the Balkans and other areas of southeastern Europe. Photograph No. HU24251 (LRDG Collection), courtesy of the Imperial War Museum.

The Raiding
Partnership

[The LRDG] provided expert knowledge of the desert and the means
to get us to the right place at the right time. We [the SAS] brought to
these ventures the necessary striking power. The resulting partnership
proved a most fruitful one.
  —Sir Fitzroy Maclean, MP, Captain, 1st SAS Regiment, 1942[1]

Auchinleck replaced the exhausted Cunningham with a new general—the
same Major General Neil Ritchie who, as deputy chief of staff, GHQ-ME,
had been the first to buy Stirling's argument for a force of airborne raiders.
That Ritchie had been elevated to lieutenant general and the command of
the Eighth Army could not have been unwelcome news to Stirling. His fear,
mounting as he brooded during the long ride back across the desert, was
that GHQ-ME would act swiftly to disband a unit so completely a failure
in its first real test. His only hope was that Ritchie, who had supported him
before, might support him again. For that reason Stirling decided that his
best approach was to seek out Ritchie himself, and urge that the SAS be
attached directly to the Eighth Army.[2]
   He found the general installed in his new headquarters and working to
prepare a new drive against Rommel. Stirling's luck, so wretched on the
Gazala raid, now turned. Not only did Ritchie grant Stirling a personal
interview, but he spoke sympathetically about the SAS's "rotten luck . . .
and the raid's having been scuppered by the weather."[3] There was no talk
of disbandment. Instead, Ritchie accepted the idea of having the SAS attached to the Eighth Army and given one more try. He also accepted the
new concept that Stirling had recently broached with Prendergast. Stirling's
new idea was that the SAS should give up on the RAF altogether. Rather,

its new means of reaching the target would be the proven LRDG. Stirling had been greatly impressed by the skill and general efficiency of Eason-smith's R1 on the Gazala operation; he believed that LRDG patrols could, with great efficiency, drop off his men in the vicinity of their targets and thereafter pick them up again for the escape into the desert. The SAS would continue to conduct its parachute training as before, but Stirling's belief was that the LRDG offered the most reliable means available for penetrating to the target and then getting back. For his part, Prendergast "had never had much faith in this parachute business at all," at least as it applied to desert operations. Ten years of exploration by motor vehicles had convinced him that, "once actually on the ground, a party of men trying to move about the desert on foot could not get far."[4] With a new approach now available and the chance for one more good try, the SAS was ready to stake its fortune on transportation provided by the LRDG.

Meanwhile Ritchie, a large man who radiated confidence, was beginning to show success in his new quest to smash Rommel.[5] In fact, he soon managed to batter Panzer Group Afrika further back into Libya and to an area of previously prepared positions known as the Gazala Line. This line Ritchie hit and then sent a second force—a full armored brigade—sweeping west around Rommel's right or desert flank. By early December this "left hook" had forced Rommel out of Gazala altogether and sent him retreating towards El Agheila, nearly 300 miles to the west and on the far side of the Libyan hump. To cut him off before he could reach El Agheila, Ritchie decided to try a second left hook, this one far more ambitious than the first. A brigade to be sent directly across the desert would seize Benghazi, a key coastal town and potentially a major chokepoint on Rommel's line of retreat along the Via Balbia. It was clear that this would involve a very difficult desert crossing of at least 200 miles. If, however, the brigade could somehow beat Rommel there, it could serve as an anvil upon which the Eighth Army could come up and hammer him from the other side.[6]

Ritchie chose for the job a unit whose motorized infantry was drawn from the Scots and the Coldstream Guards and that was supported by armored cars plus tanks and artillery. Since this left-hooking force would have to move through a considerable expanse of largely featureless desert, expert desert navigators were needed as guides. The LRDG was the obvious choice. Prendergast thus received a message telling him to send his patrols north as quickly as possible. The contingent would be led by New Zealand T1, commanded by Captain L. B. Ballantyne, a veteran of Murzuk and Kufra, and it would include two other patrols. All three hurried to reach the designated rendezvous point, only to spend five days waiting for the main force to arrive. That force's delayed arrival was caused by the need to repair or replace worn-out vehicles; it might almost have spelled the end of Ballantyne's patrol. Discovered and caught while waiting in the desert, T1 was pounded by Stukas and ME-109 fighters for nearly two hours. Only the fact that the trucks were well camouflaged and widely dispersed in wadis saved the day, and the actual damage proved surprisingly minimal. The cross-desert dash finally began on December 20, with T1 (which in the meantime had had to suffer additional air attacks) serving as lead patrol. Ballantyne sent the other two off to screen the flanks. Once the advance finally started, it made good progress and at length reached the far side of the Libyan hump. About to strike the Via at a point just south of Benghazi, however, the force ran into major German elements. These, from the 15th Panzer Division and spearheading the enemy retreat, proved too much for the blocking force's armored cars and light tanks to take on. The outnumbered and outgunned British vehicles were brushed quickly aside and the Germans continued their way east along the Via unimpeded.[7] The left hook had failed.

Still, Ritchie's advance had gone well. Despite the drag of an ever-lengthening supply line, his Eighth Army had swept west across Cyrenaica and had at last broken the siege of Tobruk begun eight months before. But Rommel had escaped from a trap that might have worked. LRDG officers believed that the Benghazi left-hook plan should have succeeded, and blamed the Eighth Army's slowness in getting the necessary units assembled.[8] By Christmas 1941, Rommel was safely installed at Agedabia, and soon withdrew to even stronger positions near El Agheila, another sixty miles further along the coast.[9]

Shrewdly chosen, the El Agheila position was protected by salt marshes and, to the south, the steep walls of a long system of wadis. Moreover, Rommel was now close to Tripoli and his source of supply and reinforcements, whereas the British supply line stretched all the way back to Egypt. While it awaited the improvement of its supply situation in preparation for the next round, the Eighth Army unleashed the LRDG on a whole series of beat-ups to keep the enemy preoccupied as much as possible. It was during this series of forays, conducted to the west of Rommel's new position, that Stirling's SAS began to succeed and come into its own as a special force. That unit had joined the LRDG at a new forward base at Jalo, far to the west of Siwa and some 150 miles south of El Agheila. It seemed, because of its proximity to the enemy rear, an excellent location from which to mount raids. Although no order had come down specifically instructing him to do so, Prendergast was already determined to do everything possible to cooperate with the SAS. It was clear to him that, by teaming up, the two units together might be able to double their striking power at this critical juncture.[10]

Their first joint operation was launched within a day or two of the move into Jalo. RAF air reconnaissance had already revealed that enemy aircraft were being concentrated on fields around Sirte, a point west along the coast from El Agheila and supposedly safely beyond the reach of the British. But in the gathering dusk, Captain C. Augustus Holliman's S1 Patrol of Rhodesians carrying a full load of Stirling's men, threaded its way towards two main airfields. One element of the SAS force—led by Stirling's second-in-command, the towering, Irish-born Lieutenant Blair "Paddy" Mayne, a champion rugby player before the war (and who had, before joining the SAS, been placed under house arrest for striking his commanding officer)—was dropped off and proceeded towards one field. The balance of the force and Stirling himself then went on to a second field and were likewise dropped off. Waiting until dark, Mayne's party (six men) crept forward, silently placing their sticky bombs on a whole variety of Italian fighters and transport planes. The charges were placed just where the RAF had told them they could do the most damage—where the wing joined the fuselage or else near the tail, either of which positions could destroy the airframe. The time-fuses were set with a short delay. Mayne then led his men up to a barracks filled with sleeping Italians, mostly ground crewmen. Easing open the door, the SAS party suddenly let fly with the concentrated firepower of Thompson submachineguns fired at close range. The Italians never had a chance. Then, just as the fuel dump and nearly thirty enemy planes began exploding from the preset charges, the SAS escaped down the same wadi by which they had approached the field. They were picked up by S1, which later retrieved Stirling also. Stirling had run into searchlights and a fully alerted perimeter defense; he had, riding with S1, ended up rampaging along the Via instead. A number of enemy vehicles were shot up. Next day the whole force narrowly missed disaster as the enemy reacted with an intensive air search of the local desert. Discovering and following S1's tracks in the sand, a pair of Luftwaffe ME-110's—fast, twin-engined fighters—approached to within a half mile of where the patrol lay hidden in some rocks. But the enemy pilots apparently lost the tracks in the glare; at any rate, they broke off the search and flew away at the last minute. S1 rode back to Jalo for more explosives. The LRDG and SAS had struck the first blow of what they soon referred to as their "raiding partnership."[11]

The raids of this new partnership continued in rapid succession in the weeks ahead. Leading another SAS party behind the lines, Lieutenant C. S. Morris (until the war, a businessman in Christchurch, New Zealand) and his T2 patrol arrived to find their assigned airfield target devoid of enemy planes. Deciding to shoot up the Via instead, the patrol used the darkness to arrive at one of the Casa Cantonieri, this particular one located near a track that led down to a small harbor's loading ramp and docks. Clustered around it were a good fifteen or twenty German vehicles, plus a mobile field kitchen. Duplicating Hay's feat of the month before, T2 and the SAS men quietly drove up and then let fly with everything they had. They destroyed most of the vehicles and killed or wounded perhaps two dozen German and Italian troops. Racing away, they paused a mile or two further on to plant mines in the road. As the patrol faded into the desert they had the satisfaction of counting seven separate explosions a few minutes later, presumably set off by the vehicles of their pursuers passing over the mines. Next, Olivey's

S2 Rhodesians guided another SAS contingent up to the large enemy field at Agedabia. By midnight the raiders had slipped through the perimeter defenses and were running from plane to plane, planting their sticky bombs. They reached the link-up point with Olivey well before dawn, having destroyed thirty-seven enemy planes, mostly outdated Italian CR-42 fighters but also some Stukas and ME-109s. This was the most successful single night's work so far, and Stirling was determined to raise the score even higher. His raids continued, and by the end of the first week of January 1942, his men had destroyed a total of ninety enemy aircraft.[12]

Yet such hit-and-run affairs were not always so one-sided. As the LRDG's intelligence officer put it, "in this business, as on other occasions, the trouble was apt to come the morning after."[13] If, the next day, enemy air patrols could locate the raiders out in the desert, then the patrol and its SAS partners could expect to pay dearly for the previous night's success. The Germans paid back Morris and T2, for example, on the first day of 1942. Spotting their tracks the morning after the raid, an ME-109, probably low on gas, made only a pass or two over their position but apparently radioed in the location. On an almost cloudless day, Morris was caught in the open with nowhere to run; the best he could do was to get his trucks as well dispersed and camouflaged as possible, and get his and the SAS men braced against the inevitable. They did not have long to wait. Minutes after the ME-109 left, the dreaded Stukas appeared, lazily circling a mile or two to the north. Then a Fiesler F1–156C Storch (Stork)—the light airplane which the Germans employed for artillery spotting and reconnaissance missions—arrived to guide the Stukas in to the attack. The Fiesler made a beeline for the patrol's position and banked away just overhead. The Stukas immediately climbed for altitude and thereafter came screaming down to attack with bombs and machinegun fire. Several trucks were hit and exploded as the ammunition and gasoline ignited. Still more Stukas appeared, and one of the SAS officers—Lieutenant Jack Lewes, the Cambridge honors student who had invented Stirling's sticky bombs—was killed in their attacks. A number of LRDG and SAS men were wounded. By the time the German planes left, Morris had lost all but one of his vehicles. He loaded up the survivors in his one truck (which also had been damaged) and limped south to Jalo. T2 had taken a beating in its "morning after," and did not become operational again until new vehicles could be sent forward to replace those lost to the Stukas.[14]

But the good results of these raids were spelled out in a series of messages sent from LRDG Group Headquarters back to the Eighth Army and GHQ-ME. Stirling—and Prendergast also—felt that, in this short period, his unit had more than proved its worth; now seemed the perfect time to try to get more men in order to expand the scope of the raids. Meanwhile, with the Germans all but driven out of Cyrenaica by Ritchie's advance, Auchinleck was basking in the glow of a successful advance and could be expected to act favorably on Stirling's request. Wangling a flight back to Cairo, Stirling, bathed and splendidly turned out in tailored battledress but still wearing proudly the beard he had grown in the desert, presented himself at GHQ-ME. He was shown in to see the C-in-C without delay. The beard offended the staff officers but seems to have amused Auchinleck. By the end of the meeting, Stirling had received permission to recruit another fifty officers and men—more than double his present strength—and had won an on-the-spot promotion to major. L Detachment, SAS, was to be given a contingent of Free French paratroopers and also some men from the Special Boat Section, a unique force raised the previous spring and whose specialty was using folbots to infiltrate enemy harbors. Stirling also decided that his organization, in keeping with its new status, now required its own special insignia. He chose a winged-dagger device, below which appeared the newly chosen motto of the SAS: "Who Dares, Wins."[15] To his parachute-trained veterans of extended operations, he also awarded a special set of wings, to be worn above the left breast pocket. In characteristic fashion, Stirling had not bothered to wait for official authorization for the new insignia. Rather, he simply began wearing them himself and counted Auchinleck's tacit acceptance of them as official permission to continue.

Prendergast's patrols were meanwhile to prepare for future operations as deep inside Tripolitania as possible. An operational directive instructed the LRDG to extend its "offensive patrols"—that is, the joint raids with the SAS—"as far back behind enemy lines as possible."[16] They were also to reconnoiter areas of Tripolitania in order to secure "topographical details" useful to "subsequent advance of other troops," and in general to report on any enemy movements or signs of new positions being prepared.[17] But getting into Tripolitania was not easy. Heading west out of Jalo, the patrols had to slip through the "El Agheila bottleneck." This was a tight, eighty-mile-long corridor of open desert stretching from the enemy positions in the north to some impassably broken ground to the south. German ground forces patrolled it intensively, and the whole expanse was easily within the fan of enemy air patrols. This forced the patrol commanders to do their moving at night or in sandstorms, and, in the daytime, to hide out in wadis. Lloyd Owens' Y2 was the first patrol to succeed in slipping through, finally reaching its assigned sector a full 550 miles to the west of Jalo. Other patrols, however, generally had a difficult time in the bottleneck. An account of Scots Guards Captain J. Alastair L. Timpson's G2 gives some idea of the problems faced. G2 was ordered to carry a special reconnaissance party behind the lines. The party included two aviators, one RAF and one Royal Navy, whose mission it was to check out prospective airfields in the direction of Tripoli. By traveling at night, G2 got past the enemy's motorized ground patrols but had several narrow escapes from Luftwaffe planes. For example, one pair of ME-109s followed Timpson's tire tracks almost to his hidden position but then broke off. Soon, however, other German planes, out in force, were crisscrossing over his position again and again, yet fortunately failed to spot any of the hidden trucks. Despite all this air activity, Timpson eventually reached his designated position: a hard-surface road north of Murzuk, remarkable for its line of crumbling Roman forts. There was plenty of Italian traffic on this road that, since the Clayton raid of the year before, had been left in peace. Timpson carried out his airfield reconnaissances and then decided to do a "proper beat-up," planting mines and ambushing several convoys. But an enemy truck escaped the ambush and alerted the enemy garrisons to the north. Timpson hid his patrol in a wadi and enjoyed watching Savoia Marchetti-79 bombers sweep in from over the horizon to bomb an empty clump of tamarisk trees; the patrol pulled out at dusk. Additional brushes with enemy planes followed. When Timpson was advised by radioed message that heavy German patrols lay in his path, he shifted course to the south and tried to push through the worst dunes the patrol had ever seen. One truck's motor gave out altogether, and the vehicle had to be abandoned (only to be recovered and repaired four months later, a particular point of pride to G2). Timpson's men finally rode back into Jalo, feeling not only the strain of a month behind enemy lines but also the satisfaction of having destroyed a number of enemy vehicles without taking a single casualty in the process.[18]

To support these deep-penetration operations while the Eighth Army stood poised to begin what was intended to be the final drive on Tripoli, Prendergast had elected to shift his full Group Headquarters out to Jalo. For nearly a month, heading back and forth from Siwa, the LRDG's Heavy Section made its long runs across the desert, hauling out the great quantity of gasoline, munitions, spare parts, and rations that would be needed to sustain the planned program of raids as the Eighth Army closed in on Rommel. Jalo became an oasis dotted with both LRDG and SAS fuel and ammunition dumps. Unfortunately, practically all of this materiel, painfully accumulated in the long and tedious treks across the desert, was about to be destroyed before it could be put to use, and both LRDG and SAS elements would be forced to beat a hasty retreat out of Jalo.[19]

In the last weeks of December 1941 and into early January 1942, Churchill had held every confidence that Ritchie's army would be able to finish off Rommel in the spring; to him, the final victory in North Africa seemed almost at hand. In reality, however, Rommel had sized up the weakness of Ritchie's exposed forward positions and the dependency of the Eighth Army on its long, overstrained supply line back to Egypt. The Desert Fox did not wait long, lashing out as soon as he could receive sufficient supplies of his own and get his forces prepared. In the third week of January these forces—now designated Panzerarmee Afrika—suddenly tore into the British near Agedabia. In little more than a week the quicksilver Rommel had gone on to smash his way forward and retake Benghazi. The British fell back in confusion, and the Germans pressed on, now fueled and sustained from the lavish stockpiles (as well as over a thousand trucks) captured from their enemies in the opening stages of this new round of battles. Rommel had mounted his second great eastward-driving offensive of the desert war; and, as had the one of the year before, this one would take him all the way across Cyrenaica.[20]

The first knowledge that Prendergast had that things were going badly was an Eighth Army message warning him to get out of Jalo as quickly as possible. It seemed that the oasis stood to be cut off at any moment. He began immediate preparations to evacuate. Unfortunately, one of his patrols—Hunter's G1, accompanying Stirling and a party of SAS raiders—was still out on a mission. The patrol's radio had been lost, and there was no way to warn them that Jalo might be in enemy hands by the time they returned. Another problem was that there was no way to save the wealth of supplies stashed in the dumps. The patrols did the best they could, mounting a round-the-clock effort to salvage as much as possible before the Germans closed in. Taking turns, they moved load after load out to a secret dump a few miles away on the edge of the Sand Sea. The extra food was distributed among Jalo's natives, Berbers friendly for the most part to the British. After that, Prendergast loaded up the unit and began the long retreat back to Siwa.[21]

G2 Patrol, under Timpson, was left behind to destroy the considerable volume of munitions that had not been moved and to await Stirling and the other Guards patrol. Timpson carried out what he called his "scorched palm" policy, first trying to blow up the extra cases of ammunition and then resorting to dumping sulphuric acid on top of them. Luftwaffe planes flew over the oasis constantly, and Timpson expected to have to make a run for it at any moment. Finally, however, the long-overdue Hunter and Stirling at last returned from their raid. Stirling was immensely pleased with himself. Not only had his men turned the tables on an Italian ambush, but they had destroyed warehouses and dockyard cranes in an enemy harbor. Then, in the darkness, they had found and blown up a batch of Afrika Korps tanker trucks. Each of these trucks could carry twenty tons (or about 4,000 gallons) of diesel fuel apiece, and the SAS had destroyed nine of them. Stirling explained that the flames from their explosions had been enough to light up "the whole sky . . . for half an hour."[22] Timpson got the combined patrols loaded up and out of Jalo only an hour before the Germans finally pulled in. By the first week of February 1942, both LRDG and SAS elements, except for one LRDG patrol which Prendergast dispatched to a small oasis in order to look for shot-down pilots and any Eighth Army troops cut off during the retreat, were again concentrated at Siwa. Prendergast had been lucky at Jalo, and he knew it: had the Germans moved faster, they might have caught and destroyed both the LRDG and the SAS in a single stroke.[23]

To the north, Ritchie's Eighth Army now installed itself behind minefields that covered a jagged, forty-five-mile-long series of positions. These began at the familiar ground of Gazala and ran down to Bir Hacheim, where the

Duke of Westminster's armored cars had, twenty-five years before, rescued the British prisoners from the Senussi. Ritchie, retreating across the very ground over which he had advanced just six weeks before, had lost heavily, including over forty tanks, artillery, a wealth of motor transport, and 1,400 men. Rommel, now facing the drag of a longer supply line, arrived to sit opposite the British positions and wait. Exhausted, both sides used the time to consolidate, repair, and get ready for the next round.[24] Prendergast himself used the lull to equip his patrols with new trucks and to send his men to Cairo for leave. Cairo was a neutral capital (King Farouk and Egypt had elected not to declare war on the Axis) whose ample and exotic pleasures offered a startling contrast to the war being fought in the desert to the west. Cooled by the Nile's waters, the city itself was untouched by the war, except for the crowds of British soldiers on leave and the belief that the whole place was supposed to be crawling with spies. It offered much to men with plenty of back pay and a powerful thirst. The favorite haunts of LRDG and SAS officers were Shepheard's or the equally splendid Continental Hotel.[25] The NCOs and "Other Ranks" usually chose a place called the Melody Club, boasting the best belly dancers in the Middle East (who performed on a stage protected from the soldiers by a barbed-wire fence). On leave and despite the strain of long periods behind the lines, LRDG and SAS troops and their officers probably "behaved . . . no worse if no better than [those of] any other unit."[26] They were aggressively proud of their elitist "desert-raider" reputation, and their sense of unit esprit could take predictable forms—fistfights expanding to full-scale brawls, and, in one wild spree, the racing of an entire patrol's vehicles up and down a Cairo main street until the arrival of the Military Police in strength.

The now-familiar pattern of joint SAS-LRDG raids resumed, this time from Siwa. Working with his new Special Boat Section elements, Stirling wanted to use folbots to plant the small mines called "limpets" on enemy ships. Benghazi harbor, 430 miles away and now far from the front line, seemed a good target. In March Olivey's S2 Rhodesians took Stirling's SAS party and two Arab agents—under Robert Melot, a Belgian-born "expert Arabist" and cotton merchant, who, like Haselden, had been made a captain in Military Intelligence—north for an attempt. On the way, Stirling's new pride and joy, a Ford station wagon painted with Afrika Korps markings and whose sides, top, and windshield had been removed to make it resemble a German vehicle called a Kfz Utility Car, and a captured Mercedes-Benz G4 staff car ran over mines. The second car caught the worst of it, and with its wounded occupants had to be sent back. The other vehicle, however, was quickly repaired. Finally, nearing dusk and after being dropped off by the patrol, Stirling and his group drove their "German" car out onto the Via Balbia itself. Their approach (Stirling drove at 70 mph, headlights bright) was nothing if not bold, but somehow got them into Benghazi. Parking the car in some rubble, they tried to launch one of their folbots, only to discover that the wind had churned up big swells and whitecaps in the harbor. It was obviously impossible to reach the ships, of which the dark silhouettes of several could be seen only a few hundred yards away. Stirling rejoined Olivey, and they decided to plant charges in a munitions dump. A month later, however, Stirling was back, this time having been guided by G2.[27] He had brought along an impressive array, "quite a notable party" of reinforcements.[28] Newly joined to the SAS was Lieutenant Fitzroy Hew Maclean, a 31-year-old product of Eton, Cambridge, and the Foreign Office, and also a serving member of Parliament (the Conservative Party). Stirling's other special participant was on loan from GHQ-ME: Lieutenant Randolph F. E. Spencer Churchill, the son of the prime minister. Like Maclean, Lieutenant Churchill was an elected member of Parliament. Accustomed as they were by now to his ability to accomplish things with a certain style, the LRDG officers were forced to give marks to Stirling for including two "Old Etonian" Tory MPs on a raiding venture against Benghazi.[29]

The approach was much as before. Robin B. Gurdon, Scots Guards, G2's new officer, had had to dodge "swarms of aircraft" as they approached through the desert. Nearing the target, Stirling loaded up his staff car and at dusk headed for Benghazi. Unfortunately, however, he managed to smash into a bump so hard that he knocked the car's front tires out of alignment. The result was a high-pitched screeching noise that, even at low speeds, could be heard for a mile. This did not faze Stirling in the slightest; he bluffed his way past an Italian roadblock on the outskirts of Benghazi and soon reached the edge of the harbor. He was well served by Maclean's excellent Italian and bluff pose as an arrogant German officer, which brushed off several Italian sentries. But they again failed to make it out to the ships they could see anchored in the harbor. The black rubber rafts brought along for this purpose refused to be inflated, probably because they had somehow been damaged in the long journey over the desert. Again frustrated, as dawn approached Stirling decided to hide out in the town during the day and try again the following night.[30] A tense day was spent, weapons at the ready, in a deserted building within sight of what seemed to be the local Gestapo headquarters (the younger Churchill, in particular, enjoying the procession of "black-booted officers striding in and out").[31] They re-emerged that night, only to be unsuccessful again: Benghazi was lit up by antiaircraft searchlights and a tanker afire in the harbor, and the Italians were blazing away at anything that moved. Stirling collected his raiders and, before dawn, drove off with nothing to show for his efforts. On the other hand, as Shaw could not help remarking, it would have been worth it just to have seen Mussolini's face could he have learned that the son of Winston Churchill himself had just spent two days in Il Duce's very own Cyrenaic capitol city.[32]

In the midst of these efforts, Prendergast was instructed to mount a series of raids against the Via Balbia in direct support of the Eighth Army. "[M]ore than half of the enemy's maintenance tonnage" was being moved from

Tripoli to Benghazi by that route, and the LRDG's role "until further orders" was "to interrupt this road movement."[33] In conjunction with RAF bombing attacks, a program of well-coordinated beat-ups was expected to cause Rommel plenty of trouble. The new orders suggested that the LRDG was now perceived—by the Eighth Army, at least—as a force whose most vital function at the moment was that of raiding. Prendergast was told to concentrate particularly on the section of the Via lying west of El Agheila. To throw off the enemy as to the exact point along the Via from which the raids were being mounted (and also to give the patrols a greater chance for survival), the LRDG began experimenting with new types of delayed-action fuses. The need was to come up with some sort of explosive device that could be planted on a passing vehicle without the enemy's knowledge. The delayed fuse of such a charge could be set to go off hours later and miles from the point on the road at which the charge had actually been planted. The enemy therefore would be led to search the wrong place: the desert area proximate to where the explosion had occurred, as opposed to the point at which the patrol had actually lain hidden and planted the charge. The only trick was to come up with a method that would work.[34]

The patrols began by trying a charge that could be snagged and picked up by the axle of the passing vehicle. When this produced poor results, they next tried a magnetic, quick-release "droppable" charge that could be suspended from a telegraph wire stretched across and above the road. This method also failed to work. Finally, they decided on a simpler but cruder expedient: a sort of satchel charge made up inside a standard Italian knapsack, and which could be thrown into the back of a passing enemy vehicle. The idea was that, at night and half asleep as their vehicles bounced over the road many miles from the front, the enemy soldiers within might not spot the lethal satchel charge they were carrying until it was too late.[35]

Timpson's G1, the inventor of this technique, was given the privilege of being first to try it out. By the time Timpson reached a scarp overlooking the Via, he could see, as the dusk settled, plenty of tempting targets passing below: staff cars, Italian and German trucks, fuel tankers, towed artillery pieces, and communications vehicles, virtually all of them heading east towards Rommel. The patrol headed down to try out the new device. The first step was to set up a fake roadblock: empty oil drums, hurricane lanterns, and signs in German and Italian instructing drivers to slow down. That done, the patrol hid and waited. A little later the first convoy appeared, headlights burning brightly. As hoped, the enemy drivers spotted the sign and duly slowed down. As the leader, Timpson (who also had the best arm) quickly darted out from the darkness to lob his charge into a big diesel truck—and found himself staring up into the face of an Italian soldier. G1's commander froze in mid-throw; the driver yelled something and sent his truck, with a great clashing of gears, lurching forward. Other attempts ended in much the same way. Exasperated with it all, Timpson eventually raced one of his own trucks onto the Via in an effort to overtake and then throw the satchel charges onto the enemy trucks. But this method also ended in failure. The next day G1 was itself attacked, just as it was setting up the antenna for the scheduled call to Siwa. As Timpson's men ran for their trucks, the enemy, an Italian motorized unit, opened fire. One LRDG soldier was killed, but G1's five trucks shot their way free of the trap and raced south into the desert.[36]

This sharp, short firefight had taken place in broad daylight and within full sight of the Via. Timpson recalled later how an enemy convoy, proceeding peacefully along, had stopped to gawk at the spectacle of a British patrol being chased into the desert less than a mile from this vital road. G1 threw off enemy planes by heading west, not south and east as the enemy would doubtless expect. It came out after a few days of lying low to plant mines and cut telegraph wires along a new part of the Via. Giving up entirely on the roadblock/satchel charge-throwing scheme, the patrol moved instead against the clusters of enemy vehicles parked at one of the local Casa Cantonieri. As before, this kind of beat-up (or "orthodox raid" as the LRDG liked to call it) was a one-sided success for the attackers. This and other operations, including the ambushing of an Auto-Saharan patrol sent out to cut off New Zealand T2 Patrol, convinced Prendergast to chuck the satchel charges business altogether and stick with the orthodox raids. As long as the patrols had the advantage of surprise, they could use the night to emerge from the desert and sting the enemy in more places than the enemy could possibly cover. These beat-ups supplemented the RAF's daylight efforts and reflected a well-conceived policy of interdicting Rommel's main supply line. They continued into the late spring of 1942 as the desert once again began to stoke up to its fearsome summer temperatures.[37] At this time word began to reach Prendergast that the Germans might be attempting a desert special operation of their own.

Certainly the British, through their use of the LRDG and SAS, had been allowed a free hand in the vast inner portions of the desert since early 1941 and the fall of Kufra. Having missed their chance to employ their Auto-Saharans for offensive action in the critical early stages, the Italians had apparently since allowed these once-excellent units to fritter away; experienced personnel were assigned to other tasks or to replace losses in conventional units, and worn-out vehicles and equipment went unreplaced. By the end of 1941, enemy forces tended not to venture below the southern edge of the Libyan plateau at all. But in March and April of 1942, information reached GHQ-ME's DMI staff that an old colleague of Prendergast's from the exploring days was back—and wearing now the uniform of a German officer. His name was, of course, Almaszy: Ladislas Edouard, Count de Almaszy, World War I fighter pilot, amateur archeologist, and fellow explorer with Bagnold, Clayton, Shaw, and Prendergast. Almaszy had been carefully watched by the British Foreign Office all through the 1930s, and he had several times reappeared in Egypt, flying down aircraft purchased by King Farouk.[38] But Shaw, who "had never trusted him to start with," and the others had long since lost contact with him.[39] In spring 1942, however, his name had suddenly started cropping up in the decrypts of coded enemy radio transmissions. From these and various other scraps, the British pieced together enough information to know that Almaszy had been made a *Hauptmann* (captain) in the Luftwaffe, and was now attached to Rommel's staff for some special purpose. Given Almaszy's desert-exploring experience, it seemed a reasonable guess that Rommel must be contemplating some sort of operation in the region below the Libyan plateau.[40]

In addition, certain suspicious signs soon began to appear. These included sets of tire tracks in locations where no British forces had recently operated, and reports, coming in from friendly Bedouin, concerning a "European officer" who had been asking for directions in odd corners of the desert.[41] What especially interested the British was that the Germans, placing total reliance upon their superbly honed blitzkrieg techniques, had not yet attempted anything in the desert below the plateau. Heretofore Rommel had viewed any sort of special venture in that arena as being wasteful of slender resources and at best a peripheral operation. In his view, the real decision was to be won in the proven blitzkrieg fashion and in the flat, excellent tank country of the Libyan plateau just inland from the coast. In a year and a half of fighting, Rommel had neither needed nor seen fit to develop anything like the LRDG or the SAS. In fact, a captured Afrika Korps major once told an LRDG officer that "we Germans couldn't do this [LRDG] sort of thing— out five hundred miles from our base for days or weeks on end. We like to go about in a crowd."[42] But while the contemplation of some sort of desert probe to the south was altogether "uncharacteristic of the Germans," there could be little doubt that Rommel would have to make use of Almaszy if he harbored serious hopes of such a move.[43] There simply was no one else available to him who was qualified for such a venture. To the British, it seemed also to mean that the Germans might at last be about to begin exploiting the inner desert for their own purposes—perhaps even to try to turn the tables on the LRDG-SAS by employing a special force of their own and with their own desert expert in command.

What Almaszy was up to was indeed ambitious, but not quite to the point of actually trying to create a desert special force for the Germans. In reality, the mission he had been given was that of getting German agents inserted in Cairo by using the desert as a safe "back door" through which to get them there. The desert would serve him as it had served the LRDG: as a vast and neutral medium, an avenue by which to outflank an enemy and reach his vulnerable rear areas. The difference was that Almaszy would be heading east, not west, as the LRDG did on its "taxi-service" missions.[44]

Almaszy was given this mission because Rommel was currently planning his greatest offensive yet, the one that would smash the Eighth Army and carry him triumphantly into Cairo. Since September 1941 and unknown to the British, he had been receiving from that city military intelligence of the most advantageous sort.[45] His unwitting source for this intelligence was none other than the U. S. military attaché in Cairo, Colonel Bonner F. Fellers, United States Army.[46] Fellers, West Point class of 1918, was an officer of considerable ability and unswerving loyalty. But for months now the Germans had been able to read virtually every coded message which he had sent out by regular dispatch from the American Embassy in Cairo. Neither Fellers nor the United States Department of State could know that, eleven months before, Italian agents had broken into the safe of the American Embassy in Rome. Every page of the State Department's secret "Black Code" had been photographed, and the agents had gotten away undiscovered. This prize the Italians had promptly shared with their German allies. Fellers himself, keenly professional and recently graduated from the U. S. Army's War College, had been handpicked in 1940 to serve as American military attaché in Cairo. It was a "plum" assignment, and Fellers was an excellent choice; he was extremely good at his job. Expected to keep Washington informed regarding the very latest British military operations in the desert, Fellers did just that. He got on quite well at GHQ-ME and, through his well-informed contacts, was given access to highly sensitive information. This information went well beyond the normal briefings, battlefield tours, and visits to units that an attaché might normally hope to be given. Fellers was given even more after Pearl Harbor and American entry into the war as Britain's ally. He filed detailed assessments of British morale, unit strengths, and abilities of individual commanders. These were regularly transmitted via the standard State Department code—unfortunately, the very one that the Germans and Italians could now read. Apparently these shrewdly formulated, extremely analytical assessments proved of "sensational value" to Rommel; at the least, they helped to give him a window on the enemy camp.[47] Indeed, the Desert Fox, in a convenient play on words, liked to call them his "little fellers."[48] The U.S. military attaché may unknowingly have given Rommel "the broadest and clearest picture of . . . [opposing] forces and intentions available to any Axis commander throughout the war."[49]

By spring 1942, however, Rommel's fear was that the British might at last somehow find out and stop the flow of this useful information—or worse, begin using it to feed him deliberately false "disinformation." Rommel thus needed Almaszy as a way to get agents installed in Cairo as a hedge, so that if the British got wise and either closed off this source at the critical moment, or began using it for their own purposes, he would still be left with a set of "eyes" in Cairo. Yet this was only one goal of what came to be called "Sonderkommando (Special Command) Almaszy."[50] The other was to exploit contacts with certain revolutionary elements within the officer corps of Egypt's armed forces. The Germans grasped only too clearly the fact that a sense of rabidly anti-British nationalism pulsed through many Egyptians.

Indeed, some of Cairo's leading citizens had rejoiced openly at the defeats which the British had suffered at Rommel's hand. The British had already secured the dismissal of the chief of the Egyptian General Staff, General Aziz el Masri Pasha, an officer notorious for his anti-British feelings. Among his circle of supporters were two junior officers of the Egyptian Army, Captain Abdel Nasser and Lieutenant Anwar el Sadat. These two future presidents of Egypt were both members of the outlawed "Free Officers Movement," and it was they whom the German agents that Almaszy was to guide across the desert were intended to contact.[51]

The process of getting the agents across the desert was called Operation Salaam. Operation Condor—the actual intelligence operations to be undertaken once the agents finally reached Cairo—would follow as the second phase. Earlier German efforts had turned out poorly. These included an attempt to land agents in the desert near Cairo by airplane as well as an attempt to kidnap General el Masri himself, and then take him back as an apparent adherent to the German cause. Almaszy was given a handful of men, apparently drawn from the elite Brandenburger Brigade, a sort of security and special operations force that functioned under the German intelligence service or Abwehr.[52] Many of the Brandenburger personnel were foreign-born *Volksdeutsche*. For this mission Almaszy drew five captured British vehicles and had them equipped with Bagnold's sun compass and the same sort of gear that the LRDG used.[53] The two Abwehr agents were Johan Eppler, age 28, a German Jew apparently born in Alexandria and converted to Islam; and Peter Sanstede, a blond-haired, muscular German who had worked as a mechanic on the East African oil rigs. The two men were given false papers, civilian clothing, portable radio sets, and 50,000 pounds in brand-new British sterling notes. The idea was that Eppler would pose as an Egyptian and Sanstede as an Irish-American. Counting Almaszy, there were eight men in all.

In mid-May 1942, Sonderkommando Almaszy left the recently evacuated LRDG base of Jalo and moved south and east into the desert. Almaszy was to make daily radio reports back to Rommel's headquarters. Running down Graziani's Palificata towards Kufra, the Germans slipped past the British garrison there and turned east towards Egypt. The Luftwaffe was to drop extra gasoline and water at designated points along the way; this would help establish dumps for future operations. Almaszy, back in the desert for the first time since 1937, had apparently lost none of his old expertise. He managed, for example, to locate a dump of water cans he had established years earlier—which, he bragged to the men of his party, had "saved the lives of Major Bagnold and his companions . . . when they had an axle-break only 24 km. from here."[54] Almaszy also ran across several abandoned Chevrolet trucks marked with Sudan Defence Force insignia. His Italian maps proved "useless" and inspired him to wonder just what Graziani's forces had been "doing [in] all the years 1931–1939." But Almaszy seems to have had trouble from the start with his handpicked Brandenburger special commandos. They were either "lazy, inept or else lacking in desert experience"; he complained (at least to his diary) that he had to "keep on asking and ordering everything." But by far the most inept and uncooperative of the lot were the two agents, whom he referred to as "Pit" and "Pan." They were easily "the most untidy fellows I've ever had under me." On the whole, however, the party made good progress. Reaching a pass near the Gilf Kebir that, Almaszy said, correctly enough, Clayton had mined the year before—"out of consideration for me"—the column hit the desert track that led east towards the Nile. At dawn next day the Germans, wearing Afrika Korps uniforms, drove boldly into Kharga Oasis. Just past its small rail station, they were halted at an Egyptian police roadblock. Almaszy put on his best "effendi" manner and told the police in good Arabic that the rest of the "inglisi" column would be coming along at any moment. With that the Germans were let through, and Almaszy pressed on.[55]

Safely out of Kharga and two weeks after leaving Jalo, the party raced across the empty desert towards the Nile. Just outside of Asyut, a town 300 miles south of Cairo, Almaszy stopped. In the distance he could see the "silver, glittering Nile pushing its way north through the huge green cultivated valley."[56] While Almaszy enjoyed the scenery, the two agents quickly changed into civilian clothes and gathered up their suitcases and documents. After a few handshakes and one last photograph, Almaszy drove them to the outskirts of Asyut. There they got out and proceeded alone. Almaszy's part of the operation was finished. He drove back, gathered up his vehicles, and faded into the desert.

The two agents had no difficulty in getting past the Egyptian police. They walked up to the rail station, bought their tickets, and caught the train for Cairo. Reaching that city, they passed through a second police checkpoint; thereafter, they installed themselves in a modest apartment in one of the suburbs. It seemed to them that their operation was already well along on the road to success.[57]

They were wrong. In fact, the British were on to them already. Almaszy, so diligent and methodical in making his daily radio reports for Operation Salaam, had already done in Operation Condor. From the time he left Jalo, the British Y Service's stations had picked up almost every one of his coded transmissions. And although many were garbled or could not be immediately decrypted, they were enough to help track his progress across the desert.[58]

After that, the indiscretions of the agents themselves had helped to spell their doom. Agent Eppler succeeded in making contact with Cairo's most famous belly dancer, a supple beauty named Hakmet Fahmi. An ardent Egyptian nationalist, Miss Fahmi had recently taken as her patriotic duty the entertainment of a British Army general staff major. A regular pattern developed. While the major was kept occupied during visits to the bedroom of her Nile houseboat, Eppler, hidden in another room, quickly sifted through the contents of that officer's briefcase. The vital information about troop movements and other matters gained in this fashion could later be radioed out to Rommel. Eppler had also met in secret with General el Masri and with Lieutenant Sadat. Sadat, a communications officer, promised to furnish extra radios should they be needed; he also helped to select an imposing residence on Cairo's Rue des Pyramids for Rommel's use when Panzerarmee Afrika finally arrived as conquerors of the city. Meanwhile, the British themselves had only to wait until Eppler grew increasingly foolhardy. That agent had recently dressed up in the uniform of a South African captain in the British forces, lavishly spending his crisp, brand-new pound sterling notes in Cairo's best nightspots. And the bar girl he had picked up was a poor choice: she happened to be none other than an agent of the Jewish Agency, then working hand-in-glove with the British.[59]

But perhaps the most crucial information had come from the shallow attack which the British had recently launched out in the desert. This attack had captured a variety of documents as well as the sophisticated, highly sensitive radio equipment employed at one of Rommel's key radio-intelligence centers. The captured documents revealed not only the specific details of the Condor mission, but also that the Germans had, beyond question, been reading Colonel Feller's dispatches all along. The end came when the two German agents, along with Hakmet Fahmi, were arrested and interrogated. At length and in possession of the agents' special code—keyed to the pages of Daphne du Maurier's novel *Rebecca*—the British could begin sending out false information to Rommel. General el Masri and Lieutenant Sadat were both imprisoned, and Captain Nasser was sent to a distant outpost in the Sudan. Colonel Fellers, who had been "deeply upset" when he learned of the role he had so unknowingly played, was kept in Cairo long enough to continue with his detailed messages, now filled with false and misleading information, every bit of it carefully designed by the British to fool Rommel; eventually he was sent to General MacArthur's staff in the Pacific theater.[60] Operation Condor, so painstakingly designed to ensure the flow of accurate intelligence to Rommel, had led to precisely the opposite result.

That it would turn out this way was not, of course, known to Almaszy as he slipped back across the desert, his part of the operation completed. Nor was any of it known at the time to the LRDG; it was all "a very high-level intelligence business."[61] Later, as scraps of information filtered down to Prendergast, he found himself somewhat disappointed that his unit had not been allowed to go after Almaszy. Instead, the LRDG had been told to stay clear of Almaszy and to let him proceed unhindered. Prendergast could not have known at the time that the Y Service's stations had been tracking their enemy carefully all along, that the counterintelligence measures were being carefully orchestrated, and that British intelligence had hopes of ultimately using Condor as a way of feeding Rommel false information. Still, and apparently acting entirely on his own, Prendergast had sent an LRDG patrol to watch the routes he guessed that Almaszy would take. His guess was good; the Sonderkommando's still-fresh tracks were indeed found, but the patrol was too late—Almaszy had already escaped to the west.[62]

Even so, the LRDG may have come closer to bagging Almaszy than Prendergast thought at the time. As indicated by Almaszy's personal diary (a copy of which was sent to Bagnold after British intelligence encountered Almaszy in Vienna just after the war), Almaszy managed to slip by two British columns and then erected markers to guide the Luftwaffe. His intention was to create a chain of secret dumps. These would support the series of LRDG-style raids he apparently had intentions of mounting against Kufra. But as he ran north, now virtually in the home stretch leading up to Jalo, he spotted "something flickering on my left front . . . in the blinding sand."[63] He quickly hid his vehicles in some dunes and got out his Zeiss binoculars for a better look. He saw "distant dark spots . . . vehicles—the enemy patrol!"[64] The "distant dark spots" were indeed vehicles belonging to the LRDG. Almaszy kept his own vehicles out of sight, and the LRDG patrol soon passed by. A day later Almaszy reached the headquarters of Panzerarmee Afrika and made his report, receiving from Rommel an on-the-spot promotion to major. In the months ahead, the LRDG continued to pick up an occasional rumor or tidbit of information about Almaszy. Eventually the LRDG occupied an oasis recently evacuated by the Germans. Its patrols found sun compasses and vehicles fitted with sand channels, radiator condensors, and other special desert gear similar to that employed by the LRDG. But there was no sign of Almaszy. Except for persistent rumors, as far as the LRDG could learn, the Desert Fox's desert expert had simply disappeared from the scene.[65]

Despite the failure of the Condor operation, a positive effect—from the German perspective—of Almaszy's brief reappearance in the desert had been to give Rommel and his staff officers their first real idea as to the nature of British special-force efforts. Before Almaszy came, bringing his personal knowledge of Bagnold, Clayton, Prendergast, and Shaw, Rommel's intelligence officers had been inclined to blame local Arabs for a good part of the raids along the Via. These local "saboteurs" were assumed to have been trained and subsidized by the British in the same way that Feisal's Arabs had been trained and paid by T. E. Lawrence in World War I. But the information which Almaszy brought back helped to give them a far clearer picture.[66] A mimeographed report, published in both German and Italian editions, was soon issued to every major unit in Panzerarmee Afrika. It declared that the LRDG "plays an extremely important part" in the British sabotage organization.[67] The "selection and training of the men," and the mobility and camouflage of the vehicles . . . have enabled . . . [this Unit] to carry out the destruction of Axis aircraft.[68] But in leaving out the SAS, the report gave no indication at all that the Germans had grasped the fact that, in actuality, two British "special raiding forces" were now being employed against them, and on a systematic basis. Until the end of the campaign, Rommel himself "used the term 'Commandos' to embrace the SAS . . . the LRDG . . . and other guerrilla type forces," apparently never learning that these comprised a variety of separate units.[69]

These units had continued to molest his supply lines all during the time that Almaszy was getting Condor across the desert, and they helped inspire GHQ-ME to concoct the most ambitious plan yet for such raids. After inserting still more radio-equipped parties of British and Arab agents into the Jebel, an LRDG patrol was to guide A Squadron, Middle East Commandos, to that same region. The Commandos were then to set up a secret desert base deep behind enemy lines and use it to mount a series of harassing attacks. The whole idea was to disrupt Rommel's offensive, the preparations for which had already been spotted by British intelligence. Timpson was shifted to G1, and the patrol was given the mission of getting the Commandos north. But the effort ended in failure almost before it began. On the way up, German planes spotted and fell upon the Commando column. Practically all of the trucks were destroyed, and the whole force took heavy casualties. Timpson picked up the survivors and limped south to Siwa. This reinforced what the LRDG had learned during Rommel's first offensive of the previous year: that a small patrol might be able to operate in the northern desert close to the Germans, but a big column (in this case, twenty large trucks loaded down with Commandos and all their supplies) was a sitting duck. GHQ-ME immediately suspended plans for a similar effort.[70]

But the joint SAS-LRDG raids continued to turn in good results. Stirling had been told by Auchinleck's director of military operations (DMO) that a special convoy of ships would try to get through to Malta. But to reach that beleaguered island, now receiving a round-the-clock pounding from the Luftwaffe, the British ships would have to run through a veritable gauntlet, fighting off swarms of attacking aircraft the whole way. The DMO indicated to Stirling that any enemy planes his men could destroy on the ground would greatly enhance the convoy's chances of survival. Thus, leading the way north, Gurdon's G2 Patrol took SAS parties towards the airfields at Benina, just east of Benghazi, and to Berka, a few miles further down the coast. Stirling led one SAS element and Mayne the second. While this force approached its targets, a second LRDG patrol, New Zealand R1, now led by former agriculture student Captain A. I. Guild, led a raiding party to hit the enemy airfield at Derna, 140 miles to the east. Guild's passengers on this trip proved a suspicious, standoffish lot. They had good reason to be: they were German Jews who had volunteered for a new British unit called the Special Interrogation Group (SIG). Wearing German uniforms and posing as Afrika Korps soldiers, they were to carry out special operations behind the lines. Their mission bordered on the suicidal. If captured, even were they not shot as spies for wearing German uniforms, they would face instant execution the moment their captors learned their true identity.[71]

On the way up, Stirling's favorite vehicle, his fake German staff car, ran over a mine and had to be left behind. Mayne's party got into a skirmish with German infantry near Berka and had to retreat. But Stirling reached his target undiscovered and slipped out onto the Benina airfield. His men quietly placed their charges on German ME-110 fighters and JU-52 transport planes, as well as on the engines and partly assembled airframes that they found inside two large hangars. Just before the fuses were set to go off, Stirling, for the *coup de grace*, led his raiders up to what he took to be the pilots' quarters, located next to the field. Easing open the door, Stirling suddenly yelled "Here, catch!" and hurled a hand grenade at a Luftwaffe officer gaping up from behind a desk. The grenade seemed to explode at almost the same instant as all the charges on the planes out on the field. The SAS parties made it back without taking a single casualty; and while waiting to pick up Stirling, Gurdon's patrol had occupied its time placing mines all along a nearby stretch of rail line.[72]

But the German Jew SIG raid on Derna meanwhile turned into a disaster. Approaching the target in their vehicles (each marked with the Afrika Korps' special swastika-and-palm insignia), the SIG men changed into their German uniforms. Each man carried a P-38 pistol, a Mauser rifle, or a Schmeisser submachinegun. As dusk neared, the SIG trucks reached the Derna track and almost immediately ran into a German military police checkpoint.[73] But their disguises worked. The Feldgendarmerietrupp NCO-in-charge told them that an "Englisch Spähtrupp" (British patrol) had just been sighted in the area and ordered them into a local staging area's compound.[74] Arriving at the compound as directed, the SIG men mingled with the hodgepodge of Italian, Luftwaffe, and Afrika Korps personnel lining up at the field kitchen for the evening meal. Next morning, their true identity still undiscovered by the Germans, they fell in at the back of the convoy and eventually reached Derna. Exactly what it was that finally gave them away remains unclear, but at dusk of their second night a detachment of German infantry suddenly surrounded their vehicles and yelled for them to surrender. At this the Jews opened up with every weapon they had. The hopelessly one-sided firefight that followed killed most of them in just moments. Already badly wounded and about to be captured, one of the SIG men apparently chose death by his own hand, pulling the pin on a hand grenade and holding it to his body as it exploded. Another, also wounded and trying to drag himself away, was captured by the Germans and shot on the spot. Of the SIG party, only two men managed to break away and finally reach the rendezvous with the LRDG.[75]

While this was going on, Stirling, still hidden out in the desert south of Benina, had decided to have another crack at Benghazi. Stirred up like angry bees after his last raid, German planes had searched every inch of the desert; they nevertheless failed to spot Gurdon's hidden LRDG patrol and its SAS party sweating it out below. Waiting until dark and borrowing one of G2's trucks, Stirling took a handful of his men to the Via. They proceeded until they came to a Feldgendarmerietrupp roadblock. Hands tightened on hidden weapons as their truck eased to a stop and a German NCO came forward. It was completely dark, but Stirling and his men were wearing British uniforms. What saved them was quick thinking by one of the SIG men whom Stirling had happened to bring along for just such an occasion. Stirling's man was a Jew who had himself served as an NCO in the old German Reichswehr until Hitler's rise to power had forced his flight to Palestine. Doing some fast talking, the SIG man, using just the right mix of bluff and soldier's slang, managed to reassure the German guards; the truck got safely through the roadblock. The party hurried on in the darkness towards Benghazi. But by the time they reached a second roadblock—this one manned by a squad of Italian Polizia Militare—the enemy had gotten wise. Both sides opened up on each other. Stirling got away again, but it was obvious that he would never make it into Benghazi now that the enemy was looking for him. Instead, he had to console himself with targets located outside the town. Within twenty minutes he and his men had located and blown up a fuel point's storage tanks and pumping equipment, as well as a motor vehicle park full of medium trucks and some large, Daimler-Benz Sd Kfz-8 half-tracks. Racing away, they were jumped by Kfz-222 armored cars. But with tracers flying, they finally managed to outrun their pursuers. Just at the point when it looked as though they would make it back to Gurdon's patrol un-scathed, the fuse to one of the sticky bombs was accidentally ignited. The whole party leaped over the side seconds before the bomb went off, com-pletely destroying G2 Patrol's loaned-out truck.[76]

Aside from the enemy vehicles Stirling's men had managed to destroy on this last effort, the raid on Benina had brought the total score of SAS-destroyed enemy planes up to 143. Starting with the raids from Jalo, in just seven months' time the LRDG and the SAS—two separate and independent units, both commanded by officers who differed markedly in personality and style of leadership—had managed to achieve a remarkable level of cooper-ation. Acting together, they had inflicted losses on the enemy to the degree that Panzerarmee Afrika had been forced to divert aircraft, troops, and ar-mored cars away from the main front.[77] Time—and the expansion of the SAS—would test how well the LRDG-SAS "raiding partnership" would fare in the more difficult operations that lay ahead.

CHAPTER 7

A Daring Gamble That Failed: The Raids on Tobruk, Benghazi, Jalo, and Barce

[The concept of disrupting] the enemy's lines of communication by raiding...had been under consideration ever since the withdrawal from Cyrenaica.

—Major General I. S. O. Playfair et al.,
The Mediterranean and Middle East, vol.4[1]

British intelligence had continued to pick up signs that Rommel was preparing to mount a new attack. Fully alerted to Panzerarmee Afrika's preparations, Ritchie had carefully arrayed the Eighth Army in a series of heavily fortified defensive positions. Protected by mines, barbed wire, trenches, pillboxes, and artillery, these formed a sort of rough triangle stretching across the desert and blocking Rommel's path. The individual strongpoints, called "boxes," had been given special names such as "Knightsbridge," "Commonwealth Keep," and so forth. It seemed impossible to believe that Rommel, even for a moment, could seriously contemplate trying to batter his way through these sprawling desert hedgehogs and the vast array of firepower concentrated in them.[2]

That was precisely the reason why he had already determined to slip around the British flank. Rather than trying to penetrate the boxes frontally, he would, instead, skirt past them and so be able to hit at them from behind. His attack began in late May 1942, and in the north. Having sent tanks and infantry forward in a quickly delivered feint, Rommel suddenly swung south towards his real objective: the lower or desert end of the British line. Surging around and past that line's southernmost box at Bir Hacheim, Rommel's tanks, armored cars, artillery, and trucks then quickly wheeled north. The British armor mounted fierce counterattacks, but the series of battles that raged in the area known as "the Cauldron" failed to stop Rommel. He managed to crack open one of the boxes and then turned to deal with Bir Hacheim, whose hard-fighting Free French defenders were able to slow down his drive on Tobruk. By mid-June, however, Rommel had taken every position in the Gazala Line, and the Eighth Army was once again in retreat towards Egypt. Tobruk—the prize denied him the year before—finally fell to Rommel nearly a month after his new offensive had commenced.[3]

For Churchill, Tobruk's loss was one of the "worst defeats" of the war.[4] The bitter news caught him at a particularly awkward moment; he was then in Washington, conferring with President Roosevelt on Allied war strategy, and the loss was hardly a testimonial to British arms. To Churchill, Tobruk's fall was "one of the heaviest blows . . . [of] the war."[5] It would force him, on his return home, to beat back a vote of censure in the House of Commons; and he had again to explain why Rommel once more stood poised at the gates of Egypt. For the British in the desert, this last of May and first three weeks of June 1942 amounted to perhaps their worst defeat of the campaign and by far its gravest crisis. Sustained by the wealth of fuel, supplies, and equipment that he had taken at Tobruk, Rommel appeared able at any moment to begin his final, victorious drive on Cairo. Everything—Egypt's capital, the British Mediterranean Fleet's base at Alexandria, the Suez Canal, perhaps even the distant oil fields of the Persian Gulf—seemed almost to be within his grasp. The fleet pulled out of Alexandria for the safety of the open sea. And in Cairo, on a day known as "Ash Wednesday," GHQ-ME began frantically to burn its secret papers before they fell into Rommel's hands.[6]

Auchinleck's response in late June was to relieve Ritchie, who had earlier done well against Rommel, and to take command of the Eighth Army himself. Three months before, Auchinleck had warned his senior commanders that "there is a real danger that . . . Rommel will turn into a kind of magician or bogeyman for our troops just because they talk so much about him."[7] Now, with the "magician" already inside Egypt and installed at Mersa Matrûh, Auchinleck's only option was to fall back and try to make a stand at some strong position where Rommel could not employ his tactical genius to slip past the British again.

The place he chose, El Alamein, was only sixty miles west of Alexandria. The advantage of El Alamein—some buildings clustered around a small desert railway station—was that the flat ground of the Libyan plateau here narrowed to a gap only thirty-five miles wide. With their right flank anchored on the Mediterranean and the impassable Qattara Depression to their left, the British could now dig in and defend on a narrow front. This meant that Rommel, on the other hand, was denied scope for the kind of outflanking moves which had succeeded so well at Gazala.[8]

Prendergast soon received orders to move the LRDG north to this new position. He and Stirling reported to Eighth Army headquarters, a complex of bunkers and sandbagged tents situated on the Alexandria road just behind El Alamein.[9] Auchinleck's chief of staff spelled out the gravity of the situation, indicating that the Germans were expected to mount an attack at any moment. Indeed, intelligence had learned that Mussolini and a full contingent of his officials, certain of victory, had already arrived in Libya in order to plan their triumphant entry into Cairo. Hitler himself, to spur on Rommel, had just promoted the Desert Fox to the rank of field marshal. The signal which Auchinleck sent out to every unit was short and to the point: "The enemy . . . thinks we are a broken army. . . . [He] hopes to take Egypt by bluff. Show him where he gets off."[10]

The first group of LRDG and SAS raiders began slipping west through the gap north of the Qattara Depression at about the same time that Rommel's lead tanks were sighted advancing to the east. Gurdon's G2 guided Stirling's men, for the first time riding in newly acquired American-built jeeps (among the very first of these four-wheel-drive vehicles to arrive in the Middle East). Each jeep was fitted with twin-mounted machineguns; the acquisition of these excellent vehicles meant that the SAS for the first time was in possession of its own form of transportation. The overall plan was for the Stirling-G2 Patrol element to link up with two LRDG patrols already being moved up from Kufra. Although all three of these elements had to dodge prowling Stukas and ME-110s, they nonetheless finally arrived at the designated point. A base camp was set up, complete with sufficient fuel, mines, and demolition charges and ammunition to give the Germans trouble over an extended period of time. The patrols then split up, Timpson's G1 taking one SAS party, Hunter's Y2 another, and Gurdon's G2 remaining with Stirling. The raiding operations that would follow were to be coordinated with Group Headquarters and the Eighth Army via Gurdon's radio.[11] After a week of staying near El Alamein, Prendergast took his remaining patrols and shifted down to Faiyum Oasis, a place which offered "a far more convenient back door" to Rommel's rear areas.[12]

Gurdon soon dropped off Stirling for a whole series of raids, and he himself shot up Afrika Korps vehicle parks and staging areas. But the intensive pace of this new program of attacks soon had its predictable effect: enemy planes began swarming after the raiders, as one LRDG officer remembered it, "like hornets from a mutilated nest."[13] And for Gurdon—Lieutenant the Honourable Robert Brampton Gurdon, eldest son of the second Baron Cransworth—luck finally ran out. His patrol tried to run south after a raid, but was caught in the open by Italian fighters. Both Gurdon and his driver were hit in the first pass, but managed to jump clear just before their flaming truck blew up. Yet Gurdon, who had been hit three times, was already done for. Although he lived long enough to get his patrol to safety, he could not survive the loss of blood. The next day his men buried him in the desert.[14] Despite the hazardous nature of the raiding operations, he was actually the first officer of the LRDG to be killed in action. He was a quiet, efficient

38-year-old who could have had a safe staff job any time he had wanted it. His death particularly affected Stirling, because Gurdon had worked with Stirling more extensively than any other LRDG patrol commander, and his abilities had very early impressed the SAS leader. Indeed, just before leaving for this last expedition, Gurdon had finally agreed to accept Stirling's offer to join his organization. Had he lived, he would have served as second-in-command of L Detachment, SAS.[15]

Meanwhile, Stirling's men were having trouble with their sticky bombs. One whole batch of fuse primers proved defective: of the forty some charges placed on enemy aircraft during one night's raid, for example, fully half failed to go off. Stirling was by now running low on explosives anyway; he therefore improvised an alternative method for destroying enemy planes. While this new method seemed almost suicidal, it worked well enough the first time it was tried. Waiting for a moonless night, Stirling led a double column of his new jeeps to the edge of an enemy airfield. He then deployed in the follow-the-leader formation called for by his new method and charged forward. The two columns of jeeps (each vehicle mounting a pair of .303 Vickers machineguns) rampaged through the parked aircraft and shot up everything. The tracers stitched into the gas tanks, blowing up about twenty planes. Although Italian fighters and a Ghibli bomber paid him back just after dawn by destroying three of his vehicles, Stirling got back to the LRDG rendezvous with no major casualties.[16] T2, now commanded by Captain N. P. Wilder, was sent to join Stirling after Gurdon's death. The Patrol was exercised in this same "jeep raid" formation and soon hit a second enemy field. Again, the new technique worked perfectly. Shooting their way through the perimeter defenses, the New Zealanders at midnight raced onto the airfield. Their machineguns destroyed fifteen ME-109Fs, a new version of that fighter only recently arrived in North Africa. But the Germans came after them in hot pursuit. At dawn, running for some low hills, Wilder spotted Afrika Korps motorized infantry advancing after him. The force was directed by a Fiesler Storch, but well-aimed shots from T2's antitank guns soon managed to knock out several of the German trucks. When the Fiesler—until now circling at a safe distance—chose to land, Wilder decided to strike back. While the rest of T2 fired furiously, he sent one of his trucks circling around. The Fiesler was by now parked on a flat stretch of desert and out of sight of the German infantry. The LRDG men raced up and captured the Luftwaffe lieutenant who was the Fiesler's pilot, and a German Army doctor. The plane was then blown up, and the patrol broke away to the south. The significance of this scrap was that it marked the first time an LRDG patrol had actually tangled with a veteran Afrika Korps unit in anything approaching a pitched battle. The New Zealanders, miraculously unwounded and quite pleased with their performance, had no doubts as to which side had gotten the best of the fight.[17]

Wilder rejoined Stirling and together they totaled up their score. Since the commencement of this current series of raids and counting the efforts since December 1941, Stirling estimated that he had destroyed nearly 200 enemy aircraft. The most recent accomplishment of what GHQ-ME called the LRDG's "incidental nuisance effort" was the demolition, by Timpson's G1 Patrol, of the single desert pipeline that supplied water to the German force at Mersa Matrûh.[18] Such efforts in themselves could not, of course, halt Rommel's advance, but they certainly did not help his progress either. Striking towards El Alamein, moreover, Rommel was soon defeated and stopped by Auchinleck. Commencing the first day of July 1942, Panzerarmee Afrika had mounted a series of furious attacks on the British positions forward of El Alamein. But aided by intensive attacks by the RAF and shored up by Auchinleck's "cool nerve and big man's calm," the Eighth Army had held in what came to be called "First Alamein," to distinguish it from the even fiercer battle to be fought there in October.[19] Auchinleck had won his battle, perhaps the most crucial of the desert war. In Churchill's phrase, he had "stemmed the adverse tide," and, as the Germans spent themselves, the British began preparations to shift over to the offensive once again.[20]

The commanding officers of both the LRDG and the SAS, but especially Stirling, given the support he had received from Auchinleck's own hand at crucial times, were thus stunned at the news that soon came out of Cairo: Auchinleck had been relieved as C-in-C Middle East. Although he had been successful in defending Egypt at the eleventh hour, First Alamein turned out to be his last battle in the desert. Early in August, he was, like Wavell before him, permitted to resign. The dismissal may have been sudden, but the reasons behind it had long been building. For two years the Prime Minister had grown increasingly frustrated with Middle East Command's "inexplicable inertia," botched battles, and long string of defeats.[21] On many occasions, just when victory seemed almost at hand despite costly losses in men and equipment, the Eighth Army had frustrated Churchill again and again by its failure to best Rommel. In the last six months in particular, and most acutely during the long retreat across Libya, Auchinleck's standing with the Prime Minister—and with the British public—had fallen. He was blamed for the shortcomings of the generals he had placed in key positions under him. These, instead of winning with the first-class material they had been provided, had consistently failed to overcome Rommel's more modest numbers and resources. At length Churchill had chosen to visit Egypt in order to judge things for himself. Accompanied by the chief of the Imperial General Staff, General Sir Alan Brooke, he had reached Egypt upon his return from Moscow and talks with Stalin and had immediately launched into a whirlwind tour of Eighth Army units. Churchill found, in his own words, "a vast but baffled and somewhat unhinged organization."[22] His conclusion was that a "drastic and immediate change should be made to impart a new and vigorous impulse . . . and . . . restore confidence in the High Command."[23] A "clean sweep" was needed, and Auchinleck had to go.[24] The requisite "new and vigorous impulse" was to come from the new team of commanders soon chosen to replace him. Designated to take over as C-in-C Middle East was General Sir Harold Alexander. The officer chosen to work directly under him, in the capacity of commander of the Eighth Army, was Lieutenant General Bernard Law Montgomery. Churchill sent the deposed Auchinleck to take over—again—from Wavell, this time as C-in-C India.[25]

Churchill's two new commanders were products of Sandhurst and of two of Britain's distinguished "public" schools—Alexander of Harrow, Churchill's old school, and Montgomery of St. Paul's.[26] Both had built up excellent reputations in the army; each differed vastly from the other in personality and method. Alexander, Irish Catholic and Irish Guards, was a son of the Earl of Caledon. Patrician, charming, urbane, and independently wealthy, he embodied many features of the British Army's "cavalier" tradition. In World War I, with the senior officers all dead, he had commanded a battalion at age 24 and had handled himself superbly. One war later, even as the Germans closed in on Dunkirk, he had insisted on dining at a table laid out with linen and silver, for the express purpose of letting his beleaguered troops see their unruffled general carrying on as usual. But if Alexander—and the sort of deftness he had shown in political mires in the Baltic and in Turkey after World War I—represented one style of command, his new subordinate, Montgomery, suggested something of the British Army's other great tradition, that of the stern, hard-fighting Puritans under Cromwell. Like that great commander, he was a no-nonsense practical soldier, a stickler for hard training and well-toughened troops. Montgomery, who neither smoked nor drank, was as self-confidently arrogant as Patton or MacArthur, and delighted in cultivating a reputation for "Bolshie" approaches to matters of military convention. This was the new command team with which Churchill hoped at last to win in North Africa. The prime minister's order was classically simple and direct: Alexander was to "take and destroy at the earliest opportunity the German-Italian Army commanded by Field Marshal Rommel."[27] And Alexander's order to Montgomery was in turn even more classically simple and direct: the General Officer Commanding Eighth Army was to go out to the desert and "defeat Rommel."[28]

Immediately Montgomery began his preparations for the great battle ultimately to be fought at El Alamein. The veterans of the Eighth Army, the men who had "borne the burden and heat of the disasters . . . and the hard slogging" of the previous summer's fighting, had seen generals come and go.[29] But despite their skepticism, Montgomery soon began to impart a new confidence, and his army gradually felt itself "braced and invigorated" by this cocky new general who employed his considerable flair for publicity to maximum effect. He was also aided by the arrival of more than 40,000 fresh troops, some 800 guns, and nearly 400 new American-built Sherman tanks. Even as Montgomery readied his plans, the Eighth Army was acquiring over Panzerarmee Afrika a nearly two-to-one advantage in tanks.[30]

In the midst of these great preparations, neither Alexander nor Montgomery could give much time to considering how best to employ the special forces they had inherited. Yet major decisions about these forces were soon required. The driving reason was that several elements in or associated with GHQ-ME's planning and intelligence levels were now trying to dismantle David Stirling's L Detachment, SAS, as a separate, independent command. They were inclined to want the SAS continued in its present raiding activities, but only as a carefully controlled element incorporated within some other unit.[31]

Stirling had just lost his benefactor, Auchinleck, and as yet had no entree with any of the new men. The question arose at this particular time principally because of the expanding operations of the super-secret Special Operations Executive (SOE). This British sabotage unit had been formed by Churchill in 1940 as an instrument for fostering resistance movements within the occupied countries. Its purpose, in Churchill's view, was to make "stabbing attacks... between the chinks of the enemy's military and economic armour"—in short, sabotage.[32] The SOE had served as one of the models for General William J. (Wild Bill) Donovan's United States Office of Strategic Services, created two years later. The SOE's Cairo-based cell had begun its operations in 1941 and had achieved considerable success, but nothing as immediately useful to British military fortunes as Stirling's raids on the enemy airfields.[33] It was now argued, however, that since both the SAS and the SOE existed primarily for sabotage, and since the SOE could claim a higher priority for arms and equipment, perhaps a greater efficiency could be achieved by merging the two. Stirling was approached on the issue of merger by officers of both SOE and GHQ-ME. Still another group of officers argued that the *de facto* relationship between the SAS and the LRDG should be formalized—that is, Stirling's force ought formally to be amalgamated with the LRDG as a sort of striking force, the whole to be commanded by Prendergast.[34]

By this time Stirling was already being characterized on Axis radio broadcasts as the British "Phantom Major" who had caused much trouble but who would be dealt with soon. Although the British did not know it, his exploits had also been given the further accolade of mention in Rommel's personal diary: to the Desert Fox he was "Colonel Stirling," leader of "the Commandos," who caused "considerable havoc and seriously disquieted the Italians."[35] But Stirling's unconventional style of command and free-and-easy organizational methods had also earned him enemies on his own side. When he was not actually on a raid, his home base in Cairo tended to be an apartment belonging to his Foreign Office brother and located in one of that city's poshest neighborhoods. Stories got out about the "tremendous parties" held there, and about Stirling's breezy attitude about security.[36] Regularly, just before an operation, it was said, SAS jeeps, bulging with weapons and equipment and obviously about to push off on some important task, could be found lined up outside. A spy need only watch for their departure and then radio out warning of an impending raid. Inside the house all kinds of sensitive military matters were discussed freely, and supposedly in front of the various nurses and other female guests invited to the place. Moreover, Stirling's servant, "a particularly fat Egyptian," from time to time took part in official business.[37] He might, for example, have to remind Stirling that "the Most Secret papers he had been looking for were under the pillow on the sofa."[38] Or perhaps he would say that GHQ-ME had just telephoned wanting to know some particular detail of the next operation, and Stirling would tell him, and it would be the servant who actually communicated this presumably highly sensitive information back to the staff. Stirling himself was absolutely convinced of the servant's trustworthiness; others, however, were not so sure.

These and other doings of Stirling's tended at once to horrify but also to fascinate the LRDG. Certainly that unit had seen Stirling in action enough to know that he was a "truly remarkable type."[39] "[Y]oung, tall, good-looking and dashing,"[40] the SAS commander had what England's poet laureate John Masefield once described as "a humorous, daredevil cock of the eye. . . . [A]ny officer having it can carry a crew into hell and back."[41] The LRDG's Prendergast was nothing like that, and probably would not have wanted to be even if he had had the choice. The phlegmatic Prendergast struck many who served with him as "slightly aloof, a cool operator with a very, very clear planning brain."[42] Stirling, especially with the "Phantom Major" billing the Germans were now giving him, was already emerging as "the romantic figure of the war in the Middle East."[43] He was not quite "another Lawrence," but his whole approach to raiding was typified by the same "light heart and cool courage." Where others plodded, "he pranced."[44]

It was precisely these "prancing" qualities which now, in the late summer of 1942, once again stood Stirling in good stead. By his audacity he had formed his L Detachment, SAS, in the first place, and by it also his unit had destroyed hundreds of enemy planes (nearly 250 by this point). Not even the most aggressive RAF fighter squadron in the Middle East could boast such a score. (Indeed, a staff officer once suggested, half seriously, that Stirling be put in for the Distinguished Flying Cross. Of course, the suggestion was flatly rejected by the RAF: as a soldier, not an airman, Stirling could not qualify for such a decoration.[45]) But if great audacity was one of his traits, Stirling soon got a chance to try his second, a special touch with the powerful. He had, early in August, already prepared and sent directly to the prime minister himself a "Most Secret" message outlining certain proposals for the employment of special forces.[46] When Churchill and his official entourage stopped in Egypt on their way back from meetings in Moscow with Stalin, Stirling at last got the chance to meet the prime minister in person. Stirling's older brother, a career Foreign Office official, working directly under the British ambassador, managed to wangle two extra invitations to the reception held in Churchill's honor. These went to Stirling and to his fellow SAS officer, Captain Fitzroy Maclean, MP. Nor could it have hurt that Churchill's own son, Randolph, had been on the SAS raid against Benghazi.[47] A luck-and-pluck endeavor of that sort was just what the prime minister—still something of a military romantic in this age of machine weapons, mass armies, and general staffs—admired above all other operations of war. Stirling proved an instant hit with him. Not only did the prime minister pronounce himself "delighted" with Stirling's account of the Benghazi raid, but he was heard, by the end of the evening, using a quotation from Byron's *Don Juan* to describe the SAS leader: Stirling was "the mildest mannered man that ever scuttled ship or cut a throat."[48] Stirling was invited back for a second evening with the prime minister. He told Churchill that his organization had from its inception "lived in constant fear of being disbanded."[49] The result of all this was that the prime minister sent Alexander a memorandum to the effect that the SAS not be put under the SOE or merged with the LRDG.[50] Instead, Stirling's organization was to be given even more jeeps and allowed to recruit additional men.

But this expansion carried with it important implications for the LRDG-SAS "raiding partnership." That partnership had, so far, worked well. The SAS's dependency upon the LRDG for transportation and navigation across the desert had been enough to impose a high degree of unity on the raiding and other types of special operations simply because it had tended to link the actions of the two units. Given this situation, Prendergast had been able to exert a considerable degree of control over every effort undertaken in this joint fashion. To the SAS might go the greater glory of conducting the bulk of the highly destructive raids on the airfields, but the LRDG called the shots. It enjoyed the status of being the controlling element, the early success story, and "the senior partner in raiding."[51] But all this now began to change. With Churchill's (and, therefore, Alexander's) backing, Stirling began to acquire more jeeps—in fact, sufficient numbers of them to move his entire command. Gone was the old dependency upon the LRDG for transportation. So also was Stirling's reliance on the LRDG for navigation. With his new backing, he was able to recruit one of the LRDG's best navigators, Corporal W. Michael Sadler, who was given a lieutenant's commission when he joined the SAS. This step meant that Sadler would navigate Stirling's future raids and that he also would train SAS personnel in those same desert-navigation techniques he had learned in the LRDG. The near-simultaneous acquisition of his own vehicles and his own navigational capability freed Stirling from relying on the LRDG at all. These steps, and the acquisition of a radio-communications capability, at once transformed the SAS into something greater than it had been before, and may indeed have been precisely what Stirling had wanted to achieve all along. It was true that his "Most Secret" message to the prime minister had proposed that various "other Special Service Units be disbanded and selected personnel absorbed, as required by

'L' Detachment."[52] This would have made possible "Unified Control" and "the allocation to L Detachment of the roles undertaken by Special Service Units."[53] No such drastic step had been brought about. But without doubt the expansion of the SAS in late summer 1942 fundamentally altered the old relationship between the two desert special forces. Whereas the LRDG had before been *de facto* the controlling element, it now had to contend with a co-equal unit, and one that in some ways soon became a rival. In the months ahead the SAS would emerge as the Eighth Army's primary unit for desert raiding, a separate striking arm and sometimes virtually a law unto itself. That this development would come at the expense of the previously unified control of raiding operations was not apparent at the time or else could not be countered, given Stirling's high-level backing.[54]

Prendergast was well aware of this changed relationship. He understood the need for his own unit to keep itself useful, and had already suggested to his officers that it might be "time for LRDG to go off and mount some big raids of our own."[55] That unit had meanwhile been continuing with its old job of ferrying out supplies to the agents hidden among the foothills of the Jebel. But it had also been given an additional task, important but unrewarding, to perform: training Eighth Army units in the techniques of desert driving and navigation. This task underscored the fact that a useful function sometimes performed by special forces in World War II was that of serving as laboratories for developing various specialized techniques, tactics, or methods that might later be adopted for use by the army as a whole. The LRDG had already, for example, received credit in a GHQ-ME general order for having developed the "Sand Channels, . . . Sun Compasses and Land Navigation [techniques]" as well as other "principles or methods . . . generally adopted as standard" by the British forces operating in the desert.[56] The general benefits of such training notwithstanding, the provision of special courses for Eighth Army armored units or for Stirling's rivals from SOE required time and personnel. Also, additional time had to be spent in training an Indian Army contingent (British-officered) which eventually joined the LRDG as the "Indian Long Range Squadron."

These training activities took up much of August. Given what was coming next, both the LRDG and the SAS, currently reorganizing, tended later to think of this time as the "August calm" and "prelude to a rather wilder September" than the two units would have preferred.[57] For the situation had changed. Rommel, attempting to break through at Alam Halfa, had recently walked into a British trap made possible by the deliberately false "little fellers" and the disinformation radioed out in the *Rebecca* code captured from Almaszy's two Condor spies. These messages had reportedly caused the unwitting Desert Fox to slap "his thighs with joy," declaring that "our spy in Cairo is the greatest hero of them all," and he had supposedly even requested OKW to award Condor the Iron Cross.[58] Led to expect only light resistance at Alam Halfa, he ran instead into the Eighth Army's well-prepared troops and massed tanks. Rommel lost nearly fifty tanks and a great quantity of motor transport, whereas Montgomery won his first desert battle.[59]

Bolstered by this success and receiving reinforcements all the time, that general anticipated mounting his big offensive sometime in September. In order to give this offensive every chance of success, the planners in Cairo began putting the finishing touches on schemes that would send raids against and cut Rommel's lengthy supply line at several key locations. These schemes would eventually employ virtually the whole array of British special forces available in the Middle East theater, and when finally put in motion, they would result in one of the biggest special forces disasters of the war.[60]

The initial inspiration for a major raiding effort in September 1942 seems to have come from Lieutenant Colonel John E. Haselden. Since his part in Keyes' ill-fated effort against Rommel's headquarters the year before, Haselden had served as the "Western Desert Liaison Officer." As WDLO, he was responsible for coordinating the various agents, British and Arab, who were sent to gather intelligence or carry out sabotage in the Jebel. But he had also had time to work out several plans for major raiding endeavors. One such plan, concerning a strike against "the enemy's lines of communication . . . [and the] shipping, harbour facilities, and fuel storage at Tobruk," was given serious consideration from about the time of "the withdrawal from Cyrenaica on."[61] Tobruk, with its excellent harbor and fuel tanks serving as the advanced base for Panzerarmee Afrika, did indeed present a choice target. A sudden strike there, delivered with the advantage of surprise, might well serve to cripple or at least hamper Rommel at the critical moment when Montgomery mounted his attack. If the harbor installations at Tobruk, and perhaps those at Benghazi as well, could be destroyed, Rommel would be forced "to use the port of Tripoli, about 1000 miles further West."[62] Moreover, the enemy garrisons at both locations were believed to be small and composed of "low category" troops.[63]

Haselden's original plan for Tobruk was relatively simple and called for a small party of Commandos to penetrate the defenses and plant explosive charges. Unfortunately, however, the plan did not long remain in this simple and uncomplicated version.[64] One of Haselden's agents, the Belgian-born Captain Vladimir Peniakoff—or "Popski" as he was known to the LRDG patrol that had just fetched him back from the Jebel—professed later to be astounded at what he had heard after returning to Cairo. And Peniakoff was hardly a stranger to risky ventures. Born of Russian *emigré* parents, he had served in the French Army in World War I and had thereafter come to Egypt, eventually achieving prosperity as a cotton factor and manager of a sugar-refining concern. A first-class intelligence agent, he had, in the last five months, dodged German and Italian patrols and had been in and out of a dozen tight spots in the Jebel. His first actual knowledge of the Tobruk plan came when he was taken into a part of GHQ-ME occupied by a section newly set up to coordinate all operations behind enemy lines.[65] It was there that his old friend Haselden began going over the preparations for hitting Tobruk.

The raid itself, Haselden explained, was set for the second week of September. At that time a force of eighty men—all posing as POWs but in reality British Commandos whose weapons would be hidden just out of view—would use this disguise to drive right into Tobruk itself. To deceive the enemy, they would ride in Afrika Korps trucks, each vehicle ostensibly driven and guarded by German troops. These guards would not be German soldiers, but a party of the SIG's German Jews dressed up as Afrika Korps soldiers. An LRDG patrol would guide the Commando-SIG force to a point near Tobruk, but would break off just short of the main desert road. Once inside the perimeter, the Commandos would quickly proceed to the harbor itself and knock out the enemy's coastal batteries. This step would clear the way for the next phase of the operation, the landing from two British destroyers and a score of PT boats and high-speed motor launches of nearly a thousand British Army and Royal Marine Commandos and assault engineers. This force, aided by surprise and with its movements carefully timed, would then push forward to blow up the fuel tanks, pumps, and other facilities in the harbor. While these operations were commencing, RAF bombing attacks would be carefully coordinated to focus attention away from the raiders. Haselden himself would go into Tobruk and command Force B, the Commando-SIG force that was to move up through the desert.[66]

Peniakoff's reaction to what Haselden described is apparent from the account that he published after the war: he had, he wrote later, promptly decided to stay clear of Haselden and his raid altogether.[67] But Peniakoff had also learned that Tobruk was not to be the only target hit at this time; there were to be three others as well. One was to be a raid mounted against Benghazi and led by David Stirling. For this effort, Stirling would be given a 220-man contingent designated Force X, which would comprise his full L Detachment, SAS, two LRDG patrols, and two light tanks furnished by the 10th Hussars. In all, Stirling's column would amount to forty vehicles of all types, and seemed an almost incredibly large force to try to slip so deeply into enemy territory.[68] The Benghazi raid's purpose was twofold. Aided by surprise, Stirling was first of all to get past the perimeter defenses and then attack any shipping that he found in the harbor. Thereafter, his Force X was to free the 16,000 or so British soldiers reportedly held in Benghazi's large POW compound. Once sprung, these POWs would be armed with captured weapons and themselves become part of the raiding force. So armed, they were to hold out long enough for a landing force, brought in by the Navy, to arrive and rescue them.[69] Its mission completed, the SAS would then fade back into the desert.

To throw off the enemy just before the Tobruk and Benghazi operations went into motion, the RAF would drop hundreds of dummy paratroopers (a trick used two years later in the D-Day invasion of Europe) on Siwa Oasis.

The LRDG would further help to throw off the enemy by staging or participating in two other raids mounted against targets well away from Tobruk and Benghazi. Guided by LRDG patrols, an entity designated Force Z—a motorized battalion of the Sudan Defence Force—would move against the old LRDG base at Jalo. The acquisition of that oasis would provide a forward base from which Stirling's SAS could later mount raids on enemy airfields, particularly as the anticipated British offensive began fighting its way west. Timed to mesh with the other three efforts, those against Tobruk, Benghazi, and Jalo, the final move planned was a raid on the enemy airfield at Barce, and would be exclusively an LRDG undertaking. Yet getting at Barce was difficult in the extreme. Once they had left the protection of the Sand Seas, the LRDG units would have to penetrate 200 miles of open desert and thick enemy patrols before reaching the safety of the Jebel's scrub-covered hills and narrow wadis. Once they were on the far side of the Jebel's hills, should something go wrong—an attack by enemy aircraft, for example—the LRDG patrols would find themselves a very long way indeed from the safety of the inner desert.[70]

These, then, were the four raids planned for September 1942. The Tobruk raid was the centerpiece and key to the whole enterprise. A "daring gamble," the thing had, in military parlance, grown out of "the contemplation of a classic type of interdiction role."[71] If Tobruk and the other raids worked, then Rommel's rear would be hit almost simultaneously at four different and widely separated points. If Peniakoff's views are of any merit—and he was proved correct by the debacle that finally resulted—he believed from the start that the whole concept was too complex to be workable. Moreover, the whole process of planning seemed from the outset to have been handled in a recklessly light-hearted manner.[72] Far from lacking in amateurish enthusiasm, staff "officers had manufactured all these schemes in order to beat Rommel on the cheap,"[73] and some of their information was incorrect. Regarding the Benghazi raid, for example, Peniakoff pointed out that there were no POW cages actually in Benghazi—all the camps were farther to the south. Regarding the undertaking of so complex and risky a set of operations in the first place, Peniakoff's bitter pronouncement was that his old friend John Haselden was "my age and should have known better."[74]

Nor was desert-agent Popski the only one who felt strong misgivings about the concept of the raids. The two special-force commanders, Prendergast and Stirling, were alike in their skepticism. The raids on Tobruk, Benghazi, Jalo, and Barce would commit seven of Prendergast's ten patrols, and all but two of these would be functioning under someone else's control during all or part of the operation. It was also argued that the involvement of so many different elements—the Royal Navy, the RAF (and now, joining in to support the RAF, recently arrived United States Army Air Forces bombers), Commandos, SIG, the SAS, and the Sudan Defence Force—would result in "a great many people tripping over each other's feet behind enemy lines."[75]

The sheer size and ambitious scope of the raids seemed to violate the idea, long-standing at GHQ-ME, that only the LRDG and the SAS "really had a right to operate that far out in the desert" on deep-penetration ventures of this sort.[76] Stirling's complaint was that the four-part, desert-wide operation would require the SAS elements to abide by a set timetable that was dangerously inflexible. This would deprive him of the kind of tactical discretion and on-the-spot control that all previous raids had shown to be essential. He said later that "the whole plan [had] sinned against every principle on which the SAS was founded."[77]

Sharing the uneasiness that Stirling and Prendergast felt about what might happen in the second week of September was the Eighth Army's commander, General Montgomery. Montgomery agreed with the senior RAF officer in the Middle East, whose view was that "the impossibility of providing fighter cover" for raids so deep behind enemy lines made the operations a poor risk at best.[78] But by the time Montgomery had arrived to take over the Eighth Army in August, the planning for the raids was already well along. He had "had no part in the making of the plans," and felt that he could not get them changed at this point, especially since many of the forces involved did not actually belong to the Eighth Army. But he made no effort to hide the fact that he "disliked the whole operation."[79] He made it clear that, in future, "any special operations taking place anywhere near Eighth Army's sector would have to come under his [Montgomery's] direct control."[80] In the end, the decision was made that the raids would go forward as planned.

To watch over them, a special combined staff was set up in Alexandria. This staff consisted of the C-in-C Mediterranean (a Royal Navy admiral), the AOC, or Air-Officer Commanding (an RAF air vice-marshal), and, from Alexander's staff, his director of military operations, Brigadier George M. O. Davy. An experienced armor officer, Davy was already troubled by the old military adage about "not being able to fight a battle by committee."[81] There seemed to be little in the way of centralized direction, and there was lacking as well "a clearcut line of authority for controlling all the various chess pieces" involved in the raids.[82] In reality, several plans—Stirling's old idea for a strike on Benghazi, the Royal Navy's hopes for a quick amphibious raid, and Haselden's original plan for a surprise blow against Tobruk—had merely been grafted onto each other and worked into a grand scheme. It was clear to Davy also that previous successes with desert special operations had acted to create a climate favorable to experimentation on this "very large and unprecedented scale."[83]

By the end of the first week of September, the forces selected to participate in the raids were ready. Guiding Haselden and his Commandos (all from D Squadron, 1st Special Service Regiment) would be Y1 Patrol, commanded by Captain David Lloyd Owen. With maps spread out before them, Haselden and Lloyd Owen went over every step of the operation: how Y1 would lead Force B north from Kufra, how they, together, would slip past the enemy patrols, approach Tobruk, and so forth.[84] The men themselves were not told of their destination until Force B had actually reached the assembly point at Kufra, although it was already clear from "rumours and the presence of the SIG German Jews that something big was on."[85] When Haselden finally let them in on their mission, the news was greeted with a low buzz of "exclamation and comment."[86] The briefing concluded, the Commando trucks were painted over with Afrika Korps markings and the various stages of the attack were rehearsed again and again. The whole force, Y1 leading, pushed off two days later.

Stirling's Force X followed not long thereafter. He had, for better control and safety in case of air attack, arrayed his force in a three-part column. When everthing was ready, Stirling, led by an LRDG patrol, moved out of the oasis and began heading north across the desert. With these two units now out of Kufra and proceeding according to schedule, the other LRDG patrols made ready for their attacks. Hunter's Y2 and R2's New Zealanders, under Captain John R. Talbot, soon linked up with the Sudan Defence Force and went over the steps for the raid on Jalo. With by far the shortest route to travel, this element, Force Z, would be the last to push off. But the Barce force, with over 650 miles of desert to cross, had already commenced the long and dangerous approach towards its objective. A full squadron of LRDG patrols—Timpson's G1, Wilder's T2, and Olivey's S2—had been gathered together and sent off under Jake Easonsmith, now a major and Mitford's replacement as squadron commander. Helping to guide the patrols would be Peniakoff and two Arab agents. Captain Richard Lawson, the LRDG's highly popular and well-respected medical officer, had at his own request been given permission to accompany the raid.[87]

Even as these four groups departed for their targets, however, the whole reason for making the raids in the first place had disappeared. The original purpose had been to hit Rommel's rear just as the Eighth Army launched its major offensive. But that offensive had recently been postponed. Despite his victory at Alam Halfa, Montgomery had concluded that the Eighth Army needed additional time in order to prepare a truly decisive, full-scale push against Rommel. Both Alexander and Montgomery were in agreement that "our preparations could not be completed in time for a September offensive"; it would be "madness to attack in September."[88] The Eighth Army's major thrust was put off until October, when Montgomery could "guarantee . . . complete success."[89] But the decision was made to go ahead with the raids as planned, GHQ-ME believing that the four raids would in the interim help keep Rommel off balance.[90] The four raiding forces were thus permitted to continue.

By dawn two days before the target date, Haselden's contingent was hidden out in a wadi some ninety miles below Tobruk. Force B's Commandos repaired breakdowns, checked weapons, and went over their plans again and again. Then, just after dawn on the day of the raid itself, Lloyd Owen led the whole column to the jump-off point, some low hills forty miles south of Tobruk and not far from the old Bir Hacheim battlefield of the previous June. The litter and burnt-out hulks of tanks and vehicles lost in that battle were all over the place and presented a somber scene. But they had so far seen no sign of enemy patrols. After an early supper, the SIG men put on their German uniforms, the Commandos climbed into their trucks, and the column pushed off. It was turning gray and cold, and the wind whipped up big dust clouds as the vehicles headed along. Lloyd Owen recalled later how "we were all rather quiet, any conversation rather forced."[91] Finally, off to the north, they spotted "small dots and clouds of dust on the horizon"—a convoy of enemy trucks moving along the main road that led into Tobruk. They had reached the point where Y1 would have to split off. After a final brief conference in which Haselden "wished us all the best of luck," he and his Commandos drove off.[92]

Y1 watched until the Commandos were practically out of sight. Just at that point, however, the patrol spotted what could only be an enemy column to the east and heading directly for Haselden. Fearing that the Commandos would be cut off, the patrol immediately raced forward, the trucks fanning out in open attack formation. They reached the enemy—an Italian motorized patrol that, fortunately for Y1, had no armored cars along for protection and did not grasp until too late that the vehicles bearing down on them were British. Y1 poured in fire at pointblank range. A number of the enemy were killed and the rest were taken prisoner. Every enemy truck was knocked out. Y1 rounded up the prisoners and moved off to a safer spot. It was by now thoroughly dark and almost time to begin the second part of Y1's operation—to knock out an enemy direction-finding station and in general to create as much havoc as possible. Haselden should by now have long since gotten inside Tobruk's perimeter. After waiting the stipulated time, Lloyd Owen began trying to make radio contact with the Commandos. But no answer came back over Y1's radio.[93]

He did not learn until much later what had happened. In the beginning, the plan seemed to go perfectly. Force B's Commandos, just as Haselden had predicted all along, succeeded in entering Tobruk without a hitch, at dusk driving right through the front gate. They got past the checkpoints and inside the perimeter with scarcely more than a wave of the hand. The column continued past the big airfield and, finally nearing the harbor, reached a point near the cove. This was the location at which they were to meet the British seaborne force that would be landed by the PTs and high-speed motor launches. It was by now thoroughly dark. So far, Haselden's plan appeared to be succeeding brilliantly; he soon got his men into position for the attack on the coast batteries. Precisely on schedule on a night that the meteorologists had correctly predicted would be pitch-black and moonless, the first RAF and USAAF bombers flew over. This was the start of the diversionary attack, and the planes began dropping their bombs in and around

Tobruk. As the enemy's antiaircraft guns and air raid sirens began opening up in full cry, the Commandos commenced their assault. At the same time, down at the cove, beacon lights were set up to guide in the motor launches and PT boats. But from here on in the operation began to go sour.[94]

Indeed the naval portion had begun to run into difficulty even before Haselden commenced his assault. The wind that had stirred up the dust clouds in the desert had also raised big rolling swells out to sea. Only a few of the special folbot parties launched from a British submarine were able to get ashore and guide in the Royal Marines landing from destroyers. Of the landing craft actually making it to shore, most ended up wide of their designated beach. Then, as the handful of Marines tried to move forward against the coastal batteries, the two destroyers, H.M.S. *Zulu* and H.M.S. *Sikh*, closed to within a mile of the shore. But both ships were repeatedly hit by the heavy volume of fire from the shore, *Sikh* so badly that she soon sank. While this was going on, the other naval force, the one intended to link up with Haselden, attempted to approach the cove. Of the few launches actually able to make out Haselden's landing lights, most were hit by heavy fire "from several directions," fire that should not have been there had the Commandos succeeded in their mission of knocking out the enemy positions guarding the cove.[95]

In fact, Haselden had already been able to knock out several of the enemy's batteries. But almost as soon as their assault began, the attacking Commandos had themselves come under attack: well-led coordinated attacks mounted by first-quality German infantry. The presence of these troops was an unpleasant surprise, since, according to intelligence, they should not have been there at all. In short order Haselden's men found themselves cut off and outnumbered. As the situation grew more desperate, Haselden finally tried to lead a breakout attempt. But his men were beaten back, and he himself was hit. Badly wounded, he died a few minutes later. Despite a desperate effort to hang on, virtually every one of his Commandos was killed or taken prisoner. With no hope now of carrying out their landings, the PT boats and launches withdrew, only to be lost at sea when German planes next day took off and pounced at first light. Yet these were only a fraction of the Royal Navy's losses resulting from Tobruk. In an attempt to save the *Zulu*, H.M.S. *Coventry*, a heavy cruiser, was dispatched to try to take the badly shot-up destroyer in tow. But German planes caught both ships, cruiser and destroyer, in the narrow waters between North Africa and Crete. Both *Coventry* and *Zulu* were sunk, each with heavy losses in men.[96] In all, during the raid and the morning that followed, three first-class warships and a number of smaller vessels were lost. The disjointed and fragmentary messages reaching GHQ-ME soon made it apparent that losses at Tobruk—Haselden's men, the naval and landing forces, and the crews of the eight British and American bombers shot down in the action—would approach 750 men. Elated over this obvious setback to the British raiding forces, Rommel in person next day "flew over

to Tobruk. . . . [to express] my appreciation to the troops for the well-con-
ducted defensive action they had fought." The British attack had "caused
us no little alarm, for Tobruk was indeed one of our most valuable
points."[97]

So also was Benghazi, some 250 miles to the west, and Stirling's venture
against it fared little better than the move against Tobruk. Force X had
gotten off to a bad start: its two light tanks had bogged down in the sand
and had had to be sent back. Then, crossing the narrow part of the Sand
Sea, the SAS drivers, many of them newly joined and on their first desert
operation, had had difficulty getting their vehicles over the dunes. But they
finally got through, and the whole column was able to dodge past Jalo and
its enemy patrols. In advance of the main force, S1 Patrol took the lead SAS
element, commanded by Major Paddy Mayne and assisted by Captain Fitzroy
Maclean, north to rendezvous with some Arab agents. These were led by
one of Peniakoff's old intelligence colleagues, Belgian-born, ex-cotton merchant Robert Melot. Melot, now in his early forties and a captain in intelligence, had been a fighter pilot in World War I. Like Peniakoff, he had,
in this war, quickly established a reputation for cool-headed, first-class intelligence work. He had been hiding out with the Bedouin since March,
eluding the swarm of enemy patrols sent after him and living off food supplied
by the LRDG.[98]

Melot met with Mayne and Maclean at the appointed location. The two
SAS officers were little impressed by Melot's prize Arab agent, who struck
them as too shifty-eyed and not altogether believable in his story of having
deserted from one of the Italians' native constabulary units. But at Melot's
insistence the man was sent into Benghazi in order to gather the latest
intelligence. He duly returned, bringing back plenty of information. Benghazi, he said, was protected by freshly laid minefields and newly arrived enemy
troops, including an Afrika Korps machinegun detachment as well as a large
force of Italian infantry. This new information was enough to convince Stirling, who by this time had arrived with the full column, that the enemy had
somehow gotten wise to the raid. He immediately radioed back to GHQ-
ME, requesting permission to throw off the enemy by shifting back the time
of the attack by at least a full day. But Stirling was told to disregard what
obviously was just "bazaar gossip" and get on with the schedule for the
raid.[99]

He thus went ahead with a full program of last-minute rehearsals and final
briefings. Each man was issued his "escape kit," consisting of extra water
and survival rations, a handful of "stay-awake" pills, a miniature compass
that looked like a button, and a silk map, secured from the RAF, of the
desert. When all was ready, the attackers moved out around dusk and headed
for Benghazi. They were led by Melot's Arab, who claimed to know the
best way down a particularly difficult escarpment just inland from the target.
But the agent instead guided them into rough terrain and a hopeless cul-de-

sac of great boulders and deep-cut wadis. In the darkness it took hours just to get all the vehicles extracted and back out onto level ground again. By now, off in the distance, the RAF was already hitting Benghazi—the cover for the raid's approach—and Stirling's column hurried to make up for lost time.[100]

It was three hours past midnight by the time his lead vehicles had reached a roadblock—merely some wooden slats stretched across oil drums—and halted. No enemy troops seemed to be about. But just as Stirling was about to motion the column forward again, enemy troops hidden off to one side suddenly opened up with a deafening burst of fire from perhaps a dozen machineguns and some 20-mm Breda cannon, as well as some heavy mortars. Stirling immediately yelled to attack, and two SAS jeeps lurched forward. They got just a few feet before incendiary bullets hit their gas tanks, blowing both up instantly. Trapped in what was obviously a well-laid ambush, the rest of the jeeps opened up with their own guns and began trying to fight their way clear. The raid against Benghazi had been caught before it could even begin. Stirling signaled the retreat, and his vehicles began racing to reach the cover of the Jebel's distant hills and wadis before the sun came up.[101]

They were caught just as they were climbing the high escarpment. Glancing back from his jeep, Maclean saw "a most unwelcome sight": from all three of the major airfields around Benghazi, enemy planes were "rising up like angry wasps."[102] The first bombers and fighters were on them in a flash. One of the SAS vehicles was hit and blown up, and then another and another. This went on all day, with the enemy sending out aircraft in fresh relays. Sundown was nearing when the last one finally flew off. Stirling rounded up his survivors; he had lost vehicles, and more than a score of his men had been killed or wounded. Disaster struck again at dawn the next day. With everyone hidden out in a wadi and supposedly safe for the moment, an SAS jeep that had been separated from the others in the previous day's confusion now came straggling in from the north, trailing a dust cloud that could be seen for miles. An Italian CR-42 fighter spotted it and sent back the position. Before the remnants of Force X could run for it, the same swarm of planes that had hit them the day before (Stirling's men were by now grimly familiar with the various markings and numerals) was on them anew. By the time the planes, having raked the wadi for hours, finally departed from this second attack, Stirling had lost twenty-five more vehicles, and still others were at least partially damaged. In all, fully three-quarters of his vehicles had been lost, and nearly a quarter of his men had been killed, wounded, or were still missing.[103]

His plan had been to limp back to Jalo, which by now should be firmly in British hands. But he arrived at that oasis to find a full-fledged firefight in progress. Force Z—Talbot's R2 Patrol and the battalion from the Sudan Defence Force—had reached Jalo on schedule four days earlier. But rather than the "low-grade Italian troops" that intelligence had promised, they found instead newly emplaced fields of mines and a resolute, obviously well-prepared enemy garrison.[104] After trying repeatedly to overcome the position, Force Z at length received orders by radio to pull out and head back to Kufra. With no other course open to them, Stirling's men and surviving vehicles joined forces with the Sudan Defence Force battalion and began the long trek down Graziani's Palificata. Further British losses were averted when Talbot's patrol, covering the withdrawal, succeeded in touching off an enemy air attack meant for the main column. But the half-dozen Italian bombers that jumped the patrol wounded a number of its men. By the time the attack was over, R2 had suffered damage to nearly every one of its vehicles.[105]

Thus, of the four raids attempted in the second week of September 1942, three—the attacks on Tobruk, Benghazi, and Jalo—had failed utterly. Moreover, Tobruk and Benghazi had cost the British greater casualties than had all previous desert-raiding operations, including the Kufra attack, combined. The only raid which proved successful was the LRDG attack on Barce, yet it also carried a high price in casualties and lost vehicles.[106]

The Barce force's first losses had occurred in the Sand Sea's dunes and far south of any enemy forces. When a vehicle flipped over in the tricky dunes, its passengers, one with a fractured skull, the other with a broken back, had had to be evacuated by air. Of his three patrols, Easonsmith had already had to divert one, Olivey's S2, to a mission other than the attack on Barce. But he had pressed on, carefully picking his way north across the miles of open desert separating him from the Jebel and his target. Reaching some low hills, he prudently left behind a truck well-stocked with extra water, food, and gasoline, to cover his line of retreat. His force at dawn reached a wadi some fifteen miles south of Barce. His own raid, like those at Tobruk and Benghazi, was set for that night. As planned, Easonsmith took Peniakoff and his two Arab agents forward on a reconnaissance.[107] They were now out of the desert and in broken terrain whose acacia trees and scattered pines suggested Greece rather than North Africa.

The vehicles were hidden under camouflage nets. Enemy planes droned overhead all day long, and the men cleaned weapons and tried to catch up on sleep. Easonsmith and Peniakoff returned from their reconnaissance and, late in the afternoon, used aerial photos and an old Italian postcard to go over the layout of Barce. At dusk they loaded up and moved out, halting later to cut telephone wires and shoot up an Italian outpost. Two hours before midnight, Easonsmith made his final deployment for the attack. While he and G1 moved against Barce itself in order to keep the enemy busy, Wilder's T2 would slant around for the attack on the airfield. Both groups then split up, each looking for the best approach to its assigned target. Easonsmith's group blundered into one of the Italian colonial settlements, scattering squawking chickens and squealing pigs off into the darkness.

Reaching the main road, he turned on his headlights—and promptly saw a pair of squat, M13/40 tanks parked on the road ahead. But the trucks raced through the roadblock before the tanks could react, and soon reached Barce.[108]

Wilder had meanwhile found his way to the airfield. Charging forward, his trucks shot down the squad of Italian infantry guarding the front gate. Skidding and dodging through the maintenance sheds and hangars, Wilder's men threw hand grenades at the windows and doors and dodged fire from the Italians. A large fuel truck was hit by machinegun fire; when it exploded, the flames lit up the entire field and revealed still more Italians coming up to chase after the raiders. Wilder's trucks then surged through the parked aircraft—SM-79s, one or two Stukas, and some Macchi fighters—pouring in incendiary bullets while the men threw more hand grenades. With a large force of Italians now shooting off flares and closing in on him from one side, Wilder ran for it. But two light tanks, their cannon already booming away, arrived to block his escape route. With not a moment's hesitation Wilder led his trucks straight at them, his own Chevrolet bouncing off one of them in a glancing blow. Then, throwing his truck into reverse, he crashed into the second tank. He and his men then leapt out of their smashed vehicle and ran for one of the jeeps as it slowed down for them. A moment later, however, this vehicle, too, was lost when, careening around a turn in the road, it flipped over; Wilder was knocked out cold and pinned underneath. The patrol got him pulled out before the Italians, now coming after them in hot pursuit, could bring their fire to bear. Even so, the last truck in line caught a full burst of fire; although the men got out before it blew up, they were captured by the pursuing Italians.[109]

While all this was going on, G1 raged through Barce. Shooting its way past the sentries, the patrol crashed through a wall and into the enemy's main barracks compound. Easonsmith blew up a dozen parked vehicles and would have done more had not a platoon of Italian tanks arrived to force him to make a run for it. Several of his men were wounded, and two jeeps, disabled by enemy fire, had to be left behind. Yet the raiding force, now reunited, managed to get out of Barce before the Italians could organize a means of blocking their escape.[110]

With less than two hours of darkness left, the patrols made for the desert. Just after dawn, however, they were ambushed by a large enemy force. Although Easonsmith again succeeded in fighting his way past his pursuers, the worst was yet to come. Spotting the patrols as they ran south, an Italian fighter called in the angry swarms of enemy planes that soon arrived to pound Easonsmith for the next four hours. He paid dearly for all the destruction he had inflicted on Barce during the previous night's work, for in these air attacks he lost all but two of his remaining vehicles, and the radio trucks of both patrols were blown up. He also lost men. A machinegun bullet tore through both of Wilder's legs, and Dr. Lawson, trying to attend to the badly wounded, had to work through a hail of enemy cannon and machinegun fire. Through all of this Peniakoff managed to demonstrate his own brand of *sang-froid* by reading, during the worst of the air attacks, a thumb-worn copy of *Paradise Lost.*[111]

Still, Easonsmith's force had destroyed or damaged fully thirty-two enemy aircraft, a figure later confirmed by intelligence. And the severity and violence of the attack had caused Barce's commander to signal his superiors that he was being hit by at least "a full force of British armoured cars."[112] The Barce operation, as part of the four-raid "daring gamble" envisioned by GHQ-ME, had been highly successful. But by the time the last enemy planes at length broke off their attack and flew north on the morning after the raid, Easonsmith was left with the dicey problem of how to get his forty-seven remaining men (nearly half of whom were wounded) and two remaining vehicles (each of which had sustained at least some damage) back over the desert to Kufra, some 800 miles to the south.[113]

CHAPTER 8

The Road Watch and the Verification of Ultra

During the vital period of Montgomery's offensive at El Alamein, the LRDG maintained a constant "Road Watch" deep behind Rommel's lines. The watchers, hidden just off the road, saw everything that passed by: exactly how many German tanks of a certain type, how much artillery, and so forth. This information was absolutely invaluable to us.
  —Colonel John W. Hackett, GSO 1 of Raiding Forces, 1942–1943[1]

Easonsmith's men, the most severely wounded riding but the rest plodding along in the sand, began moving south towards the emergency truck hidden out the day before the raid. Meanwhile, Peniakoff and Dr. Lawson were given one of the two trucks still remaining to Easonsmith and sent on ahead with the worst cases. But Lawson was low on morphine; there seemed little chance that his most critically injured charges could survive the trip across the Sand Sea.[2] Adding to their problem was the fact that Easonsmith had been unable to get off a radio message before the planes had caught him. His best chance now was to hope that his silence during the regular radio call-in times would alert Group Headquarters to send out a rescue party.[3]

That is precisely what Prendergast did.[4] Indeed, with the grim news from the other raids already filtering in, he had not waited to begin taking steps. Olivey's S2 and Lloyd Owen's Y1 were signalled to shift south and begin searching for survivors in the area below the Jebel. Lloyd Owen at length located the Peniakoff-Lawson party at an old landing ground marked by the "tail of a wrecked Hurricane fighter and odds and ends of other wrecked planes."[5] His signal soon brought in an RAF emergency medical evacuation flight. The wounded were loaded up and flown back to Cairo; fortunately, all survived. Easonsmith's main party was found and assisted on its way to the emergency truck, and thereafter the patrols, none of which had escaped damage to men and vehicles, struggled south towards Kufra.[6]

They arrived there at about the same time as the remnants of the other raiding contingents—and also a force of Luftwaffe bombers. The BBC had by some slip been permitted to announce that the raids on Tobruk, Benghazi, Jalo, and Barce had all originated from Kufra.[7] The Germans had never bothered themselves with Kufra before; they now, however, wasted no time in sending down a reprisal. Either by good luck or by good intelligence the JU-88 bombers concentrated their attention on the area harboring the LRDG patrols. A number of men were killed, and Lloyd Owen and various other survivors of the recent raids were badly wounded. The only consolation, if any, was that the patrols put out such a heavy and accurate volume of fire that they scored hits on the German planes. Indeed, two of the JU-88s crashed in flames just north of the oasis.[8]

The German air attack served to underscore the high losses already suffered in the raids. When Lieutenant Kenneth Sweating took G2 north to look for survivors from Tobruk, he found none because there were none.[9] It was true that the raids soon generated an impressive array of decorations—Easonsmith and Wilder, for example, were put in for the Distinguished Service Order, Lawson for the Military Cross, many of the NCOs and men for the Military Medal, and so on. Yet it would be at least a month before either the LRDG or the SAS would be able to undertake a major operation again. To most of the participants, the whole business of the raids, with the exception of the Barce attack, seemed "a classical balls-up" operation.[10] Prendergast believed that the Tobruk effort in particular might have stood a far better chance of success "had it been kept to its original, simple form, without the Navy and everybody else trying to get involved."[11] That the raids had turned into a debacle was abundantly obvious to their survivors. But more and more the question that began to be asked in the hospital wards, as well as in the official post-mortem held at GHQ-ME, was: Had the enemy somehow gained advance warning of the attacks? Had the Germans and Italians all along merely been waiting for the raiders, letting them drive into a well-laid ambush?[12]

A quarter of a century after the event, the comment of the British official history was that "no evidence has been found to show that the enemy had become aware of any part of the plan."[13] At the time, however, the opinion of the men who had actually made the raids was quite different. To Fitzroy Maclean of the SAS, there had been signs from the start "that too many people knew too much."[14] In a bar in Alexandria, for example, a drunken member of the seaborne landing force "was heard boasting . . . that he was off to Tobruk."[15] One of Stirling's Free French officers had heard a bartender, reputedly an enemy agent, asking pointed questions about the raids that were being planned. By the time Haselden's Commandos had departed

Kufra, the impending attacks had supposedly become "the gossip of Cairo."[16] Peniakoff's assessment was characteristically acid. What had happened, he wrote later, was that "our bright young men . . . [had simply been] far too excited to hold their tongues."[17] At the end of the day, heading straight for the "bars and clubs of Cairo," they had "discuss[ed] again their childish plans," apparently quite freely, with eager ears taking in every word they said.[18] Later that night, the next step was as old as military history. "Lovely dark Syrian heads on crumpled pillows listened carefully to their blond bedfellows. . . . [as] military plans [were] mingled with the raw pleadings of inexperienced passion."[19] This information—according to Peniakoff, at least—had soon found its way to Italian agents, who supposedly could transmit the newly gained intelligence by using a "discreet wireless set in a villa off the Pyramids Road."[20]

Certainly Tobruk's defenders had reacted with a "speed and resolution" not previously encountered on earlier raids. Just before the SAS had tried to hit Benghazi, Melot's Arab agent had told Stirling that the town bazaar "was full of the news of our impending attack."[21] Even the "actual date . . . was being freely mentioned."[22] Approaching Jalo, the attacking LRDG patrol had encountered enemy troops who obviously "had not been taken unawares."[23] A year later Peniakoff picked up additional information that tended to confirm his view that the enemy had indeed received plenty of warning. Landing in Italy as part of the invasion force that went ashore at Salerno in September 1943, he raided the headquarters of an Italian division. One of his captives turned out to be an Italian officer who, the year before, had "held an 'Intelligence' appointment on the General Staff in Cyrenaica."[24] While Peniakoff listened, the captured officer "quoted from memory our order of battle for the . . . raids." Moreover, the Italian stated that "he had got all the information complete and sorted out as early as . . . ten days before the attack." The only information he had not received concerned the actual "routes and timings of the parties moving up." These, as Peniakoff commented, were "an L.R.D.G. responsibility and they [the LRDG] were trained to keep their own counsel."[25]

Surprise, the most essential factor for success, had apparently been lost from the start. The September raids had been and would remain the largest, most complex, and most ambitious special force effort undertaken in the desert campaign. That effort had turned into the largest special force failure of the campaign. Those perhaps envious of the prestige and elite status of the LRDG, the SAS, and the Commandos had already taken to referring to these units pejoratively as "the raiding circus" or as "the private armies."[26] Certainly they enjoyed a somewhat set-apart status, the pick of the best men, and, after two years of desert fighting, a unique role among the combination of forces employed against Rommel. A defeat of this magnitude was bound to give new ammunition to those who either doubted the need for such special forces in the first place or else believed that they needed to be more tightly controlled. Montgomery, for example, was not opposed to the use of these forces, and indeed would make heavy use of them for the remainder of the campaign. Yet he "never forgave the failure of the September raids."[27] Upset by more than just the absence of proper security measures, he was inclined to fix the blame on the joint service, ad hoc headquarters that had been established for the purpose of handling the raids. Montgomery's response was, therefore, to demand that GHQ-ME turn over to his own headquarters the "overall control of every special operation... undertaken in depth [and] to the immediate front of Eighth Army."[28]

This was a step that Montgomery's superior, General Alexander, C-in-C Middle East, would not be likely to take. To do what Montgomery demanded would mean violating a principle that had been followed ever since the creation of the LRDG two years before. That principle held that overall control of deep raiding and intelligence-gathering operations should be vested not in the Eighth Army (the tactical entity), but in GHQ-ME (the strategic entity), as the higher or theater-level headquarters best able to coordinate the various functions required. In the case of the LRDG, this principle had been set out from the beginning. Bagnold had firmly declared that "the LRDG is a GHQ unit"—that is, it was to be regarded and employed as a "strategic" rather than a "tactical" force.[29] Early missions had come straight from GHQ-ME, and had been planned by its director of military operations (DMO). Thereafter, for the purpose of coordinating raids, the tendency had been to place both LRDG and SAS on an "allocation basis" under the immediate tactical control of the Eighth Army.[30] But GHQ-ME still retained overall control. Despite the problems encountered by the physical separation of the two headquarters, Eighth Army and GHQ-ME, this approach had worked well enough. In addition, Prendergast had helped to ensure its success by sending good men to serve as special liaison officers: one to the Eighth Army, and one to the DMO's staff at GHQ-ME. The officers so selected had been with the LRDG from the beginning, and possessed an extensive knowledge of special operations in the desert. It seemed to Prendergast and his staff that a major reason for the failure of the recent raids was precisely that the decision had been made to depart from the established system. The fundamental lesson of the failure seemed to be that "you could not run a complex operation of this sort by a committee"— even a joint-service committee made up of senior and experienced officers drawn from the Army, RAF, and Navy.[31]

It was nonetheless apparent to Alexander that merely continuing with the old method was no longer possible.[32] The reason was the greater number of special operations now being contemplated, as well as their greater complexity and geographical scope. Rather than accepting Montgomery's demand for total control, however, Alexander decided to entrust the coordination of all special operations to the special staff department that had been created within GHQ-ME itself, practically on the eve of the raid. The new "staff cell" or subsection would now function directly under the DMO, but with far wider powers of coordination, and was given the title of G(RF). This, in British military parlance, denoted the "G" or "Operations" element of the staff as specifically concerned with "Raiding Forces." Its purpose was just what the title implied: to coordinate the operations of the whole "raiding circus"—the LRDG, SAS, or any combination of Commando units sent to carry out deep-penetration operations behind the enemy lines.[33] The creation of G(RF) as a coordinating element with a slightly expanded charter would be the only major change the British would make for control of special desert operations in the nearly three years of such efforts.

Chosen to head the new department was Colonel John Winthrop Hackett. Active and analytical of mind, the career-soldier, Oxford-educated Hackett, already twice wounded, had seen extensive service commanding armored units in the desert. He seemed an excellent choice for G(RF), precisely because he could approach the task unhindered by any fixed or preconceived notions regarding the functioning special forces. Moreover, Hackett was excellent at staff work and detailed planning. But equally important was his potential for handling "the eccentric, independent and rather forceful types" who commanded the raiding forces—a potential ultimately to be tested to the fullest in coordination of the operations of special units deployed some hundreds of miles behind enemy lines.[34] Hackett's "brief from General Alexander [had specified] that the special forces should be treated as strategic troops," and it was therefore essential that they be retained under effective theater-level control.[35] He therefore approached his new role with determination, seeing himself as a sort of "managing director to the special forces." His job was to see that the unique capabilities and talents of these forces were made "comprehensible and palatable" to GHQ-ME and the Eighth Army—in short, "to ensure that the 'private armies' were enlisted in the public war."[36] In that sense he intended that his department serve as a planning element and immediate clearinghouse for information. Regarding the forces themselves, Hackett's view soon came to be that the LRDG's main role should primarily be one of deep reconnaissance. For Prendergast's patrols, the "destruction of long-range targets... [must always remain] a secondary role." The SAS, on the other hand, should almost exclusively be directed towards "destruction and sabotage... by stealth if possible, otherwise by force."[37] As one who would have to operate under the system coordinated by Hackett, Prendergast believed that the creation of G(RF) held promise that "all the 'funnies' of the raiding circus could be brought together under one roof."[38] He was also pleased that one of his own officers, Lloyd Owen, was temporarily assigned to Hackett's G(RF) to assist with the coordination effort. The new structure meant that special operations would be coordinated by a single officer who was directly responsible to the DMO, and thus to Alexander himself.[39]

Hence the failure of the disastrous September raids had, at least in one important sense, actually proved beneficial: it had forced the creation of a new and potentially workable mechanism for controlling a form of warfare that had served the British well since 1940. Yet, in the creation of the new mechanism, an additional factor was involved. That factor was the need for the most precise, most meticulous coordination possible of raiding operations with those intended to gather intelligence. Both were obviously regarded as crucial military undertakings, yet were also inherently incompatible with each other. Both types, it was true, relied on security and the ability to use the desert as a medium by which to reach enemy rear areas. But whereas an attack along the Via or an SAS raid on an airfield inevitably brought about a swift enemy reaction in the form of heavy air searches and ground patrols, the intelligence-gathering mission demanded that absolutely nothing what-soever be done that might alert the enemy to a British presence in the area. This was hardly a new problem, having come up again and again whenever an LRDG patrol had attempted to carry out an intelligence mission in a region also being attacked by the SAS.[40]

In this third autumn of the desert campaign, however, the problem began to take on a new and far more crucial dimension than ever before. Mont-gomery, now preparing the offensive at El Alamein, had been persuaded that an LRDG patrol should be positioned deep behind enemy lines and in such a way as to maintain a constant surveillance on Rommel's vital line of communication and supply running east from Tripoli. While no one in the LRDG could know it at the time,[41] the essential purpose of this new LRDG surveillance effort was to provide data that would be of use in the verification of information received via the "Ultra Secret."[42] That secret, perhaps the greatest and best kept of the war, was later described as a prize affording British commanders "the unique experience of knowing not only the precise composition, strength and location of the enemy's forces, but also, with few exceptions, of knowing beforehand exactly what he intended to do in the many operations and battles of World War II."[43] As a weapon for the desert campaign, however, the Ultra Secret had in some respects proved difficult to use.

For over two years, since the early spring of 1940, the British had possessed the ability to intercept and decrypt radio messages transmitted in the very highest-level, most secret, and most vital code that the Germans employed. This supreme advantage, the knowledge of which was restricted to the prime minister, his key generals and admirals, and the most select circle of intel-ligence officers, had come to be referred to as the "Ultra Secret."[44] It was based on the ability to decipher German signals encrypted through the use of a machine called the Enigma. Resembling an oversized electric typewriter, and adopted by the Germans in the late 1920s and early 1930s, the Enigma was a wonder of technological inventiveness. Most important, its codes were so complex as to be absolutely unbreakable—or so the Germans believed. Indeed, their Italian and Japanese allies had also soon adopted it. Its internal mechanism of wheels, rotors, and drums, each of which had a multiplicity of possible settings, was driven by electric circuitry, and made possible thousands and thousands of permutations. By using the appropriate key established for a particular day (a setting that "could be changed as frequently as every 24 hours"), the machine could be configured in such a way that an operational message could, in just seconds, be converted into a meaningless hodgepodge of ciphers.[45] Thus encoded, the message could then be transmitted over the air. The Enigma system was fast, efficient, and reliable. Above all, the Germans were convinced that it was secure, that it could never be broken. They were absolutely convinced, in fact, that not even the most brilliant team of codebreakers, working for years, could ever hope to "crack" an Enigma-generated message intercepted by any British or other unfriendly station that might be listening in.[46]

Unknown to the Germans, however, such a team of codebreakers had already succeeded in solving what Churchill, using the phrase he had first employed to describe the Soviet Union, might have termed a "riddle wrapped in a mystery."[47] In Britain, at a top-secret establishment called Bletchley Park, located to the west of London, special teams of cryptologists, mathematicians, language experts, and intelligence analysts had worked with feverish intensity from the opening months of the war in order to crack the Enigma's code. They were successful to the point that, by the early stages of the Battle of Britain, Bletchley's codebreakers had begun to decipher actual messages. Moreover, they had also gained considerable knowledge of the patterns of the enemy's standard transmission procedures and the keys by which the Enigma was set for its encoding operations.[48]

The mere possession of an advantage of this magnitude—the ability to gain the information contained in the enemy's most sensitive transmissions—would seemingly have been enough to guarantee success in every battle the British entered. Such, however, had not been the case in North Africa. The situation there had presented a number of practical problems which acted to limit the advantage theoretically offered by Ultra. Not only did the Germans themselves, because of security considerations, generally avoid sending out operation plans and the like over the air, but the sheer length of documents of this sort meant that they were usually delivered by courier rather than transmitted by radio in the Enigma code. Thus, it did not necessarily follow that the British, merely because they happened to be able to read some of the Enigma-coded transmissions, were able to know exactly what the enemy was planning in advance of the event.[49] Also, the Bletchley codebreakers, in contrast to their experience with the Luftwaffe, had encountered a somewhat greater degree of difficulty in breaking the Enigma keys used by the German Army (although certain German Army keys captured in Operation Crusader, for example, had thereafter "enabled [a] whole month's traffic . . . to be read [with ease]."[50] Even so, Ultra did not fail to yield a great quantity of extensive and highly useful information that gave indication of the arrival times of specific German air and ground units, their state of readiness, their need for certain types of critical spare parts, their planned movements, and so forth. Carefully compiled and analyzed, this information could indeed help to give British generals "the precise composition, strength and location of the enemy's forces."[51]

It could not, however, win the battles for them. And, by its very accuracy and completeness, the splendid advantage of the Ultra Secret could actually draw British generals into making wrong decisions where Rommel was concerned. By relying too much on the information derived from Ultra, the British had very early gotten themselves into trouble. In the first three months of 1941, for example, Wavell had received from that source accurate and extensive information regarding the arrival of Rommel's forces in Libya—information that included even the entire text of the Afrika Korps commander's very latest report to Berlin. But Ultra's generous revelations had thereafter led him to conclude that the weak strength, poor logistical situation, and lack of training of the Afrika Korps' initial elements would prevent Rommel from staging a large offensive in the immediate future. Ultra had thus permitted Wavell to arrive at a logical and reasonable estimate of his opponent's situation and prospects. It had served, that is, as the means for achieving a rational formulation of the calculus of Rommel's combat power in the early months of 1941.[52] The trouble with this formulation was that Rommel had promptly gone on to do something very different from what his actual strength (and, for that matter, the orders of his superiors) seemed to dictate.[53] He had mounted the surprise, all-out offensive in early 1941 which had thrust far into Cyrenaica and sent the British falling back to Egypt. This turn of affairs had caused Wavell to admit that "my . . . great error" was that of believing too much in the world of calculating what an enemy could do solely on the basis of his actual and available resources.[54] Wavell had, from Ultra, thus "got the message . . . but not the meaning."[55]

Nor was Wavell the only one to be led to a wrong assessment in Rommel's case becuse of the information supplied by Ultra. Churchill, in particular, was himself greatly captivated by the revelations from this new source. He had great difficulty in understanding how the British forces in the desert, armed with this unprecedented advantage in strategic intelligence, could so consistently fail to use it in order to defeat an enemy whose most sensitive and revealing signals they were reading.[56] But whereas Ultra might indeed reveal the composition and numbers of the enemy forces on hand, it did not give indications as to how these forces would actually be employed, and therein lay the problem. The decoded Enigma traffic might be "invaluable for the strategic information [it suppled]," but it was far less useful "on the tactical level."[57] The great imponderable, the gap between what the British actually knew and what the Germans actually did, remained a function of the tactical instincts and genius of Rommel himself.

Moreover, Rommel, without knowing it, had managed to add further to the British difficulties in using Ultra. By sending reports up to OKW that painted "the most pessimistic picture of his strength in armour or fuel"[58]— a picture obviously and deliberately intended to win from his superiors additional resources for the campaign in North Africa—he had succeeded in deceiving the British as to his true situation. These reports, in which the Desert Fox consistently put his worst case forward, were, like the others, duly intercepted and decoded at Bletchley and communicated to GHQ-ME. Thereafter they were used by Churchill to badger and goad GHQ-ME as to how the Eighth Army could find it so difficult to finish off Rommel, when the decrypts of his own messages had indicated that his numbers of tanks were clearly inferior to those of the British. But as first Wavell and then Auchinleck had recognized, in the fluidity of armored combat in the desert, to formulate an accurate assessment of exactly how many tanks the enemy could actually field on a given day was no easy matter. There were too many variables—such factors as tank-repair rates, the flow of spare parts, the nature of the terrain—and all had to be taken into consideration.[59] From the first, Shearer, responsible for GHQ-ME's intelligence effort, had argued that Ultra's revelations could not be taken at face value but had to be weighed against a whole variety of factors as well as information received from other sources. He remained convinced that this was the only possible means by which to obtain an accurate, balanced view. Yet this approach struck some as too conservative; ultimately, it guaranteed that his days at GHQ-ME were numbered. Under fire from London because it seemed that his estimates of Rommel's armored strength had consistently placed that strength a good deal higher than that being suggested by the Ultra decrypts, Shearer was eventually removed and sent home. That his estimates had indeed been very close to the mark all along would not become clear until much later.[60]

Shearer had, prior to his departure in spring 1942, already set in motion the steps by which the process of estimating Rommel's actual strength could be raised to a far higher level of accuracy.[61] The first such step was the creation of a new intelligence subsection, made up of officers of all three services, within the staff.[62] The function assigned to this group was that of studying, analyzing, and evaluating every phase of the process by which Rommel received his supplies, munitions, and reinforcements from across the Mediterranean. This in particular demanded the estimation of his "fuel stocks, the life-blood of the desert war."[63] It meant as well studying not just the Ultra intercepts but also such factors as the numbers and tonnages of the enemy ships making the run across the Mediterranean to Tripoli. A second need was to analyze the volume of enemy vehicular traffic that next carried the enemy's materiel east across the desert and along the Via Balbia. The matter of assessing and dealing with the enemy's Mediterranean convoys soon proved the easiest part of the whole problem. By this time, Rommel was receiving through Tripoli perhaps 60,000 of the 100,000 tons he requested each month, indicating that the German failure to neutralize or capture the island of Malta was increasingly beginning to tell. The shipping losses caused by British sea and air attacks were beginning to mount up, and would continue to do so all through 1942. Here Ultra did indeed prove a trump card: its revelations gave the British an extremely accurate picture of virtually everything sent south by sea, and enabled them to attack the convoys on a selective and devastating basis.[64]

Yet some of the enemy's resources inevitably got through. There remained also, as Shearer had argued all along, the problem of finding out what the enemy did with those resources once they had reached Tripoli and were sent to Rommel over the hard-surface, thousand-mile length of the Via Balbia. The movement of enemy convoys along the road by day could be observed by RAF reconnaissance flights, but those at night went undetected. It was this situation which led to the second of the steps that Shearer had proposed: the implementation of a round-the-clock, constant surveillance of the enemy traffic moving along the Via, such surveillance to be carried out by the LRDG. This effort, literally a counting, by type, of all enemy traffic moving over the road—in effect, a traffic "census"—eventually came to be called "the Road Watch."[65] It seemed, given the LRDG's demonstrated ability to reach the enemy's rear, an obvious solution, and one that the Germans themselves later attempted, although the surveillance team which "they positioned for a short period near the Qattara Depression was probably too far from our main lines of communication to be of any real use."[66]

Preparations for carrying out the Road Watch effort on a trial basis commenced in spring 1942. An officer, drawn from the intelligence subsection formed to analyze Rommel's flow of supplies, was dispatched to work out the steps whereby LRDG patrols could efficiently send back any information gained from watching the Via. Given that the officer so dispatched had been a university don in civilian life, it was perhaps inevitable that the LRDG soldiers referred to him as "Professor Grey Matter."[67] But he brought to the task a wealth of photographs, technical data, and information on enemy vehicle markings, as well as recognition silhouettes for the full line of German and Italian tanks, armored cars, artillery, and so on. He also developed, to help the patrols keep a running count of the various types of vehicles that they might sight, a special notebook, whose mimeographed pages contained—in addition to the technical designations and model numbers for the various types of enemy vehicles—a small silhouette of each. Using this notebook, the men watching the Via would be able to indicate, by the appropriate silhouette, the numbers of each type of vehicle they sighted. Other pages were for the numbers and types of enemy troop units observed, the types of cargo being hauled, and information concerning any special formation markings. This system would make it possible to keep a running score of the type and volume of traffic heading east towards Rommel, as well as that traveling back towards Tripoli on the return run. The information so noted could be radioed back at scheduled times. The LRDG patrol that would carry out this Road Watch mission would have to move up through the desert and then hide out a few miles south of the Via. At night, the patrol would send forward the two-man team that would do the actual watching, and the team would pick some point from which it could see the road and yet remain concealed. Then, while one man watched through binoculars, the second would note down the count in the notebook containing the silhouettes and outlines. The team would, of course, have to remain hidden out all day long and virtually under the noses of the enemy vehicles passing just a few hundred yards away along Rommel's single and vital line of communication. If about to be captured, the team was either to bury its notebook in the sand or else try to tear up and scatter the pages. Under no circumstances was the enemy to learn that the British were mounting a systematic, day in–day out surveillance effort at this location so deep behind the lines.[68]

Nor, for that matter, could Prendergast or his key officers be told that the ultimate purpose of their Road Watch mission was far more than they realized at the time—that the real reason for it was to provide a source of data crucial to the balanced evaluation of the information provided by Ultra, that is, to assist GHQ-ME's intelligence staff in the verification and assessment of Ultra by supplying empirical data gained from actual observation in the field. Certainly the first indication that these men ever had about the existence of something so sensitive as Ultra was the publication, some thirty years later, of F. W. Winterbotham's book, *The Ultra Secret*. That work was the first actual acknowledgement that the British had been able to read the German code all through World War II. To be sure, the existence of the Ultra Secret was hardly the sort of information that could be entrusted to men about to conduct a special operation 600 miles behind enemy lines. As far back as the opening stages of the desert campaign, with the Long Range Patrols about to push off on their first mission, Shearer had personally found himself hard pressed not to reveal to Bagnold the good news that their side possessed the ability to intercept and read messages sent in the highest-level code used by the Italians.[69] To have done so would obviously have violated the old intelligence rule about "the need to know" and the compartmentation of sensitive knowledge. After all, had Bagnold somehow been taken, his captors might have gained far more than just the knowledge that their code had been broken. The Italians used virtually the same model of the Enigma machine as the Germans. It was not, therefore, beyond the realm of possibility that Bagnold's captors might, by putting two and two together, have arrived at the correct conclusion—to be shared with their German allies— that their efficient, supposedly foolproof Enigma system had, in fact, been compromised. The great prize of Ultra could thus have been lost in the first stages of the war, just at the point when it was beginning to pay off. Nor was that the only example of an occasion when the existence of Ultra could not be revealed to the officers controlling the special operations effort in the desert, even though the information so supplied often had a direct bearing on their efforts. The first indication, for example, that desert-expert Almaszy had reappeared in Libya and was about to attempt the Salaam-Condor mission had come from Ultra. The fact that Almaszy's name kept cropping up on Ultra intercepts had quickly alerted British intelligence to the possibility of enemy efforts in the region south of the Libyan plateau.[70] Once again, however, this was not the sort of information that could be shared with men whose missions regularly took them behind enemy lines. Therefore the LRDG's patrols, aware only that they were to conduct a hazardous and difficult intelligence-gathering mission, but with no way of knowing that the real purpose of that mission was to help verify what Ultra had revealed, prepared to begin the Road Watch. In time, the demands of carrying out this mission would exceed even those of the raiding effort, and the mounting of the Road Watch itself would become the most important single contribution made by the LRDG to the winning of the desert campaign.[71]

Prendergast had already selected the optimal spot for the surveillance effort. The point chosen seemed absolutely the last place where the enemy would expect to find a British patrol lurking. Fully 600 miles behind the lines, in a spot where no raiding operations had been conducted in the recent past, the Via Balbia passed over a quiet sector of desert. That sector, about fifty miles to the west of El Agheila, was remarkable for the great, gleaming arch of white marble that straddled the Via. The arch itself could be seen for miles, having been raised ten years before by Mussolini to commemorate the Italian conquest of North Africa. (It bore inscriptions in Latin as well as bas-relief scenes depicting Mussolini as conquering emperor.)[72] The advantage of "Marble Arch" (to use the term by which the LRDG and SAS invariably referred to it and to the region immediately around it)—other than the unlikelihood of the enemy's ever suspecting anything so far to the rear— was that, just a few miles to the south, shallow wadis offered a good approach and cover adequate to hide the vehicles. The first Road Watch patrol duly arrived at this spot in March 1942, just after Rommel had launched the sudden offensive that drove the Eighth Army all the way back to Gazala. As planned, the patrol hid its trucks and then began sending forward a surveillance team each night. The effort of watching the road managed to prove at once both nerve-straining and monotonous. The men conducting the surveillance suffered from heat and thirst as the hours dragged by. As one of them described it later, "You look at your watch at 11 and look again four hours later and it's 11:15."[73]

This trial period showed that three patrols were required to carry out the watch—one actually watching at Marble Arch, one on the way up to relieve it, and one heading back to base. The initial effort convinced Prendergast that ten days to two weeks should be fixed as the limit for keeping a patrol on station.[74] Each patrol was given a set call-time for radioing back to base whatever information it had gained. Should something really big appear along the Via—a large convoy, perhaps, or an unusually heavy volume of new tanks—then the patrol was to send back a message on "flash" priority. But the first few patrols in spring 1942 saw nothing. Indeed, two weeks passed with very little traffic at all. Just after Easonsmith's R1 took over, however, the Road Watch suddenly began sighting considerable enemy movement. A message radioed back to Group Headquarters indicated that, in the space of a single morning, his patrol had counted more than a hundred enemy tanks being towed east on tractor-trailer lowbed trucks. A second message indicated the passage, in Rommel's direction, of still more Panzer Mk IIIs and IVs, as well as a considerable force of armored cars, both German and Italian. Several enemy units were identified. At night, the surveillance team crawled almost to the edge of the road and attempted to identify vehicles by silhouette or by the noise of their engines.[75] In the days ahead, additional messages followed, giving GHQ-ME precisely the kind of information that would make possible the gauging of the enemy's strength in a balanced and accurate way. Churchill had again been badgering for an immediate British attack against Rommel's ostensibly weak forces. Armed with the latest Ultra, a decrypt of Rommel's most recent situation report to OKW (in which the Desert Fox had again deliberately played down the amount of armor actually available to him), he had complained to GHQ-ME that Rommel "had in forward area 159 serviceable tanks and Italians 87, or barely half the number you credited them with."[76] But the information now coming in from the Road Watch soon confirmed GHQ-ME's original assessment that the actual enemy strength in tanks was in fact much greater than that indicated in the reports that Rommel was sending up to OKW. The Road Watch thus, in the first weeks of its trial effort, was already beginning to serve as an effective means of assessing Ultra revelations, and thereby helping to avoid the kinds of intelligence blunders that had already proved costly. Its role was analogous, indeed, to that of the Australian and British "Coast Watchers" who, six months later and halfway around the world, hid out in the Solomon Islands to maintain a surveillance of the Japanese naval and air forces moving down "the Slot" towards Guadalcanal.[77] As did those of the Road Watch in the desert, their reports helped to fill in the gap between what could be learned from decrypted messages sent in the enemy's code, and what the enemy might actually be doing with the forces available to him.

But obtaining this information was risky in the extreme. Bedouin shepherds had several times wandered close to where Easonsmith's trucks lay hidden, and once an Italian soldier had chosen to relieve himself just yards from the watch team's hiding place, a clump of brush. But the biggest scare had come a few days later when an entire German convoy—perhaps 200 troops and a score of trucks or armored cars—had pulled off the Via to laager up for the night. Their dispersed vehicles had formed a perimeter that had completely encircled the position where Easonsmith's watchers lay hidden. His men had managed, by remaining motionless, to avoid detection; eventually, after a very long night, they succeeded in getting away.[78] The information which they and succeeding teams provided was employed to good effect by the officer named to replace Shearer, Colonel Francis W. de Guingand. The new DMI found their reports particularly useful in the compilation of highly detailed "intelligence summaries," published on at least a weekly basis and distributed to the staffs of the key operational formations. The extremely accurate and detailed content of these summaries reflected the fact that, "week after week [and] 24 hours a day . . . a two-man post was on the road [and maintaining] the watch."[79] This team saw everything, and noted such details as the passage east along the Via of "so many vehicles [of a particular type], carrying an estimated so many unsunburnt troops with clean uniforms[, and] so many German Mark III tanks."[80] De Guingand later pronounced this sort of intelligence as "invaluable . . . to Headquarters . . . [and to] the DMI in particular."[81] The Road Watch "provided . . . certain facts on which [rather precise] calculations of enemy strength can be based." Without the Road Watch reports, "we should frequently have been in doubt as to the enemy's intentions . . . and our estimate of enemy strength . . . far less accurate and accepted with far less confidence."[82]

Therefore the Road Watch continued. Prendergast was told that the LRDG's role of "gaining information about enemy road movements" was of such vital importance that it must "on no account be jeopardized by other operations."[83] But "other operations"—especially the SAS attacks intended to interdict the road or to hit the airfields further on—had nonetheless several times threatened the security of the surveillance effort. This situation reflected the basic special-operations incompatibility of trying to run the watch and yet mount raids in the same general vicinity. As the intensity of LRDG beat-ups along the Via (for Prendergast was obliged simultaneously to maintain both the Road Watch and to keep up the interdiction effort) and Stirling's airfield raids had increased, the enemy had taken steps to block the raiders. Italian troops soon began stretching fifty miles of barbed-wire concertina fence across the desert just south of El Agheila, an obstacle that forced the Road Watch patrols to loop around it, far to the south. Also, after their reconnaissance planes had spotted the patrols' tire tracks left along the new route, the Germans seeded the detour with mines. Several LRDG trucks moving up towards Marble Arch were lost or damaged as a result.[84] Even so, the surveillance effort continued and the vital information was kept flowing. For example, information from Ultra, supplemented by what the Road Watch teams had seen, soon enabled the Eighth Army to know almost the exact date of Rommel's attack on the Gazala line.[85] Again, however, not even Ultra and the Road Watch could give warning of Rommel's intention to outflank the British positions; the unknown element remained, as always, Rommel's propensity to do the unexpected. As DMI, de Guingand "kept in constant touch with the Long Range Desert Group" in these months, and the watch was kept up until midsummer 1942, having been maintained continuously since the first week of March.[86] But late in July it was finally suspended, "by orders from GHQ-ME." The reason for stopping this "most tedious but enormously successful effort" at this juncture was strategic in nature.[87] Rommel's eastward drive had now taken Tobruk, and this new conquest had given him a forward port and therefore reduced his dependency on Tripoli. In short, his supplies could now come in by ship through Tobruk, rather than by the long journey over the Via Balbia from Tripoli. Thus, the rationale for keeping the watchers positioned far to the west at Marble Arch had disappeared. The next step was to look for a suitable location further to the east, one from which the Road Watch could keep surveillance of the traffic that now flowed out of Tobruk. But no location could be found, the "country east of Tobruk . . . [being] too open and dangerous and too close to the main body of Rommel's forces."[88] The watch was therefore halted, and the LRDG for the moment switched back to the task of conducting raids with the SAS.

Although the Road Watch had been discontinued after only four months' duration, it had, during this period, proved its value again and again. Its success during the spring and early summer thus provided the background to Montgomery's insistence, in autumn 1942 and after a three-month suspension, that the watch be reinstituted as a means of supporting his offensive at El Alamein. In his view, the Road Watch could help to narrow the odds by making it possible for him to weigh any information received through Ultra with additional data secured from a watch point located deep in enemy territory. It meant that when the Eighth Army's offensive commenced, he would have, in addition to superior numbers and resources, the advantage of a "window on the enemy's rear."[89]

His superiority in numbers soon included 1,029 tanks (many of them the new American-built Shermans) as against 496 German and Italian tanks, some 195,000 British as against 104,000 German and Italian troops, and 1,200 RAF and USAAF planes against fewer than 700 operational enemy aircraft. Montgomery planned to attack on October 23. As his preparations for the battle at El Alamein went forward, a second force—a massive Anglo-American undertaking under General Dwight D. Eisenhower—commenced the steps that would enable it, far to the west, to land on the coast of French North Africa. These landings, code-named Operation Torch, were intended to ensure that Rommel would be caught between two large and powerful forces and eventually crushed.[90]

But the key to winning at El Alamein, as Montgomery viewed it, was tactical surprise. Since such previous offensives as Crusader had tried to outflank Rommel by slicing through the desert and then hooking up towards the coast, he decided instead to concentrate his resources for a heavy, bludgeoning blow in the north. To hide, however, the massive preparations for such an attack through a desert as open and "as flat and hard as a billiard table"—as de Guingand (who was now shifted up from DMI to become

Montgomery's chief of staff) put it—was difficult in the extreme.[91] Therefore, to deceive the enemy into believing that the main thrust of his attack
would come, as had Crusader, from around the desert flank, Montgomery
prepared an elaborate facade of bogus supply dumps and unit concentrations,
to include the laying out of dummy tanks and a lengthy water pipeline. As
intended, these conspicuous "preparations" were duly picked up by Luftwaffe reconnaissance flights, and the aerial photographs so secured were studied in detail at Rommel's headquarters. Not only were German attentions
kept riveted on the desert flank, but, even better, the Germans concluded
that no British attack need be expected until sometime in November. In
reality, the attack would come in October and far to the north of the desert
flank. When it finally commenced, fully four British infantry divisions and
three armored divisions would, after a massive artillery bombardment and
the clearing of paths through the minefields by combat engineers, advance
to smash Panzerarmee Afrika in its own forward positions.[92]

Montgomery's meticulous preparations for what he called Operation Lightfoot—the offensive at El Alamein—proceeded according to schedule. He
had already, from Ultra, gained one particularly useful piece of information:
Rommel, ordered back for a rest and a meeting with Hitler and Mussolini,
had recently departed North Africa. Also, just days before the El Alamein
offensive was to be launched, Ultra intercepts told Montgomery that Panzerarmee Afrika had on hand perhaps a week's supply of fuel at most for its
tanks. This low level was a direct result of the heavy air and naval campaign
being mounted against the enemy shipping that attempted the run across
the Mediterranean. Ultra gave the British the exact cargoes carried in these
ships; frequently, it gave as well their specific departure dates and estimated
times of arrival. Armed with this information, British aircraft and submarines
operating from Malta and North Africa had pounced on convoys and reduced
Panzerarmee Afrika's intake of supplies to a maximum of about 6,000 tons
per month. In the period immediately prior to El Alamein, for example,
fully twenty Axis ships, carrying perhaps thirty percent of Rommel's needed
supplies, were sent to the bottom. The reports which Panzerarmee Afrika
radioed up to OKW—reports which laid out in detail the logistical plight it
now faced in the desert—could only help further to seal its doom, since
much of this information was almost immediately picked up through Ultra.[93]
Owing to this and to the work of the special intelligence entity that Shearer
had pushed for back in the spring, Montgomery was, by the eve of El
Alamein, in possession of "the most detailed picture of the enemy that a
general had so far had in the war."[94]

But he wanted an even more detailed picture than that. The ability of
the Germans to bounce back, and particularly their ability to recover, repair,
and render operational once more their damaged tanks, had impressed and
dismayed the British throughout the desert campaign.[95] To what degree
might that ability prove a factor in the coming offensive? With the Eighth

Army's year-and-a-half experience of being surprised by the Germans when their actions seemed out of character with the picture supplied by Ultra, Montgomery was insistent that every intelligence resource available to him be employed. When his army jumped off on Lightfoot, he wanted a way to monitor exactly what was going on behind his enemy's lines. He had long since recognized that the "LRDG was a prime source of information, valuable information."[96] This time the Road Watch was to function as a sort of insurance policy, a way of comparing Ultra's revelations with what was really taking place far across the desert and on the other side of Panzerarmee Afrika.

Thus late in September, Prendergast received orders to begin moving up his patrols. The watch site was again to be Marble Arch, unused and unvisited since midsummer. It was again regarded as a viable position from which to do the surveillance since, according to the plan, British and American aircraft would, as soon as Lightfoot opened, hit the ports of Tobruk and Benghazi so hard that the bulk of the enemy's supplies would once more have to come in through Tripoli. But the Road Watch effort was to be just one of several special operations being planned to support the offensive.[97] In Cairo, a coordinating conference called by Brigadier Davy, Alexander's DMO, was attended by Colonel Hackett of G(RF) and representatives from the LRDG, the SAS, and various intelligence elements associated with GHQ-ME. The conference went over the planning for a whole series of reconnaissance and raiding endeavors intended to assist the Eighth Army's advance. It was left open to the LRDG—which Hackett had come to regard as "basically a beautifully organized reconnaissance force that enjoyed a good raid now and then"—to make, in addition to the Road Watch effort, "attacks on [any suitable] long-range targets that presented themselves."[98] Also, in order to help "define the respective roles of the SAS and the LRDG," GHQ-ME had recently issued Operation Instruction no. 144.[99] This document, which reflected the new strength of Hackett's G(RF) department, was an attempt to establish a formalized definition of the roles these two special forces were to play, and it seemed especially necessary at this particular point. Not only was one of these special forces, Stirling's, about to become larger and more powerful still, but both the LRDG and SAS were to be joined by yet another force formed for desert special operations. This situation led to fears—only too real in light of the recent Tobruk-Benghazi disasters—that they might indeed all end up "tripping over one another behind enemy lines."[100]

The new force being raised would be trained and led by Peniakoff. Its official designation, PPA, actually stood for "Popski's Private Army," although the title originally was "No. 1 Demolition Squadron."[101] The PPA was the brainchild of Hackett, who was determined to unleash, at the critical moment when the El Alamein offensive opened, as many raiding forces as possible against Panzerarmee Afrika's airfields, supply lines, and logistical facilities. The goal was interdiction: to molest and disrupt the flow of fuel and supplies along the 1,200 miles of Via separating the Germans and the

Italians from their principal base at Tripoli. Since the LRDG and SAS would obviously be pushed to the limit in carrying out their respective tasks, Hackett felt that this expansion of the raiding forces was appropriate and called for.[102] Rather than bringing into existence a new and entirely separate unit, however, he had originally requested that a small, additional force be raised and placed under the LRDG. Peniakoff would lead it but would take his orders from Prendergast. This proposed arrangement was not destined to work out. Although Peniakoff may have been a self-described "passionate champion" of the LRDG, regarding that unit as "the finest body of men in any army," he, on the other hand, was not held in comparable esteem by Prendergast's officers.[103] They saw Peniakoff as a "colourful character" who had indeed performed very "gallant work" behind enemy lines, but they harbored doubts about his judgment and methods.[104] Peniakoff and the first men he managed to recruit were permitted to spend just one week as officially part of and subordinated to the LRDG. At the end of that time, they were informed that "the organizational structure of things in LRDG just did not allow for a full extra squadron." Therefore, Peniakoff, at least according to his account, was "thrown back on my own."[105]

Following the pattern of the other special units, he promptly went out and had "a Cairo Jew" make up an official insignia for his PPA: a silver, sixteenth-century mariner's astrolabe, done up in miniature, to be worn on a black Tank Corps beret similar to the one that Montgomery himself wore.[106] But his main problem was and remained recruiting. Unable to obtain volunteers from the LRDG, SAS, or Commandos, Peniakoff wound up instead with men drawn mostly from various motor transportation units. They had had no combat experience at all. Nor were his officers particularly strong: several were rejects from other units. Of these original volunteers, both officers and men, only two actually remained with him to the end. The others were not lost in the attrition of combat, however, Peniakoff had himself simply "dropped" them because they had not proved "as solid and purposeful as I would have wished."[107] Still, once he had gained his initial complement of twenty-two men and the six jeeps he had been given, he pressed on with a program of LRDG-assisted training intended to get his force—the third desert-raiding unit formed since 1940—ready and prepared to strike when the moment came.

Peniakoff was not the only special-force leader currently grappling with the problems of recruitment. Capitalizing on the favorable impression he had made on Churchill back in August, Stirling meanwhile was trying to expand the SAS so as to be able to concentrate on a variety of "shorter-range attacks on enemy communications and establishments."[108] Indeed, the strength of the SAS was to be increased to that of a full regiment.[109] To attain this new strength, he wished "to hand pick his new recruits . . . [from among] the desert-trained men [in] the best regiments in the army."[110] But in this endeavor he ran afoul of Montgomery himself, who soon took steps to block the recruitment of good men needed in their conventional units. At length deciding to take his case straight to the top, Stirling, accompanied by Hackett, drove out for an audience at the Eighth Army's headquarters near El Alamein. The meeting was hardly a success—in fact, Hackett remembered "a tremendous row" between Montgomery and Stirling. The two had never met before, and Stirling, who had seen his share of generals come and go in the desert campaign, perhaps failed to let himself be suitably impressed by "Monty's cocksure ways."[111] On the other side, the request by Stirling for top-quality men struck Montgomery as "quite arrogant." "What," he finally asked Stirling, "makes you think you can use these men to greater advantage than I can myself? The answer is 'no.'"[112] Stirling was later somewhat mollified by de Guingand, the chief of staff, who promised to do his best to see that the SAS got the pick of any troops arriving from Britain. But as both men recognized, these troops, as new to the desert as they were to combat, would have to be put through the hastiest of training programs if they were to have any part in the offensive now just weeks away.[113]

Only the LRDG remained free of these difficulties. One of its major advantages, indeed, was that its personnel had remained largely stable throughout the campaign. There was, after the major expansion in late 1940, no wholesale acquisition of new men. Volunteers could be hand-picked to fill vacancies. Nor did there occur anything like the same level of vacancies due to combat losses that characterized line units. Hackett described the three special units as "elite," but with the LRDG being perhaps "the most difficult unit to get into in the whole theatre: many good men always wanted to join."[114] Thus a small contingent from the Grenadier Guards, the senior Foot Guards regiment in the British Army, had arrived to take the place of the men lost or wounded in the September raids.[115] With this relatively small addition in personnel, the unit could be readied to carry out its assigned tasks for Lightfoot, of which the Road Watch was already regarded as the most crucial. LRDG Operation Instruction No. 62 thus sent Y1 Patrol, now led by Lieutenant E. F. Spicer, north in order to be ready to conduct, until relieved, a "traffic census" at the Marble Arch site.[116] Spicer's men departed Kufra on October 20, three days before the start of Lightfoot. They were, however, to stay clear of Marble Arch proper and to hold off on commencing the actual watch until receipt of a radioed order to do so. This order would be sent only after the go-ahead was received from the Eighth Army. The reason for delaying until the last possible moment was to reduce chances of the watch's being discovered, thereby possibly tipping off the enemy that something major was afoot.[117]

Three days after Y1 had left Kufra and precisely at 9:40 at night on October 23, nearly a thousand British guns opened up in full fury on the enemy positions forward of El Alamein.[118] The offensive caught Panzerarmee Afrika totally by surprise, and its command posts and communications were momentarily thrown into confusion by the sudden violence of the barrage. Yet the enemy resistance proved surprisingly effective. Enemy artillery, including the deadly 88–mm guns, quickly zeroed in on the masses of British troops and tanks trying to push through the minefields; Montgomery's losses began mounting up at an alarming rate. For the next three days and in the face of heavier and heavier casualties, the Eighth Army doggedly kept trying to advance. The bleak reports reaching London caused Churchill's confidence in Montgomery momentarily to flag. In despair the prime minister asked General Sir Alan Brooke, the CIGS, if "we . . . [had] a single general who could . . . win [even] a single battle."[119] When the news reached Rommel, he hurriedly flew back to the desert to take command. But in this period that Montgomery called "the real crisis of the battle," the British kept on, no matter how high the losses.[120] For the enemy, too, was meanwhile taking heavy losses, being steadily worn down in a World War I–style contest of attrition. When part of the Afrika Korps was stopped cold in its attempt to stage a counterattack, Montgomery seized the moment to send General Freyberg's tanks and New Zealanders advancing through a sector south of the main battlefield. Although this thrust likewise resulted in high losses, it exacted an even greater cost from the Germans, especially in armor.[121]

This outcome and the continuing pressure in the north forced Rommel, eleven days into the battle, to radio a grim message to OKW. His signal detailed Panzerarmee Afrika's enormous losses and also indicated that he should began retreating immediately were any large part of his army to be saved. This assessment provoked Hitler's immediate order that the Panzerarmee must "hold on, not . . . yield[ing] a step."[122] Instead of retreating, Rommel was to offer his troops "only one path—the path that leads to victory or death."[123] Two days after the sending of the OKW message, however, Rommel finally concluded that, with or without the Führer's permission, he had no choice but to retreat. Both the text of the first signal and that of Hitler's response to it reached Montgomery's hands a short while after being plucked from the ether for decoding at Bletchley. The Ultra Secret decrypts of these signals encouraged Montgomery in his view that the Eighth Army's efforts to wear down the enemy were working. If he could keep pounding away, victory was in sight.[124]

He soon had additional confirmation of this from the Road Watch. Six hundred miles to the west of the battle raging at El Alamein, Spicer's Y1 Patrol had finally received word to commence its surveillance at Marble Arch. Slipping past enemy air patrols, Spicer moved to get his Road Watch team in position by dawn. At first the watchers saw little: as late as October 30, perhaps a hundred vehicles at most were passing along the Via in front of the team's hiding place.[125] This seemed hardly the start of the general retreat that the Ultra decrypts were soon suggesting. Yet on November 4, just one day after the breaking of Rommel's first OKW message—the one requesting "either aid . . . or permission to retreat lest his force . . . be annihilated"—

the situation began changing with dramatic suddenness.[126] From dawn to dusk on that day, a veritable flood of enemy vehicles could be seen streaming west along the Via Balbia. Indeed, in just one day the watchers counted no fewer than 3,500 enemy vehicles, all rolling west and apparently carrying the remnants of Panzerarmee Afrika. And when Y1 was relieved by R2 Patrol, the scene became even more dramatic. For the next six days, until November 14, R2 counted nearly sixty tanks and armored cars of different sorts, a torrent of light vehicles, staff cars, and sidecar motorcycles, and nearly 7,000 trucks, each of them filled to overflowing with German and Italian infantry. There were also nearly 30 large tanker trucks, a dozen or more of the large armored personnel carriers used by the Germans, and some 68 large artillery pieces. Finally, in that time approximately 400 "miscellaneous vehicles" (most of which had passed by at night, when exact identification was impossible), and an estimated 42,500 German and Italian troops traveled by to the west. The figure of 42,500 troops, it should be noted, represented just under half of Rommel's total strength in men. So intensive did the withdrawal become that whole columns of enemy vehicles completely overflowed the Via and spilled out onto the bordering desert. This off-the-road traffic nearly swarmed over the watch site and soon forced R2 to give up the Road Watch altogether and flee to the south.[127]

But not before the radio messages to GHQ-ME and the Eighth Army had told all that R2 had seen. Received from a point deep behind enemy lines, they offered Montgomery—four days after Ultra had alerted him to Rommel's plight—the advantage of positive verification of a key intelligence source. Aerial reconnaissance flights also picked up the swarms of enemy vehicles choking the Via, but only the Road Watch could provide a precise, comprehensive, hour-by-hour description of the enemy movement that flowed along to the west.[128] It saw, indeed, what aerial reconnaissance flights, given the technological limitations of that day, could never see.[129]

The watch continued. G2, the next patrol up, abandoned the Marble Arch site completely and shifted to a point forty miles west. The region crawled with enemy units trying to regroup after the retreat, but the patrol maintained the flow of information.[130] G(RF)'s Hackett was fulsome in his praise. Beginning, he said, with the crucial stage at the height of El Alamein and continuing thereafter "for seven vital weeks in the Autumn during the offensive," the watch went on without pause, twenty-four hours a day.[131] The Germans apparently picked up the Road Watch signals "all the time, but were fooled since the watch site was only a few miles from the sea. The enemy's DF [radio direction finding] types thus could never be sure if we had sent parties ashore from submarines or high-speed launches or what."[132] Moreover, "the value of the information that the patrols were radioing back to us was of a really monumental sort. It gave us a window on the Germans, a way to see what they were really up to."[133]

As an example, the Road Watch sent back sufficient information to make it clear that Rommel probably would not try to hold at El Agheila as he had the year before. He was too weak and, as the watch indicated, most of his forces had by now been shifted too far to the west.[134] The watch was useful in still another way as well. Rommel, losing ship after vital ship at sea, was growing increasingly suspicious. After the British—aided, of course, by Ultra's precise information—had succeeded in finding and annihilating a convoy hidden by fog, he demanded that all possible sources of leakage be investigated thoroughly. These included "wireless interdiction, Italian treachery and the [whole question of the] security of the Enigma system."[135] Rommel's radioed demand for such an investigation was intercepted and decoded at Bletchley, and it immediately caused the British considerable anxiety. Was the priceless advantage of the Ultra Secret, just when the Eighth Army was apparently at last well on its way to defeating Rommel, now about to be found out? And the corollary question was: Might not the Germans, if they learned the truth, suddenly begin using it to feed the British false information? In the anxious days ahead, the intelligence experts analyzed every detail of the intercepted enemy transmissions. As they did so, they were increasingly reassured by the information that the Road Watch continued to send back. When considered against all other factors, these reports seemed only to confirm the picture formed by the Ultra decrypts.[136] The analysts could find no apparent gap between what Ultra said and what was indicated by the actions of the enemy forces operating in the desert. In the end and despite Rommel's intuitive suspicions about "the security of the Enigma system," the British could conclude that the enemy had failed after all to catch on to the fact that their encryptographic system was, in reality, only too vulnerable. The Road Watch patrols in this period thus served a second vital function. They not only provided GHQ-ME and the Eighth Army with "a window on the Germans," as Hackett had put it, but they also served as a way of helping to confirm, by their field observations, that the Ultra Secret yet remained a secret. Finally, as Montgomery commenced driving west in pursuit, the Road Watch effort helped assuage the old "fear of Rommel suddenly debouching in surprising strength," as he had in earlier periods of the campaign.[137] By exploiting to the maximum the unique capabilities of a special force, the British had devised a balanced and effective intelligence-gathering apparatus. It was one that freed them from relying too much on Ultra, at least in those ways that had left them vulnerable in the past.

The period of Rommel's retreat across the desert led, if anything, to increased demands on the Road Watch. GHQ-ME's intelligence staff pressed the LRDG, through Hackett's G(RF), to keep the information coming at all costs; Prendergast therefore doubled the number of patrols so committed. How demanding and dangerous that effort could be was made clear by the experiences of G1 patrol from late November until mid-December 1942. On the move north towards the Via, Captain Timpson (recovered from injuries sustained in the Sand Sea during the September raids) had had to dodge mines and use a route which exposed his patrol to enemy air observation. He was eventually spotted by an enemy plane, which quickly called in a large force of Afrika Korps motorized infantry and armored cars. When this and a second column were about to cut him off, he yelled for his patrol to make a run for it. Only Timpson, seven men, and two trucks and a jeep, however, managed to escape the trap. His other twelve men and their vehicles were captured—the biggest single LRDG "bag" the Germans had so far brought off. The only bright spot was that Timpson had managed to save his radio truck. When he learned that a second or backup patrol, T2, had also run into trouble and been forced back, he knew that he had to press on with the Road Watch effort exclusively with what he had.[138]

Down to only a handful of men, he at length reached a point where a rocky rise overlooked the Via and where he could look north to see the blue Mediterranean. The main Luftwaffe fighter fields were just a few miles to the east, and Timpson's watch teams began spotting heavy enemy ground and air traffic almost immediately. They also saw, and reported by radio, the movement close to shore of several enemy tankers attempting to make emergency runs of fuel to Rommel. But short of sleep from maintaining a constant watch on this short-handed basis and tired out by the seventeen-mile trek on foot between the watchpoint and their base camp, Timpson and his men were beginning to run out of food (most of their rations had been lost when the rest of the patrol had been captured). It had also grown bitterly cold. Desperate enough to try to pass himself off as a German officer, Timpson bartered some goat's milk from an Arab. Finally trading his khaki shirt (ever the Guards officer, Timpson quipped that he hoped the Arab would not spot him by the Jermyn Street address of his London tailor sewn in the collar), he got back to his men as quickly as possible, skin of goat's milk in hand. He also had a brush with a downed Italian pilot, but again managed to pass as a German. Yet G1's time was running out. One member of the patrol, injured earlier, soon developed blood-poisoning and a 103°-plus temperature. Enemy planes began circling the area, tipped off by the patrol's tracks or by alert German DF operators. One of his watch teams was captured when a German infantry battalion pulled off the Via and camped right on top of its position. Even so, just before capture, the team succeeded in burying its "papers and traffic census." The Germans caught two British soldiers who wore neither badges nor insignia to identify them as members of the LRDG.[139]

Timpson himself was, a day later, almost captured in the same manner. On this occasion a German unit, pulling off the road at dawn, parked its vehicles in such a way that the low cluster of tamarisk where G1's commander lay hidden was encircled. For the rest of the day and into the night, Timpson had to lie motionless, enduring not just the cooking smells wafting over from the Germans' field-kitchen, but also the strains of the various "outdated American jazz numbers" coming from a nearly radio truck.[140] Several times enemy soldiers nearly stumbled onto his hiding place. Still, he managed to slip away that night, having spent a full day in the middle of an enemy laager. Yet he had not been distracted to the point of failing to carry on with the Road Watch mission: he had spent the entire day, in fact, counting every enemy vehicle that moved west along the Via. Timpson and what was left of his patrol were finally relieved on December 14, having maintained the watch without a break since November 29. Hackett spoke of this effort as a "wonderfully unique information-securing operation . . . [and] altogether a beautiful piece of work."[141] G1's brand of pluck and determination similarly impressed Brigadier Davy, GHQ-ME's DMO. "No matter what the odds against them," as he later recalled, "LRDG always gave us a constant watch, a constant view."[142] Because of their help, "we always knew exactly how many enemy tanks and how much artillery and so forth to expect. The SAS and, to some extent, the PPA—which would become more valuable later on—were also highly useful to us." But in late 1942, "LRDG was the key. Absolutely everything that passed along the road was seen and reported to us [at GHQ-ME]. From an intelligence point of view, the [LRDG] Road Watch was an absolutely priceless asset."[143]

CHAPTER 9

The Last Act: A Left Hook Around the Mareth Line

I would like you to know how much I appreciate the excellent work done by your patrols.... Without your careful and reliable reports the launching of the "left hook" would have been a leap in the dark.
—General Sir Bernard L. Montgomery to
Officer Commanding LRDG, 2 April 1943[1]

The Road Watch continued. Yet, as Brigadier Davy commented, "the odds against its successful accomplishment unfortunately were heightened at this time by the raiding actions of the other special force, the SAS."[2] Raiding operations were suddenly being mounted in the very area where the Road Watch teams lay hidden. Newly expanded into the full 1st SAS Regiment, Stirling's original L Detachment, SAS, had grown "from a small band of fifty...into a much larger force with its own transport, navigators, and signals."[3] In fact, Stirling's men had become "a sort of LRDG of their own."[4] That unit now comprised, in addition to its original nucleus, the new volunteers received from the troop drafts recently arrived from Britain, the remnants of two Commando units, some Greek volunteers, and—by virtue of what Hackett called "a loose and friendly alliance"—the Special Boat Section as well.[5] In all, Stirling had three full squadrons, each amounting to eight independent, jeep-equipped patrols. In Britain an additional full SAS Regiment, the 2nd, also intended for operations in North Africa, had been raised by Stirling's older brother—thereby permitting wags to comment that they finally understood what the letters "SAS" stood for: "Stirling and Stirling."[6]

Plagued by problems of organizing and training his greatly enlarged force, however, Stirling had been unable to play as large a part as he would have liked in Lightfoot. But following El Alamein, Montgomery gave his permission for the 1st SAS to conduct extensive raids along the Via to the west of El Agheila. The plan was that these raids would cause sufficient havoc to prevent Panzerarmee Afrika's support elements from moving supplies along the road at night. If prevented from operating under cover of darkness, the enemy vehicles would, according to the theory, be left with no choice but to move by day, when the RAF could pounce.[7]

It was this series of interdictive efforts that had thus begun erupting along the Via and practically right on top of the Road Watch. The patrol which relieved Timpson's G1 was horrified to watch as, a day later, the SAS "shot up the road and [enemy] camps in the near vicinity."[8] This action brought heavy ground and air searches of the region near the watch site. When the Germans at length stumbled onto one of the LRDG forward camps, they closed in to attack with armored cars and Afrika Korps infantry. Only the patrol commander and two of his men got away; six other LRDG soldiers were killed or captured.[9]

Theoretically, this problem—SAS beat-ups stirring up the pot to the extent that enemy patrols looking for the SAS raiders happened instead onto LRDG Road Watchers—should have been prevented by the coordinating actions of Hackett's G(RF) section. Certainly Hackett had taken steps. He had, for example, chosen a longitudinal meridian in the desert as a line of demarcation by which to keep the two units clear of each other. The SAS thus got everything to the east of the meridian, the LRDG everything to the west. But controlling the SAS from Cairo could be more easily said than done. Davy recalled that the LRDG "had been good from the start, always responsive to orders. But its offshoots—and the SAS was one—could be very difficult to handle."[10] Perhaps the problem was bound to arise anyway, once the SAS had gained its own vehicles and become independent of the LRDG. The old "raiding partnership," lasting until early summer 1942, was gone. The partners were, by the divergent nature of their missions, in some respects now in competition with each other. There also were limits as to how much control could actually be exerted by radio from Cairo. Hackett complained that it could be "rare to get a reply" once a radio message had been sent to the SAS.[11] In truth, G(RF)'s head was himself reluctant to try to impose too much control. Deep in the desert and faced by situations that changed rapidly, the special-force commander on the spot sometimes seemed the individual best qualified to make decisions about what targets to hit.[12]

Hackett admittedly had come to regard the leaders of the raiding forces as "special types indeed." Stirling seemed easily "the real star" of the special forces that operated in the desert.[13] He was aggressive, ruthless, and had the true soldier's gift for smelling out an enemy's weak points. Prendergast, on the other hand, was "a different species." His mission "was watching, and he was cool, reserved, and efficient," managing to control the actions of his patrols from a central base hundreds of miles away from the scene of the actual operations.[14] Stirling's style was that of "looking round for good things to put bombs on," and he always insisted on leading his raiders in person.[15] Even Montgomery had apparently become impressed by Stirling's abilities. By December Hackett was sending Stirling messages indicating that "Army Commander feels your activities could have decisive effect on the course of battle."[16] It was in this period that Hackett had firmly and repeatedly instructed Stirling to stay clear of the Road Watch area. Yet his messages were not enough. There were "simply too many fat targets," and the SAS had hit them.[17] On another occasion G(RF) radioed Stirling to leave unmolested a particular rail line—"We may need it for the offensive." But Stirling's radioed reply had come back quickly: "Very sorry. Railway blown up at X and Y and Z. Couldn't resist it!"[18]

Stirling's plan had been to hit the enemy at least once every night at some point along the 200–mile stretch of Via lying between El Agheila and Tripoli. But the same spate of attacks that brought the Germans down on the Road Watch patrols also brought them down on Stirling. Rommel had lately become increasingly exasperated with these "British Commandos."[19] They had "succeeded again and again in shooting up supply lorries behind our lines, laying mines, cutting down telephone poles and [carrying out] similar nefarious activities."[20] Inspecting his desert flank during this period, the Panzerarmee's commander found "the tracks of the British, probably made by some of Stirling's people."[21] Within a few days, "Stirling's people" began to take undue losses. A dozen SAS officers and men were killed or captured, the unit's biggest losses since the Benghazi fiasco of three months before.

Meanwhile, Montgomery was bearing down on El Agheila. He already knew from Ultra and the Road Watch's confirming reports that the Desert Fox had shifted the bulk of his forces west and out of El Agheila. Sizeable elements, however, had been left there to delay the Eighth Army, and early in December, Montgomery decided to trap them. His plan was to use a left hook by which to turn the enemy's "inland flank while pinning him down by a frontal attack near the coast."[22] This was a maneuver similar to the one that had been tried the year before at Benghazi. It had failed at that time largely because the flanking force had taken too long to get started. For this new attempt, General Freyberg's 2nd New Zealand Division, backed up by a full armored brigade, would try to move across the desert south of El Agheila. The New Zealanders would then hook north so as to strike the Via just beyond the old Road Watch site at Marble Arch. If this maneuver could be carried out quickly enough, the enemy forces still in El Agheila would be cut off and cornered before they could get away.[23]

This left hook, involving a distance of some 200 miles, would be made through a "tract of desert that was not very well known and [which was] expected to prove difficult."[24] As in the attempt of the year before, the LRDG was again instructed to provide guides and advanced reconnaissance. Prendergast chose one of his best patrols—appropriately enough, R1, which had participated in the previous attempt and which was made up of New Zealanders.[25] Moreover, its commander, Captain Browne, was himself well-known to Freyberg's staff. Maintaining radio silence, R1 linked up with the lead elements of the division and the left-hook effort commenced. Browne carefully led the way through a bad area crisscrossed by deep wadis. He marked the route of advance by setting out iron posts, each fitted with a small, black-painted tin triangle easy to spot against the yellow-white sand. For movement at night, hurricane lanterns, shaded by being placed inside tin cans with one side cut off, served as beacons for the tanks and truck-mounted infantry. The force moved west and then turned north, and, despite the rough ground, made remarkably good progress. Less than twenty-four hours before Montgomery's main attack opened, Freyberg's entire division had reached its designated point on the Via and was all set to trap the Germans. Despite the rapid progress, however, the whole effort went for naught. Just before Freyberg cut the Via, Rommel, tipped off by Luftwaffe air reconnaissance and several radio intercepts, had guessed the coming of this "classical outflanking move."[26] In the nick of time he had managed to get the last of his forces pulled out, just before the jaws of the trap snapped shut. Thus, at El Agheila, the Eighth Army attacked only empty positions; Rommel's forces were already fading back along the coast towards new positions at Buerat and Homs.[27]

Yet Freyberg's efficiency in carrying out the left-hook attempt soon encouraged Montgomery to try another. He sent the New Zealand Division, Browne's R1 again leading, through the desert to cut off Nofilia, a point just inland from the coast and located about where the Via abruptly turned north. The position was held by forces left behind as a rear guard, and Montgomery was convinced that they could be trapped. Indeed, the BBC and Radio Cairo chose at this point to announce that Panzerarmee Afrika had already been "bottled up" and that Montgomery was now merely "hammering home the cork."[28] Their announcement, however, proved premature. Rommel succeeded once again in slipping his forces away just in time; again, the left-hook body arrived to cut off an empty position.[29] The failure of this second attempt was the fault neither of Montgomery nor of Freyberg's New Zealanders, who had managed to negotiate some extremely difficult terrain. The fault, rather, lay with the Road Watch. Had that endeavor been functioning properly, it could have sent back warning at the first signs of the German pullout and in time for Montgomery to have adjusted accordingly, perhaps picking a point further west. But the Road Watch was not working properly. The patrol currently assigned to the watch had recently been forced away from the road at the critical moment. Instead of keeping a watch team on the Via day and night, the patrol had been forced to run south and lie low in the desert just to save itself. The reason was simple: the program of SAS attacks. The pace of Stirling's raids had recently picked up again, and an unfortunate by-product of the enemy reaction to them was that the Road

Watch had been stopped precisely at the moment when it could have been most effective in giving advanced warning of the enemy's sudden retreat up the Via.[30]

Thus, despite Montgomery's two aggressive attempts to employ desert left hooks, the enemy had gotten safely away both times. That the attempts had not altogether been a failure, however, was soon borne out by Ultra intercepts. The effect of these was to indicate that, "since the battle of El Alamein, Rommel has had the tendency to look over his shoulder . . . showing nervousness at the danger of a British outflanking movement."[31] This contributed to Rommel's eventually falling all the way back to Tunisia, giving up even his key port of Tripoli without a fight and departing Tripolitania—and Libya—altogether. He fixed his hopes on the Mareth Line—the extensive, twenty-mile-long belt of thick minefields, bunkers, and barbed wire-protected fortifications which the French had completed in 1939 and which had been intended to block an Italian attack from Libya. By occupying and defending the Mareth Line's strong positions, Rommel could hope to fight, at least for a time, Montgomery's pursuing army to a standstill.[32]

Far to the west, the success of the Torch landings posed for him, however, the dilemma of a second Allied force in North Africa. Once the Anglo-American forces under Eisenhower had gained possession of Oran and Casablanca, they would be free to push east and come at Rommel while Montgomery kept up the pressure from the other side. Hitler promised to send additional German forces as soon as possible. These would include crack airborne formations, the latest models of the FW-190 fighter plane, and numbers of the lethal new Pzkw V1 or "Tiger" tank. Hitler also began dispatching south the vanguard of what, under General Jürgen von Arnim, would grow into a second full Panzerarmee in North Africa, the 5th.[33] Yet despite his strong position at Mareth and the imminent arrival of these new forces, Rommel had already become convinced that Africa was lost.[34] At this time, according to Major the Count de Almaszy, Rommel sent for his desert expert and painted the grimmest possible picture. "You are a Hungarian," Rommel told Almaszy, and "can leave us at any time. If I were you, I should get out while the going's good. We are going to lose this war."[35]

Certainly Rommel was rapidly losing his few remaining outposts in the desert. Prendergast sent three LRDG patrols down to help Leclerc's Free French forces as they moved north for "le conquête du Fezzan." Leclerc had spent much of the preceding year, frequently with the assistance of LRDG patrols, sending periodic forays against the Italian outposts in that region. The audacity of these pinprick raids had managed to win a tribute from the official German armed forces journal, *Die Wehrmacht*. "By taking skillful advantage of . . . weather and violent sandstorms," noted that organ in May 1942, "the de Gaullists surprise the defenders of . . . small forts . . . [and our] southern advance posts."[36] Their raids completed, the attackers quickly "dodge away on their fast vehicles to reappear several hours later, or in the night, at a position 60 or 70 miles away."[37] Now, with Rommel falling back to the west, Leclerc moved rapidly to take the Italian outposts that still covered his flank. The five LRDG patrols sent to assist Leclerc were to raid the southern airfields from which the Italians might send air attacks against the advancing Free French. These raids were in the main successful, although some Italian planes did manage to escape and later inflicted heavy losses on Leclerc's columns. But the French picked up outpost after outpost as they came north from Chad. One of Leclerc's best units was led by Jacques Massu, the veteran of Clayton's Murzuk raid two years before. In January 1943 and 1,600 miles from their starting point, Leclerc's men at last took Murzuk, the final large Italian strongpoint left in the Fezzan. With it they acquired 700 prisoners, a score of fieldpieces, and three dozen armored cars, as well as trucks and other vehicles. The fall of Murzuk meant that, east and south of the Mareth Line, the entire inner desert was now in British or Free French hands.[38]

Meanwhile, the Road Watchers, during the last days of 1942, had literally run out of places from which they could watch the enemy. Neither the difficult, broken terrain near Rommel's new Mareth Line position nor the high concentration of enemy units in that region could permit the sort of surveillance effort which had proved so useful when the armies had faced each other in open desert. The LRDG, after an incredible period of good luck in which the enemy never succeeded in catching and destroying an entire Road Watch patrol, thus received orders to call off a program that had run continuously since the start of the El Alamein offensive two months before.[39] Its termination released patrols needed for the new reconnaissance effort that Montgomery now demanded. At the same time, Peniakoff and his PPA were instructed to accompany the LRDG to its new base much farther to the west. Peniakoff was anxious to begin his "demolition operations," and had been told by Hackett to operate under the overall direction of the LRDG. Initially, he had foreseen "some difficulty" in getting Prendergast to "burden his patrols with 'passengers,'" but the LRDG soon put the PPA to good use in helping to set up a line of dumps that would support the operations of both units behind enemy lines.[40] This was a necessary first step to comply with Montgomery's requirement that the LRDG undertake a series of deep reconnaissances far to the west. One particularly difficult obstacle—a wide cut in the desert known as Wadi Tamet—demanded careful attention because it blocked the line of advance. To find passable routes over it, Prendergast sent out a surveying party escorted by Browne's R1. But the Germans had anticipated just such a move and had already taken steps. When the patrol tried to pass through an area heavily seeded with mines, Browne was badly wounded and the South African engineer officer riding with him was killed. Three days later, the patrol was ambushed by German armored cars. R1's radio truck and a jeep were knocked out; three New Zealanders and a Royal Engineers officer and his sergeant were cap-

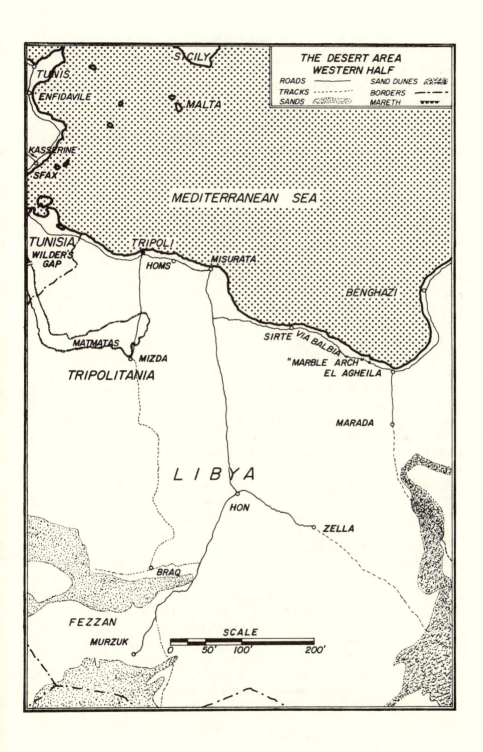

THE DESERT AREA
WESTERN HALF

ROADS ——————
TRACKS ------------
SANDS ⬡⬡⬡⬡

SAND DUNES ⬡⬡⬡
BORDERS —·—·—·
MARETH ⵜⵜⵜⵜ

SICILY

TUNIS

ENFIDAVILE

MALTA

KASSERINE

SFAX

MEDITERRANEAN SEA

TUNISIA
WILDER'S
GAP

TRIPOLI

HOMS

MISURATA

BENGHAZI

MATMATAS

MIZDA

TRIPOLITANIA

SIRTE VIA BALBIA

"MARBLE ARCH"
EL AGHEILA

MARADA

L I B Y A

HON

ZELLA

BRAQ

FEZZAN

MURZUK

SCALE

0   50'   100'   200'

tured. Yet the remnants of the patrol managed to get away, bringing with them the carefully marked maps completed just before the armored cars had caught them.[41]

Hard on the heels of R1's ambush, Prendergast sent out another patrol. This one was the Guards Patrol, now recombined since its losses the month before had rendered impossible the operation of the two G Patrols separately. Under Lieutenant the Honourable Bernard Bruce, an Oxford graduate and nephew of the tenth earl of Elgin, the patrol began probing a second major wadi that blocked the Eighth Army's forward movement. Bruce was joined by an experienced tank officer, Major J. D. Player, flown down from the 7th Armoured Division in order to gauge the possibility of another left-hook attempt. The patrol's other task was to carry a set of the new code ciphers to Stirling, whose 1st SAS had recently shifted forward to operate from a fort earlier abandoned by the Italians. The codebooks were dropped off and the patrol pushed west. Traveling through bitterly cold weather that, fortunately, was sufficiently overcast to keep the enemy's planes from flying, the patrol brushed past German armored cars to outrun them in an open stretch. Finally Bruce reached his area and there split his patrol into two teams, the better to carry out the assigned reconnaissance.[42]

He took one team, Major Player the other. The teams fanned out and tried to avoid contact with the enemy, whose air and ground patrols had several times been spotted off in the distance. Bruce's team almost immediately found an "impassable escarpment"—one of the largest they had ever seen and one not marked on any of their captured Italian maps. It was obvious that the Eighth Army could never hope to get its tanks and trucks over this obstacle. Guided by some Bedouin (who instantly spotted the LRDG soldiers as "Ingleezi"), however, Bruce located two points which would be "quite passable for a force of all arms."[43] This information was radioed back to the Eighth Army. When Player's team failed to show up at the appointed rendezvous, Bruce, with maps and vital information to get back, at length had to slip his vehicles past large concentrations of German units. To speed things up, Prendergast radioed him to report directly to the Eighth Army's headquarters. When G Patrol's commander finally arrived at that location, he was immediately taken before the staff and Montgomery himself. Montgomery pronounced Bruce's information "just what I wanted," and promptly began using it to develop plans for another left-hook effort.[44]

Bruce did not learn until later what had happened to Player and the rest of the patrol. Forced off their route by thick enemy patrols, the second team had reached the rendezvous four days late. Player drove forward in the dark, heading towards what he took to be Bruce's trucks. These turned out to be not LRDG trucks at all but German armored cars. Captured, Player and his LRDG sergeant were forthwith taken to Rommel's headquarters for interrogation. Rommel's chief of staff, Colonel (later Major General) Fritz Bayerlein, listened while they repeated the prescribed name-rank-and–service-number responses. Finally giving up on the questioning as hopeless, Bay-erlein, in good English, said, "Here, have some of your own cigarettes," tossing Major Player a fresh pack of Players.[45] For his part, the resourceful Player managed to break out of an Italian POW cage not long afterwards and eventually made it back to his own lines.

Less than three days after G Patrol's return from the escarpment, Mont-gomery attempted a left hook. The patrol was given the task of guiding three large units. Bruce dropped off his best navigator at the 7th Armoured Division's headquarters, and deposited a second one at Freyberg's New Zealand Division. Bruce himself linked up with the 4th Light Armoured Brigade, the formation which would have by far the most arduous terrain to negotiate. The operation commenced, with the brigade making good prog-ress until it came to the same steep escarpment Bruce had found two weeks before. Bruce was unable to convince the 4th Light Armoured's commander that the escarpment was totally impassable, and that his best chance was to use the alternate route that G Patrol had located. He ultimately took some satisfaction in the fact that the full squadron of armored cars sent down the escarpment required three full days just to find a way back out again. But the brigade commander's obstinacy had delayed the left hook and effectively wrecked the operation. Rather than being cut off, Rommel's forces once again had time to break away from an exposed position.[46]

They fell back to join the rest of Panzerarmee Afrika, now engaged in improving the "strongest position" in North Africa, the Mareth Line.[47] That line stretched from the Mediterranean down to the rugged chain of foothills in the south. Its system of fortifications blocked a natural corridor and the one route by which the Eighth Army could advance up the coast. The positions themselves extended down to and were tied in with the range of steep hills, the Matmatas, that lay just inland. This line of hills ran generally north and south in the desert and then bent around to the northwest, thus effectively sheltering the Mareth Line's right flank.[48] Still more difficult ob-stacles lay to the west and south, just beyond the hills: a series of desert salt lakes and mudflats, which the Bedouin called *chotts*. Angling south from the Matmatas and the easternmost chott was the largest single Sand Sea to be found in either the Libyan desert or the Sahara, the Grand Erg Oriental. The various hills and salt flats were barriers restricting and channelizing an Eighth Army whose experience for the past two years had been the flanking movements and sweeping maneuvers made possible by the open terrain of the Libyan desert. Here, however, the terrain favored the Germans who held the narrow gateway to southern Tunisia. The existence of the difficult barriers flanking the Mareth Line seemed to restrict the Eighth Army to only one possible course of action: to attempt, by frontal assault, to smash through the very center of the German-held fortifications—and to pay a high price in the process. It seemed clear from the map that Montgomery had at last run out of open desert and territory where left hooks might be used to outflank Rommel and thus pry him loose from his very strongest positions.[49]

Late in January 1943, Montgomery sent for Prendergast. The Eighth Army's commander explained that, very soon, he would have to move against the Mareth Line, and that frontal attacks there would be exceedingly bloody. They might, indeed, cost the British more casualties even than El Alamein's 13,500 killed, wounded, or missing. Moreover, such attacks might fail to win success.[50] Montgomery explained that he already knew plenty about the Mareth Line—he happened, in fact, to have in his headquarters no less than the French engineer officer who had helped lay it out, as well as the former French chief of staff in Tunisia who had presided over its construction. These two officers provided a vast amount of information. They also planted the germ of a concept that, could the maneuver be carried off, might yet enable the British to outflank the Mareth Line and thus avoid the necessarily high casualties to be incurred in attempting to take it by frontal assault.[51]

The premise that they advanced was based, however, on fairly thin evidence—a single report completed years before and whose conclusions, relative to the right flank of the Mareth Line, had never been put to any sort of realistic test. The French officers indicated that, in 1938, a veteran Saharan soldier, General Catroux, had been able to complete a reconnaissance of the region just inland from the Mareth Line. His report had offered the speculation (Catroux was then, of course, concerned solely with an Italian invasion) that it might be theoretically possible for a force of perhaps one or two very lightly equipped but first-quality enemy divisions to skirt past the Matmata hills and then move north to go around and above the flank of the Mareth fortifications. Several gaps, potentially useful as avenues of approach, were mentioned in his report. Nonetheless, an attack of that sort—even if one were possible, and if one of the gaps did turn out to be passable—would be an extremely risky undertaking at best. Certainly the terrain through which such an attack would have to proceed was marked on the French maps as *terrain chaotique*. Nor did the two French officers offer any real encouragement that a practicable route could be found to the north of the gaps, all of which lay well to the south of the Mareth Line.[52] A force attempting to get over the steep-sided desert hills might get itself hopelessly bogged down, thus giving Panzerarmee Afrika plenty of time to spot it and react accordingly. Even so, the Catroux report had at least given Montgomery the idea. He now needed something far more solid on which to go before he committed forces—as he put it—to such a "leap in the dark."[53] Although an extensive RAF photoreconnaissance effort would be mounted, aerial photographs alone were of little use in determining whether armor, artillery, and motorized infantry could actually negotiate a particular region of desert terrain. Thus, by the time Prendergast returned south to his Group Headquarters, he understood very clearly that the LRDG's crucial mission at this point was to find a way whereby the Eighth Army could outflank the Mareth Line.[54]

His first step was to see to the establishment of advanced dumps for supporting the deep probes the patrols would have to make as they began exploration of possible routes.[55] He dispatched Easonsmith, by RAF plane, on a liaison visit to Algeria to Lieutenant General Sir Kenneth A. N. Anderson's British First Army, now advancing east as part of Eisenhower's Allied Expeditionary Force. There, Easonsmith arranged for cooperation in the form of a fuel dump that would service any patrols that made it that far west. Every possible step would be taken to prevent the enemy from getting suspicious about heavy reconnaissance activity to the west and south of the Mareth Line. The patrols would radio back their information in a special cipher code which Bagnold, then deputy signal-officer-in-chief, GHQ-ME, had recently devised.[56] Throughout the campaign Rommel had been "well served by his field intelligence"[57] and by his radio intercept service, but, as far as the British could tell, the Germans had failed to break this new code. Prendergast also acted to improve the procedures for LRDG cooperation with conventional forces in left-hook efforts. Montgomery had already selected Freyberg's New Zealanders for the outflanking attempt around Mareth, if a way for such a move could be found. Prendergast therefore arranged for Captain Browne, his most experienced "left-hooking" patrol commander, to be attached to the headquarters of the 2nd New Zealand Division. Browne's mission there was to offer expert advice and to assist in the putting together of the most accurate and detailed maps possible of the region through which the attempt would be made.[58] These included a sand table model, constructed to scale, which would be revised and refined according to the latest information radioed in by the patrols. The 2nd New Zealand Division's key staff officers would then use the model in order to study the terrain and to brief commanders, most particularly those who would lead the advanced elements. Overall, this process permitted a high degree of speed and efficiency, and suggested a level of special force–conventional element tactical cooperation not previously attained.[59]

The first patrols pushed off on their probes less than a week after Prendergast's meeting with Montgomery. But the enemy patrolling activity south of Mareth was heavy. S1 Patrol, for example, accompanied by some of Peniakoff's men and exploring a possible route, ran into a strong Italian force and some German armored cars. The patrol got free but, in the process, lost three vehicles and one man killed. Additional losses were incurred as the process of investigating the Matmata hills south of Mareth continued.[60]

Fittingly enough, given that it was New Zealanders who had been selected to make the flanking attempt, a New Zealand patrol became the first one actually to find a way through the hills.[61] That patrol, T1, a veteran of the Murzuk raid and of Clayton's ambush south of Kufra, also won the honor of being the first British unit actually to cross the frontier from Tripolitania into Tunisia. Its initial explorations, however, were disappointing. Several promising cuts in the hills proved to be nothing but cul-de-sacs; the line of 300-to-600-foot-high Matmatas in this sector appeared unbroken. So also was the sector further to the west and south, each potential spot turning out to be choked with soft sand through which the 2nd New Zealand Division could never hope to get its vehicles. Finally, far to the south and almost sure that it would have to return to base empty-handed, the patrol found what Montgomery needed—a narrow opening in the hills with flat, open desert just beyond. T1 pushed through this gap and explored to the west. There was very little room for maneuver once out of the gap: the impassable dunes of the Grand Erg Oriental were just off to the west. Yet the patrol brought back quite enough information to make it clear that Freyberg's men could get through the gap and then turn north to outflank the Mareth Line.[62]

At 2nd New Zealand Division headquarters, Browne, assisted by engineer officers, therefore molded his sand table model to show a path through the barrier. In the days ahead, Prendergast sent out additional patrols to explore the area north of what, at Eighth Army headquarters, was already being referred to as "Wilder's Gap" in honor of the veteran patrol commander who had found it.[63] The need now was to locate a suitable route by which Freyberg's force could, once through the gap, hook in through the Matmatas from north and west of the Mareth Line. A likely spot seemed to be the area just below a ridge line identified on the French maps as the Jebel Tebaga. The investigation of this region fell to Lieutenant R. A. Tinker's T2 Patrol, accompanied by Peniakoff and most of his PPA force. Tinker set up an advanced fuel dump and then ventured into the Grand Erg Oriental. His patrol had seen nothing like its "dirty brown, powdery, silt-like sand" in the Libyan desert; not even Bagnold's tried-and-true methods seemed to work in the dunes.[64] But Tinker discovered that, by trying to stay clear of the worst dunes and keeping to the edge of the Grand Erg, he could still move forward. He was convinced that a fairly large motorized force could make adequate if not rapid progress through this narrow region lying between the Erg and the steep Matmatas.[65]

Tinker did not gain this information without cost, however. He had already spotted columns of Italian armored cars busily ranging the desert floor near the line of hills and, through his binoculars, had seen German infantry digging in on the far crests. Local Bedouin may have tipped off the enemy to his presence. At any rate, while he and Peniakoff were out exploring routes, ME-109 fighters suddenly swept in from the north to attack T2's base camp. In just seconds nine trucks and a jeep were on fire and exploding, one of them the radio vehicle. Five New Zealanders were wounded, and the patrol's entire reserve of gasoline went up in flames. With only three jeeps left and almost no fuel (he was then some 450 miles from the LRDG's base), Tinker decided to strike out for the friendly forces nearest his present location. These, he reasoned, would most probably be the U. S. II Corps, at this moment pushing from Algeria towards Tunisia and the Kasserine Pass. If he could link up with the Americans, he could also radio his reconnaissance information through to the Eighth Army.[66]

With the wounded (some of whom had suffered painful burns) loaded on the jeeps and everyone else walking, Tinker got his patrol away before enemy ground forces could arrive to follow up the air attack. He got to the edge of the Chott el Jerid and threaded his jeeps over its narrow camel track—thus, by necessity, making the first successful crossing by motor vehicle of this quagmire of coagulated mud, salt, and sand. Days after the ME-109 attack, Tinker finally ran into the first advanced American units. The Americans, still new to the war, had seen nothing like this British desert patrol, and at first Tinker had trouble getting them to believe that he had actually crossed the desert through the enemy lines from the Eighth Army. But eventually, after being taken to II Corps headquarters, he was conveyed to British First Army headquarters and from there got his messages sent to Montgomery.[67]

It was while arrangements were being made to get them back to the Eighth Army that T2 and the PPA managed a few days' recuperation amidst the pleasures of an exotic, *Beau Geste*-style Saharan outpost called Tozeur. The town was sheltered by lush date palms and peopled by burnoused men, veiled women, and swaggering Zouaves, Spahis, and Foreign Legionnaires who seemed straight out of central casting, and its Hôtel Trans-Atlantique was thick with war correspondents. Peniakoff grumbled later that some of these had contrived to fill the "men with whiskey," thereafter concocting "incredible fables out of their drunken ramblings."[68] But the desert campaign's foremost war correspondent, the Australian Alan Moorehead, was there and formed a rather different impression of the occasion. Certainly Tinker's and Peniakoff's men deeply impressed him. He wrote later of meeting these "survivors of a unit of the Long Range Desert Group," the "picked men . . . who for two years had been making stupendous trips behind enemy lines."[69] They struck him as almost "unrecognizable as soldiers . . . [being] black-bearded up to the eyebrows . . . [and with] their young faces . . . burnt almost henna-red by the sun. They wore ragged shorts and shirts bleached white by the sun . . . [and] native sandals. In place of helmets . . . they had khaki native cloths that kept the sun off the backs of their necks."[70] Moorehead had covered the British and Empire-Commonwealth units fighting in the desert since the beginning, but he was particularly taken with these special-forces soldiers. "They showed just what the desert will do to white men, how reliant it will make them and how tough." These men "loved their life . . . of going on, of discovering new places and breaking open new trails."[71]

Actually, Tozeur fell not long thereafter to a mobile column of German armored cars and motorized infantry. But its loss was only a small setback for the Allies compared to what was happening elsewhere at the same time. Choosing his moment carefully, Rommel had once again contrived to do the unexpected. With Montgomery edging towards him from one direction and Eisenhower's Allied Expeditionary Force slowly closing in on him from another, Rommel had decided to hit the Allies at their weakest point. His attentions were drawn to the southern or right flank of the broad front of British, Free French, and American units advancing into Tunisia from Algeria. While von Arnim's 5th Panzerarmee held in the north, Rommel, with timing reminiscent of his best days in the desert, had, in the third week of February, quickly lashed out. With German movements sheltered by a billowing sandstorm and preceded by intensive Luftwaffe attacks, Rommel sent his panzers straight into the exposed elements of the U.S. II Corps at Kasserine Pass.[72]

The American commander, Lieutenant General Lloyd R. Fredendall, was caught totally by surprise. The inexperience of the Americans and Eisenhower's divided, overcomplex Allied command structure had together handed Rommel precisely the opening he needed. Also, through Ultra, Eisenhower had "for several days" been receiving strong indications of an impending German attack—but an attack that would take place in the northern sector.[73] The intelligence officer on Eisenhower's staff, British Brigadier Eric E. Mockler-Ferryman, had been led by Ultra "to believe that [only] a feint would be made where the [real] attack actually occurred."[74] That is, he believed, the Germans would merely feint at Kasserine, thereafter making their real attack in the north. Mockler-Ferryman had spent the previous two years working with Ultra, but this did not prevent his misjudging what the decrypted signals were revealing about German intentions. The old problem with Ultra surfaced once again. Ultra may indeed have created for "top Allied commanders . . . the unique experience of knowing not only the precise composition, strength and location of the enemy's forces, but also, with few exceptions, of knowing beforehand exactly what he intended to do."[75] Unfortunately, Rommel's attack at Kasserine Pass was clearly one of those "few exceptions." In the event the Americans, by dint of hard fighting, finally did manage to hold Rommel; his offensive was stopped before it could achieve any decisive strategic results. He himself wrote later that while "the American troops could not yet be compared with the veteran troops of the Eighth Army . . . the tactical conduct of [their] defense had been first class. They had recovered very quickly after the first shock."[76] Eisenhower replaced the hapless Fredendall with Lieutenant General George S. Patton, Jr. Mockler-Ferryman also was relieved because he had been "too wedded to one type of information [i.e., Ultra]."[77] His replacement, Brigadier K. W. D. Strong, was an intelligence officer who was "never satisfied with his information," but who would instead bend every effort to procure it, and weigh what he received, from every possible source—"spies, reconnaissance . . . any means available."[78]

As has been noted, the essential purpose of the LRDG Road Watch had been to prevent just such a reliance on only one source. The year before,

GHQ-ME's Brigadier Shearer had been replaced because he had, it was charged, relied too "insufficiently on Ultra."[79] Thereafter, the Road Watch program had been initiated. But the terrain of Tunisia was quite different from that of Libya. No longer was there a lengthy, open desert flank on which the LRDG could conveniently sit and watch unobserved every vehicle that passed along Rommel's line of communications. The effect of Tunisia's hilly, mountainous terrain was to mask the German movements from their enemies. Hidden behind a protective range of mountains, Rommel had been able to carry out his tactical deployments largely unobserved. Even had the terrain been more conducive to Road Watch operations, none of the LRDG patrols was available for such a task. At the time of the Kasserine battles, they were all committed to the search for a way around the Mareth Line. Moreover, the LRDG's patrols belonged to Britain's desert army, the Eighth Army. There had apparently been no thought of assigning them to screen the advance of Eisenhower's Anglo-American and Free French Allied Expeditionary Force.[80]

Meanwhile, the Germans' taking of Tozeur had the effect of leaving several LRDG and PPA elements dangerously short of fuel. Almost out of gasoline, Bruce's G Patrol, for example, had to give up trying to make it all the way back to the LRDG base. Instead, as had Tinker earlier, Bruce drove north into Algeria. His plan was to reach a friendly headquarters as quickly as possible, and thereby get his crucial maps dispatched by air over to Montgomery.[81] G Patrol slipped past the enemy and finally fetched up at a desert airfield from which Major General James H. Doolittle's Northwest African Strategic Air Force's divisions, groups, and wings were daily rising to pound the enemy-held port of Tunis.[82] Doolittle, the famous air racer, had led the famous B-25 raid on Tokyo the previous spring. Bruce's men apparently made an instant hit with the gaggle of B-17 and B-24 bomber pilots at the base: "Ayrabs in jeeps" is how the Americans reportedly referred to G Patrol.[83] The curious flyers strolled in from their missions and gawked as G Patrol played its "desert raiders" role to the hilt. As Bruce recalled, the sight of the patrol in its "desert-camouflaged vehicles bristling with guns" was something that, as even the Americans were prepared to admit, "had Hollywood beat."[84] Bruce's only complaint was predictable: in contrast to a British officers' mess, the comparable messes of the Americans were "disappointingly dry" of spirits. The patrol was at the point of being taken up for a ride in a B-17 when word came that Bruce was to head back immediately.[85]

He did not discover until later just how lucky he had been to dodge the heavy enemy patrols covering Mareth. In fact, the Germans had just managed to bag a major prize indeed: none other than the "Phantom Major" of special forces himself, the officer whom correspondent Moorehead described as "the most resourceful adventurer of the desert war"—David Stirling.[86] The founder and commander of the 1st SAS Regiment and destroyer of "more enemy aircraft than . . . any of the famous Allied air 'aces'" had been caught in a wadi forty miles north of Mareth, sound asleep.[87]

Stirling had pushed off on his last mission early in January with two main objectives in mind.[88] The first was to raid the enemy's road network north of Mareth, and "to put, by explicit request of Montgomery, every possible pressure on the German rear."[89] The second was to conduct reconnaissance and to report back on the nature and extent of the enemy's defensive positions. But Stirling had one additional goal as well: to try, if possible, to get through the enemy lines and go all the way to Anderson's First Army in the north. In attempting this last undertaking, however, Stirling had in mind a further purpose which he did not bother to disclose to Hackett or to the Eighth Army. Stirling believed that if his force could actually become the first unit to get through and reach Anderson, such an accomplishment would materially help the case for getting the two existing SAS regiments raised to full brigade status. Raised to this new status, the brigade would, of course, be commanded by David Stirling, and it would be able to mount special operations on a scale far grander than ever before.[90]

The 2nd SAS Regiment—the one formed and commanded by his brother, Lieutenant Colonel William Joseph Stirling, also of the Scots Guards—had recently arrived in North Africa for operations in support of the First Army.[91] Stirling's own reading of his fortunes at the moment had apparently led him to determine that it was now "vital to get instructions and support from a more important formation than Middle East Headquarters."[92] His idea was that, by getting through the enemy lines and thence up to Anderson, he would be in a position to work directly in order to acquire "the sympathy of the top brass of the First Army." He had two reasons for this view. First, it seemed to him that becoming "the first fighting unit to . . . [establish] contact between the Eighth and the First Armies" would be an important achievement in itself.[93] Second, it would afford him an opportunity to try his quiet but effective and Churchill-touted brand of personal dynamism on a new set of general officers. This might facilitate the arguing of the case for merging the two SAS regiments into a full and separate SAS brigade. "A little additional prestige . . . [gained from this bold passage through the lines] would," he thought, "come in handy."[94]

Yet the LRDG patrol reports now coming in indicated increasingly heavy enemy activity around Mareth, and G(RF)'s Hackett told Stirling to be exceedingly careful. In fact, Hackett expressly instructed Stirling to avoid altogether the dangerous corridor formed by Gabes on the coast and the edge of the Chott el Jerid in the west.[95] That region, which the Eighth Army referred to as the "Gabes Gap," was no more than sixty miles wide. Both then and by radio messages later, Hackett warned Stirling in strong terms to stay clear of this narrow gap. Hackett knew that an enemy intelligence directive had recently given warning to all units of "acts of sabotage by

English patrols." The directive both outlined the raiding techniques of the LRDG and SAS and indicated that "operations carried out recently . . . with the use of special vehicles reveal that this special form of warfare, highly developed by the English, is now being used in Tunisia. Further operations of this kind must [therefore] be expected."[96] Also, Stirling was warned to be particularly alert to possible treachery by the local Arabs, whom intelligence viewed as being firmly under the control of the enemy. None of this fazed Stirling in the slightest, however. Dividing his force and pushing into enemy territory, he struggled for several days through some of the Grand Erg's difficult dunes.[97] Meanwhile, his two groups maintained radio contact with each other, making the mistake of "frequently . . . [signalling] their positions."[98] At length Stirling decided to begin his raids by pushing directly up through the narrow Gabes Gap—exactly the thing he had been told not to do. The first of his parties moved off at dusk. Unknown to Stirling, it soon ran into three Afrika Korps armored cars and, in the confusion, lost its crucial radio jeep, which meant that it could offer no warning of the heavy enemy activity. Even so, the remainder of the party was able to carry out mining attacks against a railroad. Yet it soon ran into more armored cars, which, this time, were backed up by Afrika Korps infantry. Trying to get away, the party and its one surviving officer were at the point of asking local Bedouin for help when they were surrounded and captured by a company of Italian motorized infantry.[99]

Stirling's group had pushed off not long after the first. Late in the afternoon, German reconnaissance planes spotted his vehicles, but he decided to press on just the same. The party kept moving through the night. Just before dawn he hid his jeeps in a twisting, brush-covered wadi.[100] Sentries were posted and everyone else, thoroughly exhausted from a hard travail through rough country, went to sleep in the wadi. So also, apparently, did the sentries. At midafternoon on a cold, clear day, the two guarding the wadi's entrance were "awakened by a steady crunch, crunch against the rocky surface."[101] They woke up too late, and stared into the muzzles of German submachineguns. The surprise was complete; within seconds a full company of enemy troops was pouring into the wadi. Stirling and all of his men were captured, the Germans rounding them up and herding them out onto the floor of the desert. Stirling was amazed at what he saw: completely encircling the wadi were armored halftracks, armored cars, and the best part of a battalion of German troops. Addressing him in good English, his captors—who took no pains to hide their glee—told Stirling that they were a new and special unit only recently sent to North Africa for the express purpose of "track[ing] down the SAS."[102] Moreover, the German officer in command told Stirling that his unit had just happened to pick this particular spot for a routine training exercise. Going through the drill for cordoning off an area, the commander had by chance sent a patrol to the very wadi where Stirling and his men were hidden. What had begun as a training exercise for

German troops new to the desert had ended up netting "the Phantom Major" and his "notorious SAS leaders."[103] Within a day or two, Axis radio stations were announcing that the "famous Colonel Stirling" had been captured and was now a prisoner of war.[104]

Yet Stirling was hardly one to give up easily. He had, moreover, also managed to save his RAF "button" escape compass. When it was dark, after having spent the day locked up in a makeshift prisoner of war compound, he suddenly, on the pretext of asking for a cigarette, contrived to break away from his guards. He ducked their shots and eventually sought refuge in a house owned by "a gold-ringed, apparently well-off, portly Arab."[105] The Arab told Stirling that he had previously helped "other shot-down British airmen" to escape.[106] Yet it was probably this same Arab who turned Stirling in. At any rate, a day later, the Bedouin shepherd ostensibly guiding Stirling to safety suddenly pulled out a Beretta pistol. Stirling was held at gunpoint until Italian troops, arriving in trucks as if on cue, came up to retake the SAS leader. That night, Stirling was taken to an airfield and flown to Italy in a Luftwaffe Ju-52 transport.[107] His career of causing trouble for the enemy did not, however, cease now that he was a prisoner. Over the next year he escaped with such regularity that he was eventually, after a final hunt had run him down again, taken to perhaps the most notorious of the German prisoner of war camps, Colditz. A castle situated high on top of a mountain, Colditz was the supposedly escapeproof place which the Germans reserved for the most difficult of their Allied prisoners. Its stringent security was too much even for the daring and resourcefulness of David Stirling, and he spent the rest of the war there.

The loss of the SAS leader was almost immediately felt on the British side. Hackett and GHQ-ME had first learned of Stirling's capture from the signal which Rommel had flashed to OKW in the Enigma code. (In an interview conducted two years before Winterbotham's book first revealed the Ultra Secret, all that Hackett could say was that "we had had all the Germans' high-level ciphers all the time, but they didn't know it.")[108] Stirling may indeed, as Hackett indicated, have been caught "doing precisely what I had told him not to do."[109] It would, nevertheless, become quite clear to him that, at least in its North Africa operations, the SAS never again quite matched "the drive, audacity, or destructiveness" which had characterized its efforts when Stirling was in command.[110] The officers who succeeded him either lacked his skill in leading operations, or else they lacked his gift for sensing where best to strike in order to inflict the maximum dislocation on the enemy.

Nor had the PPA quite measured up to the early hopes for what it might accomplish in the way of harassing Rommel's rear areas and lines of communication. The restrictive nature of the Tunisian terrain made it difficult to get at the enemy with the same degree of access characteristic of the earlier period in Libya. In addition, Peniakoff chafed under the burden of having to coordinate operations with the LRDG. As quickly as he could, he seized the opportunity to try to get himself temporarily attached to the First Army—in other words, to get free of the Eighth Army and thus of LRDG control, and this despite the rather liberal "roving commission" established by Prendergast that had instructed the PPA leader to harass the enemy at "my discretion and according to my judgment."[111] As the desert campaign approached its final act, the LRDG, as in the beginning, would once again come to play the dominant and crucial special-force role.

Montgomery was now far along in his preparations for the move against the Mareth Line. Desert Fox Rommel—now raised to the title of commander, Heeresgruppen (Army Group) Afrika, and controlling both his and von Arnim's armies—had long since been alert to the possibility of another left-hook attempt. Late in January, a conference at his headquarters examined just such a possibility, and General Catroux's 1938 report alluding to possible gaps in the Matmatas was discussed in detail.[112] Rommel remarked to an Italian general that "in Africa, there is no defense line that cannot be outflanked, and that goes for this line at Mareth, too."[113] Rommel could not know that first Wilder's patrol and then Tinker's had already found passable routes by which to outflank Mareth. In the past, however, the presence of these LRDG patrols poking around on his flanks had often presaged a British left hook, and Rommel was thinking about one now. His response was therefore to try to hit Montgomery with a spoiling attack before the latter could move. His hope was to catch the Eighth Army's forward units "off-balance," and to hit them sufficiently hard to "interfere with . . . [the] preparations" for the impending drive on Mareth.[114]

Early in March, he dispatched his tanks against Montgomery's advanced elements. The attack was to have caught the British by surprise; instead, the German armor lurched forward into a trap. RAF air reconnaissance and excellent radio-intercept work by the British Y Service had alerted Montgomery, and, by the end of the day, his antitank guns had knocked out over forty enemy tanks. This defeat proved to be Rommel's last battle in the desert. Three days later the Desert Fox, "his former fiery spirit . . . burning low," flew north.[115] He informed Hitler that North Africa was lost, and that as many of the German troops there as possible should be saved before it was too late. The Führer sent Rommel on convalescent leave and placed von Arnim in command in North Africa.[116]

Meanwhile, under General Patton, a rejuvenated and more seasoned U. S. II Corps prepared to come at von Arnim from the other side. Also, General Sir Harold Alexander was appointed "Commander of the Group of Armies operating in Tunisia," a step which at last placed the Allied armies under firm and unified operational control.[117] Eight days after Rommel's spoiling-attack attempt, Montgomery issued his detailed plans for the attack on the Mareth Line. The night of March 20 was set as the jump-off date. The plan called for the Eighth Army's 30th Corps to attack frontally against the line's eastern flank—"to break in, roll it up from east and north, destroy or prevent the escape of the garrison, and then . . . [to] advance and capture Gabes."[118] That portion of the plan involving special operations and concerning the LRDG in particular was the left-hook attempt. Montgomery relied upon this maneuver to threaten the enemy from the flank and rear at precisely the same time that the 30th Corps was commencing its attack against the Mareth Line. As indicated, the left-hook effort would be led by the 2nd New Zealand Division. Joined by an armored brigade and backed up by Leclerc's Free French "L" Force, Freyberg would command a formation including the 2nd New Zealand Division and designated the New Zealand Corps.[119]

The LRDG patrol reports brought back during the previous month indicated that the New Zealand Corps would have to pass through territory considered arduous but passable. In terms of total distance to be traveled, the route itself—dipping south through the desert and then around the Mareth flank—amounted to more than 200 miles. This long haul would require the staging of vast amounts of gasoline in secret dumps in order to fuel the movement of a full corps' complement of tanks and trucks. Thus, night after night before the maneuver commenced, every available motor transport unit was used to haul thousands of tons of fuel to the series of dump areas whose location, just east of Wilder's Gap, the LRDG had already pinpointed. By daybreak each morning, every drum of fuel was hidden away and camouflaged against the chance of discovery by enemy aircraft.[120]

For weeks, Prendergast had kept Tinker's T2 Patrol, which he had selected to guide the left hook, working in the closest possible cooperation with Freyberg's key staff officers. Just before the move began, Tinker's patrol of New Zealanders, accompanied by an engineer officer, pushed west through Wilder's Gap to begin marking out the route of advance. They employed the same system of metal stakes hung with black triangles that had worked so well in the El Agheila left-hook attempt of three months before. Tinker also attached one of his most practiced navigators to the headquarters of the 2nd New Zealand Division. This individual would have the task of guiding the provost section actually charged with controlling the division's forward movements. When all was ready, Freyberg's advanced units quickly moved across the desert and arrived at Wilder's Gap, their first stop. The Germans, by this point, had already guessed that something was up, but when a force of Afrika Korps armored cars attempted to investigate, it was driven off by heavy fire. Finally, under cover of darkness and guided by T2, Freyberg's 25,600 men, riding in trucks, jeeps, Bren-gun carriers, tanks, and armored cars, began moving north through Wilder's Gap. Twenty-four hours later, the 30th Corps' attack on the Mareth Line proper commenced.[121]

Von Arnim was ready for it. The British infantry and engineers were at first able to fight their way forward into the Mareth defenses, but were stopped when their heavy tanks were held up by a rain-swollen wadi. When von Arnim counterattacked with the 15th Panzer Division, Montgomery realized that the frontal-assault portion of the thrust against the Mareth Line was doomed. He decided, therefore, to throw his available weight behind the left hook. This decision thus converted the New Zealanders' "subsidiary flanking manoeuvre into the principal stroke."[122] In order "to reinforce General Freyberg as strongly as possible," Montgomery ordered a full armored division—the 1st Armoured Division, consisting, in addition to its personnel, of some 1,200 tanks and vehicles—to hook around and then link up with the New Zealanders.[123] T2 Patrol therefore received orders to intercept and then guide forward the 1st Armoured Division.

Meanwhile, Freyberg's force had continued to make good progress up the narrow corridor lying between the Grand Erg's dunes and the Matmatas. The route was cut by wadis and was full of patches of soft, powdery sand. The advancing column raised clouds of dust easily spotted by the enemy. Even so, the lead elements, ably guided by Tinker's navigator, soon reached the hills near what was called the "Tebaga Gap." When the news of their arrival reached him, von Arnim, fully appreciating the threat to his right flank and rear, shifted two of his best divisions, the 21st Panzer and the 164th Light Africa, over to block the gap. RAF and USAAF bombers (these last being flown by some of the same American pilots whom Bruce's patrol had met the month before) were quickly called in to pound the German units trying to hold the line.[124]

Tinker's T2 met and guided the 1st Armoured Division through Wilder's Gap and then north towards Tebaga. Despite breakdowns and several traffic jams along the way, the move was made with remarkable speed. It marked, indeed, the first time that a full armored division, British or German, had attempted to move through country as difficult as that to be found in this portion of the desert. Yet the tanks managed to negotiate the bad wadis and soon joined forces with Freyberg. Attacking late in the afternoon and with the "sun [supposedly] blinding the enemy's eyes," the 1st Armoured's tanks punched through the ruins of a Roman wall and surged into the Tebaga Gap.[125] But the Germans fought back fiercely and finally halted the attack. Even so, the left hook had already achieved its purpose. Three days before and sixty miles to the north and west, Patton's II Corps had lashed out at the 10th Panzer Division at El Guettar. Von Arnim's conclusion was that Patton's advance would soon cut him off in the north. At the same time, Montgomery renewed the pressure at Mareth. To get out of the trap, von Arnim began pulling his units out of the Mareth positions before he could be pinned between Patton in the north and Montgomery in the south. His withdrawal was completed in less than seventy-two hours. The LRDG-guided desert left hook, the largest—and last—of the desert campaign, had done its work well. It had applied pressure at precisely the right moment, and the Germans had been pried loose from a position which had beaten the frontal assault mounted by a full corps.[126]

Montgomery pursued as von Arnim retreated north towards Tunis, his last port. For von Arnim, and for those surviving Afrika Korps soldiers who had first laid eyes on their desert battleground two years and three months before, the end in North Africa was already in sight. They were being backed into an ever-smaller pocket in Tunisia's northeast corner. The Allied forces closed in on them from three directions. "Rivalry between American and British troops for the victory honours was matched by rivalry between the two British Armies," the First and the Eighth.[127] This rivalry served to spur on the attack that, in April and May, steadily wore down the German and Italian formations attempting to hold onto the little territory that still remained to them. Hitler ordered the Germans to resist to the last bullet and the last man, but, in the first week in May, the British fought their way into Tunis itself. Five days later, von Arnim surrendered, with over 250,000 German and Italian soldiers, and a vast booty of guns, tanks, and vehicles. General Alexander signalled Churchill that "all enemy resistance has ceased . . . [and] we are masters of the North African shores."[128]

For the three desert special forces, the LRDG, SAS, and PPA, the last act had been the actions preliminary to and during the Mareth left hook. After Mareth, the Eighth Army had lurched out of its customary sands and north into the brush-dotted hills and green valleys of Tunisia. The special forces had run out of the desert country that had facilitated their operations.[129] Even before that, the game had changed. As Peniakoff, just before Mareth, had recognized, his unit no longer had a desert open into which it could vanish. The situation was now different; gone was the desert flank open for a thousand miles.[130] In Tunisia, in order to get at the enemy, the PPA had had to find a gap, slip through it to make the raid, and then run back, hoping always that the gap had not already been closed.[131] With the Germans retreating north, Montgomery realized that "there will be no further scope for . . . [this type of special operation] in the country we are now entering."[132] On the second day of April, the LRDG patrols were released from Eighth Army control and sent back to GHQ-ME.

For the LRDG patrols in particular, the 1,200-mile trip back along the Via Balbia, past El Agheila, Benghazi, Barce, and Tobruk, held plenty of memories for men who had spent two years watching or raiding along that road when Rommel had stood poised and ready to strike into Egypt. Sixteen LRDG soldiers—three officers and thirteen men—plus the rather greater numbers of SAS, Commando, and SIG soldiers who had ridden with them, lay buried somewhere in the vast sands that stretched off to the south. Another two dozen LRDG soldiers were prisoners or were listed as missing in action. But Egypt now became a backwater of the war as the action shifted north and across the Mediterranean. At the request of GHQ-ME, some of the LRDG patrols were briefly sent into the desert to search for salvageable vehicles among the thousands of hulks left behind in the wake of the Eighth Army's advance. Other patrols were dispatched to "show the flag" in several captured oases, and to support British civil affairs officers sent to administer Libya.[133] Also, much of the LRDG was disbanded, including the Guards Patrol and portions of the New Zealand patrols. Having suffered "crippling losses" in the battles around Mareth, the Grenadier, Coldstream, and Scots Guards battalions that had so readily furnished their excellent volunteers in the early stages of the campaign were now forced to ask for them back.[134] Many of the New Zealanders were similarly recalled to the 2nd New Zealand Division that, along with the Germans' 90th Light Division, had comprised what Moorehead thought of as "the elite of the British and German armies" in the long desert campaign.[135] Yet these men were reluctant to leave the LRDG. They found themselves poring "over maps of the world, searching in desperation for another desert...[in which to operate]." One of the LRDG's departing New Zealanders even told Moorehead that "we got a tip ...that they might have a job for us in China [fighting the Japanese]."[136] He and his comrades were hopeful that they might be sent to the Gobi desert, but just now there seemed to be no enemies to fight in those far regions.[137] After nearly three years in which the desert had been used to best advantage in order to strike at and disrupt the enemy, to watch his movements, or to guide conventional forces in sudden flanking attacks, the war had seemingly left behind the very first of the units formed for special operations in the desert, and at that very moment when its accomplishments had won for it a level of prestige freely acknowledged by every British unit that had fought in the campaign.[138]

Epilogue

The last war spawned a surprising number of special units and formations...[but these] did not give, militarily, a worthwhile return for
the resources in men, material and time that they absorbed.
—Field Marshal Sir William Slim, *Defeat Into Victory*[1]

The stock of special operations and of the forces that carried them out "had,
at least at GHQ [Middle East], been high from the beginning."[2] This "sometimes unrealistic faith" in what small units of the LRDG, SAS, PPA, and
Commando type might accomplish amounted almost to a "cult of special
forces."[3] It remained clear that a succession of key generals had chosen to
rely upon such forces as a means by which to cope with the problems of
warfare in that region. The result was that by spring 1943 their prestige
virtually ensured that new roles would be found for them as the war shifted
to the other side of the Mediterranean. For example, the desert patrols of
the proven LRDG were probably in no real jeopardy of disbandment, even
though the actual focus of operational commitment had now moved well
away from the desert habitat which had shaped them since 1940.[4]

In fact, Prendergast—and likewise the leaders of the SAS and PPA—had
commenced searching for a new role just after the Mareth operation. In
Prendergast's case, one was soon found. As the Allies began looking ahead
to the impending thrust across to Sicily and Italy, GHQ-ME's planners
concerned themselves with the feasibility of staging a number of secondary
and supporting operations. These, it was envisioned, would be mounted on
the right flank of that drive and would be diversionary in nature. In one of
them, a small contingent of British forces, to be spearheaded by the LRDG,

would be shipped north into the Aegean Sea, thence to occupy various of the small islands situated between the Greek and the Turkish coasts.[5]

A GHQ-ME directive of April 1943 specified that Prendergast was to begin transforming his patrols into units "able to operate by jeep or on foot in mountainous country . . . with Patriot forces."[6] The "Patriot forces"—local partisan bands to be supplied with arms and explosives—would be used to raid, harass, and in general make trouble for the Germans. The hope was that these guerrillas would succeed in tying down large numbers of enemy troops. The plan seemed, as far as the theory went, a workable one. As things turned out, however, the LRDG's participation in the first of these operations ultimately proved a disaster more costly to the unit than the nearly three years of desert operations combined.

In the summer of 1943, selected patrols began training in landing operations conducted from submarines and destroyers. Other elements moved up into the rugged highlands of Syria to begin learning the techniques of mountain warfare. No portion of the LRDG, however, had time to complete a full program of training before events compelled action in a new and unfamiliar zone of operations. The Allies, having by now taken Sicily, were moring quickly against Italy itself. At the same time the Germans, in order to cover the Greek flank, began shifting units down into the Aegean Sea's Cyclades and Dodecanese chains of islands. It was this step which precipitated the immediate commitment of the desert patrols to their new arena. Hastily pressed into service as a force by which to interfere with the enemy's new thrust, the LRDG, reinforced by volunteers newly recruited to replace the departed Guardsmen and New Zealanders, was taken by ship across the Mediterranean.[7]

The initial operations went well. (Indeed, some of the efforts with local partisan forces would later be expanded, by novelist Alistair Maclean, into the fictional account entitled *The Guns of Navarone*.) Still, it greatly alarmed Prendergast to note how operations on these small islands imposed new and "distinctly unfavourable conditions."[8] These went against "principles considered essential to the success of the LRDG, principles that ran back to the earliest days [of the desert campaign]."[9]

The most obvious difference was that the unit was no longer a motorized, self-contained force operating in a region whose ground and conditions it knew better than did the enemy. Put another way, it was a special force that "could no longer be regarded as the master of its own element."[10] Also, with the shift in arena there had come "a loss in mobility, of independence of movement."[11] The LRDG, as an improvided raiding force, now had to be carried to the scene of its operations by small landing craft furnished and controlled by the Royal Navy. Once ashore, and functioning now in terrain altogether too rugged for vehicles, it was deprived of the mobility, speed, and flexibility of movement that had spelled success in the desert. The loss of its vehicles, its customary mode of conveyance, meant also the loss of the old advantage of heavy firepower. Since the patrols now had to operate on foot, they could carry only fairly light weapons. And whereas in the past, after a raid, the patrols could make a run for the safety of the desert, they were now to be stuck on some small island, a situation which afforded enemy forces a far better chance of hunting them down. Finally, these factors in combination greatly reduced the range of options, the types of maneuvers— "the bag of tricks, as it were"—available to the patrol commanders.[12]

Disaster overtook them within a month of their arrival in the Dodecanese Islands. Prendergast, soon elevated to second-in-command of the British raiding forces operating in the Aegean, arranged for Lieutenant Colonel J. R. Easonsmith to succeed him as commanding officer of the LRDG. But in October 1943—against the recommendation of both Prendergast and Eason-smith—the unit was ordered to embark in motor launches and move north in order to capture a small island. The operation went badly from the start. On the way up, Luftwaffe aircraft spotted and pounced on the flotilla, with the result that crucial folbots were lost to strafing attacks before most of the raiders could be landed.[13] Of the LRDG soldiers who actually made it ashore, most were ultimately lost to the Germans. These losses included Captain Richard Lawson, the medical officer who, the year before, had won the Military Cross for his part in the Barce raid, and had been "thrilled and honoured to be offered the chance to join the LRDG."[14] Lawson was wounded and captured; he and a number of the others spent the rest of the war in a German prisoner-of-war camp.[15]

Other and even heavier losses were soon sustained on Leros, the major island held by the British in the Dodecanese chain and against which the Germans at length mounted a small but determined air and naval assault. Preceded by fighters and Stukas, JU-52 transport planes landed several battalions of German airborne troops on a narrow strip of land lying in the middle of the island. A second wave of airborne troops followed the first, with additional enemy units being brought in by sea. These forces quickly pushed out of their initial lodgements and against the single British brigade— plus the collection of small units that included the LRDG—trying to hold Leros. In the rocky hills and defiles of that island's broken terrain, the combat developed into a series of sharp, disjointed engagements fought out between small units. It was one of these actions that claimed the life of the LRDG's new commanding officer. As the British situation deteriorated, Easonsmith took a reconnaissance party forward in an effort to scout enemy positions. Circling around for a better approach, he stumbled instead into a German ambush and was killed. Within a day the Germans were in full control of the island. Virtually the only troops to escape them were a mixed group of LRDG soldiers and elements of Major the Earl Jellicoe's Special Boat Squadron, Stirling's old raiding partners from the several attempts on Benghazi. These men escaped by seizing and then making off with an enemy motor launch, and were eventually picked up by a British destroyer.[16]

Prendergast, who, after Easonsmith's death, had resumed command of the LRDG, also managed to get away. By dodging German patrols, he and the others were able to hide out in the hills long enough to radio out a call for help. At night, six days after the rest of the island's defenders had surrendered, an RAF air-sea rescue launch finally slipped in to take them to safety. As late as two weeks after the surrender, handfuls of LRDG soldiers were still escaping from the island.[17]

Following the disaster at Leros (in the nearly three years of the desert campaign, no enemy force had ever succeeded in pinning and attacking the LRDG in its own base) the remnants of the unit were brought back across the Mediterranean. Although Prendergast's men and the other special-force troops had given a good account of themselves and, here and there, had managed to slow down and even stop the German paratroopers' advance, the fiasco all but terminated the participation of New Zealand troops in the LRDG. Leros brought up the awkward Gallipoli-era issue of whether New Zealand troops should be employed directly under British command.[18] In planning the Dodecanese effort, GHQ-ME had apparently neglected to obtain in advance the permission of New Zealand authorities for committing the LRDG's New Zealand troops to what was regarded as a whole new series of operations.[19] Those authorities now, therefore, requested the immediate return of all such troops to their original New Zealand units. Although a hastily worked out compromise in the end permitted a handful of officers and men to stay, most of the LRDG's New Zealanders—or approximately one-half of the unit—now departed. Of these, most were sent to Italy to rejoin their parent 2nd New Zealand Division and would, early in 1944, take part in the heavy fighting for Monte Cassino.[20] Their departure and the high casualties in the islands reduced the LRDG to a fraction of its former strength. It seemed entirely possible also that the British troops still remaining in the unit would be pulled out in order to replace the heavy losses already sustained in the Italian fighting. In short, a force formed for desert warfare seemed, nine months after the conclusion of the desert campaign, about to be disbanded.[21]

But the special forces still had friends in high places. Hackett had left GHQ-ME and now commanded a parachute brigade in Italy.[22] But Brigadier George Davy, who had recently served as deputy chief of staff at Allied Force Headquarters in Algiers, and had thus "been out of contact with the special-forces business for six months," now came back.[23] Early in 1944, he was named commander of a composite force designated Land Forces Adriatic. Consisting of a single Commando brigade, some artillery units, and a mountain battalion, Davy's "odds and ends had quite a large job to do." His command was to "do everything possible in order to mount attacks against the enemy elements located on the mainland of Greece, Albania and Yugoslavia," provided that those elements were located "within reach of the coast, or were on an island."[24] In short, with the very meager forces available to him, Davy was to keep as many German troops tied down as possible. One of his first demands was "to have LRDG and any other special forces available put under me, and they promptly were."[25]

Davy's request reflected his faith in the capabilities of special-force units. He had "never doubted" that the LRDG could, despite the recent disasters in the islands, "perform quite as well as a raiding-reconnaissance force [on the southern periphery of Europe]" as it had during the height of the desert campaign.[26] The LRDG's Aegean setbacks had come "because no one had properly considered what to do with the patrols, after they ran out of desert." The basic concept was sound; the needs now "were 'repairs' and the proper medicine." Davy's solution was to have the LRDG "trained extensively in seaborne and airborne operations for use . . . in Italy and the Balkans." Its patrols would form his advanced raiding parties for Land Forces Adriatic. But "the main emphasis," as in the last stages of the desert campaign, "would continue to be on the reconnaissance role.[27]

Prendergast's talents were meanwhile required elsewhere. Posted back to Britain, he was, following training in parachute operations, assigned to the Special Operations Executive and a mission in support of the D-Day invasion of France. His new function envisioned a landing behind enemy lines and, in conjunction with OSS teams furnished by the American forces, a program by which to organize and coordinate the actions of the French resistance effort. With the loss in action of Easonsmith and the departure of Prendergast to the SOE, the logical choice to take over command of the LRDG was David Lloyd Owen. YI's old patrol commander, he had served most recently as commander of B Squadron during the fiasco in the islands, and he possessed an unrivalled grasp of LRDG operations. Lloyd Owen thus took over in 1944 as the fourth and last commanding officer of the unit, and continued in that capacity for the rest of the war and until the unit's disbandment in spring 1945.[28]

Like Prendergast, Lloyd Owen was a practical and efficient organizer. He began by stressing training in those techniques which the bitter experience of the Aegean operations had shown to be crucial. Although the basic patrol-and-squadron structure was retained, various changes were accomplished. These had, overall, the effect of altering the essential mode of tactical employment of the LRDG to the degree that, in the opinion of Brigadier Davy, a "rather different type of special unit emerged." The desert veterans were given training in parachute operations, and in raiding and reconnaissance missions on skis and in mountainous terrain. This sort of internal reorganization, plus the intensive training effort undertaken in early spring 1944, went far towards helping the unit adapt itself to the conditions of its new theater of operations. During the next year, both in the Balkans and across the Adriatic in northern Italy, the LRDG proved itself able to send back useful information and also—as GHQ-ME's April 1943 directive had required—to operate with "Patriot forces" behind German lines. They raided a whole series of lucrative targets, and numbers of enemy troops were kept busy trying to cope with the LRDG and the various guerrilla elements. In short, the unit again demonstrated its ability to maintain pressure on the enemy from the rear. In addition, numbers of downed RAF and USAAF pilots and crewmen were rescued, including ten Americans pulled from a 15th Air Force B-24, crash-landed and sinking in the Adriatic, and eventually returned to friendly lines.[29]

Thus, from Lloyd Owen's takeover in 1944 until the surrender of Axis forces in Europe in 1945, the LRDG continued—as Davy had believed that it could—to function with considerable effectiveness as a special force. But in June 1945, two years and one continent removed from its original desert habitat, it was finally disbanded by decision of the British War Office. That decision foreclosed any possibility of the unit's being employed against the Japanese, although Lloyd Owen had already undertaken to explore such a role.[30] Field Marshal Sir Harold Alexander, now supreme Allied commander in Italy, indicated to Lloyd Owen that the "news of the War Office decision . . . must have come to you as a great shock—as it did to me."[31] Lieutenant General Sir Bernard Freyberg noted that "[n]obody realizes better than I do the extent to which . . . [the LRDG's] work contributed to the success of the North African campaign. . . . [I]t will always be a source of pride and satisfaction . . . that New Zealanders were able to play a part in . . . [the LRDG's] long series of brilliant operations."[32] But the decision was final. When the War Office was faced with the problems of demobilizing a mass army of citizen soldiers, such special units as the LRDG, regarded as unique to the war just fought, would be among the first to go.

Joining the LRDG in disbandment were its two main partners in raiding—those other special forces originally formed to meet the requirements of the desert campaign. It was not lost upon and indeed was a source of some little pride to members of the LRDG that their unit had, by its "long series of brilliant operations," as Freyberg had put it, helped to make possible the early successes of Stirling's L Detachment, Special Air Service, and of Peniakoff's PPA.[33] Like the desert campaign's original special force, however, these units also were no longer needed. The war against Japan ended before serious consideration could be given to adapting the SAS to operations perhaps in China, Indochina, Burma, or Manchuria, although "speculation about such a role [had] abounded just prior to [that unit's] disbandment."[34] In the British Army during the post-World War II demobilization, forces of this type were, in a period of budgetary stringency, regarded as luxuries for which there was neither a need nor the resources to maintain them. Their personnel either returned to civilian life, or, in the case of the handful of regulars involved, were transferred to other units and military assignments of a more conventional nature.[35]

That conventional soldiers in plentiful ranks had been skeptical of the special-forces approach all along can hardly seem surprising.[36] The pronouncement of one of the most highly regarded British generals of the war, Field Marshal Sir William Slim (who had commanded during the difficult campaign against the Japanese in Burma), was that the British Army in World War II had "spawned a surprising number of special units and formations ... each trained, equipped, and prepared for some particular type of operations."[37] These had, on the whole, turned out to be "expensive, wasteful, and unnecessary."[38] Such groups of "super-soldiers" had consumed good men, scarce equipment, and generous amounts of training time, and yet they had carried out only a limited number of missions. Moreover, the notion that units of this type could be used only for certain operations had generated jealousy in nonspecial units, and what Slim saw as the "cult" of special forces. The overall effect was "undoubtedly to lower the quality of the rest of the army—both by skimming the cream off it, but [also] by encouraging the idea that only specially equipped *corps d'élite* could be expected to undertake ... [those most obviously demanding, the most clearly hazardous missions]."[39] The only exception to this might be the type "of special unit ... designed to be employed in small parties, usually behind the enemy, on tasks beyond the normal scope of warfare in the field."[40] Such a unit would have exclusive responsibility for deep-penetration raiding and reconnaissance activities—precisely the kinds of operations that conventional units could not accomplish unless afforded additional training and specialized equipment. Properly handled and coordinated from the highest levels, units of this variety might be capable of achieving truly "strategic results."[41]

After the war, Slim's way of thinking—undoubtedly reinforced by Winston Churchill's regaining the prime ministership in 1951—at length helped get the Special Air Service resurrected and into combat, this time as part of the counterinsurgency effort mounted in Malaysia in the early 1950s.[42] Nor did such forces thereafter disappear from the British array: both the SAS and a Royal Marines unit claiming descent from Jellicoe's World War II Special Boat Squadron saw action in the Falklands War of 1982.[43] This and other examples constitute ample evidence for some that the British have a particular bent towards reliance upon special forces. Six years after the end of World War II, addressing a meeting of the Royal United Services Institution, the same Colonel Hackett who had headed the G(RF) section in GHQ-ME advanced a "national characteristics" explanation. One of the basic reasons why the British had been willing to employ special forces, he said, was the "national temperament." This had disposed them, he argued, "to find an open flank wherever there is blue water," and was the natural legacy of some centuries of maritime ascendancy.[44] Reinforced by a sort of "adventurous individualism," the tendency could quite easily be transposed to a situation in land warfare—not least to "the small raiders' paradise" of the North African desert.[45] Their enemies also occasionally indulged the British with testimonials along this line. When they lost Stirling, declared Rommel, the British had "lost the very able and adaptable commander of the desert group which had caused us more damage than any other British unit of equal strength."[46] And, commented Generalmajor von Holzendorff, whereas British generalship was often on the "very methodical" side, not so the British special forces. These had been "master[s] in small-scale warfare (commando raids, long-range reconnaissance in the desert), and [had] worked with sportsmanlike skill."[47]

The handful of regular officers who had emerged as the masters of this "small-scale warfare" fared well in their subsequent British Army careers.[48] Neither Stirling of the SAS nor Peniakoff of the PPA had been career officers; both left the army at the end of the war.[49] But three of the LRDG's four commanding officers—Easonsmith, the fourth, and the only nonregular, was killed in action late in 1943—had been careerists. All three—Bagnold, Prendergast, and Lloyd Owen—eventually attained at least the rank of brigadier, with Lloyd Owen, who had joined the LRDG as a junior officer, gaining promotion to major general before his retirement thirty years later. By that time he had served in Malaya, as a brigade and regional force commander, as General Officer Commanding Cyprus District during the mid-1960s, and as chief of the officer-selection program in the British Army.[50] Hackett attained the highest rank of the group—full general—as well as a knighthood. He had left GHQ-ME to take command of a parachute brigade, thereafter seeing action in Italy and at Arnhem in 1944. By the time he retired in 1968 to become principal of King's College, University of London, he had held a variety of staff appointments and served in NATO as commander of the British Army of the Rhine.[51] In Lloyd Owen's words, the LRDG had "rescued me from a rather humdrum assignment and given me a chance to show what I could do."[52] Coming at the right moment, the involvement with desert special operations had perhaps helped each of these men "to show what I could do."

That they had been successful owed rather more to individual abilities, the availability of a critical mass of desert expertise, and good strategic judgment on the part of at least one theater commander than to any guidance set forth in official doctrine. Nearly a decade before, in his *Lectures on F. S. R. III*, British armored-warfare theorist Major General J. F. C. Fuller had declared that "how to make use of . . . [motorized scouting and raiding] forces . . . is one of the new and by no means least important problems of war which now faces us."[53] Concerning such forces, however, the *Field Service Regulations* offered little beyond a few generalized comments. Despite the long experience of Air Control in Iraq, the *FSR* made no attempt to clarify in detailed fashion the role of motorized reconnaissance forces in a desert environment. And while neither Fuller's writings nor those of Basil H. Liddell Hart in the same period could in fairness be described as shedding much additional light on the problem, Bagnold, for his part, admitted later that he had "never much bothered to read . . . [either of these two authors] before the war anyway."[54]

Of necessity, therefore, and by its very nature the desert special-operations effort had developed and taken on a form quite apart from the conventional armor-artillery-infantry campaign waged along the Mediterranean littoral. Moreover, it had evolved through several main phases, as the basic strategies by which the British conducted such operations were themselves shifted from one to another. The first strategy employed—filling the summer and remaining months of 1940 and resulting in the raising of the LRDG—was in essence a delaying strategy. As an instrument of strategic deception, it succeeded in its purpose of buying time for the improvement of British conventional forces. Commencing as a stopgap and coming hard on the heels of the Commando attacks already being mounted from Britain, it did not fail to encourage a belief in the efficiency of special operations.[55] During the period of this delaying effort, distance and coordination problems ensured that the special-operations venture would remain a dimension strategically in consonance with but operationally separate from the conventional campaign conducted in the Libyan plateau. The arrival of the Germans, however, soon necessitated the adoption of a second strategy, a raiding strategy, that was directly keyed to the support of the British conventional forces. The period of this essentially interdictive strategy lasted through the summer of 1942 and the arrival of British reinforcements in overwhelming strength. It supported offensives or, when Italo-German forces drove to the gates of Egypt and British fortunes fell to their nadir, paralleled the efforts of the RAF to molest an enemy supply effort strained by distance. As a psychological concomitant of their physical destruction, the raids were intended to "affect the enemy's morale . . . [and] engender considerable uneasiness in the mind of the enemy [commander]."[56] While unrealistic expectations regarding this "handsome-profit-in-proportion-to-the-cost"[57] endeavor brought about the ill-conceived raids of September 1942, the advent of LRDG Road Watch and scouting/guiding capabilities led to a strategy of integrating special-force operations with those of the conventional forces. What was most crucial during the period of this integrated strategy, however, was less the ability of the special forces to reconnoiter routes or conduct a Road Watch than the improved performance of British conventional elements. Only when these had reached a level of operational skill approaching that of their enemies could the capabilities offered by the special forces be exploited to the fullest.[58]

The chief flaw of the desert special-operations venture was not so much the proliferation of forces (targets and opportunities for their employment existed virtually until the end of the campaign) but the failure to devise a controlling apparatus to keep pace with that proliferation.[59] The structure was workable but loose. Hackett's G(RF) section represented an attempt to set up "a clearing house . . . by which to juggle conflicting types of operations."[60] The attempt proved effective. How much more effective it might have proved had it been expanded into something more substantial—a "Joint

Desert Special Operations Command," perhaps—must remain an unanswered question with contemporary implications for soldiers. Joining the desert forces under one command while yet preserving their unit identities and basic missions was a control measure that arguably offered prospects for better coordination and greater efficiency. No such attempt was made, however, not least because of adroit political maneuvering on the part of at least one of the special-force principals. Also, in the critical period when such a move might have been attempted, the attentions of Alexander and Montgomery and their staffs were understandably absorbed by the problems of Alam Halfa and El Alamein.[61] As Prendergast commented many years later, "What we had probably worked about as well as could be expected under the circumstances."[62]

"What we had" had first taken form in 1940 in response to perceptions of strategic exigency, unusual circumstances of geography and habitat, and the instructive precedent of Lawrence and the Light Cars of World War I. The availability of men with exceptional desert expertise became for Wavell the means of fleshing out a vague concept of "motor guerillas." The special forces that evolved from this beginning made possible a collective response to the conditions of the desert, becoming the instrumentality by which the British extended their reach to wage war in an additional arena of the campaign. A succession of British theater commanders in the Middle East grasped and exploited the situation to advantage, achieving in the process a conceptual synthesis regarding the employment of these forces. If not the decisive agency in achieving the final outcome in the desert, the special forces were at least a factor. They were the means by which the British exploited and their enemies failed to exploit the North African desert as a strategic ally.

Notes

ABBREVIATIONS USED IN NOTES

CID	Committee of Imperial Defence (British)
CIGS	Chief of the Imperial General Staff
C-in-C	Commander-in-Chief
COS	Chiefs of Staff (British)
DAK	Deutsches Afrika Korps
DF	Direction-Finding
DMI	Director of Military Intelligence
DMO	Director of Military Operations
DSO	Companion of the Distinguished Service Order
Dtd/dtd	Dated
ed.	edited (by), edition
FO	Foreign Office (British)
FRS	Fellow of the Royal Society
G(RF)	General Staff Operations, Raiding Forces
GHQ-ME	General Headquarters, Middle East
GOC-in-C	General Officer Commanding-in-Chief
HMSO	Her Majesty's Stationery Office
HQ-BTE	Headquarters, British Troops in Eygpt
IWM	Imperial War Museum

JCS	Joint Chief of Staff (U.S.)
LAMB	Light Armoured Motor Battery
LCP	Light Car Patrol
LHCMA	Liddell Hart Centre for Military Archives, King's College
LRDG	Long Range Desert Group
Ltr/ltr	Letter
MC	Military Cross
MEF	Middle East Forces
MHRC	Military History Research Collection
MoD	Ministry of Defence (British)
nd	no date
np	no place, no publisher
OBE	Officer, Order of the British Empire
OCMH	Office of the Chief of Military History
OKH	Oberkommando des Heeres (German Army High Command)
OKW	Oberkommando der Wehrmacht (German Armed Forces High Command)
OSS	Office of Strategic Services (U.S.)
PPA	Popski's Private Army
PR	Photographic Reconnaissance
PRO	Public Record Office
Pzkw	Panzerkampfwagen (armored fighting vehicle)
RAF	Royal Air Force
RAMC	Royal Army Medical Corps
RASC	Royal Army Service Corps
RE	Royal Engineers
RGS	Royal Geographical Society
RN	Royal Navy
SAS	Special Air Service
SBS	Special Boat Section/Squadron
Sd Kfz	Sonderkraftfahrzeug (armored special-purpose vehicle)
SIG	Special Interrogation Group
Sigint	Signal Intelligence (intelligence gained from interception and decryption of enemy signals)
Soe	Special Operations Executive (British)
USGPO	United States Government Printing Office

WO   War Office (British)

W/T   Wireless Telegraphy

Y   Y Service (interception, decryption, and analysis of enemy tactical messages)

CHAPTER 1

1. T. E. Lawrence, *Seven Pillars of Wisdom: A Triumph* (9th ed.; Harmondsworth, Middlesex, Eng.: Penguin Books, 1971), p. 612.

2. Basil H. Liddell Hart, *A History of the World War, 1914–1918* (reprint ed.; Portway, Bath, Eng.: Cedric Chivers, 1968), pp. 398–99.

3. For Lawrence, see Sir Ronald Storrs, "Lawrence," *The Dictionary of National Biography* (3rd ed.; Oxford: Oxford University Press, 1961), pp. 528–31; Basil H. Liddell Hart, *Colonel Lawrence: The Man behind the Legend* (New York: Dodd, Mead, 1934); Suleiman Mousa, *T. E. Lawrence: An Arab View* (Oxford: Oxford University Press, 1966); John E. Mack, *A Prince of Our Disorder: The Life of T. E. Lawrence* (Boston: Little, Brown, 1978); Desmond Stewart, *T. E. Lawrence: A New Biography* (New York: Harper & Row, 1977); and Stanley and Rodelle Weintraub, eds., *Evolution of a Revolt: Early Postwar Writings of T. E. Lawrence* (University Park: Pennsylvania State University Press, 1968).

4. *The Times History of the War* (London: The Times, 1916), vol. 9, p. 312.

5. The standard work on the Senussi is E. E. Evans-Pritchard, *The Senussi of Cyrenaica* (Oxford: Clarendon, Press, 1949). See also Major General George MacMunn et al., *History of the Great War Military Operations: Egypt and Palestine from the Outbreak of War with Germany to June 1917*, vol. 1, pt. 1 (London: HMSO, 1928), pt. 1, pp. 101–3; and Majid Khadduri, *Modern Libya: A Study in Political Development* (Baltimore: Johns Hopkins University Press, 1963), p. 15.

6. MacMunn et al., *Military Operations: Egypt and Palestine*, pp. 107–8; and *The Times History of the War*, pp. 281–315.

7. Captain Charles E. Callwell, *Small Wars: Their Principles and Practice* (3rd ed.; London: Harrison for HMSO, 1903), pp. 1–3.

8. See WO 95/Ind. 29771, *Order of Battle, Troops in Egypt from November 1914–April 1918;* and MacMunn et al., *Military Operations: Egypt and Palestine*, vol. 1, pt. 1, pp. 136–38, and app. 2, p. 389.

9. Major George Inchbald, *Camels and Others: The Imperial Camel Corps in World War I* (London: Johnson, 1968), pp. 18, 33.

10. For the Camel Corps, see Ian L. Indriess, *The Desert Column* (Sydney: Augus & Robertson, 1932); and for remarks on later operations against the Turks see Lawrence, *Seven Pillars of Wisdom*, pp. 554–607.

11. Richard M. Ogorkewicz, *Armor: A History of Mechanized Forces* (New York: Frederick A. Praeger, 1960), pp. 169, 237.

12. Ibid., pp. 424–26; Basil H. Liddell Hart, *The Tanks: The History of the Royal Tank Regiment and Its Predecessors: Heavy Branch Machine-Gun Corps, Tank Corps and Royal Tank Corps, 1914–1945*, vol. 1, (New York: Frederick A. Praeger, 1959), pp. 18–21; and MacMunn et al., *Military Operations: Egypt and Palestine*, vol. 1, pt. 1, p. 139.

13. WO 95/4478, *War Diaries, Egyptian Expeditionary Force, Desert Mounted Corps:*

Light Car Patrols; see especially diary entry of 15 July 1915. MacMunn et al., *Military Operations: Egypt and Palestine,* vol. 1, pt. 1, p. 138n.

14. Lieutenant General Sir John Maxwell, quoted in *The Times History of the War,* p. 293.

15. See the descriptions in war correspondent W. T. Massey's *The Desert Campaigns* (New York: Putnam, 1918), pp. 145–46; MacMunn et al., *Military Operations: Egypt and Palestine,* vol. 1, pt. 1, pp. 133–34; and *The Times History of the War,* pp. 310–14.

16. Khadduri, *Modern Libya,* pp. 10–16.

17. Sir John Slessor, *The Central Blue* (London: Cassell, 1956), pp. 15–18, 650–55; and MacMunn et al., *Military Operations: Egypt and Palestine,* vol. 1, pt. 1, pp. 135–39.

18. MacMunn et al., *Military Operations: Egypt and Palestine,* vol. 1, pt. 1, pp. 142–44; and WO 95/4478, *War Diaries, E.E.F . . . Light Car Patrols.*

19. Massey, *Desert Campaigns,* p. 162.

20. Captain Claude H. Williams, "Light Car Patrols in the Libyan Desert" (typescript copy lodged in Royal Geographical Society, London), pp. 16–18.

21. Ibid.

22. "Report of H. W. Hodgson, Brigadier General, Commanding Siwa Column, dtd 9th February 1917" (copy lodged in Royal Geographical Society, London), pp. 1–10.

23. Williams, "Light Car Patrols," pp. 19–21.

24. "Report of H. W. Hodgson, Brigadier General," section no. 3 (cover sheet) and p. 1 (annotation).

25. General Sir Archibald P. Wavell, *The Palestine Campaigns* (3rd ed.; London: Constable, 1941), p. 38.

26. Alexander H. C. Kearsey, *Operations in Egypt and Palestine, 1914 to June, 1917, Illustrating the Field Service Regulations* (2nd ed.; Aldershot, Eng.: Gale & Polden, 1931), p. 31.

27. Dr. John Ball, *Notes on Recent Determinations of Geographical Positions in the Libyan Desert* (Cairo: Survey Department, Survey of Egypt, 1919), pp. 1–6; *Who's Who in 1940: An Annual Biographical Dictionary* (London: Adam & Charles Black, 1940), p. 144; and interview with Brigadier Ralph A. Bagnold, OBE, FRS, Mark Beech, Edenbridge, Kent, Eng., 31 May 1972.

28. Ball, *Notes,* p. 1; and Bagnold interview, 31 May 1972. Ball, "Desert Survey," in Egypt, Ministry of France, *The Survey of Egypt, 1898–1948: Survey Department Paper No. 50,* G. W. Murray, ed. (Cairo: Survey of Egypt, 1950), outlines the contributions of the LCPs, 1915–1918.

29. See W. B. Kennedy Shaw, *Long Range Desert Group: The Story of Its Work in Libya, 1940–1943* (reprint ed.; Portway, Bath, Eng.: Cedric Chivers, 1970), pp. 11–12; D. Newbold, "Survey Methods and Results," *Geographical Journal* 78 (December 1931), app. 1, pp. 526–29; and Dr. John Ball, *Desert Reconnaissance by Motor-Car: Primarily a Hand Book for Patrol Officers in Western Egypt* (copy lodged in Royal Geographical Society) (Cairo: np, 1917).

30. Lieutenant General Sir Archibald P. Wavell, *Allenby: A Study in Greatness* (New York: Oxford University Press, 1941), p. 188; Liddell Hart, *History of the World War,* p. 398; and Cyril Falls, "Allenby," *The Dictionary of National Biography* (3rd ed.; Oxford: Oxford University Press, 1961), pp. 7–18.

31. Stanley and Rodell Weintraub, *Evolution of a Revolt,* pp. 1–10.

32. Lowell Thomas, *With Lawrence in Arabia* (Garden City, N.Y.: Garden City/ The Century, 1924), pp. 3–10. The literature on Lawrence is extensive, and researchers will wish to consult Great Britain, Imperial War Museum, *Thomas Edward Lawrence: A List of References by and on Colonel T. E. Lawrence in the Imperial War Museum* (London: Imperial War Museum Library, 1952).

33. Lawrence, quoted in Liddell Hart, *History of the World War*, p. 280.

34. Lawrence, *Seven Pillars of Wisdom*, pp. 172, 193–202.

35. A brief summary of early topographic work is in WO 32/10776, *Historical Sketch of the Directorate of Military Intelligence During the Great War*. See also Cyril Falls et al., *History of the Great War Military Operations: Egypt and Palestine, From June 1917 to the End of the War*, vol. 2, pt. 2 (London: HMSO, 1930), p. 406; Wavell, *Palestine Campaigns*, pp. 97–99; and C. S. Jarvis, *Arab Command: The Biography of Lieutenant Colonel F. W. Peake Pasha* (London: Hutchinson, 1942), p. 31.

36. Wavell, *Allenby*, p. 193n.

37. Stewart, *T. E. Lawrence*, p. 132.

38. Basil H. Liddell Hart, *T. E. Lawrence: In Arabia and After* (London: Jonathan Cape, 1948), p. 428; Liddell Hart, *Colonel Lawrence*, pp. 354–65.

39. A. J. P. Taylor, *English History: 1914–1945* (New York: Oxford University Press, 1965), p. 149.

40. Stewart, *T. E. Lawrence*, pp. 292–306.

41. Lord Moran, *Churchill Taken from the Diaries of Lord Moran: The Struggle for Survival, 1940–1965* (Boston: Houghton Mifflin, 1966), p. 113.

42. Shelford Bidwell, "Irregular Warfare: Partisans, Raiders and Guerillas," *Journal of the Royal United Services Institute for Defence Studies*, 122 (September 1977), p. 80.

CHAPTER 2

1. Major Ralph A. Bagnold, *Libyan Sands: Travel in a Dead World* (London: Hodder & Stoughton, 1935), pp. 18–19.

2. Interviews with Brigadier Ralph A. Bagnold, OBE, FRS, Mark Beech, Edenbridge, Kent, Eng., 1972 and 1976. On British forces, see WO 33/1002, *Order of Battle of the Egyptian Expeditionary Force, Middle East Area, January 1921 to August 1922 (Parts I–XVI)*.

3. T. E. Lawrence, quoted in *The Sunday Times* (London), 22 August 1920, p. 7.

4. Howard M. Sachar, *The Emergence of the Middle East, 1914–1924* (New York: Alfred A. Knopf, 1969), pp. 366–82; Sir John B. Glubb, *War in the Desert: An RAF Frontier Campaign* (London: Hodder & Stoughton, 1960), p. 69; and Basil H. Liddell Hart, *The Tanks: The History of the Royal Tank Regiment and Its Predecessors: Heavy Branch Machine-Gun Corps, Tank Corps and Royal Tank Corps, 1914–1945*, vol. 1, (New York: Frederick A. Praeger, 1959), pp. 208–9.

5. Wing Commander R. H. Peck, "Aircraft in Small Wars," *Journal of the Royal United Service Institution* 73 (August 1928), p. 543.

6. Air Marshal Sir John B. Glubb, "Air and Ground Forces in Primitive Expeditions," and Squadron Leader G. E. Godsave, "Armoured Cars in Desert Warfare," in *Journal of the Royal United Service Institution* 71 (November 1926), pp. 777–84; and 76 (May 1931), pp. 396–406, respectively. See also AIR 5/Series 2: 1264/11J3/29/ 129, *Iraq: Patrol Car Situation Reports, 1929;* and AIR 5/Series 2: 1212/11J1/133/23, *Armoured Cars Policy: Palestine, Transjordan, Iraq, 1933–1942*.

7. Desmond Stewart, *T. E. Lawrence: A New Biography* (New York: Harper & Row, 1977), pp. 304–5; Stanley and Rodelle Weintraub, eds., *Evolution of a Revolt: Early Postwar Writings of T. E. Lawrence* (University Park: Pennsylvania State University Press, 1968), pp. 1–21; and Basil H. Liddell Hart, *Colonel Lawrence: The Man behind the Legend* (New York: Dodd, Mead, 1934), pp. 354–65.

8. John W. Gordon, "Mechanized Forces to Control Desert Tribes: Italian, French, and British Approaches, 1919–1934," in *Proceedings of the First Meeting of the French Colonial Historical Society*, ed. Alf A. Heggoy (Athens, Ga.: French Colonial Historical Society, 1976), pp. 116–23.

9. See Ministère des Armées, État-Major de l'Armée de Terre, Service Historique, Archives Historique Contemporaines, Maroc, *Confins Sahariens (Avril 1934)/* Carton M. Kech/30; and *Cies Sahariennes/*Carton A3/34; Algerie, *Programme de Pénétration Saharienne: Mission des Compagnies Sahariennes, Territoires du Sud, 1927–1935/* Carton Algerie/37; Colonel A. Fagalde, "French North Africa," and Vice Admiral C. V. Usborne, "The French Campaign in Morocco," both in *Journal of the Royal United Service Institution* 71 (May 1926), pp. 281–92, and 81 (August 1936), pp. 505–75, respectively. See also Frank E. Trout, *Morocco's Saharan Frontiers* (Geneva: Librairie Droz, 1969), p. 239; Alan Scham, *Lyautey in Morocco: Protectorate Administration, 1912–1925* (Berkeley: University of California Press, 1970), pp. 44–47; Jean Gottmann, "Bugeaud, Gallieni, and Lyautey: The Development of French Colonial Warfare," in *Makers of Modern Strategy: Military Thought from Machiavelli to Hitler*, ed. Edward M. Earle (2nd ed.; Princeton: Princeton University Press, 1971), pp. 234–54; General George Catroux, "L'achèvement de la pacification Marocaine," *Revue Politique et Parlementaire* 161 no. 479 (1934), pp. 24–46; and Leon Lehuraux, *Le Conquérant des Oasis, Colonel Theodore Pein* (Paris: Librairie Plon, 1935).

10. General George Catroux, "La position stratégique de l'Italie en Afrique du Nord," *Politique Étrangère* (June 1939), pp. 271–81; and W. K. McClure, *Italy in North Africa: An Account of the Tripoli Enterprise* (London: Constable, 1913), pp. 36–37, 139. For Graziani, see Marshal Rodolfo Graziani, *Africa Settentrionale, 1940–1941* (Rome: Danesi, 1948).

11. Great Britain, War Office, *Military Report on Libya, 1936 (Amended to 1940)* (London: HMSO, 1936), p. 6a; *Military Report on the North-Western Desert of Egypt, 1937 (Amended to 1939)* (London: HMSO, 1937), pp. 41–50; and ltr, Major General David L. Lloyd Owen, CB, DSO, OBE, MC, to author, dtd 29 June 1971.

12. "The Operations of the Italian Air Force in North Africa, 1929–1931 (Compiled from Information Supplied by the Italian Air Ministry)," *Journal of the Royal United Service Institution* 78 (May 1933), pp. 374–80; and Bagnold interviews.

13. Lieutenant Colonel A. G. Coppi, "Recent Operations of the Italian Troops in Libya," *Journal of the Royal United Service Institution* 74 (February 1929), pp. 166/ A, 169, 172b/B; and D. M. Smith, *Mussolini's Roman Empire* (New York: Viking, 1976), pp. 32–43.

14. Bagnold, *Libyan Sands*, pp. 244–51; and Bagnold interviews.

15. Captain Paul Moynet, *Victory in the Fezzan* (London: Fighting France Publications, 1944), p. 5.

16. Bagnold interviews.

17. While it is customary (and convenient) to speak of the Libyan desert's inhabitants as "Arabs," the majority of the population is made up of Berbers. For the Arab invasion, see John B. Glubb, *The Great Arab Conquests* (London: Hodder & Stoughton,

1963), pp. 260–61. For descriptions of the topography and climate, see Edwin D. McKee, ed., *A Study of Global Sand Seas* (Geological Survey Professional Paper 1052) (Washington, D.C.: NASA, USGPO, 1979); Harold D. Nelson, ed., *Libya: A Country Study* (3rd ed.; Washington, D.C.: USGPO, 1979), esp. pp. 61–120; and Richard F. Nyrop, ed., *Egypt: A Country Study* (4th ed.; Washington, D.C.: USGPO, 1983), esp. pp. 51–104; Dr. John Ball, "Problems of the Libyan Desert," *Geographical Journal* 70 (August 1927), pp. 105–28.

18. J. N. L. Baker, *A History of Geographical Discovery and Exploration* (New York: Houghton Mifflin, 1932), p. 316; W. B. Kennedy Shaw, *Long Range Desert Group: The Story of Its Work in Libya, 1940–1943* (reprint ed.; Portway, Bath, Eng.: Cedric Chivers, 1970), pp. 45–46; 79–80; Lieutenant Colonel N. B. de Lancey Forth, "More Journeys in Search of Zerzura"; and "Obituary for Lieut.-Col. Newell Barnard de Lancey Forth," both in *Geographical Journal* 75 (January 1930), pp. 48–59; and 81 (May 1933), p. 479, respectively.

19. J. J. Clarke, "Military Technology in Republican France: The Evolution of the French Armored Force, 1917–1940" (Ph.D diss., Duke University, 1968), pp. 95–96; Ball, "Problems of the Libyan Desert," and *Contributions to the Geography of Egypt* (Cairo: Government Press, Bulâq, 1939); and Ahmed Hassanein Bey, "Through Kufra to Darfus," *Geographical Journal* 64 (October 1924), pp. 273–91.

20. Bagnold interviews; *Who's Who in 1969: An Annual Biographical Dictionary* (London: Adam & Charles Black, 1969), p. 126; and ltrs, Brigadier Ralph A. Bagnold to author, dtd 2 November 1969 and 14 February 1970. For Enid Bagnold, see Enid Bagnold, *Enid Bagnold's Autobiography* (Boston: Little, Brown, 1969), esp. p. 75.

21. Bagnold interviews.

22. Bagnold interviews. See also Bagnold, *Libyan Sands*, pp. 18–28, 83–88. For navigation, see Douglas Newbold, "Survey Methods and Results," *Geographical Journal* 78 (December 1931), app. 1, pp. 526–33.

23. Bagnold interviews. See also Bagnold, *Libyan Sands*, pp. 51–55; and "Major R. A. Bagnold on Cairo-Siwa Motor Trip," *The Times* (London), 3 July 1928, p. 15a.

24. Bagnold interviews. See also Bagnold, *Libyan Sands*, pp. 139–69; "Journeys in the Libyan Desert 1929 and 1930," *Geographical Journal* 78 (July 1931), p. 13; and ltr, Ralph A. Bagnold to Arthur R. Hinks, FRS, Secretary of RGS, dtd 2 July 1929 (*Correspondence File, R. A. Bagnold and RGS, 1929–1938*, Royal Geographical Society).

25. Ltr, Bagnold to Arthur R. Hinks, RGS, dtd 6 August 1929. Additional information provided by Bagnold interviews, and interviews with Brigadier Guy L. Prendergast, DSO, Fort Augustus, Inverness-shire, Scotland, 1972 and 1976.

26. Bagnold, *Libyan Sands*, pp. 150–52, as are quotations which follow.

27. Ibid., pp. 156–58, amplified by Bagnold interviews. See also "Major R. A. Bagnold on Libyan Desert Expedition," *The Times* (London), 3 January 1931, p. 3.

28. Bagnold, *Libyan Sands*, p. 151.

29. Ibid., p. 18. See also Bagnold, "Journeys in the Libyan Desert 1929 and 1930," pp. 17–19; and ltr, Bagnold to Secretary, RGS, dtd 30 December 1929.

30. Bagnold, "A Further Journey through the Libyan Desert," *Geographical Journal* 82 (July 1933), pp. 103–7.

31. Newbold, "Survey Methods," p. 529; and ltr, W. B. Kennedy Shaw to author, dtd 4 November 1969.

32. Bagnold interviews.

33. Ibid.

34. Bagnold, *Libyan Sands*, pp. 170–221; ltr, Bagnold to Secretary, RGS, dtd September 1932; *The Times* (London), 3 January 1931, p. 3; and Bagnold, "Journeys in the Libyan Desert 1929 and 1930," p. 34.

35. Kennedy Shaw, *Desert Group*, p. 199.

36. Bagnold interviews; Prendergast interviews; Bagnold, *Libyan Sands*, pp. 260–70; and "Major R. A. Bagnold—Libyan Desert Expedition Leaves Cairo," *The Times* (London), 28 September 1932, p. 11.

37. Bagnold interviews. Ltr, Bagnold to author, dtd 14 February 1970.

38. Bagnold interviews.

39. Bagnold, *Libyan Sands*, p. 277.

40. Ibid., p. 282.

41. Bagnold interviews.

42. Ibid., and Prendergast interviews. See Bagnold, *Libyan Sands*, pp. 272–84.

43. Ltr, Bagnold to author, dtd 2 November 1969; Bagnold interviews; and Foreign Office files J1101/1101/66, *RA (Maj) Bagnold: Exped. to Libyan Desert;* J768/768/16, *Bagnold: Expedition Across Libyan Desert;* and J23/23/66, *Maj R. A. Bagnold: Libyan Expedition: Report and Maps.*

CHAPTER 3

1. Ltr, Brigadier Eric J. Shearer, CB, CBE, MC, to author, dtd 11 January 1972.

2. See, for example, "Request of Mr. W. B. Kennedy Shaw," *RGS Committee Minutes: Expedition Committee*, minutes of 12 November 1934, p. 135; and Shaw, "An Expedition in the Southern Libyan Desert," *Geographical Journal* 87 (March 1936), pp. 193–221.

3. Wing Commander H. W. G. J. Penderel, "The Gilf Kebir," *Geographical Journal* 83 (June 1934), pp. 449–56; F. J. R. Rodd, "A Reconnaissance of the Gilf Kebir by the Late Sir Robert Clayton East Clayton," *Geographical Journal* 81 (January 1933), pp. 248–54; FO 371/18033 (and 4 and 5), *Almaszy, Count: Expedition to Libyan Desert* (J683/I/66); FO 371/24630, *Almaszy, Count Laszlo: Reasons against his Return to Egypt* (J712/J1101/192/16); and FO 371/15257, *Almaszy, L. E. de* (C5983/5983/21).

4. *Kufra: Italian Official Documents Referring to Mr. P. A. Clayton and Wing Commander H. W. G. J. Penderel and Their Expeditions to the Gilf Kebir, 1933* (Royal Geographical Society, Dept. of Archives and MSS: papers captured by Free French Forces and presented to RGS by Lieutenant Colonel W. B. Kennedy Shaw).

5. Interviews with Brigadier Ralph A. Bagnold, OBE, FRS, Mark Beech, Edenbridge, Kent, Eng., 1972 and 1976. See also WO 32/3536, *Anglo-Egyptian Sudan-Italian Boundary: 1933–1935.*

6. WO 32/3536, *Anglo-Egyptian Sudan-Italian Boundary: 1933–1935;* ltr, Brigadier Ralph A. Bagnold, OBE, FRS, to author, dtd 14 February 1970; and interview with Brigadier Ralph A. Bagnold, 21 June 1976.

7. Howard M. Sachar, *Europe Leaves the Middle East, 1936–1954* (New York: Alfred A. Knopf, 1972), pp. 22–30; Major General I. S. O. Playfair et al., *The Mediterranean and Middle East*, vol. 1, *The Early Successes against Italy (to May 1941)* (London: HMSO, 1954), pp. 2–3; and General Sir Edmund Ironside, *Time Unguarded: The Ironside Diaries, 1937–1940* (New York: David McKay, 1963), p. 25.

8. WO 32/3543, *Appreciation on 12.10.35 by the General Officer Commanding, British*

Troops in Egypt, of the Probable Situation at the end of October in the Event of an Italian Offensive from Libya, pp. 1–10.

9. W. B. Kennedy Shaw, *Long Range Desert Group: The Story of Its Work in Libya, 1940–1943* (reprint ed.; Portway, Bath, Eng.: Cedric Chivers, 1970), p. 15.

10. *GOC-BTE Appreciation, 12 October 1935*, pp. 1–12. Unless otherwise noted, all quoted material in this paragraph is from this source.

11. Ibid., p. 1; Playfair, *Mediterranean*, vol. 1, p. 4, gives a figure of 80,000.

12. WO 32/4169, *The Defence of Egypt, Appendix "A", Egyptian Military Intelligence, 21 March 1937, in Anglo-Egyptian Cooperation in the Defence of Egypt: 1937–1940*, p. 1.

13. For full text of treaty, see Great Britain, Foreign Office, *Cmd. 5360: Treaty of Preferential Alliance: Britain and Egypt, August 26, 1936* (London: HMSO, 1937). See also Sachar, *Europe Leaves the Middle East*, pp. 22–30; P. J. Vatikiotis, *The Egyptian Army in Politics: Pattern for New Nations?* (Bloomington: Indiana University Press, 1961), esp. pp. 4–28, 238–59; and WO 106/1594B, *Middle East, 1937–1938, Lectures by M. I. 2(a) at M. A.'s Conference: 22.6.37*, pp. 3–4.

14. WO 32/4169, *The Defence of Egypt, Appendix "A" . . . 21 March 1937*, pp. 2–3. See also ltrs, Major General J. H. Marshall-Cornwall, Chief British Military Mission to Egypt, to: Egyptian Minister for War, dtd 13 July 1937 and 4 January 1938; Under Secretary of State, the War Office, dtd 4 November 1937 and 9 January 1938; and ltr, Major General R. H. Haining to Major General Marshall-Cornwall, dtd 25 March 1937; in WO 32/4166 and 32/4167, *British Military Mission to Egypt—Reorganization of Egyptian Army: Span 1936–1938*.

15. WO 32/10125, *Army Council Instructions to General Officer Commanding-in-Chief in the Middle East, July 1939*.

16. For Wavell, see John Connell, *Wavell: Soldier and Scholar* (New York: Harcourt, Brace and World, 1965), esp. pp. 34, 204–15.

17. Ibid., pp. 176–80.

18. Ltrs, Shearer to author, dtd 8 November 1971, 22 December 1971, and 6 February 1972.

19. Bagnold inverviews.

20. Ibid.; and Bagnold, "Early Days of the Long Range Desert Group," *Geographical Journal* 105 (January 1945), pp. 30–31.

21. John W. Gordon, "The 'Lawrence Legend' and British Plans for a Tribal Revolt in Libya, 1935–1940," in *Proceedings of the Conference on War and Diplomacy, 1976*, ed. David H. White (Charleston, S.C.: The Citadel, 1976), pp. 74–80.

22. Quoted in Connell, *Wavell*, p. 175.

23. Bagnold interviews. See also WO 201/2555, *Provisions of Arms for the Bedouins in the Western Desert, August 1939 to April 1940;* WO 201/254, *Notes on Preparation for Tribal Warfare in Libya and Italian East Africa, October 1939–April 1940;* WO 201/336, *Tribal Action in Libya, April-December 1940;* and WO 201/327, *Appreciation Regarding [a] British Offensive into Libya, August-October 1939*.

24. Connell, *Wavell*, p. 220, as is quotation in sentence which follows.

25. Ltr, GOC-in-C, Middle East, to Director of Military Intelligence, dtd 27 April 1940, in WO 201/336.

26. T. E. Lawrence, *Seven Pillars of Wisdom: A Triumph* (9th ed.; Harmondsworth, Middlesex, Eng.: Penguin Books, 1971), p. 192.

27. Playfair, *Mediterranean*, vol. 1, pp. 101–8, 206–12; and W. G. F. Jackson, *The Battle for North Africa, 1940–43* (New York: Mason/Charter, 1975), pp. 5–7.

28. *GOC-BTE Appreciation, 12 October 1935*, p. 6. See also teleg. GOC-in-Chief, Middle East to CIGS, WO, dtd 8 September 1939, in WO 106/2034.

29. Bagnold interviews.

30. Bagnold, "Early Days of the LRDG," p. 30. See also Major R. A. Bagnold, "Mechanical Mobility," *Journal of the Royal United Service Institution* 76 (August 1931), pp. 595–608; Royal Geographical Society, *Correspondence File: Bagnold-RGS Letter File, 1929–1938;* and Bagnold, *The Physics of Blown Sand and Desert Dunes* (New York: William Morrow, 1941).

31. Bagnold interviews.

32. Bagnold, "Early Days of the LRDG," pp. 31–32.

33. Bagnold interviews.

34. Bagnold, "Early Days of the LRDG," p. 31.

35. Bagnold interviews. See also Playfair, *Mediterranean*, vol. 1, pp. 206–7.

36. Bagnold interviews; and ltr, Bagnold to author, 19 February 1972.

37. Bagnold, "Early Days of the LRDG," p. 32. See also WO 201/807, *War Diary and Narrative, Long Range Desert Group, June 1940–November 1940*, esp. Formation of the Long Range Patrol . . . to September 1, 1940; and ltr, Bagnold to author, 2 November 1969.

38. Ltr, Bagnold to author, 2 November 1969.

39. Playfair, *Mediterranean*, vol. 1, pp. 109–24.

40. Bagnold interviews.

41. Ibid.; and ltr, Bagnold to author, 2 November 1969.

42. Bagnold interviews.

43. Wavell, quoted in Connell, *Wavell*, p. 180.

44. WO 193/150, *General Staff Report of the Raising of Insurrections: Possibility of Guerrilla Activities*, dating back to 1938, spoke of the "special purpose of guerilla [sic] activities."

45. See U.S., War Department, "Organization and Training of British Commandos," in *Tactical and Technical Trends No. 1* (Washington, D.C.: Military Intelligence Service, 1942), pp. 11–17; Brigadier Bernard Fergusson, *The Watery Maze: The Story of Combined Operations* (New York: Holt, Rinehart and Winston 1961), esp. pp. 15–23; Colonel J. F. C. Fuller, *British Light Infantry in the Eighteenth Century* (London: Hutchinson, 1925); and John W. Gordon, "The U.S. Marine Corps and an Experiment in Military Elitism: A Reassessment of the Special Warfare Impetus, 1937–1943," in *Changing Interpretations and New Sources in Naval History: Papers from the Third United States Naval Academy History Symposium*, ed. Robert W. Love (New York: Garland, 1980), pp. 362–73.

46. For the relationship between special forces and politicians, see Eliot A. Cohen, *Commandos and Politicians: Elite Military Units in Modern Democracies* (Cambridge, Mass.: Center for International Affairs, Harvard University, 1978), esp. pp. 37–44.

47. Interviews with General Sir John W. Hackett, GCB, CBE, DSO, MC, King's College, London, 1972.

48. See WO 32/9660, *Notes on Long Range Desert Patrols*, dtd January 1941; Bagnold interviews; Bagnold, "Early Days of the Long Range Desert Group," pp. 33–34; and Kennedy Shaw, *Desert Group*, pp. 15–28.

49. Bagnold interviews; Playfair, *Mediterranean*, vol. 1, pp. 294–96; and Kennedy Shaw, *Desert Group*, pp. 19–21.

50. Bagnold, "Early Days of the LRDG," pp. 33–35; and WO 201/807, *War Diary and Narrative, Long Range Desert Group, June 1940–November 1940*.

51. Bagnold interviews.

52. *Instructions for Use of Bagnold Sun-Compass*, nd, in J. P. Stocker Papers, Long Range Desert Group Collection of Major General David L. Lloyd Owen, Imperial War Museum.

53. WO 201/807, Formation of the Long Range Patrol . . . to September 1, 1940; R. L. Kay, *Long Range Desert Group in Libya, 1940–41* (Wellington, N.Z.: War History Branch, Department of Internal Affairs, 1949), pp. 3–5; Bagnold interviews; and WO 201/2200, *Vehicles for the Long Range Desert Group, October 1940–October 1943*.

54. Bagnold interviews.

55. Ltr, Major General David L. Lloyd Owen, CB, DSO, OBE, MC, to author, dtd 5 March 1970.

56. Ltrs, Shearer to author, dtd 8 and 16 November and 22 December 1971, and 6 February 1972.

57. Playfair, *Mediterranean*, vol. 1, pp. 113–18, 206–9.

58. WO 201/807, Formation of the Long Range Patrol; Bagnold, "Early Days of the LRDG," pp. 34–35; and Kennedy Shaw, *Desert Group*, pp. 32–33.

59. Connell, *Wavell*, pp. 244–45. See also WO 201/807, Formation of the Long Range Patrol.

60. Kennedy Shaw, *Desert Group*, p. 27; ltr, Shearer to author, dtd 11 January 1972.

61. Bagnold interviews.

62. See WO 201/807, Long Range Patrols, Operation Order no. 1, dtd 4 September 1940.

CHAPTER 4

1. Interviews with Brigadier Ralph A. Bagnold, OBE, FRS, Mark Beech, Edenbridge, Kent, Eng., 1972 and 1976, amplifying ltr, Bagnold to author, 2 November 1969.

2. WO 201/807, *War Diary and Narrative, Long Range Desert Group, June 1940–November 1940*, esp. Formation of the Long Range Patrol . . . to September 1, 1940; Long Range Patrol Operation Order no. 1, dtd 4 September 1940; and Brigadier Ralph A. Bagnold, "Early Days of the Long Range Desert Group," *Geographical Journal* 105 (January 1945), p. 35.

3. See the account in R. L. Kay, *Long Range Desert Group in Libya, 1940–41* (Wellington, N.Z.: War History Branch, Department of Internal Affairs, 1949), p. 5.

4. WO 201/807, Report on a Reconnaissance of Central Libya . . . LRP; Bagnold, "Early Days of the LRDG," p. 35; W. B. Kennedy Shaw, *Long Range Desert Group: The Story of Its Work in Libya, 1940–1943* (reprint ed.; Portway, Bath, Eng.: Cedric Chivers, 1970), pp. 33–34; and Bagnold interviews.

5. Bagnold interviews.

6. Bagnold, "Early Days of the LRDG," p. 35.

7. Ibid.

8. WO 201/807, Formation of the Long Range Patrol, app. 2. See also Kennedy Shaw, *Desert Group*, app. 5, pp. 248–49. Interview with Richard P. Lawson, MD, Calne, Wiltshire, Eng., 2 June 1972. Medical information relating to the LRDG is

in Lawson, "LRDG Medical Diary, 1942–1943," copy lodged in Imperial War Museum.

9. Interviews with Major General David L. Lloyd Owen, CB, DSO, OBE, MC, Norwich, Norfolk, England, 1972, 1976, 1983. See Major General I. S. O. Playfair et al., *The Mediterranean and Middle East*, vol. 1, *The Early Successes against Italy (to May 1941)* (London: HMSO, 1954), pp. 209–12; and Bagnold, "Early Days of the LRDG," p. 36.

10. Ltr, Bagnold to author, dtd 2 November 1969.

11. Kennedy Shaw, *Desert Group*, pp. 46–47.

12. Bagnold, "Early Days of the LRDG," p. 37. For British plans for a counter-stroke, see WO 201/327, *Appreciation Regarding [a] British Offensive into Libya, August-October 1939;* W. G. F. Jackson, *The Battle for North Africa, 1940–43* (New York: Mason/Charter, 1975), pp. 27–46; Correlli Barnett, *The Desert Generals* (New York: Ballantine Books, 1972), pp. 1–56; and Playfair, *Mediterranean*, vol. 1, pp. 258–65. For the Y Service, see F. H. Hinsley et al., *British Intelligence in the Second World War: Its Influence on Strategy and Operations*, vol. 1 (New York: Cambridge University Press, 1979), p. 21n.

13. Bagnold interviews. See also Kay, *Long Range Desert Group in Libya*, pp. 5–7; and WO 201/807, esp. Formation of the Long Range Patrol . . . LRDG, app. 2, dtd 25 November 1940.

14. Bagnold, "Early Days of the LRDG," p. 37.

15. Ltr, Brigadier Eric J. Shearer, CB, CBE, MC, to author, dtd 11 January 1972; and Shearer's comments in "Discussion" following presentation at RGS of Bagnold, "Early Days of the LRDG," pp. 44–45.

16. Michael Crichton-Stuart, *G Patrol* (London: William Kimber, 1958), pp. 22–29. See also David Erskine, *The Scots Guards, 1919–1955* (London: William Clowes & Sons, 1956), pp. 74–75.

17. For the Yeomanry Patrol, see David L. Lloyd Owen, *The Desert My Dwelling Place* (London: Cassell, 1957); and Lloyd Owen, *Providence Their Guide: A Personal Account of the Long Range Desert Group, 1940–45* (London: Harrap, 1980), esp. pp. 38–40.

18. Bagnold interviews; Kay, *Long Range Desert Group in Libya*, p. 7; WO 201/807, esp. appendix 4: Long Range Desert Group: Establishment Authorized on 22nd November 1940; and Formation of the Long Range Patrol . . . October-November 1940.

19. Bagnold interviews.

20. Bagnold, "Early Days of the LRDG," pp. 37–38.

21. WO 201/807, Formation of LRP, app. 6, Rpt of a visit to Fort Lamy by Major R. A. Bagnold; Crichton-Stuart, *G Patrol*, p. 29; and Playfair, *Mediterranean*, vol. 1, pp. 296–97.

22. Churchill, quoted in Jackson, *Battle for North Africa*, p. 46.

23. Bagnold interviews; WO 201/807, LRDG Operation Order no. 3, nd.

24. Compare Kennedy Shaw, *Desert Group*, pp. 54–55, with Crichton-Stuart, *G Patrol*, pp. 32–33; and John W. Gordon, "The 'Lawrence Legend' and British Plans for a Tribal Revolt in Libya, 1935–1940," in *Proceedings of the Conference on War and Diplomacy, 1976*, ed. David H. White (Charleston, S.C.: The Citadel, 1976), p. 78.

25. Crichton-Stuart, *G Patrol,* p. 37.

26. Ltr, Major General David L. Lloyd Owen to author, dtd 5 March 1970.

27. Bagnold interviews.

28. Bagnold, "Early Days of the LRDG," p. 38.

29. Kennedy Shaw, *Desert Group,* p. 58.

30. Crichton-Stuart, *G Patrol,* pp. 40–43; and ltr, W. B. Kennedy Shaw to author, dtd 4 November 1969.

31. WO 201/808, *War Diary and Narrative, Long Range Desert Group, December 1940–March 1941,* Summary of the Fezzan Operation undertaken by two Long Range Patrols under Captain P. A. Clayton, January/41.

32. Kennedy Shaw, *Desert Group,* pp. 60–67; and Kay, *Long Range Desert Group in Libya,* pp. 8–25.

33. Bagnold, "Early Days of the LRDG," p. 38.

34. Bagnold interviews.

35. Kennedy Shaw, *Desert Group,* p. 70. See also Crichton-Stuart, *G Patrol,* p. 55; and WO 201/808, Summary of Operations from Faya towards Kufra . . . LRP/G/5 of 31.1.41.

36. See the account in Lloyd Owen, *Providence Their Guide,* pp. 34–35.

37. Kennedy Shaw, *Desert Group,* p. 70.

38. Ibid., and the accounts in Crichton-Stuart, *G Patrol,* pp. 59–63; and Kay, *Long Range Desert Group in Libya,* pp. 25–27. For the *Lady Be Good,* see files held in Imperial War Museum, and Dennis E. McClendon, *Lady Be Good: Mystery Bomber of World War II* (Fallbrook, Calif.: Aero Publishers, 1982).

39. For cipher codes, see WO 201/807, app. II, Special Instructions for the use of the stencil cipher; Crichton-Stuart, *G Patrol,* p. 64; and Captain Paul Moynet, *Victory in the Fezzan* (London: Fighting France Publications, 1944), pp. 12–20.

40. Bagnold, "Early Days of the LRDG," p. 39.

41. Bagnold interviews.

42. Ibid., and WO 201/808, esp. ltr, GOC-in-Chief, ME, to OC, LRP, dtd 1 October 1940.

43. Bagnold, "Early Days of the LRDG," p. 38.

44. Playfair, *Mediterranean,* vol. 1, pp. 257, 366–69; and Barnett, *Desert Generals,* pp. 50–56.

45. Jackson, *Battle for North Africa,* p. 69.

46. Ronald Lewin, *Ultra Goes to War: The First Account of World War II's Greatest Secret Based on Official Documents* (New York: McGraw-Hill, 1978), pp. 160–61.

47. Hinsley et al., *British Intelligence in the Second World War,* vol. 1, pp. 386–98; Major General I. S. O. Playfair et al., *The Mediterranean and Middle East,* vol. 2, *The Germans Come to the Help of Their Ally (1941)* (London: HMSO, 1956), pp. 10–17; Jackson, *Battle for North Africa,* pp. 93–98.

48. Larry H. Addington, *The Blitzkrieg Era and the German General Staff, 1935–1941* (New Brunswick, N.J.: Rutgers University Press, 1971), pp. 160–63.

49. Lewin, *Ultra Goes to War,* p. 161.

50. Crichton-Stuart, *G Patrol,* p. 68.

51. Hanson Baldwin, "Desert Fighters," *New York Times,* 13 February 1941; "British Explorers Led Desert Raiding Units," *New York Times,* 14 February 1941; and "Harrassing the Italians in the Heart of Libya," *Egyptian Mail,* 14 February 1941.

CHAPTER 5

1. Ltr, General Sir Neil Ritchie, GBE, KCB, DSO, MC, to author, dtd 29 March 1972.

2. WO 201/808, *War Diary and Narrative, Long Range Desert Group, December 1940–March 1941*, Cyrenaica Comd. Operation Instructions no. 7/dtd 21 March 1941. See also F. H. Hinsley et al., *British Intelligence in the Second World War: Its Influence on Strategy and Operations*, vol. 1 (New York: Cambridge University Press, 1979), p. 399; and Major General I. S. O. Playfair et al., *The Mediterranean and Middle East*, vol. 2, *The Germans Come to the Help of Their Ally (1941)* (London: HMSO, 1956), pp. 8, 30–34. General Neames's Cyrenaica Command (CYRCOM) became "the reconstituted Western Desert Force" in April 1941.

3. Michael Crichton-Stuart, *G Patrol* (London: William Kimber, 1958), pp. 70–81. WO 201/809, *War Diary and Narrative, Long Range Desert Group, April 1941–August 1941*, Operations of "A" Squadron; Cyrenaica Comd. Operation Instruction no. 7/dtd 31 March 1941.

4. WO 201/809, Operations of "A" Squadron; WO 201/809, Movements of "A" Squadron LRDG under the orders of HQ. Cyrenaica Force; Patrol Report 31.3.41–10.4.41 by detachment "G" Patrol.

5. Interviews with General Sir John W. Hackett, GCB, CBE, DSO, MC, King's College, London, 1972.

6. Alan Moorehead, *The March to Tunis: The North African War, 1940–1943* (New York: Harper & Row, 1967), pp. 9, 20–21. For Battleaxe, see Correlli Barnett, *The Desert Generals* (New York: Ballantine Books, 1972), pp. 59–69.

7. WO 32/10126, *Lessons from Cyrenaica: Span 1941–1942*, esp. Co-operation in Battle, dtd 8 February 1942; and WO 201/357, *Lessons of the Campaigns in the Western Desert: Operation "Battleaxe," June–November 1941*. See also Generalmajor Hans-Hennig von Holzendorff, "Reasons for Rommel's Success in Africa 1941–42," MS #D-024, OCMH, 1947; and Generalmajor Alfred Toppe, "German Experiences in Desert Warfare during World War II," MS #P-129, OCMH, 1952 (both lodged in U. S. Army Military History Institute, Carlisle Barracks, Pa.).

8. W. B. Kennedy Shaw, *Long Range Desert Group: The Story of Its Work in Libya, 1940–1943* (reprint ed.; Portway, Bath, Eng.: Cedric Chivers, 1970), pp. 21, 47.

9. Interviews with Brigadier Ralph A. Bagnold, OBE, FRS, Mark Beech, Edenbridge, Kent, Eng., 1972 and 1976.

10. WO 201/808, Long Range Desert Group, Opn Order no. 6/dtd 7 March 1941; and Brigadier Ralph A. Bagnold, "Early Days of the Long Range Desert Group," *Geographical Journal* 105 (January 1945), pp. 40–42.

11. Bagnold interviews.

12. WO 201/809, Operation Directive to Officer Commanding, Long Range Desert Group/dtd 10 July 1941.

13. Interviews with Brigadier Guy L. Prendergast, DSO, Fort Augustus, Inverness-shire, Scotland, 1972 and 1976.

14. Ibid.

15. Bagnold, "Early Days of the LRDG," pp. 41–42; and WO 201/809, Occupation of the Kufra Oases by the LRDG, esp. Provision of Aircraft for the LRDG (nd).

16. Bagnold interviews.

17. Ibid.

18. Ltr, Brigadier Eric J. Shearer, CB, CBE, MC, to author, dtd 11 January 1972.

19. Kennedy Shaw, *Desert Group*, p. 87.

20. Bagnold interviews.

21. Prendergast interviews.

22. See WO 201/809, Change of Command of LRDG, 1941.

23. Kennedy Shaw, *Desert Group*, p. 106.

24. Ibid, p. 106n. See also Vladimir Peniakoff, *Private Army* (London: Jonathan Cape, 1950), pp. 196–99. Interviews with Major General David L. Lloyd Owen, CB, DSO, OBE, MC, Norwich Norfolk, Eng., 1972, 1976, and 1983.

25. WO 201/809, Composite patrol (Lt. Easonsmith) 10 June-3 July 1941; WO 201/809, Reconnaissance Report, Y Patrol/dtd 4.8.41; Lloyd Owen interviews, and Peniakoff, *Private Army*, pp. 64, 77, 195.

26. Prendergast interviews. See also WO 201/809, Patrol Report, G Patrol, 25 March-25 August 1941; and the account in Crichton-Stuart, *G Patrol*, pp. 84–87.

27. WO 201/810, *War Diary and Narrative, Long Range Desert Group, August 1941–November 1941*, esp. pp. 1–6, MS narrative; and Prendergast interviews.

28. Hackett interviews. By the end of 1941, four New Zealanders, for example, had been awarded commissions. R. L. Kay, *Long Range Desert Group in Libya, 1940–41* (Wellington, N.Z.: War History Branch, Department of Internal Affairs, 1949), biographical notes, pp. 32–33.

29. Barnett, *Desert Generals*, p. 74. See also Major General I. S. O. Playfair et al., *The Mediterranean and Middle East*, vol. 3, *British Fortunes Reach Their Lowest Ebb* (London: HMSO, 1960), pp. 1–3.

30. Playfair, *Mediterranean*, vol. 3, pp. 3–9.

31. Auchinleck, quoted in Barnett, *Desert Generals*, p. 74.

32. Prendergast interviews.

33. Extensive efforts by the LRDG preceded the formulation of these ambitious plans.

34. See Brigadier Bernard Fergusson, *The Watery Maze: The Story of Combined Operations* (New York: Holt, Rinehart and Winston, 1961), pp. 94–105; Elizabeth Keyes, *Geoffrey Keyes: VC, MC, Croix de Guerre* (London: George Newnes, 1956), esp. pp. 136–208; Playfair, *Mediterranean*, vol. 3, pp. 21–22; Hinsley, *British Intelligence in the Second World War*, vol. 2 (New York: Cambridge University Press, 1981), p. 303n; and Anthony Cave Brown, *Bodyguard of Lies* (New York: Harper & Row, 1975), pp. 94–95. Prendergast interviews; and WO 201/727, *Personal File on Lieutenant-Colonel Haselden, 5 March 1942–28 July 1942 (Raiding Forces, GHO Middle East)*.

35. See WO 201/747, *MO3 Battle File: SAS Regiment; WO 201/721, MO3 History of the SAS, 1941–1942;* and WO 201/2624, *War Establishment, 1st Special Air Service Regiment, and Provision of Personnel for Irregular Commandos, September 1940–September 1942*. Ltr, General Sir Neil Ritchie to author, dtd 29 March 1972. For accounts of the SAS, see Virginia Cowles, *Who Dares, Wins (Formerly The Phantom Major)* (New York: Ballantine Books, 1959); and Philip Warner, *The Special Air Service* (London: William Kimber, 1971).

36. Ltr, General Sir Neil Ritchie to author, dtd 29 March 1972; Playfair, *Mediterranean*, vol. 3, p. 17; and Prendergast interviews, amplifying the account given in Cowles, *Who Dares, Wins*, pp. 6–17.

37. Cowles, *Who Dares, Wins*, pp. 18–28.

38. Hackett interviews. See WO 201/811, *War Diary and Narrative, Long Range Desert Group, November 1941–February 1942*, Eighth Army Operation Instruction no. 16/dtd 10 November 1941/to Capt. D. Stirling, L Sec. I SAS Bde.

39. WO 201/811, Some Account of the Part Played by LRDG in the Operation of 9th Army in Cyrenaica in November-December 1941, esp. pp. 1–4; and Keyes, *Geoffrey Keyes*, pp. 209–21.

40. Keyes, *Geoffrey Keyes*, pp. 222–32. Hinsley, *British Intelligence in the Second World War*, vol. 2, p. 303 (and note), indicates that, "having already disclosed that Rommel had flown to Rome on 1 November, the Army Enigma reported that he would return to north Africa on the evening of 18 November. . . . [This news] was obviously received too late to stop the operation."

41. WO 201/811, Eighth Army Operation Instruction no. 11/dtd 7 November 1941; Keyes, *Geoffrey Keyes*, pp. 233–72; David J. C. Irving, *The Trail of the Fox: The Search For the True Field Marshal Rommel* (New York: E. P. Dutton, 1977), pp. 114–16; and Basil H. Liddell Hart, ed., *The Rommel Papers* (New York: Harcourt, Brace, 1953), pp. 156, 292.

42. Cowles, *Who Dares, Wins*, pp. 28–32.

43. Hackett interviews.

44. WO 201/811, Special Instructions to Capt. Easonsmith O. C. Patrol R1/dtd 15/11/41; Cowles, *Who Dares, Wins*, pp. 33–36; and Prendergast interviews.

45. Barnett, *Desert Generals*, p. 110.

46. See Playfair, *Mediterranean*, vol. 3, pp. 33–71.

47. WO 201/811, Long Range Desert Group, Mid-November Operations in Cyrenaica: Operation Instruction no. 20 (given verbally)/dtd 15–11–41; Eighth Army Operation Instruction no. 18/dtd 11 November 1941; Prendergast interviews; and Lloyd Owen interviews.

48. WO 201/811, Mid-November Operations in Cyrenaica: Operation Instruction no. 22 (sent by W(T)/dtd 24/11/41).

49. For Italian armored developments between the wars, see John J. T. Sweet, *Iron Arm: The Mechanization of Mussolini's Army, 1920–1940* (Westport, Conn.: Greenwood Press, 1980), esp. pp. 175–90, and app. 2, pp. 195–99.

50. WO 201/811, Recce. Report no. 20 (G1 Patrol)/dtd 5/12/41.

51. WO 201/811, Recce. Report no. 20 (Y1 Patrol)/dtd 8.12.41, and LRDG's Part in the 8th Army's Offensive: The Second Phase: 6–24 Dec. 41; Prendergast interviews; Lloyd Owen interviews, and account in David L. Lloyd Owen, *The Desert My Dwelling Place* (London: Cassell, 1957), segments of which are contained in Kennedy Shaw, *Desert Group*, pp. 113–17.

52. Playfair, *Mediterranean*, vol. 3, pp. 58–62.

CHAPTER 6

1. Fitzroy Maclean, *Eastern Approaches* (London: Jonathan Cape, 1950), pp. 193–94.

2. Interviews with Brigadier Guy L. Prendergast, DSO, Fort Augustus, Inverness-shire, Scotland, 1972 and 1976.

3. Virginia Cowles, *Who Dares, Wins (Formerly The Phantom Major)* (New York: Ballantine Books, 1959), p. 38.

4. Prendergast interviews. See also WO 201/721, *MO3 History of the SAS, 1941–1942*.

5. For Ritchie, see Correlli Barnett, *The Desert Generals* (New York: Ballantine Books, 1972), pp. 119–25.

6. Major General I. S. O. Playfair et al., *The Mediterranean and Middle East*, vol. 3, *British Fortunes Reach Their Lowest Ebb* (London: HMSO, 1960), pp. 61–85.

7. WO 201/811, *War Diary and Narrative, Long Range Desert Group, November 1941–February 1942*, Patrol Report, T1, 2–25 December 1941/dtd 24.12.41; Playfair, *Mediterranean*, vol. 3, pp. 85–86; R. L. Kay, *Long Range Desert Group in Libya, 1940–41* (Wellington, N.Z.: War History Branch, Department of Internal Affairs, 1949), p. 32; ltr, Lieutenant Colonel Paul R. Freyberg (Second Baron Freyberg), OBE, MC, to author, dtd 30 March 1972; and ltr, Freyberg to Brigadier Eric J. Shearer (and forwarded to author), dtd 14 November 1971.

8. Prendergast interviews.

9. Playfair, *Mediterranean*, vol. 3, p. 92.

10. WO 201/811, LRDG's Part in the 8th Army's Offensive, The Second Phase. 6–24 December 1941, esp. p. 3. Playfair, *Mediterranean*, vol. 3, p. 89; and Prendergast interviews.

11. WO 201/811, Patrol Report, S1, 8–16 December 1941/dtd 18.12.41; WO 201/721, *MO3 History of the SAS, 1941–1942;* and Cowles, *Who Dares, Wins,* pp. 39–51.

12. WO 201/811, Patrol Report, T2, 10–19 December 1941/dtd 24.12.41; Patrol Report, S2, 13–23 December 1941/dtd 25.12.41; LRDG's Part in the 8th Army's Offensive, The Third Phase, 25 December 1941–5 February 1942; and R. L. Kay, *Long Range Desert Group in the Mediterranean* (Wellington, N.Z.: War History Branch, Department of Internal Affairs, 1950), p. 3.

13. Ltr, W. B. Kennedy Shaw to author, dtd 4 November 1969, and closely following Kennedy Shaw, *Long Range Desert Group: The Story of Its Work in Libya, 1940–1943* (reprint ed., Portway, Bath, Eng.: Cedric Chivers, 1970), pp. 125–26.

14. WO 201/811, LRDG's Part in the 8th Army's Offensive, The Third Phase, 25 December 1941–5 February 1942, esp. pp. 2–3; Kay, *Long Range Desert Group in the Mediterranean*, pp. 3–4; and Cowles, *Who Dares, Wins*, pp. 62–63.

15. Prendergast interviews, and Cowles, *Who Dares, Wins*, pp. 68–70.

16. WO 201/811, Eighth Army Operation Instruction no. 32/dtd 22 December 1941 (L. O./Liaison Officer).

17. Ibid.

18. WO 201/811, Patrol Report, G2, 26 December 1941–15 January 1942/dtd 16.1.42; interviews with Major General David L. Lloyd Owen, CB, DSO, OBE, MC, Norwich, Norfolk, England, 1972, 1976, and 1983. See Michael Crichton-Stuart, *G Patrol* (London: William Kimber, 1958), pp. 114–21.

19. WO 201/811, LRDG's Part in the 8th Army's Offensive, The Third Phase, 25 December 1941–5 February 1942; and Prendergast interviews.

20. Playfair, *Mediterranean*, vol. 3, pp. 135–54. See also Barnett, *Desert Generals*, pp. 128–34; and Basil H. Liddell Hart, ed., *The Rommel Papers* (New York: Harcourt, Brace, 1953), pp. 191–225.

21. WO 201/811, Patrol Report, G1, 16–31 January 1942/dtd 7.2.42.

22. Cowles, *Who Dares, Wins*, p. 84.

23. WO 201/811, LRDG's Part in the 8th Army's Offensive, The Third Phase,

25 December 1941–5 February 1942; Crichton-Stuart, *G Patrol*, pp. 123–24; and Prendergast interviews.

24. Playfair, *Mediterranean*, vol. 3, pp. 197–221.

25. Lloyd Owen interviews.

26. Kennedy Shaw, *Desert Group*, pp. 145.

27. WO 201/812, *War Diary and Narrative, Long Range Desert Group, February 1942–April 1942*, "A" Sqdn, LRDG, Operation Instruction no. 20/dtd 15 March 1942; Patrol Report, S2, 15 March–1 April 1942/dtd 3.4.42; Cowles, *Who Dares, Wins*, pp. 89–100; and Maclean, *Eastern Approaches*, pp. 190–212.

28. Prendergast interviews.

29. Ibid.

30. WO 201/813, *War Diary and Narrative, Long Range Desert Group, April 1942–May 1942*, LRDG's Part in the 8th Army's Operations, The Fifth Phase, April 19–May 26, 1942, esp. pp. 53–58; Crichton-Stuart, *G Patrol*, pp. 137–40; Maclean, *Eastern Approaches*, pp. 213–25.

31. Cowles, *Who Dares, Wins*, p. 105.

32. Kennedy Shaw, *Desert Group*, p. 161.

33. WO 201/813, Eighth Army Operation Instruction no. 60/dtd 23 April 1942; LRDG's Part in the 8th Army's Operations, The Fifth Phase, April 19–May 26, 1942, esp. p. 57.

34. Prendergast interviews.

35. Ibid.

36. WO 201/813, LRDG Operation Instruction no. 35/dtd 6.5.42; Patrol Report, G1 8–28 May 1942/dtd 30.5.42; and Crichton-Stuart, *G Patrol*, pp. 141–53.

37. WO 201/813, Patrol Report, G1, 8–28 May 1942/dtd 30.5.42.

38. See WO 201/725, *Enemy Long Range Activities, June-July 1942*, esp. ltrs, DMI, GHQ MEF, to LRDG ("Germans in Sahara") and GHQ MEF to Eighth Army dtd 23 and 24 July 1942, respectively. FO 371/15257, *Almaszy, L. E. de: Flight from Lympne to Wadi Halfa and Back (1931)/C5983/5983/21;* FO 371/15679, *Almaszy: Aeroplane Crash (1931)/W10742/10742/50;* and *Almaszy: Projected Flying School . . . (1940)/J-186/192/16,* etc; Paul Carell, *The Foxes of the Desert* (New York: Bantam Books, 1972), pp. 208–9.

39. Ltr, Brigadier Ralph A. Bagnold, OBE, FRS, to author, dtd 14 February 1970 and amplified in Bagnold interviews.

40. Ronald Lewin, *Ultra Goes to War: The First Account of World War II's Greatest Secret Based on Official Documents* (New York: McGraw-Hill, 1978), pp. 176–77.

41. Prendergast interviews.

42. Quoted in Kennedy Shaw, *Desert Group*, p. 172.

43. Lewin, *Ultra Goes to War*, p. 175.

44. Bagnold interviews; and ltr, Bagnold to author, dtd 14 February 1970, indicating that "He [Almaszy] and I had long talks together in Cairo in 1951 just before he died."

45. Wilhelm F. Flicke, *War Secrets in the Ether*, pt. 3, trans. R. W. Pettengill, (Washington: National Security Agency, 1954), pp. 154–60 (copy marked "Army War College Library, Carlisle Barracks, PA.")

46. U. S. War Department, *Official Army Register (January 1, 1940)* (Washington, D.C.: USGPO, 1940), p. 257; and F. H. Hinsley et al., *British Intelligence in the Second*

World War: Its Influence on Strategy and Operations, vol. 2, (New York: Cambridge University Press, 1981), pp. 331, 361, 640n.

47. Lewin, *Ultra Goes to War,* pp. 175–77.

48. David J. C. Irving, *The Trail of the Fox: The Search for the True Field Marshal Rommel* (New York: E. P. Dutton, 1977), p. 152.

49. David Kahn, *Hitler's Spies: German Military Intelligence in World War II* (New York: Macmillan, 1978), p. 193.

50. Lewin, *Ultra Goes to War,* pp. 175–76.

51. P. J. Vatikiotis, *The Egyptian Army in Politics: Pattern for New Nations?* (Bloomington: Indiana University Press, 1961), pp. 6, 205.

52. For the *Lehrregiment Brandenburg,* see Playfair, *Mediterranean,* vol. 3, p. 22n; Carell, *Foxes of the Desert,* pp. 209–14; Anthony Cave Brown, *Bodyguard of Lies* (New York: Harper & Row, 1975), pp. 104–106; Herbert Kriegsheim, *Getarnt, Getäuscht und Doch Getreu: Die Geheimnisvollen "Brandenburger"* (Berlin: Bernard & Graefe, 1959), pp. 283–319; and Werner Brockdorff, *Geheimkommandos des Zweiten Weltkrieges* (Munich: Welsermahl, 1967), pp. 170–89.

53. Bagnold interviews; and ltr, Bagnold to author, dtd 14 February 1970.

54. "Almaszy 'Diary'" (Typescript extracts in possession of Brigadier Ralph A. Bagnold; forwarded to Bagnold by Intelligence Organization, Allied Commission for Austria, British Troops in Austria, 16 December 1949), pp. 2–22. Unless otherwise noted, all quoted material in this paragraph is from "Almaszy 'Diary'."

55. Ibid.

56. Ibid., pp. 23–24.

57. Brockdorff, *Geheimkommandos,* pp. 170–89.

58. See "Almaszy 'Diary'," pp. 17–19; Hinsley, *British Intelligence in the Second World War,* vol. 2, pp. 377–78; and Lewin, *Ultra Goes to War,* p. 177, quoting a former British intelligence officer, who recalled that "we followed them all the way."

59. Cave Brown, *Bodyguard of Lies,* pp. 110–11.

60. Ibid., p. 102. See U.S. Department of the Army, *Official Army Register,* vol. 1, *United States Army Active and Retired Lists (1 January 1949)* (Washington, D.C.: USGPO, 1949), p. 673.

61. Prendergast interviews.

62. Kennedy Shaw, *Desert Group,* pp. 168–77.

63. "Almaszy 'Diary'," p. 40.

64. Ibid.

65. Prendergast interviews.

66. "Almaszy 'Diary'," pp. 4–14; and Carell, *Foxes of the Desert,* pp. 216–19.

67. Quoted in Kennedy Shaw, *Desert Group,* p. 165.

68. Ibid.

69. Liddell Hart, *Rommel Papers,* p. 292 and note. See also WO 201/2136, *Summary No. 539: Appendix—British Commandos for Special Tasks* (GHQ-ME translation of a captured German document).

70. WO 201/814, *War Diary and Narrative, Long Range Desert Group, May 1942–September 1942,* "A" Squadron, 1st Special Service Regiment, Patrol Report, 4–18 June 1942/dtd 20.6.42; and Crichton-Stuart, *G Patrol,* p. 150.

71. WO 201/727, *Personal File on Lieut.-Colonel Haselden,* esp., for SIG, "Capt. Buck's Party," rpt/dtd 7 July 1942; WO 201/721, *MO3 History of the SAS, 1941–1942;* Cowles, *Who Dares, Wins,* pp. 110–13; and, for the SIG, Major General I. S. O.

Playfair et al., *The Mediterranean and Middle East*, vol. 4, *The Destruction of the Axis Forces in Africa* (London: HMSO, 1966), p. 21 and note.

72. 201/813, LRDG Operation Report no. 38, G2 Patrol/dtd 28.5.42; Cowles, *Who Dares, Wins*, pp. 113–22; and Crichton-Stuart, *G Patrol*, pp. 137–38.

73. WO 201/721, *MO3 History of the SAS, 1941–1942;* and Cowles, *Who Dares, Wins*, pp. 111–19.

74. See the account in Cowles, *Who Dares, Wins*, pp. 114–19.

75. Prendergast interviews.

76. WO 201/814, LRDG, Operation Report no. 45, G2 Patrol/dtd 22.6.42; WO 201/721, *MO3 History of the SAS;* Cowles, *Who Dares, Wins*, pp. 128–31; and Crichton-Stuart, *G Patrol*, pp. 139–40.

77. See Playfair, *Mediterranean*, vol. 3, pp. 89, 358; and Cowles, *Who Dares, Wins*, p. 252, for claims as to enemy aircraft destroyed.

CHAPTER 7

1. Major General I. S. O. Playfair et al., *The Mediterranean and Middle East*, vol. 4, *The Destruction of the Axis Forces in Africa* (London: HMSO, 1966), p. 20.

2. Correlli Barnett, *The Desert Generals* (New York: Ballantine Books, 1972), pp. 137–56; and Major General I. S. O. Playfair et al., *The Mediterranean and Middle East*, vol. 3, *British Fortunes Reach Their Lowest Ebb* (London: HMSO, 1960), pp. 215–16.

3. Ibid., pp. 223–75; and Basil H. Liddell Hart, ed., *The Rommel Papers* (New York: Harcourt, Brace, 1953), pp. 191–232.

4. Playfair, *Mediterranean*, vol. 3, p. 274.

5. Winston S. Churchill, *The Second World War*, vol. 4, *The Hinge of Fate* (Boston: Houghton Mifflin, 1950), p. 383.

6. Alan Moorehead, *The March to Tunis: The North African War, 1940–1943* (New York: Harper & Row, 1967), pp. 354–55.

7. David J. C. Irving, *The Trail of the Fox: The Search for the True Field Marshall Rommel* (New York: E. P. Dutton, 1977), p. 6.

8. See WO 32/1012G, Memo, GOC-in-C, MEF, to Commander Eighth Army . . . [etc.]: Co-operation in Battle/dtd 8 February 1942. For a description of the "Alamein Line," see Playfair, *Mediterranean*, vol. 3, pp. 331–35.

9. WO 201/814, *War Diary and Narrative, Long Range Desert Group*, LRDG's Part in the 8th Army's Operations, The Seventh Phase, June 29th-September 11th, 1942: Eighth Army Operation Instruction no. 99 (To: Major Stirling) dtd 16 July 1942.

10. Barnett, *Desert Generals*, p. 200.

11. WO 201/814, LRDG Operation Report no. 50, G2 Patrol, July 3rd to 18th, 1942/dtd 23.7.42; LRDG Operation Instruction no. 51, G1 Patrol/dtd 30/6/42; WO 201/721, *MO3 History of the SAS, 1941–1942;* and WO 201/747, *MO3 Battle File: SAS Regiment*.

12. Interviews with Brigadier Guy L. Prendergast, DSO, Fort Augustus, Inverness-shire, Scotland, 1972 and 1976.

13. Michael Crichton-Stuart, *G Patrol* (London: William Kimber, 1958), p. 157.

14. WO 201/814, LRDG Operation Report no. 50, G2 Patrol . . . dtd 23.7.42.

15. Virginia Cowles, *Who Dares, Wins (Formerly The Phantom Major)* (New York: Ballantine Books, 1959), p. 158.

16. WO 201/721, *MO3 History of the SAS, 1941–1942.*

17. WO 201/814, LRDG's Part in the 8th Army Operations, The Seventh Phase, June 29th-September 11th, 1942. For the ME-109F, see Playfair, *Mediterranean,* vol. 3, app. 9, p. 453.

18. WO 201/814, LRDG Operation Report no. 54, T1 Patrol, 7/7/42 to 29/7/42/ dtd 5th August 1942. See also Cowles, *Who Dares, Wins,* pp. 161–79.

19. Barnett, *Desert Generals,* p. 217.

20. Quoted ibid., p. 251.

21. For Churchill's long unhappiness with Auchinleck, see esp. Churchill, *The Hinge of Fate,* pp. 408–24.

22. Playfair, *Mediterranean,* vol. 3, p. 367.

23. Ibid.

24. See Churchill, *The Hinge of Fate,* pp. 415–17.

25. Ibid., p. 367; and W. G. F. Jackson, *The Battle for North Africa, 1940–43* (New York: Mason/Charter, 1975), pp. 258–64.

26. For Alexander, see Nigel Nicolson, *Alex: The Life of Field Marshal Earl Alexander of Tunis* (New York: Atheneum, 1973); for Montgomery, Nigel Hamilton, *Monty: The Making of a General, 1887–1942* (New York: McGraw-Hill, 1981).

27. Playfair, *Mediterranean,* vol. 3, p. 369.

28. Nicolson, *Alex,* p. 167.

29. Playfair, *Mediterranean,* vol. 3, pp. 370–71.

30. Ibid., vol. 4, pp. 3–11.

31. WO 193/616, *SOE Middle East Series—Gen'l 14 Jan 41–14 Sept. 43;* and WO 201/728, *Reorganization of Special Forces in the Middle East, July-August 1942.*

32. M. R. D. Foot, *SOE in France: An Account of the Work of the British Special Operations Executive in France 1940–1944* (London: HMSO, 1966), p. xvii. See also WO 193/620, *Reorganization of SOE in Middle East and Control of G(R) Funds.*

33. Foot, *SOE in France,* pp. 4–14, 31–32.

34. Cowles, *Who Dares, Wins,* p. 154; and Prendergast interviews.

35. Liddell Hart, *Rommel Papers,* p. 292.

36. Interviews with General Sir John W. Hackett, GCB, CBE, DSO, MC, King's College, London, 1972.

37. Ibid. See also the account in Cowles, *Who Dares, Wins,* pp. 138–40, quoting Lieutenant Carol Mather, SAS.

38. Hackett interviews. See also Fitzroy Maclean, *Eastern Approaches* (London: Jonathan Cape, 1950), pp. 405–406.

39. Interviews with Major General David L. Lloyd Owen, CB, DSO, OBE, MC, Norwich, Norfolk, England, 1972, 1976, and 1983.

40. Vladimir Peniakoff, *Private Army* (London: Jonathan Cape, 1950), p. 273.

41. John Masefield, *The Taking of the Grey* (New York: Macmillan, 1934), p. 17.

42. Interview with Richard P. Lawson, MD, Calne, Wiltshire, Eng., 2 June 1972.

43. Hackett interviews.

44. Peniakoff, *Private Army,* p. 273.

45. Hackett interviews.

46. WO 201/728, *Reorganization of Special Forces in the Middle East, July-August 1942,* Stirling to Prime Minister, dtd 9 August 1942.

47. Cowles, *Who Dares, Wins*, pp. 190–91; and Maclean, *Eastern Approaches*, p. 227.

48. Cowles, *Who Dares, Wins*, p. 191.

49. Ibid.

50. Ibid.

51. Hackett interviews.

52. WO 201/728, Stirling to Prime Minister, dtd 9 August 1942.

53. Ibid.

54. Prendergast interviews.

55. Ibid.

56. GHQ MEF General Order 108/dtd 4.2.44, quoted in W. B. Kennedy Shaw, *Long Range Desert Group: The Story of Its Work in Libya, 1940–1943* (reprint ed.; Portway, Bath, Eng.: Cedric Chivers, 1970), p. 40. Also, planning was initiated that called for the sending of elements of Transjordan's Arab Legion (created by "Glubb Pasha," the British Army's Colonel Sir John Bagot Glubb) to it for special desert training. WO 201/2587, *Attachment of the Arab Legion to the Long Range Desert Group for Training, 1942*.

57. Prendergast interviews.

58. Anthony Cave Brown, *Bodyguard of Lies* (New York: Harper & Row, 1975), p. 113.

59. Playfair, *Mediterranean*, vol. 3, pp. 379–91; and Winston S. Churchill, *The Hinge of Fate*, pp. 488–92.

60. Playfair, *Mediterranean*, vol. 4, pp. 1–21.

61. Ibid., p. 20. See also WO 201/727, *Personal File on Lieutenant-Colonel Haselden, 5 March 1942–28 July 1942, Raiding Forces, GHQ Middle East*.

62. Colonel John W. Hackett, "The Employment of Special Forces," *Journal of the Royal United Service Institution* 97 (February 1952), p. 34.

63. Kennedy Shaw, *Desert Group*, p. 184.

64. Lloyd Owen interviews; and ltr, Lloyd Owen to author, dtd 1 April 1971.

65. Peniakoff, *Private Army*, pp. 192–93.

66. WO 201/815, *War Diary and Narrative, Long Range Desert Group, September 1942–January 1943*, LRDG Operations, September 11th-October 23rd, 1942; and Playfair, *Mediterranean*, vol. 4, p. 21n.

67. Peniakoff, *Private Army*, pp. 193–94.

68. Playfair, *Mediterranean*, vol. 4, p. 21n; and WO 201/721, *MO3 History of the SAS, 1941–1942*.

69. Peniakoff, *Private Army*, p. 194.

70. WO 201/815, LRDG Operation Instruction no. 57/dtd 28 August 1942; Playfair, *Mediterranean*, vol. 4, p. 21; and R. L. Kay, *Long Range Desert Group in the Mediterranean* (Wellington, N.Z.: War History Branch, Department of Internal Affairs, 1950), pp. 6–7.

71. Hackett, "Employment of Special Forces," p. 34. See also WO 201/753, *Small Combined Operations and Raids, July-December 1942*.

72. Peniakoff, *Private Army*, pp. 193–94.

73. Ibid.

74. Ibid.

75. Prendergast interviews. For the air force, see Wesley F. Craven and James

L. Cate, *The Army Air Forces in World War II*, vol. 2, *Europe: Torch to Pointblank* (reprint ed.; Washington: USGPO, 1983), pp. 31–33.

76. Lloyd Owen interviews.

77. Stirling, quoted in Cowles, *Who Dares, Wins*, p. 188.

78. Playfair, *Mediterranean*, vol. 4, p. 20.

79. Ibid.

80. Hackett interviews.

81. Interview with Brigadier George M. O. Davy, CB, CBE, DSO, London, 8 June 1972. See also Kennedy Shaw, *Desert Group*, pp. 183–84.

82. Prendergast interviews.

83. Hackett interviews.

84. WO 201/815, LRDG Operation Instruction no. 56/dtd 17th August 1942; LRDG Operation Report, "Agreement," Y1 Patrol/dtd 23/9/42.

85. Lloyd Owen interviews.

86. David L. Lloyd Owen, *Providence Their Guide: A Personal Account of the Long Range Desert Group, 1940–45* (London: Harrap, 1980), pp. 104–105.

87. Lawson interview. See also Lloyd Owen, *Providence Their Guide*, pp. 105–106; and Cowles, *Who Dares, Wins*, pp. 180–94.

88. Montgomery of Alamein, *The Memoirs of Field-Marshal the Viscount Montgomery of Alamein, K. G.* (New York: World, 1958), p. 107.

89. Ibid.

90. Cowles, *Who Dares, Wins*, p. 187.

91. Lloyd Owen interviews.

92. Ibid.

93. WO 201/815, LRDG Operation Report, "Agreement," Y1 Patrol/dtd 23/9/42; and Lloyd Owen interviews.

94. WO 201/742, *Reports on Operations at Tobruk, 14 September-13 November 1942;* WO 201/740, *Report on the Raid on Tobruk, 13–14 September 1942;* Craven, and Cate *Army Air Forces in World War II*, vol. 2, pp. 28–33; and Playfair, *Mediterranean*, vol. 4, p. 22.

95. Playfair, *Mediterranean*, vol. 4, p. 22.

96. Ibid., pp. 22–23.

97. Liddell Hart, *Rommel Papers*, p. 291.

98. See WO 201/739, *Reports on Operation "Caravan" (Raids on Barce, Benghazi, and Tobruk);* Maclean, *Eastern Approaches*, pp. 230–34; and Cowles, *Who Dares, Wins*, pp. 191–94.

99. Maclean, *Eastern Approaches*, pp. 235–36.

100. Ibid., pp. 237–39; and Cowles, *Who Dares, Wins*, pp. 195–96.

101. WO 201/735, *Reports on Operations at Benghazi, September 1942.*

102. Maclean, *Eastern Approaches*, p. 239.

103. WO 201/735, *Reports on Operations at Benghazi, September 1942;* and Hackett interviews.

104. Hackett interviews.

105. WO 201/815, LRDG Operations, The Eighth Phase, September 11th-October 23, 1942.

106. Prendergast interviews.

107. Lawson interview; WO 201/815, Report on Operation "Caravan," G1 and

T1 Patrols, 1–25 September 1942/dtd 27 September 1942; and Peniakoff, *Private Army*, pp. 198–205.

108. WO 201/739, *Reports on Operation . . . Barce . . . ;* and Crichton-Stuart, *G Patrol*, pp. 161–65.

109. WO 201/815, Report on Operation "Caravan," Operation Report no. 57/dtd 27 September 1942; and Kay, *Long Range Desert Group in the Mediterranean*, pp. 7–8.

110. WO 201/815, Report on Operation "Caravan," Operation Report no. 57/dtd 27 September 1942; and Crichton-Stuart, *G Patrol*, pp. 166–69.

111. Lawson interview; and Peniakoff, *Private Army*, pp. 213–20.

112. Lawson interview. See also Playfair, *Mediterranean*, vol. 4, p. 23.

113. Kay, *Long Range Desert Group in the Mediterranean*, pp. 7–9.

CHAPTER 8

1. Interviews with General Sir John W. Hackett, GCB, CBE, DSO, MC, King's College, London, 1972.

2. WO 201/815, *War Diary and Narrative, Long Range Desert Group (Phases 8 and 9) Sept 1942–Jan 1943*, LRDG Operation Report no. 57 ("Caravan"), G1 and T1 Patrols/dtd 27 Sept 42; interview with Richard P. Lawson, MD, Calne, Wiltshire, Eng., 2 June 1972; and Vladimir Peniakoff, *Private Army* (London: Jonathan Cape, 1950), pp. 210–21.

3. WO 201/815, LRDG Operation Report no. 57.

4. Interviews with Brigadier Guy L. Prendergast, DSO, Fort Augustus, Inverness-shire, Scotland, 1972 and 1976.

5. Interviews with Major General David L. Lloyd Owen, CB, DSO, OBE, MC, Norwich, Norfolk, England, 1972, 1976, and 1983. See also WO 201/740, *Report on the Raid on Tobruk*.

6. WO 201/815, LRDG Operation Report no. 56 ("Agreement"), Y1 Patrol/dtd 23 Sept 42.

7. David L. Lloyd Owen, *Providence Their Guide: A Personal Account of the Long Range Desert Group, 1940–45* (London: Harrap, 1980), p. 114; and WO 201/721, *MO3 History of the SAS, 1941–1942*.

8. Lloyd Owen interviews.

9. WO 201/815, LRDG Operation Report no. 60, G2 Patrol/dtd 18 October 1942.

10. Lloyd Owen interviews.

11. Prendergast interviews.

12. See WO 201/742, *Reports on Operations at Tobruk, 14 September-13 November 1942*.

13. Major General I. S. O. Playfair et al., *The Mediterranean and Middle East*, vol. 4, *The Destruction of the Axis Forces in Africa* (London: HMSO, 1966), p. 23.

14. Fitzroy Maclean, *Eastern Approaches* (London: Jonathan Cape, 1950), pp. 228, 261.

15. Ibid., p. 229.

16. Crichton-Stuart, quoted in Lloyd Owen, *Providence Their Guide*, p. 114.

17. Peniakoff, *Private Army*, p. 194.

18. Ibid.

19. Ibid.

20. Ibid.

21. Maclean, *Eastern Approaches*, p. 235.

22. Ibid.

23. W. B. Kennedy Shaw, *Long Range Desert Group: The Story of Its Work in Libya, 1940–1943* (reprint ed.; Portway, Bath, Eng.: Cedric Chivers, 1970), p. 196.

24. Peniakoff, *Private Army*, p. 195.

25. Ibid.

26. Prendergast interviews.

27. Hackett interviews.

28. Ibid.

29. WO 201/2200, *Vehicles for the Long Range Desert Group, October 1940–1943*, esp. Situation re L.R.D.G. and Kufra, dtd 30.4.41, p. 1.

30. Prendergast interviews.

31. Ibid. See also Colonel John W. Hackett, "The Employment of Special Forces," *Journal of the Royal United Service Institution* 97 (February 1952), p. 34.

32. Lloyd Owen, *Providence Their Guide*, p. 105, argues that "without Colonel [John W.] Shan Hackett they [the September raids] would have been an even bigger fiasco than they unhappily turned out to be."

33. Hackett interviews; and WO 201/728, *Reorganization of Special Forces in the Middle East, July-August 1942*.

34. Hackett interviews.

35. Ibid.

36. Ibid.

37. Ibid. See also WO 201/752, *Appointment of a Commander, Raiding Forces, October-November 1942*.

38. Prendergast interviews.

39. Ibid.

40. Hackett, "Employment of Special Forces," p. 32.

41. Interview with Brigadier Ralph A. Bagnold, OBE, FRS, Mark Beech, Edenbridge, Kent, Eng., 21 June 1976; Prendergast interview, 29 June 1976; and Lloyd Owen interview, 9 June 1976.

42. F. W. Winterbotham, *The Ultra Secret* (New York: Dell, 1974), p. 17.

43. Ibid.

44. See U.S., War Department, *German Operational Intelligence* (np: German Military Documents Section, Adjutant General's Office, 1946), esp. p. 138; and Wilhelm F. Flicke, *War Secrets in the Ether*, pt. 3, trans. R. W. Pettengill, (Washington, D.C.: National Security Agency, 1954), esp. p. 182, neither of which indicates any German awareness that the system had been compromised. For Ultra, see F. H. Hinsley et al., *British Intelligence in the Second World War: Its Influence on Strategy and Operations*, vol. 1 (New York: Cambridge University Press, 1979–   ), I, App. 1, pp. 487–95; Winterbotham, *The Ultra Secret*, esp. pp. 15–35; and Ronald Lewin, *Ultra Goes to War: The First Account of World War II's Greatest Secret Based on Official Documents* (New York: McGraw-Hill, 1978), esp. pp. 25–72.

45. F. H. Hinsley, *British Intelligence in the Second World War*, vol. 1, (New York: Cambridge University Press, 1981), p. 487.

46. Hinsley, *British Intelligence in the Second World War*, vol. 2, esp. app. 1, pt. (ii), pp. 643–49.

47. Churchill, quoted in Lewin, *Ultra Goes to War*, p. 25.

48. Hinsley, *British Intelligence in the Second World War*, vol. 1, app. I, pp. 487–95.

49. Ibid., esp. pp. 397–98.

50. Ibid., vol. 2, app. 4, p. 662.

51. Winterbotham, *Ultra Secret*, p. 17.

52. Hinsley, *British Intelligence in the Second World War*, vol. 1, pp. 386–93; Lewin, *Ultra Goes to War*, pp. 159–61; and Larry H. Addington, *The Blitzkrieg Era and the German General Staff, 1865–1941* (New Brunswick, N.J.: Rutgers University Press, 1971), pp. 162–63.

53. David J. C. Irving, *The Trail of the Fox: The Search for the True Field Marshal Rommel* (New York: E. P. Dutton, 1977), p. 81.

54. Wavell, quoted in Lewin, *Ultra Goes to War*, p. 160.

55. Ibid.

56. Ibid., pp. 162–63.

57. Hinsley, *British Intelligence in the Second World War*, vol. 1, p. 394.

58. Lewin, *Ultra Goes to War*, p. 174.

59. Ltr, Brigadier Eric J. Shearer, CB, CBE, MC, to author, dtd 11 January 1972.

60. Hinsley, *British Intelligence in the Second World War*, vol. 2, pp. 333–34, 356, 381, 429, 445.

61. Ltr, Shearer to author, dtd 11 January 1972.

62. Lewin, *Ultra Goes to War*, pp. 171–73.

63. Martin van Creveld, *Supplying War: Logistics from Wallenstein to Patton* (New York: Cambridge University Press, 1977), p. 194.

64. Hinsley, *British Intelligence in the Second World War*, vol. 2, pp. 399–425, and app. 17, "Contribution of Sigint to Axis Shipping Losses on North African Routes June to October 1942," pp. 728–38.

65. Prendergast interviews.

66. Lloyd Owen interviews. See also Lewin, *Ultra Goes to War*, p. 177n.

67. Michael Crichton-Stuart, *G Patrol* (London: William Kimber, 1958), p. 134; and Lloyd Owen interviews.

68. WO 201/812 and 813, *War Diary and Narrative, Long Range Desert Group*, esp. LRDG's Part in the 8th Army Offensive, 4th phase, and LRDG's Part in the 8th Army Operations, 5th Phase, April 19–August 26, 1942, detail the early Road Watch efforts undertaken under Prendergast's direction; Prendergast interviews.

69. Ltr, Shearer to author, dtd 22 December 1971.

70. Lewin, *Ultra Goes to War*, pp. 175–77.

71. Ltr, Major General Sir Francis de Guingand, KBE, CB, DSO, to author, dtd 15 March 1972; and Hackett interviews.

72. Prendergast interviews.

73. Kennedy Shaw, *Desert Group*, p. 210.

74. Prendergast interviews.

75. WO 201/812 and WO 201/813, *War Diary and Narrative, Long Range Desert Group*, esp. LRDG's part in the 8th Army Offensive.

76. Lewin, *Ultra Goes to War*, p. 174. For a detailed discussion of the problem of counting the operational tanks available to Rommel, see Hinsley, *British Intelligence in the Second World War*, vol. 2, pp. 354–57.

77. For the Coastwatchers, see Eric A. Feldt, *The Coastwatchers* (Oxford: Oxford University Press, 1946).

78. WO 201/812 and WO 201/813.

79. Hackett, "Employment of Special Forces," p. 30.

80. Ibid.

81. Ltr, de Guingand to author, dtd 15 March 1972.

82. WO 201/771, memo, DMI to DMO, GHQ-ME, dtd 14 December 1942 ("Intelligence Value of LRDG Road Watch"). Road Watch information is in WO 201/540, *Director of Military Intelligence, Middle East: Weekly "Desert" Intelligence Reviews, 5 January-13 August 1942;* WO 201/2173, *Daily Intelligence Summaries, September 1942– January 1943;* and WO 201/2171, *Daily Intelligence Summaries, 1 January, 1942–15 November 1942.*

83. Crichton-Stuart, *G Patrol,* p. 141.

84. Prendergast interviews.

85. Hinsley, *British Intelligence in the Second World War,* vol. 2, pp. 360–62.

86. Ltr, de Guingand to author, dtd 15 March 1972.

87. Prendergast interviews.

88. Ibid. See also Major General Sir Francis de Guingand, *Operation Victory* (New York: Charles Scribner's Sons, 1947), p. 110.

89. Hackett interviews.

90. Playfair, *Mediterranean,* vol. 4, p. 30; Denis Richards et al., *Royal Air Force, 1939–1945,* vol. 2, *The Fight Avails* (London: HMSO, 1954), p. 233; W. G. F. Jackson, *The Battle for North Africa, 1940–43* (New York: Mason/Charter, 1975), pp. 274–83; and Correlli Barnett, *The Desert Generals* (New York: Ballantine Books, 1972), pp. 284–86.

91. De Guingand, quoted in Anthony Cave Brown, *Bodyguard of Lies* (New York: Harper & Row, 1975), p. 117.

92. Jackson, *Battle for North Africa,* pp. 265, 283–86; de Guingand, *Operation Victory,* pp. 152–62; and Playfair, *Mediterranean,* vol. 4, pp. 4–7.

93. Lewin, *Ultra Goes to War,* p. 266; Major General I. S. O. Playfair et al., *The Mediterranean and Middle East,* vol. 3, *British Fortunes Reach Their Lowest Ebb* (London: HMSO, 1960), pp. 326–28; Playfair, *Mediterranean,* vol. 4, p. 26; and Hinsley, *British Intelligence in the Second World War,* vol. 2, pp. 417–29.

94. Cave Brown, *Bodyguard of Lies,* p. 121.

95. Bagnold interviews.

96. Hackett interviews. Ltr, de Guingand to author, dtd 15 March 1972, emphasizes the LRDG's role in the Road Watch but offers no specific linkage to Ultra.

97. See, for example, WO 201/815, LRDG Operations: The Ninth Phase: October 1942–January, 1943; LRDG Operation Instruction no. 47/dtd 14 October 1942; Minutes of the Libyan Sub-Committee Meeting...ISLD (AB)/dtd 1–2 October 1942.

98. Hackett interviews.

99. Ibid.

100. Peniakoff, *Private Army,* p. 238.

101. WO 106/2332, *Popski's Private Army: No. 1 Demolition Squadron PPA: Historical Summary.*

102. Hackett interviews.

103. Peniakoff, *Private Army,* p. 238.

104. Ltr, Major General David L. Lloyd Owen, CB, DSO, OBE, MC, to author, dtd 1 April 1971.

105. Peniakoff, *Private Army*, p. 241.

106. Ibid., p. 242.

107. Ibid., p. 244.

108. Hackett interviews.

109. WO 201/747, *MO3 Battle File: SAS Regiment.*

110. Virginia Cowles, *Who Dares, Wins (Formerly The Phantom Major)* (New York: Ballantine Books, 1959), pp. 202–204.

111. Hackett interviews.

112. Ibid. A similar account is given in Cowles, *Who Dares, Wins*, pp. 202–203.

113. Ltr, de Guingand to author, dtd 15 March 1972.

114. Hackett interviews.

115. Crichton-Stuart, *G Patrol*, p. 174.

116. WO 201/815, LRDG Operations: The Ninth Phase: October 1942–January 1943.

117. Prendergast interviews.

118. For the battle, see Generalmajor Alfred Toppe et al., "German Experience in Desert Warfare in World War II," MS #P-129, OCMH, 1952, pp. 45–48; Playfair, *Mediterranean*, vol. 4, pp. 35–72; and Field Marshal Lord Carver, *El Alamein* (London: Batsford, 1962).

119. Arthur Bryant, *The Turn of the Tide, 1939–1943: A Study Based on the Diaries and Autobiographical Notes of Field Marshal the Viscount Alanbrooke* (London: Collins, 1957), p. 512, quoting Churchill.

120. Montgomery of Alamein, *The Memoirs of Field Marshal the Viscount Montgomery of Alamein, KG* (New York: World, 1958), p. 117.

121. Playfair, *Mediterranean*, vol. 4, pp. 56–76.

122. Hitler, quoted in Lewin, *Ultra Goes to War*, p. 268, which differs slightly from Basil H. Liddell Hart, ed., *The Rommel Papers* (New York: Harcourt, Brace, 1953), p. 321.

123. Liddell Hart, *Rommel Papers*, p. 321.

124. Hinsley, *British Intelligence in the Second World War*, vol. 2, pp. 449–52, 450n.

125. WO 201/815, LRDG Operations: The Ninth Phase: October 1942–January 1943.

126. Hinsley, *British Intelligence in the Second World War*, vol. 2, p. 448.

127. WO 201/815, LRDG Operations: The Ninth Phase: October 1942–January 1943.

128. Ibid.; and Prendergast interviews.

129. For example, as late as the Battle of Gazala (May-June 1942), "photographic reconnaissance of enemy armour was quite inadequate . . . because only 20" lens cameras were available and low flying was practically impossible." Hinsley, *British Intelligence in the Second World War*, vol. 2, p. 358n.

130. WO 201/815, LRDG Preliminary Report no. 65, G2 Patrol, Tripoli Road Watch/dtd 8/12/42.

131. Hackett, "Employment of Special Forces," p. 30.

132. Hackett interviews.

133. Ibid.

134. Kennedy Shaw, *Desert Group*, p. 213.

135. Cave Brown, *Bodyguard of Lies*, pp. 128–29.

136. Winterbotham, *Ultra Secret*, pp. 119–23; and Hinsley, *British Intelligence in the Second World War*, vol. 2, p. 596.

137. Barnett, *Desert Generals*, p. 311.

138. WO 201/815, LRDG Instruction no. 70/dtd 19 November 1942; LRDG Operation Report no. 70, G1 Patrol/dtd 29 December 1942; and Prendergast interviews.

139. WO 201/815, LRDG Operation Report no. 70, G1 Patrol/dtd 29 December 1942; and the account in Crichton-Stuart, *G Patrol*, pp. 176–88.

140. Crichton-Stuart, *G Patrol*, p. 186.

141. Hackett interviews.

142. Interview with Brigadier George M. O. Davy, CB, CBE, DSO, London, 22 May 1972.

143. Ibid.

CHAPTER 9

1. WO 201/816, *War Diary and Narrative, LRDG, Phase 10, January 1943–March 1943*, Main HQ Eighth Army, MEF to OC, LRDG, Memo, B. L. Montgomery to Prendergast/dtd 2 April 1943.

2. Interview with Brigadier George M. O. Davy, CB, CBE, DSO, London, 22 May 1972.

3. W. B. Kennedy Shaw, *Long Range Desert Group: The Story of Its Work in Libya, 1940–1943* (reprint ed.; Portway, Bath, Eng.: Cedric Chivers, 1970), p. 221.

4. Davy interview. See also WO 201/728, *Reorganization of Special Forces in the Middle East, July-August 1942;* and WO 201/721, *MO3 History of the SAS, 1941–1942.*

5. Interviews with General Sir John W. Hackett, GCB, CBE, DSO, MC, King's College, London, 1972.

6. Ibid.

7. WO 201/815, *War Diary and Narrative, LRDG, Ninth Phase, October 1942– December 1942*, Eighth Army Operation Instruction no. 6/dtd 3 January 1943 (to Comd SAS Regt); and Hackett interviews.

8. WO 201/815, GHQ MEF Operation Instruction no. 144/dtd 22 September 1942; and LRDG Operations: The Ninth Phase: October 1942–January 1943.

9. Ibid.

10. Davy interview.

11. Colonel John W. Hackett, "The Employment of Special Forces," *Journal of the Royal United Service Institution* 97 (February, 1952), p. 32, amplified in Hackett interviews.

12. Hackett interviews.

13. Ibid.

14. Ibid.

15. Hackett, "Employment of Special Forces," p. 32.

16. Virginia Cowles, *Who Dares, Wins (Formerly The Phantom Major)* (New York: Ballantine Books, 1959), p. 214.

17. Hackett interviews.

18. Hackett, "Employment of Special Forces," p. 32, amplified in Hackett interviews.

19. Basil H. Liddell Hart, ed., *The Rommel Papers* (New York: Harcourt, Brace, 1953), p. 292.

20. Ibid., p. 378.

21. Ibid., p. 379.

22. Major General I. S. O. Playfair et al., *The Mediterranean and Middle East*, vol. 4, *The Destruction of the Axis Forces in Africa* (London: HMSO, 1966), p. 221. See also WO 201/815, 2 NZ Div Adm Instruction no. 19/dtd 13 December 1942 w/Operation Order no. 28/dtd 13 December 1942, and Operation Order no. 29/dtd 16 December 1942.

23. See Liddell Hart, *Rommel Papers*, pp. 348–73.

24. Playfair, *Mediterranean*, vol. 4, p. 222.

25. Interviews with Brigadier Guy L. Prendergast, DSO, Fort Augustus, Inverness-shire, Scotland, 1972 and 1976.

26. Ibid.

27. W. G. Stevens, *Bardia to Enfidaville* (Wellington, N.Z.: War History Branch, Department of Internal Affairs, 1962), p. 57.

28. David J. C. Irving, *The Trail of the Fox: The Search for the True Field Marshal Rommel* (New York: E. P. Dutton, 1977), p. 252.

29. Liddell Hart, *Rommel Papers*, p. 374.

30. WO 201/815, LRDG Operations: The Ninth Phase: October 1942–January 1943; and Prendergast interviews.

31. Irving, *Trail of the Fox*, p. 254.

32. Liddell Hart, *Rommel Papers*, pp. 388–94. For Ultra intercepts during this period, see F. H. Hinsley et al., *British Intelligence in the Second World War: Its Influences on Strategy and Operations*, vol. 2 (New York: Cambridge University Press, 1981), pp. 579–81.

33. Playfair, *Mediterranean*, vol. 4, pp. 109–191, analyzing Torch.

34. Liddell Hart, *Rommel Papers*, pp. 359–69; and Irving, *Trail of the Fox*, p. 246.

35. Ltr, Brigadier Ralph A. Bagnold, OBE, FRS, to author, dtd 14 February 1972.

36. Paul Moynet, *Victory in the Fezzan* (London: Fighting France Publications, 1944), pp. 24–25.

37. Ibid., p. 33.

38. WO 201/815, LRDG Operation Report no. 54, T1 Patrol, "A" (NZ) Squadron/dtd 28/12/42; and GHQ MEF Operation Instruction no. 151/dtd 15 November 1942; Eighth Army Operation Instruction no. 6/dtd 21 December 42.

39. WO 201/815, LRDG Operations: The Ninth Phase: October 1942–January 1943; and Prendergast interviews.

40. Vladimir Peniakoff, *Private Army* (London: Jonathan Cape, 1950), p. 261.

41. WO 201/816, LRDG Operations: The Tenth Phase: January 24th, 1943–March 29th, 1943. See also the account in R. L. Kay, *Long Range Desert Group in the Mediterranean* (Wellington, N. Z.: War History Branch, Department of Internal Affairs, 1950), p. 11.

42. WO 201/816, LRDG Operation Instruction no. 84/dtd 30 January 1943; LRDG Operation Report no. 84/dtd 21 February 1943; and the account in Michael Crichton-Stuart, *G Patrol* (London: William Kimber, 1958), p. 192.

43. Montgomery, quoted in Crichton-Stuart, *G Patrol*, p. 194.

44. Prendergast interviews.

45. See Crichton-Stuart, *G Patrol*, p. 195.

46. WO 201/816, LRDG Operations: The Tenth Phase: January 24, 1943–March 29th, 1943; and Playfair, *Mediterranean*, vol. 4, p. 234.

47. But see Rommel's assessment of Mareth in Liddell Hart, *Rommel Papers*, pp. 392–93; and Hinsley, *British Intelligence in the Second World War*, vol. 2, pp. 460, 579–81, 584.

48. Playfair, *Mediterranean*, vol. 4, pp. 330–33.

49. W. G. F. Jackson, *The Battle for North Africa, 1940–43* (New York: Mason/Charter, 1975), pp. 329, 337, 341, 346–51, 354–64.

50. Prendergast interviews.

51. Playfair, *Mediterranean*, vol. 4, p. 333n; and Kennedy Shaw, *Desert Group*, p. 234.

52. Liddell Hart, *Rommel Papers*, p. 392; and Playfair, *Mediterranean*, vol. 4, p. 333n.

53. Prendergast interviews.

54. Ibid.; and WO 201/816, LRDG Operations: The Tenth Phase: January 24, 1943–March 29th, 1943.

55. WO 201/815, LRDG Memorandum: Tunisia as Field of Operation/dtd 18 January 1943.

56. Prendergast interviews.

57. F. H. Hinsley, *British Intelligence in the Second World War*, vol. 1 (New York: Cambridge University Press, 1979), p. 399.

58. WO 201/816, LRDG Operations: The Tenth Phase: January 24th, 1943–March 29th, 1943.

59. Kay, *Long Range Desert Group in the Mediterranean*, p. 12.

60. WO 201/816, LRDG Operations: The Tenth Phase: January 24th, 1943–March 29th, 1943.

61. Ibid.

62. Ibid.; Kay, *Long Range Desert Group in the Mediterranean*, p. 12; see also the account in Major General Sir Francis de Guingand, *Operation Victory* (New York: Charles Scribner's Sons, 1947), pp. 235–36.

63. Playfair, *Mediterranean*, vol. 4, p. 333n.

64. Peniakoff, *Private Army*, p. 279.

65. WO 201/815, LRDG Operation Report no. 58/dtd 14 February 1943.

66. Ibid.

67. Kay, *Long Range Desert Group in the Mediterranean*, pp. 12–21.

68. Peniakoff, *Private Army*, p. 301.

69. Alan Moorehead, *The March to Tunis: The North African War, 1940–1943* (New York: Harper & Row, 1967), p. 487.

70. Ibid.

71. Ibid.

72. See Jackson, *Battle for North Africa*, pp. 332–33; Playfair, *Mediterranean*, vol. 4, pp. 287–313; and Liddell Hart, *Rommel Papers*, pp. 397–408.

73. Captain Harry C. Butcher, quoted in Ronald Lewin, *Ultra Goes to War: The First Account of World War II's Greatest Secret Based on Official Documents* (New York: McGraw-Hill, 1978), pp. 273–74.

74. Ibid. See also Captain Harry C. Butcher, *My Three Years with Eisenhower* (New York: Simon & Schuster, 1946), pp. 265–66.

75. F. W. Winterbotham, *The Ultra Secret* (New York: Dell, 1974), p. 17.

76. Liddell Hart, *Rommel Papers*, p. 407.

77. Stephen E. Ambrose, *The Supreme Commander: The War Years of General Dwight D. Eisenhower* (Garden City, N.Y.: Doubleday, 1970), p. 173.

78. Butcher, quoted in Lewin, *Ultra Goes to War*, p. 274. See Hinsley, *British Intelligence in the Second World War*, vol. 2, pp. 573–92, for an analysis of the intelligence situation before the battle.

79. Lewin, *Ultra Goes to War*, p. 274. See also Hinsley, *British Intelligence in the Second World War*, vol. 2, p. 333, for a discussion of the position of DMI within the GHQ-ME staff.

80. WO 201/815, Memorandum for G-3, Allied Force Headquarters: Subject: LRDG Patrols/dtd 14 January 1943; and Prendergast interviews.

81. WO 201/816, LRDG Operation Report no. 84 (Cont'd), G Patrol/dtd (?) 1943.

82. Wesley F. Craven and James L. Cate, *The Army Air Forces in World War II*, vol. 2, *Europe: Torch to Pointblank* (reprint ed.; Washington: USGPO, 1983), pp. 118–19.

83. Crichton-Stuart, *G Patrol*, pp. 202–3.

84. Ibid.

85. Ibid.

86. Moorehead, *March to Tunis*, p. 488. See also Liddell Hart, *Rommel Papers*, p. 393.

87. David Erskine, *The Scots Guards, 1919–1955* (London: William Clowes & Sons, 1956), p. 75.

88. WO 201/815, Operations of S.A.S. Regt: Period 1 January–15 February (Approx)/dtd 7 January 1943.

89. Hackett interviews.

90. Cowles, *Who Dares, Wins*, p. 233.

91. Erskine, *Scots Guards*, app. E, p. 584.

92. Cowles, *Who Dares, Wins*, p. 233.

93. Ibid.

94. Ibid.

95. Hackett interviews.

96. Intelligence Report: Acts of Sabotage by English Patrols/dtd 4 February 1943/ XXI, HQ Armored Division "Centauro" (131).

97. WO 201/815, Operations of S.A.S. Regt . . . /dtd 7 January 1943.

98. Cowles, *Who Dares, Wins*, p. 235.

99. Ibid., p. 241.

100. Hackett interviews.

101. Cowles, *Who Dares, Wins*, p. 243.

102. Ibid.

103. Ibid., p. 245.

104. Hackett interviews. See also Liddell Hart, *Rommel Papers*, p. 393.

105. Cowles, *Who Dares, Wins*, p. 247.

106. Hackett interviews.

107. Liddell Hart, *Rommel Papers*, p. 393. See also Erskine, *Scots Guards*, p. 75.

108. Hackett interviews.

109. Ibid.

110. Ibid.; a point suggested also in Hackett, "Employment of Special Forces," p. 35.

111. Peniakoff, *Private Army*, pp. 305–6.

112. Playfair, *Mediterranean*, vol. 4, p. 333n.

113. Rommel, quoted in Irving, *Trail of the Fox*, p. 265.

114. Liddell Hart, *Rommel Papers*, pp. 415–16.

115. Playfair, *Mediterranean*, vol. 4, pp. 324, 329.

116. Liddell Hart, *Rommel Papers*, pp. 416–20.

117. Eisenhower's Directive to Alexander, quoted in Jackson, *Battle for North Africa*, p. 353.

118. Playfair, *Mediterranean*, vol. 4, p. 320.

119. WO 201/815, Notes on Conference . . . General Leclerc/dtd 22 November 1942; de Guingand, *Operation Victory*, pp. 239–40; and Playfair, *Mediterranean*, vol. 4, p. 320. See also WO 201/594, *General Leclerc and Force "L": Future Operations under Eighth Army, January-April 1943;* and Howard W. Holmes, "Leclerc: The Man and the March," *Infantry* 56 (May/June 1966), pp. 24–28.

120. WO 201/816, LRDG, A (NZ) Squadron Reports, Operation with Eighth Army/dtd 9 April 1943.

121. Ibid. See Liddell Hart, *Rommel Papers*, p. 420; Playfair, *Mediterranean*, vol. 4, p. 337; and de Guingand, *Operation Victory*, pp. 246–47.

122. Playfair, *Mediterranean*, vol. 4, p. 341.

123. Ibid.

124. Ibid., pp. 343–45; WO 201/816, LRDG . . . Report . . . dtd 9 April 1943; and the account in Kay, *Long Range Desert Group in the Mediterranean*, p. 22.

125. Playfair, *Mediterranean*, vol. 4, p. 347.

126. WO 201/816, LRDG Operations: The Tenth Phase: January 24th, 1943–March 29th, 1943. That Rommel had from the start anticipated just such a move is apparent from Liddell Hart, *Rommel Papers*, pp. 392–422.

127. Jackson, *Battle for North Africa*, p. 378.

128. Alexander, quoted in Playfair, *Mediterranean*, vol. 4, p. 459. See also Moorehead, *March to Tunis*, pp. 579–80.

129. WO 201/816, LRDG Operations: The Tenth Phase: January 24th, 1943–March 29th, 1943.

130. Peniakoff, *Private Army*, p. 305.

131. Ibid.

132. Ltr, Montgomery to Prendergast, dtd 2 April 1943, quoted in Kennedy Shaw, *Desert Group*, p. 238. See also WO 201/816, Eighth Army Operation Instruction no. 3/dtd 21 March 1943.

133. Prendergast interviews.

134. Crichton-Stuart, *G Patrol*, p. 206.

135. Moorehead, *March to Tunis*, p. 580.

136. Ibid., p. 489.

137. Peniakoff, *Private Army*, p. 323.

138. Moorehead, *March to Tunis*, p. 249.

EPILOGUE

1. Field Marshal Sir William Slim, *Defeat into Victory* (New York: David McKay, 1961), pp. 455–57.

2. Interview with Brigadier George M. O. Davy, CB, CBE, DSO, London, 22 May 1972.

3. Interviews with General Sir John W. Hackett, GCB, CBE, DSO, MC, King's College, London, 1972.

4. Ibid.

5. WO 201/816, *War Diary and Narrative, Long Range Desert Group*, LRDG Operations: The Tenth Phase, January 24th, 1943–March 29th, 1943, p. 4; WO 201/816, MOST SECRET Cipher Message, GHQ-ME to Eighth Army, dtd 15 March 1943; R. L. Kay, *Long Range Desert Group in the Mediterranean* (Wellington, N.Z.: War History Branch, Department of Internal Affairs, 1950), p. 24; and David L. Lloyd Owen, *Providence Their Guide: A Personal Account of the Long Range Desert Group, 1940–45* (London: Harrap, 1980), pp. 125–33.

6. WO 201/817, *War Diary and Narrative, Long Range Desert Group, April 1943–September 1943*, LRDG Operations: The Eleventh Phase (Training and Re-equipping), March 30, 1943–September 10, 1943, p. 1A. See also WO 201/817, GHQ Directive no. 165/dtd 2 June 43.

7. WO 201/817, Long Range Desert Group, "B" Squadron Training Directive no. 1, dtd 28/5/43; and interviews with Major General David L. Lloyd Owen, CB, DSO, OBE, MC, Norwich, Norfolk, Eng., 1972, 1976 and 1983.

8. Interviews with Brigadier Guy L. Prendergast, DSO, Fort Augustus, Inverness-shire, Scotland, 1972 and 1976. Alistair Maclean's *The Guns of Navarone* (London: Collins, 1957) was made into a film in 1959.

9. Prendergast interviews.

10. Ibid.

11. Ibid.

12. Davy interview.

13. WO 201/818, *War Diary and Narrative, Long Range Desert Group, September 1943–November 1943* (Aegean Ops), Operations in Aegean, 11/9/43 to 30/11/43.

14. Interview with Richard P. Lawson, MD, Calne, Wiltshire, Eng., 2 June 1972.

15. Ibid.

16. Brigadier C. J. C. Molony et al., *The Mediterranean and Middle East*, vol. 5, *The Campaign in Sicily 1943 and the Campaign in Italy, 3rd September 1943 to 31st March 1944* (London: HMSO, 1973), pp. 531–59; and Kay, *Long Range Desert Group in the Mediterranean*, p. 31.

17. WO 201/818, Operations in Aegean; and Lloyd Owen, *Providence Their Guide*, pp. 140–48.

18. Prendergast interviews.

19. Davy interview.

20. Brief biographical information on some of the LRDG's New Zealanders is found in Kay, *Long Range Desert Group in the Mediterranean*, pp. 32–33.

21. Lloyd Owen interviews. See also WO 201/818, Operations in Aegean, esp. p. 9.

22. Hackett interviews.

23. Davy interview.

24. Ibid.

25. Ibid.

26. Ibid.

27. Ibid.

28. WO 201/818, Report by Col. G. L. Prendergast . . . dtd (?) 1943; Prendergast interviews; M. R. D. Foot, *SOE in France: An Account of the Work of the British Special Operations Executive in France 1940–1944* (London: HMSO, 1966), pp. 385–418, esp. table 5, p. 403, reflecting Prendergast as commander of the "Parot" mission in the Vosges; Lloyd Owen, *Providence Their Guide*, pp. 149–57; Lloyd Owen interviews; and Davy interview.

29. Davy interview.

30. Lloyd Owen interviews.

31. CONFIDENTIAL ltr, Field Marshal The Hon Sir H. R. L. G. Alexander, GCB, CSI, DSO, ADC, to Lt-Col D. L. Lloyd Owen, DSO, MC, Commanding Long Range Desert Group/dtd 26th June, 1945, reproduced on plate facing p. 191, Lloyd Owen, *Providence Their Guide*.

32. Ltr, Lieutenant-General Sir B. C. Freyberg, VC, to Lt. Col. D. L. Lloyd Owen, DSO, MC, dtd 12th July, 1945, reproduced on plate facing p. 191, Lloyd Owen, *Providence Their Guide*.

33. Ibid.

34. Lloyd Owen interviews.

35. Hackett interviews.

36. For perceptions of another special force, see John W. Gordon, "The U.S. Marine Corps and an Experiment in Military Elitism: A Reassessment of the Special Warfare Impetus, 1937–1943," in *Changing Interpretations and New Sources in Naval History: Papers from the Third United States Naval Academy History Symposium*, ed. Robert W. Love (New York: Garland, 1980), pp. 362–73.

37. Slim, *Defeat into Victory*, pp. 455–56.

38. Ibid.

39. Ibid.

40. Ibid., p. 457.

41. Ibid.

42. On the SAS since World War II, see Tony Geraghty, *Inside the SAS: 1950 to 1980* (New York: Ballantine Books, 1982).

43. Max Hastings and Simon Jenkins, *The Battle for the Falkland Islands* (New York: Norton, 1983); Presentation on SAS and SBS operations, Seminar on Military Elite Forces, U. S. Marine Corps Command and Staff College, Quantico, VA, 15 October 1982.

44. Colonel John W. Hackett, "The Employment of Special Forces," *Journal of the Royal United Service Institution* 97 (February 1952), p. 27.

45. Ibid., pp. 27, 36.

46. Rommel, quoted in Basil H. Liddell Hart, ed., *The Rommel Papers* (New York: Harcourt, Brace, 1953), p. 393.

47. Generalmajor Hans-Hennig von Holzendorff, "Reasons for Rommel's Success in Africa 1941–42," MS #D-024, OCMH, 1947, p. 12.

48. Regarding the British Army officer corps, see Christopher B. Otley, "The Origins and Recruitment of the British Army Elite, 1870–1959," (doctoral diss., University of Hull, 1965); Correlli Barnett, *Britain and Her Army, 1509–1970* (London: Allen Lane, 1970), pp. 487–88; and E. S. Turner, *Gallant Gentlemen: A Portrait of the British Officer, 1600–1956* (London: Michael Joseph, 1956), pp. 311–12.

49. For the role of elite units as "leadership nurseries," see Eliot A. Cohen,

Commandos and Politicians: Elite Military Units in Modern Democracies (Cambridge, Mass.: Center for International Affairs, Harvard University, 1978), pp. 33–34.

50. Information from personal interviews and from *Who's Who: An Annual Biographical Dictionary* (London: Adam & Charles Black), vols. for 1969–1982.

51. Hackett interviews. After retiring from the British Army, Hackett served as principal of King's College, University of London.

52. Lloyd Owen interviews.

53. Major General J. F. C. Fuller, *Armored Warfare: An Annotated Edition of Lectures on F. S. R. III (Operations Between Mechanized Forces)* (2nd ed.; Harrisburg, Pa.: Military Service Publishing Company, 1943), pp. 4–5. See also Great Britain, War Office, *Field Service Regulations*, 3 vols., *Operations-General (1935)* (London: HMSO, 1935), vol. 2, pp. 176–86.

54. Interviews with Brigadier Ralph A. Bagnold, OBE, FRS, Mark Beach, Edenbridge, Kent, Eng., 1972 and 1976.

55. WO 193/150, *General Staff Report on the Raising of Insurrections: Possibility of Guerilla Activities*, a report originating in the late 1930s, had concentrated on operations in Europe. For the Commandos, see Brigadier Bernard Fergusson, *The Watery Maze: The Story of Combined Operations* (New York: Holt, Rinehart and Winston, 1961), pp. 46–69.

56. Ltr, General Sir Neil Ritchie, GBE, KCB, DSO, MC, to author, dtd 29 March 1972.

57. A phrase used by Hackett, "Employment of Special Forces," p. 36.

58. Ltr., GOC-in-C, Eighth Army, MEF, to OC, LRDG, dtd 2 April 1943, reproduced in W. B. Kennedy Shaw, *Long Range Desert Group: The Story of Its Work in Libya, 1940–1943* (reprint ed.; Portway, Bath, Eng.: Cedric Chivers, 1970), p. 238. For the Eighth Army, see W. G. F. Jackson, *The Battle for North Africa, 1940–43* (New York: Mason/Charter, 1975), pp. 353–88; and for Montgomery, Nigel Hamilton, *Master of the Battlefield: Monty's War Years, 1942–1944* (New York: McGraw-Hill, 1983), esp. pp. 183–95.

59. Lloyd Owen, *Providence Their Guide*, p. 46, indicates that, in August 1941, GHQ-ME had contemplated using Bagnold to raise and employ "up to five formations similar to the LRDG." These were to have been controlled "from a special section of the Operations Branch in Cairo." Shortages of men and equipment, however, brought the plan to naught. Amplified in Bagnold, Prendergast interviews.

60. Hackett interviews.

61. Davy interview.

62. Prendergast interviews.

Essay on Sources

Since this work is amply footnoted by chapter, this essay concentrates on those collections of official records and major sources of documentary and printed information available to any researcher of British special operations in North Africa in World War II.

Primary Sources

Organizational Records

While certain classes of papers, judged inappropriate or too sensitive for release, were either destroyed or "retained in department of origin at the time of the transfer of the class," the great quantity of the official evidence relevant to the British experience in the War of 1939–1945 began to become accessible to researchers after 1970. Such material is lodged in the Public Record Office, as are records for the War of 1914–1918 and the interwar decades. The published *Guide to the Contents of the Public Record Office* and the War Office Class Lists assist the researcher in identifying those files germane to his program of investigation. Given the obvious cruciality of official documents to a study of special operations, this essay identifies (1) the major records class-listings and (2) the numbers and titles of the groups filed therein. These records are here considered in three general categories: War of 1914–1918; Developments Between the Wars; and War of 1939–1945.

Within the first category, War of 1914–1918, important records relating to the employment of forces in the Western Desert are contained in War Office (WO) 95, *War Diaries, War of 1914 to 1918*. Highly useful to the researcher are 4465, *War Diaries, Egyptian Expeditionary Force: No.'s 2, 4, 5, and 6 Light Car Patrols, March 1918–October 1918;* 4478, *War Diaries, Egyptian Expedi-*

tionary Force, Desert Mounted Corps: Light Car Patrols; and 4516, *War Diaries, Egyptian Expeditionary Force, 5th Cavalry Division: Light Car Patrols 1918– 1919.* Several important operational and intelligence files are contained in WO 32, Registered Papers, General Series, including 10778, *Formation of an Intelligence Corps for Egypt, 1916–1917.*

Within the second category, Developments Between the Wars, such issues as mechanization, imperial defense, and the role of British forces in Egypt led to important strategic and operational assessments. These influenced the overall climate of military thinking in which the decision to form desert special forces eventually was taken. In WO 32, Registered Papers, General Series, particular attention was given to 4169, *Anglo-Egyptian Cooperation in the Defence of Egypt: Span 1937–1940;* 3543, *Appreciation on 12.10.35 by the General Officer Commanding, British Troops in Egypt, of the Probable Situation at the end of October in the event of an Italian Offensive from Libya;* 10125, *Army Council Instructions to the General Officer Commanding-in-Chief in the Middle East, July 1939;* and 4173, *Mediterranean and Middle East—Arrangements for Strengthening the Defences of Egypt, October 1937: Span 1937–1940.* WO 33, Reports and Miscellaneous Papers, contains strength returns, tables of organizations, and reports on mechanization. WO 106, Directorate of Military Operations and Intelligence, is highly useful for its periodic intelligence assessments, and AIR 5/Series 2 deals with the Air Ministry's armored-car operations in Iraq. Foreign Office files were also consulted, chiefly with a view towards intelligence on inner-desert activities conducted by the Italians. Regarding French developments, classes consulted at the Château de Vincennes, Paris, were in Ministère des Armées, État-Major de l'Armée de Terre, Service Historique, Archives Historiques Contemporaines, Maroc, and included: *Cies Sahariennes* (A 3/34); *Bulletins de Renseignements des Questions Musulmanes* (RP/ 10); *1927–29; Assassinat de M. Estienne* (Rabat/28); and in Ministère de la Guerre . . . 1930–1933, *Motorisation 1930–1933* (C/10); *Confins Sahariens (Avril 1934)* (M. Kech/30); *Programme de Pénétration Saharienne: Mission des Compagnies Sahariennes, Territoires du Sud, 1927–1935* (Algerie/37); and *Affaire du Djebel Arlah (8 Decembre 1928), Affaire de Djihari (14 Octobre 1929): Rapports; Enquêtes, Maroc 1928–29* (Maroc/F-3).

As to the final category, most of the key special-forces files are located in WO 201, War of 1939 to 1945, Military Headquarters Papers, Middle East Forces. The most important of these collections are 807–819, *Colonel Prendergast Papers: Long Range Desert Group Diary and Narrative;* 747, *MO 3 Battle File: SAS Regiment;* and 2624, *War Establishment, 1st Special Air Service Regiment.* Other files deal with issues ranging from operations to command relationships. Important material bearing upon the overall issue of special operations in the Middle East is in WO 32, Registered Papers, General Series; WO 106, Directorate of Military Operations and Intelligence; WO 169, War of 1939 to 1945, War Diaries, Middle East Forces; and in WO 193, Directorate of Military Operations Collection Files.

Important materials are also held outside the custody of the Public Record Office. In addition to maps, the Imperial War Museum, Lambeth, holds collections of useful photographs which, arranged in albums, may be consulted under such headings as "LRDG," "SAS," and "PPA." The National Portrait Gallery, London, houses photographs of key figures, and, useful for photographic depictions of different types of geological features, the Mobil Oil Corporation, New York, maintains an extensive collection.

Supporting its officer education effort, the British Army Staff College, Camberley, has both a library and an archive of research materials, including reports, essays, course outlines, and special lectures. Relevant to the larger issue of forces for special operations, the Office of the Chief of Military History Collections at the U.S. Army Military History Institute, Carlisle Barracks, Pennsylvania, and the James C. Breckinbridge Library, Education Center, U.S. Marine Corps Development and Education Command, Quantico, Virginia, contain such highly useful items as copies of transcribed oral history interviews. The General Mark W. Clark papers and the Vice Admiral Friedrich Ruge Collection, both held in the Department of Archives and Museum, The Citadel, Charleston, South Carolina, are helpful less for their information on special forces than for the insights offered regarding various techniques of command employed in World War II.

Individual Papers

In addition to the repository at Churchill College, Cambridge, the scholar should consult the Bulletins of the National Register of Archives, London. The largest institutional collections of papers dealing with desert exploration and with World War II in the desert are held at the Imperial War Museum, Lambeth; the Liddell Hart Centre for Military Archives, King's College, London; the Royal Geographical Society, London; and the British Museum, London. These yield collections that cover significant portions of an officer's career, or those that encompass important aspects of special operations and desert exploration. In the Imperial War Museum, The Long Range Desert Group Collection of Major General D. L. Lloyd Owen (1917–   ) also contains selected papers of W. B. Kennedy Shaw and Richard P. Lawson, MD. Lodged in the LHCMA, King's College, are papers of Major General J. F. C. Fuller (1878–1966); Major General Sir Francis W. de Guingand (1900–1979); and General Sir John W. Hackett (1910–   ). At the Royal Geographical Society, in addition to maps and reports, the Department of Archives and Manuscripts contains a Bagnold-RGS Letter File, 1929–1938. Major papers of T. E. Lawrence are held in the British Museum, at Harvard University, and at the University of Texas. Private collections consulted were those of Brigadier R. A. Bagnold; the late Brigadier G. M. O. Davy; Richard P. Lawson, MD; and Brigadier Guy L. Prendergast.

Printed Primary Sources

Published documents and reports also yielded substantial information on topics having to do with special operations. In addition to those already cited, major repositories surveyed were the Air Department Library and the Army Library (now the Central and Army Library), Ministry of Defence, Whitehall. Admiralty, Air Ministry, Foreign Office, War Office, and Parliamentary reports were consulted, as were various reports and studies compiled by the Survey of Egypt. Employed in conjunction with these were two highly useful American military publications: United States, War Department, *Handbook on the British Army* (Washington: USGPO, 1943), and *British Military Terminology* (Washington: USGPO, 1943), as were a variety of campaign studies. Providing additional clarification and perspective were United States Joint Chiefs of Staff, *Department of Defense Dictionary of Military and Associated Terms* (Washington: USGPO, 1984); Department of the Army, *Special Military Operations* (Washington: USGPO, 1972), and *Special Warfare, U.S. Army* (Washington: USGPO, 1962); Department of the Navy, *Special Operations: U.S. Marine Corps* (Washington: USGPO, 1984); and Frank R. Barnett, B. Hugh Tovar, and Richard H. Shultz, eds., *Special Operations in U.S. Strategy* (Washington, D.C.: NDU Press, 1984.)

Of the memoirs left by participants in the desert campaigns of both World Wars, any listing must, of course, include T. E. Lawrence, *Seven Pillars of Wisdom: A Triumph* (9th ed.; Harmondsworth, Middlesex, Eng.: Penguin Books, 1971). Less known memoirs of World War I are Oliver Hogue, *The Cameliers* (London: Melrose, 1919); Ian L. Idriess, *The Desert Column* (Sydney: Angus & Robertson, 1932); W. T. Massey, *The Desert Campaigns* (New York: Putnam, 1918); and Sam C. Rolls, *Steel Chariots in the Desert: The Story of an Armoured Car Driver with the Duke of Westminster in Libya and in Arabia with T. E. Lawrence* (London: Jonathan Cape, 1937). For the process of post-World War I desert exploration, Major Ralph A. Bagnold, *Libyan Sands: Travel in a Dead World* (London: Hodder & Stoughton, 1935) may be used with Major Claude S. Jarvis, *Three Deserts: The Author's Experiences in the Egyptian Deserts* (London: Murray, 1936); and G. W. Murray, *Dare Me to the Desert: A Record of Travel in the Libyan Desert and Sinai* (London: Allen & Unwin, 1967). Accounts of actions against desert tribesmen are in Sir John B. Glubb, *War in the Desert: An RAF Frontier Campaign* (London: Hodder & Stoughton, 1960); Marshal Rodolfo Graziani, *Africa Settentrionale, 1940–1941* (Rome: Danesi, 1948); and Squadron Leader G. E. Godsave, "Armoured Cars in Desert Warfare," *Journal of the Royal United Service Institution* 71 (May 1931), pp. 396–406.

Of the commanders of the three main World War II desert special forces, none produced a book-length memoir, although Bagnold, "Early Days of the Long Range Desert Group," *Geographical Journal* 105 (January 1945), pp. 30–46, provides an excellent brief account of the first unit of that type.

Among the most satisfactory accounts by participants are W. B. Kennedy Shaw, *Long Range Desert Group: The Story of Its Work in Libya, 1940–1943* (reprint ed.; Portway, Bath, Eng.: Cedric Chivers, 1970); and Major General David L. Lloyd Owen, *The Desert My Dwelling Place* (London: Cassell, 1957), and *Providence Their Guide: A Personal Account of the Long Range Desert Group, 1940–45* (London: Harrap, 1980), this last particularly so because it covers the entire period of the unit's existence. Vladimir Peniakoff, *Private Army* (London: Jonathan Cape, 1950), sometimes reads as if "Popski" were writing as a second Lawrence. Other excellent accounts are Malcolm James, *Born of the Desert* (London: Collins, 1945); Sir Fitzroy Maclean, *Eastern Approaches* (London: Jonathan Cape, 1950); Michael Crichton-Stuart, *G Patrol* (London: William Kimber, 1958); and W. E. Benyon Tinker, *Dust upon the Sea* (London: Hodder & Stoughton, 1947). Important memoirs by general officers are Field Marshal Earl Alexander, *The Alexander Memoirs, 1940–1945: Field Marshal Earl Alexander of Tunis* (New York: McGraw-Hill, 1962); Major General Sir Francis de Guingand, *Operation Victory* (New York: Charles Scribner's Sons, 1947); Montgomery of Alamein, *Memoirs* (New York: World, 1958); Field Marshal the Viscount William Slim, *Defeat into Victory* (New York: David McKay, 1961), for his ideas on the role of special forces; and Field Marshal the Earl Wavell, *Generals and Generalship (The Lees-Knowles Lectures at Trinity College, Cambridge, 1939)* (2nd ed.; New York: Macmillan, 1943), and *Soldiers and Soldiering or Epithets of War* (London: Jonathan Cape, 1953); and, given his strong advocacy of the special-operations approach, Sir Winston S. Churchill, *The Second World War*, vol. 4, *The Hinge of Fate* (Boston: Houghton Mifflin, 1950).

Journals and Newspapers

As a source of participant accounts and vital contemporaneous information, journals and newspapers contain much data regarding individual careers and key developments. In the area of desert exploration, the single most important British source for this study was the *Geographical Journal*, published since 1893 by the Royal Geographical Society, London. For British professional military writing of the 1920s and 1930s particularly useful sources were *The Journal of the Royal United Service Institution;* the *Army Quarterly* (incorporating the *United Service Magazine*); the *Cavalry Journal* (now *The Royal Armoured Corps Journal*); *Tank: the Journal of the Royal Tank Regiment; The Royal Air Force Quarterly;* and *The Royal Engineers Journal.* For French desert efforts during the interwar era, *Revue Militaire, Revue de Cavalrie,* and *L'Aéronautique* were important, as, for the Italian ones, were *Esercito e Nazione* and *Nazione Militare.* The important British newspapers were, of course, *The Times* of London and, for Egypt, the *Egyptian Gazette*, the *Egyptian Mail*, and the *Middle East Digest*.

Interviews and Correspondence

Efforts to establish contact with a variety of experts and participants in the desert explorations or in the campaign which followed yielded a rich correspondence and detailed, lengthy responses to questions. A program of personal interviews followed, such being initiated in a three-phase process over the years 1972–1983. Some participants who had earlier responded to written questions could not be reached for interview. Those who could, however, provided insights and information not available elsewhere and which greatly expanded upon the documentary evidence. Responding either to questionnaires or granting personal interviews were Brigadier Ralph A. Bagnold, the late Brigadier George M. O. Davy, Colonel Paul Richard Second Baron Freyberg, the late Major General Sir Francis de Guingand, General Sir John W. Hackett, Major William B. Kennedy Shaw, Richard P. Lawson, MD, the late Captain Sir Basil H. Liddell Hart, Major General David L. Lloyd Owen, Sir Fitzroy Maclean, MP, Brigadier Guy L. Prendergast, General Sir Neil Ritchie, and the late Brigadier Eric J. Shearer.

Secondary Sources

Bibliographies

An appropriate beginning point for many aspects of British military history is Robin Higham, ed., *A Guide to the Sources of British Military History* (Berkeley: University of California Press, 1971). Great Britain, Public Record Office, *The Second World War: A Guide to the Documents in the Public Record Office* (Public Record Office Handbooks no. 15) (London: HMSO, 1972) is essential for the primary-source holdings for World War II, as are the various Parliamentary bibliographic aids and those published for the Imperial War Museum. A. S. White, *A Bibliography of Regimental Histories of the British Army* (London: Stockwell, 1965) is also useful. Although no satisfactory bibliography of special forces and their operations is available in that work or elsewhere, the researcher may nevertheless usefully turn to Hope Miller and William A. Lybrand, *A Selected Bibliography on Unconventional Warfare* (Washington, D.C.: Special Operations Research Office, The American University for Department of the Army, 1961); United States, Department of the Army, *United States Army Special Warfare School Library Handbook and Bibliography* (Fort Bragg, N.C.: Special Warfare Center, 1962); and United States Army War College Library, *Special Warfare* (Carlisle Barracks, Pa.: USAWC, 1983) for assistance.

Official Histories

With the exception of R. L. Kay's brief *Long Range Desert Group in Libya, 1940–41*, and his *Long Range Desert Group in the Mediterranean* (Wellington,

N.Z.: War History Branch, Department of Internal Affairs, 1949 and 1950, respectively), there are no published official monographs dealing with special operations in the desert campaign. However, certain of the volumes comprising the series of British official histories produced for both World Wars remain indispensable to a study of those operations. For World War I, the Official Military Histories edited by Brigadier General Sir J. E. Edmonds provide detailed, small unit-based accounts of the Western Desert campaign. Far less detailed are the World War II Official Military Histories of the Mediterranean and Middle East theaters, produced under the editorship of Major General I. S. O. Playfair. These volumes nevertheless attempt to weave the efforts of all three British services into a single account. Generally more satisfactory for the detail of their operational narratives are the comparable Australian, Indian, New Zealand, and South African volumes, which may be supplemented by United States official histories, both Army and Army Air Forces. Given the significance of "Sigint" to the outcome of the North African campaign, F. H. Hinsley et al., *British Intelligence in the Second World War: Its Influence on Strategy and Operations*, 3 vols. (New York: Cambridge University Press, 1979–   ), remains essential to an assessment of the relationship between special forces and intelligence. Likewise useful in providing a context for special and unconventional operations are M. R. D. Foot, *SOE in France: An Account of the Work of the British Special Operations Executive in France 1940–1944* (London: HMSO, 1966); and *War Report of the OSS*, History Project, Strategic Services Unit, Office of the Assistant Secretary of War, War Department, Washington, D.C., Kermit Roosevelt, ed., vol. 2 (New York: Walker, 1976).

Studies of Special Forces

Although military units of the elite and special variety have been a distinctive feature of the twentieth-century military experience, the corpus of studies about them is an extremely limited one at best. Such forces, which often inspire in their partisans powerful cult feelings and in their orthodox soldier detractors strong animosities, have tended to generate emotion in equal measure to rational analysis. Particularly needed, therefore, are sober, systematic assessments of their operational contributions (successful and otherwise) and of their relationship to the fundamental issues of strategy, civil-military relations, and national military structure.

Representing attempts to come to grips with these issues are Roger A. Beaumont, *Military Elites: Special Fighting Units in the Modern World* (New York: Bobbs-Merrill, 1974); Eliot A. Cohen, *Commandos and Politicians: Elite Military Units in Modern Democracies* (Cambridge, Mass.: Center for International Affairs, Harvard University, 1978); M. R. D. Foot, "Special Operations I and II," in *The Fourth Dimension of Warfare*, ed. Michael Elliott-Bateman (New York: Praeger, 1970), pp. 19–51; Colonel John W. Hackett,

"The Employment of Special Forces," *Journal of the Royal United Service Institution* 97 (February 1952), pp. 26–41; Otto Heilbrunn, *Warfare in the Enemy's Rear* (New York: Praeger, 1963); James Ladd, *Commandos and Rangers of World War II* (New York: St. Martin's Press, 1978); Edward Luttwack et al., *A Systematic Review of "Commando" (Special) Operations 1939–1980* (Potomac, Md.: C & L Associates, 1982); and William Seymour, *British Special Forces* (London: Sidgwick & Jackson, 1985). Among studies of specific units, campaigns, concepts, or individual leaders are James Altieri, *The Spearheaders* (Indianapolis: Bobbs-Merrill, 1960); Werner Brockdorff, *Geheimkommandos des Zweiten Weltkrieges* (Munich: Welsermahl, 1967); Robert D. Burhans, *The First Special Service Force: A War History of the North Americans 1942–1944* (Washington: *Infantry Journal*, 1942); Rupert Butler, *Hand of Steel* (London: Hamlyn, 1980); G.B. Courtney, *SBS in World War Two* (London: Panther Books/Granada, 1983); Virginia Cowles, *Who Dares, Wins (Formerly The Phantom Major)* (New York: Ballantine 1959); Roy Farran, *Winged Dagger* (London: Collins, 1948); Herbert Kriegsheim, *Getarnt, Getauscht und Doch Getreu: Die Geheimnisvollen "Brandenburger"* (Berlin: Bernard & Graefe, 1959); Gordon Landsborough, *Tobruk Commando* (London: Cassell, 1956); James Lucas, *Kommando: German Special Forces of World War Two* (London: Arms and Armour Press, 1985); Albert H. Paddock, *U.S. Army Special Warfare: Its Origins: Psychological and Unconventional Warfare, 1941–1952* (Washington, D.C.: USGPO, 1982); Charles Messenger, *The Commandos 1940–1946* (London: William Kimber, 1985); F. O. Miksche, *Secret Forces* (Westport, Conn.: Greenwood Press, 1970); Charlton Ogburn, *The Marauders* (New York: Harper, 1956); Hilary St. G. Saunders, *The Green Beret* (London: Michael Joseph, 1949); Otto Skorzeny, *Skorzeny's Secret Missions* (New York: E. P. Dutton, 1951); Helmuth Spaeter, *Die Brandenburger: Eine Deutsche Kommandotruppe* (Munich: Walter Angerer, 1978); John Strawson, *A History of the SAS Regiment* (London: Martin Secker & Warburg, 1984); Arthur Swinson, *The Raiders: Desert Strike Force* (New York: Ballantine, 1971); Charles L. Updegraph, *Special Marine Corps Units of World War II* (Washington, D.C.: History and Museums Division, Headquarters, U.S. Marine Corps, 1972); Philip Warner, *The Special Air Service* (London: William Kimber, 1972), and *The Secret Forces of World War II* (London: Granada Publishing, 1985); Charles Whiting, *Skorzeny* (New York: Ballantine, 1972); Len Whittaker, *Some Talk of Private Armies* (Herpenden, Herts.: Albanium Publishing, 1984); and Peter Young, *Storm from the Sea* (London: William Kimber, 1958).

General Reference Works and Special Subjects

Of necessity the task of evaluating the desert special-forces experiment demands examination of a range of issues beyond those immediately associated with the initial decision for formation. At a minimum, such an examination must include the various institutional practices shaping the British

Army of World War II, as well as those factors which helped to make the desert campaign an arena of blitzkrieg warfare. Among the works consulted on these and other topics were Larry H. Addington, *The Blitzkrieg Era and the German General Staff, 1865–1941* (New Brunswick, N.J.: Rutgers University Press, 1971); Captain Charles E. Callwell, *Small Wars: Their Principles and Practice* (2nd ed.; London: Harrison, 1903); Peter Calvocoressi, *Top Secret Ultra* (New York: Pantheon Books, 1980); Charles Cruickshank, *Deception in World War II* (London: Oxford University Press, 1979); *Dictionary of National Biography*, 1900–1950 (London: Oxford University Press, 1912–1959); Raymond Dronne, *Le Sermont de Koufra* (Paris: Editions du Temps, 1965); Arthur Ehrhardt, *Kleinkrieg: Geschichtliche Erfahrungen und Künftige Möglichkeiten* (Potsdam: Ludwig Voggenreitter, 1944); Chris Ellis, *Military Transport of World War I* (London: Blandford, 1970); John Ellis, *The Sharp End: The Fighting Man in World War II* (New York: Charles Scribner's Sons, 1980); E. E. Evans-Pritchard, *The Senussi of Cyrenaica* (Oxford: Clarendon Press, 1949); Brian Gardner, *The Public Schools: An Historical Survey* (London: Hamish Hamilton, 1973); Josef Garlinski, *Intercept: The Enigma War* (New York: Charles Scribner's Sons, 1979); Major General Sir Charles Gwynn, *Imperial Policing* (2nd ed.; London: Macmillan, 1939); W. C. G. Henneker, *Bush Warfare* (London: Hugh Rees, 1907); Michael Howard, *Studies in War and Peace* (London: Temple-Smith, 1970), and *The Mediterranean Strategy in the Second World War* (London: Weidenfeld & Nicolson, 1968); Brian Johnson, *The Secret War* (London: British Broadcasting Corporation, 1978); David Kahn, *Hitler's Spies: German Military Intelligence in World War II* (New York: Macmillan, 1978); Ronald Lewin, *Ultra Goes to War: The First Account of World War II's Greatest Secret Based on Official Documents* (New York: McGraw-Hill, 1978); Jay Luvaas, *The Education of an Army: British Military Thought, 1815–1940* (Chicago: University of Chicago Press, 1964); Kenneth Macksey, *Armoured Crusader: Major General Sir Percy Hobart* (London: Hutchinson, 1967); Edwin D. McKee, ed., *A Study of Global Sand Seas* (Geological Survey Professional Paper 1052) (Washington, D.C.: NASA, USGPO, 1979); Richard M. Ogorkiewicz, *Armoured Forces: A History of Armoured Forces and Their Vehicles* (2nd ed.; London: Arms and Armour Press, 1970); Christopher B. Otley, "The Origins and Recruitment of the British Army Elite, 1870–1959" (doctoral diss., University of Hull, 1965); V. J. Parry et al., *War, Technology and Society in the Middle East* (London: Oxford University Press, 1975); *The Statistical Digest of the War* (London: HMSO, 1951); Samuel A. Stouffer et al., *The American Soldier*, 2 vols. (Studies in Social Psychology in World War II) (Princeton: Princeton University Press, 1949); John J. T. Sweet, *Iron Arm: The Mechanization of Mussolini's Army, 1920–1940* (Westport, Conn.: Greenwood Press, 1980); Sir Percy Sykes, *A History of Exploration* (3rd ed.; New York: Harper, 1961); Wilfred P. Thesiger, *Arabian Sands* (New York: E. P. Dutton, 1959); Martin van Creveld, *Supplying War: Logistics from Wallenstein to Patton* (New York: Cambridge University Press, 1977); P. J. Vatikiotis, *The Egyptian Army in Politics: Pattern for New Nations?* (Bloomington: Indiana University Press, 1961); Philip E. Vernon, *Personnel Selection in the British Forces* (London: University of London Press, 1949); War Department, *Military Dictionary: English-Italian* (Washington, D.C.: USGPO, 1943); *Military Dictionary: English-German* (Washington, D.C.: USGPO, 1943); A. S. White, "The Army List," *Journal of the Society for Historical Research* 25 (1947); 45, no. 181 (1967); and F. W. Winterbotham, *The Ultra Secret* (New York: Dell, 1974).

Index

Abassia Ordnance Depot, 46
Afrika Korps, 66, 70, 138
Agedabia, 89, 91, 93
Ahmed, Sayed, 6, 7, 8, 9, 10
Ain Dalla, 53
"Air Control" formula, 17, 19, 39
Aircraft: in desert campaign of World War I, 8; in desert campaign of World War II, 42, 63–64, 70, 71, 84, 91, 112, 124–25, 127, 132, 175, 181; for desert exploration, 29; in Senussi campaign, 20, 21
Alam Halfa, 118–19, 123, 188
Albania, Italian invasion of, 37
Alexander, Gen. Sir Harold, 114, 115, 117, 123, 134, 135, 173, 176, 184
Allenby, Sir Edmund, 12, 13, 17, 18, 37
Almaszy, Ladislas Edouard, Count de, 33–34, 98–104, 118, 142, 159
Anderson, Sir Kenneth A. N., 165, 170
Anglo-American Expeditionary Force, 168, 169
Anglo-Egyptian Treaty (1936), 36
Aosta, Duke of, 39
"Arab 'G' Expansion Scheme," 38
Arabian Desert, location of, 1
Arab Revolt, in World War I, 2, 13, 14

Armored cars: use of to control Bedouins, 18–19; use of in Senussi campaign, 19, 21
"Ash Wednesday," 110
A Squadron, 69, 72, 74–75, 76, 105
Asyut, 102
Auchinleck, Sir Claude, 71–74, 77, 84, 86, 87, 92, 110, 111, 113–14, 115, 139
Auto-Saharan company (Italy): and British exploration of desert, 29–31; desert capabilities of, 35–36; and the Libyan operations, 41–42, 56, 57, 64–65, 72, 98; in Senussi campaign, 20–21; and the Siwa diversion, 39–40

Bagnold, Ralph Alger, 17, 35, 40, 42–46, 76–77, 101, 104, 134, 141, 165, 186; as civilian, 40; desert explorations of, 23–25, 26–31; early career of, 23–24; and the Long Range Patrols, 45, 58, 67, 69, 72, 73, 74; recall of, to army service in 1939, 40–41; transfer of, to India, 25–26; writings of, 40, 53
Balbo, Italo, 22, 41, 42, 49
Ball, Dr. John, 11, 12, 23, 25

Ballantyne, L. B., 64, 88–89
Barce raid, 121, 128–30, 132, 181
Battleaxe, 71
Bayerlein, Fritz, 162–63
BBC, 132, 158
Beda Littoria mission, 79, 81–82, 84
Bedouin, British attempts to contain,
    17–18
Benghazi raid, 88, 107, 117, 119, 120–
    21, 126–27, 128, 132, 133, 147
Benina, 105
"Big Cairn," 54, 56
Bir Hacheim, 7, 94, 109–10, 124
"Black Code," 100
Bletchley Park, 137, 139, 150, 152
Britain, Battle of, 44, 47, 137
Brooke, Sir Alan, 113
Browne, Tony, 86, 158, 160, 165
Bruce, Bernard, 162, 163, 169, 175
B Squadron, 72, 76, 183

Cairo Citadel, 30, 38
Camel, use of for desert travel, 4, 23
Camel Corps, in World War I, 4, 5–6,
    8, 13
Casa Cantonieri, 90, 98
Catroux, Gen., 164, 173
"Cauldron," 110
Chad Province, 41
Chevrolet truck, use of for desert oper-
    ations, 46–47, 54, 56
Chott el Jerid, 167, 170
Churchill, Randolph F. E. Spencer, 96,
    117
Churchill, Winston, 17; in World War
    I, 5, 7; in World War II, 17, 44, 60,
    66, 70–71, 77, 93, 110, 113, 114,
    116–17, 138, 143, 148, 150, 176, 185
Citroen-Kégresse caterpillar, use of, for
    desert travel, 23, 27
Clayton, Patrick, 33–34, 45, 48, 49–50,
    53–54, 56, 58, 60–64, 65, 93
Clayton, Sir Robert, 33
Colditz, 172
Coldstream Guards, 59
Commando raids, 78–79, 105
"Commonwealth Keep," 109
Continental Hotel, 95

Crichton-Stuart, 61, 62, 75–76, 85
Croucher, Lance Corporal, 46
Crüwell, Ludwig, 86
Cunningham, Sir Alan, 77, 79, 84, 87
Cyrenaica, 20, 66, 91, 94, 119, 133,
    138

Dalla oasis, 28–29
Dardanelle campaign, British failure in,
    1
Davy, George M. O., 122, 147, 154,
    155, 182–83
D-Day landing, 79, 183
De Gaulle, Charles, 60
De Guingand, Francis W., 144, 145–
    46, 149
Derna, 105, 106
Desert Reconnaissance by Motor-Car, 12
Desert special force: establishment of,
    33–51; first mission of, 53–67. See
    also Long Range Desert Group;
    Long Range Patrols; Popski's Private
    Army; Special Air Service
"Desert-walloping," 28
"DesForce" staff, 69
Dieppe raid, 79
Die Wehrmacht, 159
Dodecanese Islands, 181
Donovan, William J., 115
Doolittle, James H., 169
D'Ornano, Lt. Col., 61, 62, 63

Easonsmith, J. R., 75, 81, 83, 88, 128,
    129–30, 131, 132, 143, 165, 181, 182
Egypt: granting of independence by
    Britain, 36; relations with Great Brit-
    ain, 36–37
Egyptian Expeditionary Force, in
    World War I, 12
Eight Army, 77–78, 87, 93, 94–95, 96–
    97, 99, 109, 110–11, 114, 118–19,
    123, 134, 150, 151
Eisenhower, Dwight D., 145, 159, 168
El Agheila, 67, 88, 89, 142, 157, 158,
    174
El Agheila bottleneck, 92
El Alamein, 6, 110, 111, 113, 114, 136,

145, 146, 147, 149, 151–52, 156, 159, 188

11th Hussars, 75–76

El Guettar, 175

Enigma code system, 136–37, 138, 141–42, 172

Eppler, Johan, 101–3

Estienne, Gen. J. E., 23

Ethiopian Crisis, 34–35, 36, 38

Fahmi, Hakmet, 102–3

Faiyum Oasis, 111

Falklands War of 1982, 185

Farouk, King, 23, 37, 95, 99

Faya, 64

Feisal, Prince, 2, 12, 13

Fellers, Bonner F., 100, 103

Fezzan, 20

Fifth light Division, 66

First Alamein, 113

Folbot operations, 78, 81, 95–96

Force B, 120, 122–23, 124

Force X, 120, 123, 126, 127

Force Z, 121, 123, 127–28

Forth, N. B. de Lancey, 23

Fredendall, Lt. Gen. Lloyd R., 168

Free French Allied Expeditionary Force, 169, 174

Free Officers Movement, 101

Freyberg, Sir Bernard, 45, 59, 157, 158, 163, 165, 174, 175, 184

Fuller, J. F. C., 37, 71, 186

G (Guards) Patrol, 59, 60, 61, 62, 69, 75–76, 162–63, 169

G1 Patrol, 76, 85, 94, 97–98, 111, 123, 128, 129, 154, 156

G2 Patrol, 76, 92–93, 94, 96, 105, 106–7, 111, 132

Gabes, 170

Gabes Gap, 170, 171

Gariboldi, Italo, 66

Gazala Line, 88, 109–10, 144

Gazala raid, 84, 87, 94

General Headquarters, Middle-East (GHQ-ME), establishment of, at Cairo Citadel, 38, 44

General Officer Commanding British Troops in Egypt (GOC-BTE), 35

"Ghiblis," 58

Gilf Kebir, conquest of, 33, 34, 102

Giraud, General Henri, 19–21

Grand Erg Oriental, 163, 166

Graziani, Rodolfo, 20–23, 49, 57, 59, 65, 72, 128

Great Britain: desert campaign of during World War I, 1–15

G(RF), 135, 147, 152, 156–57, 170, 185, 187

Grenadier Guards, 149

Grosvenor, Hugh Richard Arthur, 7

Guderian, Heinz, 71

Guild, A. I., 105

Gurdon, Robert Brampton, 96, 106, 111–12

H. M. S. *Coventry*, 125

H. M. S. *Sikh*, 125

H. M. S. *Talisman*, 81

H. M. S. *Torbay*, 81

H. M. S. *Zulu*, 125

Hackett, John Winthrop, 131, 135, 147, 149, 151, 152, 154, 155, 156, 157, 160, 170, 172, 187

Halder, Franz, 66–67

Half patrols, 76

Hart, Basil H. Liddell Hart, 1, 14, 37, 71, 186

Haselden, John E., 75, 79, 81, 82, 119, 120, 121, 123, 124–25, 132–33

Hautecloque, the Viscount de, 63

Hay, Anthony, 85, 90

Hejaz, Arabs, 13

Hitler, Adolf, 39, 66, 146, 150, 159, 173

Hobart, Percy C. S., 42

Holliman, C. Augustus, 89–90

Hunter, Anthony, 94, 111

Iraq: British campaign to control Bedouin tribesmen in, 17–18; as British mandate, 31

Italy: Auto-Saharan company of, 20–21, 29–31, 35–36, 39–40, 41–42, 56, 57, 64–65, 72, 98; Egyptian offensive of,

56–57; Ethiopian invasion of, 34–35, 36, 38; Libya offensive of, 20–22, 39–40

Jalo raid, 89, 91, 92, 93, 102, 104, 107, 121, 126, 127–28, 132, 133
Jarabub oasis, 9
Jebel, 105, 131
Jebel al Akdar, 70, 75
Jebel al Uwaynat, 29
Jebel Tebaga, 166
Jeep raid formation, 112
Jeeps, use of, in desert campaigns, 111, 117
Jellicoe, Earl, 181
"Jerry cans," 70
Jihad, and the desert campaign of World War I, 1–2
Joint Desert Special Operations Command, 187–88
Jones, Lady Enid Bagnold, 24
Jones, Sir Roderick, 24

Kamal-al-Din, Prince, 23, 25, 27
Kasserine Pass, 167, 168, 169
Keyes, Geoffrey C. T., 78, 79, 81–82,
Keyes, Sir Roger, 78
Kharga Oasis, 102
Khyber Pass, 25
"Knightsbridge," 109
Krim, Abd el, 19
Kufra oasis, 20, 21, 22, 23, 30, 41, 42, 72, 74, 101, 104, 111

Lady be Good crew, 64, 83
Land Forces Adriatic, 182, 183
Lawrence T. E., 1, 2, 12–13, 14–15, 17–19, 37, 38, 104, 108
Lawson, Dr. Richard, 123, 129–30, 131, 132, 181
Laycock, Robert E., 78, 81, 82
"Layforce," 78–79
Lazarus, Lt. Kenneth, 76
L Detachment, 80, 81, 92, 112, 115, 116, 117–18, 120, 184
Leclerc, Col., 63, 64–65, 159, 160, 174
"Leopards," 44
Leros, 181, 182

Lewes, Jack, 91
Lewes bombs, 81
Lewis guns, 48
Libya: as a base of Senussi operations in World War I, 6; Italian forces in, 20–22, 39–40
Libyan Sands: Travels in a Dead World (Bagnold), 40
Light Armoured Battery, in World War I, 5
Light Car Patrols, in World War I, 6, 8, 9, 10, 11, 14, 23, 36, 188
Limpets, 95
Lloyd Owen, David L., 86, 92, 122–24, 131, 132, 135, 183–84, 186
Long Range Desert Group (LRDG), 59; acquisition of aircraft by, 73; change of name to Long Range Desert Group, 59; disbanding of, 184; formation of, 46; joint operations with SAS, 94–95, 98, 99, 105, 107, 111, 115, 117, 118; joint operations with SOE, 115; lowpoint of existence, 73; need of, for friend in headquarters, 74; operations of, 56–57; recruitment efforts of, 59, 76–77; reputation of, 76–77; raids by, into enemy territory, 58–59, 60–67, 69–86, 96–98, 103–7, 110, 112–13, 116, 121, 132, 133, 136, 140–42, 144–45, 147, 148, 149, 153, 156, 159–60, 162, 164–65, 171, 173, 174, 175, 176, 179–84, 187; split of into half patrols, 76; use of for strategic defense, 72–73
Long Range Patrols, 44, 45, 50; formation of, 44, 46; makeup of, 45; movement of, into desert, 50–51, 53; operations of, 53–54, 57–58; organization of, 48; outfitting of, 47–48, 72–73; raids of, into enemy territory, 58–59
Lorrenzini, Maggiore, 30, 31, 41, 43, 56, 57

Maclean, Fitzroy, 87, 96, 117, 126, 127, 132

"Marble Arch," 142, 144, 145, 147, 149, 150, 157
Mareth Line, 159, 160, 163, 165, 166, 169, 173, 174–75, 177
Masefield, John, 116
Massu, Jacques Emile Charles Marie, 61, 62, 160
Matruh, 6
Mayne, Blair "Paddy," 90, 126
Melody Club, 95
Melot, Robert, 95, 126, 133
Mersa Matruh, 113
Mitford, E. C., 45, 48, 54, 56, 57–58, 69, 70, 74–75
Mockler-Ferryman, Eric E., 168
Model A Ford, use of for desert exploration, 26–27, 28
Model T Ford: adaptation of to meet desert environment, 11; use of, for desert exploration, 24
Monte Cassino, 182
Montgomery, Bernard Law, 114, 115, 119, 122, 123, 134, 136, 145, 146, 147, 148–49, 150, 151, 155, 156, 157, 158–59, 162, 164, 165, 168, 173, 174, 175, 176
Moorehead, Alan, 71, 167–68
Moreschini, Capitano, 64, 65
Morris, C. S., 90
"Motor guerrilla," 37–38
Motor Machinegun Battery, in World War I, 5
Motor vehicles, use of, for desert warfare, in World War I, 4–8
Murray, Sir Archibald, 2, 4–6, 9, 10, 12
Murzuk: fall of, 160; raids on, 59, 60, 61–62, 74, 93
Mussolini, Benito, 20, 34, 37, 39, 43, 66, 111, 142, 146

Nasser, Abdel, 101
Neame, Sir Philip, 69–70
New Zealand Corps, 174
New Zealand Division, inclusion of, in desert special force, 46, 47–48
Nofilia, 158
Northwest Frontier, 25

O'Connor, Richard, 58, 63, 66, 69–70
Olivey, John, 90–91, 95, 123, 131
Operation Compass, 58, 59, 60, 66
Operation Condor, 101, 102, 103, 104, 118
Operation Crusader, 77–78, 79, 81, 84, 137–38
Operation Lightfoot, 146, 147, 149, 155–56
Operation Salaam, 101, 102
Operation Torch, 145

Palificata, 53, 54
Palestine: as British mandate, 31; in World War I, 13
Panzerarmee Afrika, 93, 104, 107, 109, 113, 114, 147
Panzer Group Africa, 77, 86, 88
Paratrooper operations, 78, 79–81, 120
Pash, Aziz el Masri, 101
Pasha, Ja'far, 6
Patriot forces, 180, 183–84
Patton, George S., Jr., 168, 173, 175
Penderel, H. W. G. H., 29, 30, 33, 34
Peniakoff, Vladimir (Popski), 119, 120, 121, 126, 130, 131, 133, 147, 148, 160, 167–68, 172–73, 176
Physics of Blown Sand and Desert Dunes (Bagnold), 40
Player, J. D., 162, 163
Playfair, I. S. O., 109
Popski's Private Army (PPA), 147, 160, 167, 172–73, 176, 179, 184
Prendergast, Guy, 45, 73, 74, 76, 77–78, 84–85, 91, 92, 93, 94–98, 103–4, 110–11, 116, 117, 118, 131, 132, 142, 148, 152, 157–58, 162, 164, 165, 179–80, 181, 182, 183, 186, 188
"Professor Grey Matter," 140

Qattara Depression, 35, 110, 111, 140

R Patrol, 48, 58
R1 Patrol, 76, 81, 83, 88, 143, 157–58, 160, 162
R2 Patrol, 76, 86, 127, 151
Radio Cairo, 158
Rebecca code, 118

Regia Aeronautica, 20
Revolt in the Desert (Lawrence), 14
Rhodesian Patrol, 76
Riff War, 19
Ritchie, Neil M., 69, 80, 87, 88, 91, 93, 94–95, 109, 110
Road Watch mission, 131, 140–45, 147, 149–54, 155–58, 159, 160, 168–69, 187
Rohlfs, Gerhard, 23
Rommel, Erwin, 66–67, 69, 70, 71, 77, 78–79, 82, 84, 86, 88, 89, 93, 94, 97, 99, 100, 104, 109, 111, 113, 118, 119, 123, 125–26, 133, 136, 138, 141, 142, 143, 145, 150–52, 157, 158, 159–60, 165, 167–68, 173, 185–86
Roosevelt, Franklin D., 110
Royal Air Force (RAF), desert operations of, 18–19, 73, 84, 120, 121, 173, 182, 187
Royal Corps of Signals, 24
Royal Flying Corps' No. 17 Squadron, 2
Royal Geographical Society, 26, 29, 33Royal Naval Air Service (RNAS), in World War I, 5
Royal Tank Regiment, 24

S (Southern Rhodesia) Patrol, 59
S1 Patrol, 89–90, 165
S2 Patrol, 86, 95, 123, 128
Sadat, Lt. Anwar el, 101, 103
Sadler, Corp. W. Michael, 117
Sahara Desert, 1
Sand Sea, 22, 33, 35; crossing of, 55–56
Sanstede, Peter, 101–3
Scorched palm policy, 94
Scots Guards, 59
2nd New Zealand Division, 39, 165–66, 174, 177, 182
Selassie, Haile, 34
Senussi: British encouragement of revolt of, 38; in desert campaign of World War I, 2, 4–6, 9–10, 12, 18, 19
September raids, 133–34, 135–36
7th Armoured Division, 39, 41
7th Panzer "Ghost" Division, 67

Seven Pillars of Wisdom (Lawrence), 14, 38
Shaw, William Kennedy, 28, 29, 35, 45, 47, 48, 50, 58, 72
Shearer, Eric J., 33, 49, 50, 58, 59, 73–74, 75, 139, 146, 169
Shepheard's Hotel, 38, 80, 95
Sidi Rezegh, 84
"Sigint" (Signals Intelligence), 79, 82
Signal-flag system, use of by desert special force, 48–49
Sinai Desert, location of, 1
Sirte, 89
Siwa Oasis, 50, 72, 74–75, 94, 98, 105, 120–21; Italian attempt to sieze, 39–40
Siwa campaign, in World War I, 7–11
"Siwa diversion," 39
Slessor, Sir John, 8
Slim, Sir William, 179, 185
Small Wars: Their Principles and Practice, 2, 4
Somme, battle of, 7
Special Boat Squadron, 80, 92, 95, 155, 181, 185
Special Air Service (SAS): joint raids with LRDG, 94–95, 98, 99, 105, 107, 111, 115, 117, 118; operations of, 80, 82–83, 87, 90–91, 94, 105, 111, 112, 121–22, 127, 132, 136, 142, 147, 148–49, 155, 157, 162, 170, 171–72, 176, 179, 184
Special Interrogation Group (SIG), 105, 106, 107, 120, 121, 123, 124
Special Operations Executive (SOE), 115, 183
Spicer, E. F., 149, 150
Steele, D. G., 48, 58
Sticky bombs, 80–81, 91, 112
Stirling, David, 79–83, 87, 90, 91, 94, 95, 105, 106, 110–12, 115–17, 120, 122, 132, 148–49, 155–57, 169–72, 185–86
Stirling, William Joseph, 170
Strong, K. W. D., 168
Sudan Colonial Service, 28
Sudan Defence Force, 74, 101, 121, 123, 127

Sudan Defence Force Mobile Machine-
gun Company, 74
Sun compass, 11–12, 47–48
Sweating, Kenneth, 132

T Patrol, 48, 60, 61, 62, 63, 64, 65
T1 Patrol, 76, 88–89, 165–66
T2 Patrol, 76, 81, 82, 91, 98, 112, 123,
128, 166, 167, 174, 175
Talbot, John R., 123, 127
Tanks, use of for desert warfare, 7
Tara-Moorina survivors, 7
Tebaga Gap, 175
Tebu, 29
Theodolite, 28, 47, 48
"Thermos bombs," 70
Thomas, Lowell, 13–14
Timpson, J. Alastair L., 92–93, 94, 97–
98, 105, 111, 113, 123, 152–54, 156
Tinker, Lt. R. A., 166–67, 174, 175
Tobruk, 109–10, 145; siege of, 70–71,
89
Tobruk garrison, 84
Tobruk raid, 109–10, 119, 123–26, 128,
132, 133, 147
Tozeur, 167, 169
Transjordan, as British mandate, 31
Tripolitania, 20, 66, 92, 165–66
Turkey, and the desert campaign of
World War I, 1–2

Ultra secret, 136–42, 143, 144, 146,
150, 151, 152, 157, 159, 168, 172
Ultra Secret, The (Winterbotham), 141,
172
U.S. II Corps, 167, 168, 173, 175
Uwaynet, exploration of, 29, 33, 43

Via Balbia, raids against, 85–86, 96–97,
139–40. *See also* Road Watch mission
Von Arnim Jürgen, 159, 168, 173, 174–
76

W Patrol, 48, 54, 56, 57–58
"Wacos," 73
Wadi Halfa, 30, 72
Wadi Tamet, 160
Wavell, Archibald, 10–11, 18, 37, 39,
40–41, 43, 44, 45, 58, 59, 60, 65–66,
70–71, 71–72, 113, 138
Western Desert Force: in World War I,
2, 6; in World War II, 66, 69, 77
Wilder N. P., 112–13, 123, 128, 129
Wilder's Gap, 166, 174, 175
Wilson, Lt. Gen. Sir Henry, 42–43
Winterbotham, F. W., 141, 172
World War I, desert campaigns of, 1–15
World War II: and desert missions
against the Germans, 69–86; first de-
sert missions, 53–67; early desert
raids in, 87–107; and exploration of
the desert, 17–31, 33; formation of
desert special force, 33–51; and the
Mareth line, 155–77; raids on Tobruk, Benghazi, Jalo, and Barce,
109–30; and the Road Watch, 131–54

Y (Yeomanry) Patrol, 59, 62, 69, 76
Y1 Patrol, 76, 86, 122, 124, 131, 149,
150
Y2 Patrol, 76, 86, 92, 111
Y Service, 173

Zionist rebellion, 37

About the Author

JOHN W. GORDON is Professor of History at The Citadel in Charleston, South Carolina. He is the co-editor of *Proceedings of The Citadel Conference on War and Diplomacy, 1977* and *Selected Papers from The Citadel Conference on War and Diplomacy, 1978*, and he has contributed articles and essays to *Franklin D. Roosevelt: His Life and Times, Delaware History, Curricula and Course Development in Peace and Conflict Studies*, and *Marine Corps Gazette*.

Recent Titles in
Contributions in Military Studies

The Tainted War: Culture and Identity in Vietnam War Narratives
Lloyd B. Lewis

Shaping a Maritime Empire: The Commercial and Diplomatic Role of the American Navy, 1829–1861
John H. Schroeder

The American Occupation of Austria: Planning and Early Years
Donald R. Whitnah and Edgar L. Erickson

Crusade in Nuremberg: Military Occupation, 1945–1949
Boyd L. Dastrup

The Dogma of the Battle of Annihilation: The Theories of Clausewitz and Schlieffen and Their Impact on the German Conduct of Two World Wars
Jehuda L. Wallach

Jailed for Peace: The History of American Draft Law Violators, 1658–1985
Stephen M. Kohn

Against All Enemies: Interpretations of American Military History from Colonial Times to the Present
Kenneth J. Hagan and William R. Roberts

Citizen Sailors in a Changing Society: Policy Issues for Manning the United States Naval Reserve
Louis A. Zurcher, Milton L. Boykin, and Hardy L. Merritt, editors

Strategic Nuclear War: What the Superpowers Target and Why
William C. Martel and Paul L. Savage

Soviet Military Psychiatry: The Theory and Practice of Coping with Battle Stress
Richard A. Gabriel

A Portrait of the Israeli Soldier
Reuven Gal

The Other Price of Hitler's War: German Military and Civilian Losses Resulting from World War II
Martin K. Sorge

The New Battlefield: The United States and Unconventional Conflicts
Sam C. Sarkesian